# THE SONGS OF EDVARD GRIEG

To the memory of John Horton

# THE SONGS OF
# EDVARD GRIEG

BERYL FOSTER

Scolar Press

Published by
SCOLAR PRESS
Gower Publishing Company Limited
Gower House
Croft Road
Aldershot
Hants GU11 3HR
England

Gower Publishing Company
Old Post Road
Brookfield
Vermont 05036
USA

**British Library Cataloguing in Publication Data**
Foster, Beryl
   The songs of Edvard Grieg.
   1. Norwegian music. Grieg, Edvard, 1843–1907
   I. Title
   780′.92′4

   ISBN 0–85967–791–5

**Library of Congress Cataloging-in-Publication Data**
Foster, Beryl.
   The songs of Edvard Grieg / Beryl Foster.
   p.   cm.
   Includes bibliographical references and index.
ISBN 0–85967–791–5
   1. Grieg, Edvard, 1843–1907.   Songs.   2. Songs—History and criticism.   I. Title.
ML410.G9F6 1990
782.42′092—dc20      90–37497      CIP
                                   MN

Printed in Great Britain by
Billing & Sons Ltd, Worcester

# Contents

# Preface

To those outside Scandinavia music in Norway is generally viewed in terms of Hardanger fiddles and Grieg. A detailed knowledge of either would appear to be limited; the composer at least is still chiefly known to the general public only by his Piano Concerto and the two orchestral suites from the incidental music to *Peer Gynt*, although many pianists and singers, professional and amateur, will have performed some of his smaller works. Unfortunately, because of his lack of output in the larger forms, Grieg has frequently been dismissed as a miniaturist and, as with any composer known by a handful of popular compositions but generally not in greater depth, that very popularity is often maligned. Debussy was referring to the *Elegiac Melodies* when he made his famous remark, 'on a dans la bouche le goût bizarre et charmant d'un bonbon rose qui serait fourré de neige',[1] but it is a view of Grieg's music still all too widely held. In more recent times Grieg's life and works have also been subjected to crass popular image-making in the American musicals *Norwegian Nights*, produced in New York in 1936, and *Song of Norway*, New York 1951.

This book is concerned with Grieg as a composer of songs, of all his music still the least appreciated form. One of the most famous, *Jeg elsker dig* (I love you), is from a group entitled *Hjertets Melodier* (Melodies of the Heart), a description that epitomizes all his songs, for here more than anywhere else Grieg's development both as artist and human being is most closely reflected. The result is an extremely varied repertoire for any singer, which contains many excellent and a number of truly great songs, yet until now no comprehensive study of this oeuvre has been made. Previously, the most comprehensive surveys have been Astra Desmond's article in *Grieg. A Symposium*[2] and John Horton's chapter in his biography of Grieg,[3] although these necessarily comprise only brief descriptions of the principal opus numbers with comments on the most interesting musical points, translations and editions. More detailed analyses of a number of the songs are given by Finn Benestad and Dag Schjelderup-Ebbe in *Edvard Grieg, mennesket og kunstneren* (. . . the Man and the Artist),[4] but here too, some of them are cursorily dismissed and several are not mentioned at all.

I have periodically over the last ten years sung through all of Grieg's songs and have, where possible, featured a number of them in recital programmes and this book is written with performance firmly in mind. I have dealt here with all the songs Grieg wrote, excepting only *Ich denke dein* which is no longer extant, placing them as far as was practical in chronological order of composition and viewing them against the background of the composer's life and other works. With the exception of those few songs written to German texts (and the one in English), I have referred to them all by their original Norwegian or Danish titles with, at first mention, a literal English translation of that title immediately following and with a copious use of opus numbers, in order to avoid any confusion that might arise from using the titles of the various published translations. Those familiar with the Norwegian language will appreciate that many changes have taken place between the Dano-Norwegian orthography of Grieg's time and that of the modern *riksmål* or official language. However, as the older spelling is still in use in most Scandinavian editions and also in the volumes of songs (vols 14 and 15) of the *Grieg Gesamt-Ausgabe* (cited henceforth as *GGA*), published by Peters,[5] although not in Benestad and Schjelderup-Ebbe's book, it has seemed expedient for me to retain the titles and quote texts in the form they appear in the manuscript or first edition. Thus some of the spelling is not as it would be found in modern Norwegian — for example, *Spillemænd* (Minstrels), op. 25 no. 1, would now appear as 'Spillemenn' — except for such names as 'Solveig', where the original 'Solvejg' might be thought unnecessarily archaic. I have also retained 'Christiania' as the name of the Norwegian capital. This was the name in use throughout Grieg's lifetime; the city did not revert to its ancient name, Oslo, until 1924.

Unless otherwise indicated in the Notes, the passages quoted from Grieg's many letters are all my own translations from the originals. For the correspondence between Grieg and Delius, I am indebted to Lionel Carley's *Delius. A Life in Letters*, Vol. I: *1862–1908* (Scolar Press 1983). I acknowledge my gratitude to the literature listed in the Bibliography and offer grateful thanks, too, to Dr William Halverson and Mr Rolf Kr. Stang of the United States for permission to discuss and quote from their English translations used in the *GGA*. Thanks are also due to Professor Dag Schjelderup-Ebbe and the Grieg Committee for their permission to see these translations before publication and for making copies available to me. I am particularly grateful to Professor Nils Grinde of Oslo University, who has edited the songs for the *GGA*, for answering a number of queries and for sharing with me some of the more recent scholarship with regard to Grieg's songs.

I am indebted to the authorities of Bergen Public Library for permission to quote from the manuscripts of Grieg's songs and the many letters which are in the Grieg Collection there. I am grateful, too, to Messrs Stainer and Bell and to Messrs Ashdown (Elkin Edition, Norwich) for copying archive material for me. Passages from the following are also quoted by kind permission: Eivind Groven's comments on and diagram of the Hardanger fiddle scale, from Kristian Lange, *Norwegian Music – A Survey* (English edition), 1971, p.15 and the excerpt from Willy Dahl, *Ibsen* (in the series *Norske forfatter i nærlys*), 1974, p.32 (H. Aschehoug & Co., Oslo); Niels Gade, *Min lille Fugl* from *Den danske romance – Gade, Hartmann, Rung* (Edition Wilhelm Hansen, Copenhagen); Eyvind Alnæs, *Borte* and Agathe Backer Grøndahl, *Der skreg en Fugl* (Norsk Musikkforlag A/S, Oslo); Roger Quilter, *Now sleeps the crimson petal* (Boosey & Hawkes Music Publishers Ltd, London); Grieg, *Den blonde Pige II* (Prof. Nils Grinde).

My thanks and gratitude are also due to many more people who have helped me in various ways during the time I have been working on this book, but in particular to the following: first and foremost to John Horton, whose idea it was that I might specialize in Scandinavian song and for his subsequent interest and encouragement, who, sadly, died a few months before the publication of this book; to Karen Falch Johannessen and Lise McKinnon of Bergen Public Library for all their help and advice so generously given; to Torbjørn Støverud for reading and offering some corrections and additions to the Discography; to Diane Sævig, singer and teacher, for answering my queries about the performance of Grieg's songs and their place in the modern repertory; to Rolf Davidson, former Rektor of Bergen Music Conservatory, for allowing me free access to the library there; and by no means least to Marianne and Eilif Serck-Hanssen for their most generous hospitality on so many occasions.

St. Albans,                                                                                           BF
May 1990

## Notes

1   Debussy's review in *Gil Blas* of a concert of Grieg's music held under the auspices of Edouard Colonne, Paris, April 1903.
2   *Grieg. A Symposium*, ed. Gerald Abraham, 1948.
3   John Horton: *Grieg*, 1974, pp.165–95.
4   Finn Benestad and Dag Schjelderup-Ebbe: *Edvard Grieg, mennesket og kunstneren* (E.G., The Man and the Artist), 1980.
5   *Grieg Gesamt-Ausgabe/Samlede Verker/Complete Works* (cited hereafter as *GGA*), Vols 14 and 15, musical ed. Nils Grinde, ?1990.

# 1 Folk-song to Art-song

Grieg wrote at least one hundred and eighty songs; of these one is no longer extant and another thirty remain, either complete or in sketches, only in manuscript.[1] There are also fifty-eight works for mixed or male-voice choir and for solo voice with choir. Thus, excluding folk-song arrangements, Grieg composed more vocal music than piano and chamber works together. This alone would make the songs especially noteworthy. Add to it that they were written throughout his life (from op.2 to op.70), show all the high and low points in his development as a composer and reflect his innermost feelings – 'written with my heart's blood', as he frequently described several of them – and they become a most crucial part of his musical oeuvre. Yet if one were to ask most non-Scandinavian singers to name some of his songs, few could probably list more than half a dozen, and of these it is likely that at least one or two would not be known as Grieg wrote them, thanks – or rather, no thanks – to the treatment many of them have received from publishers and translators.

In the history of music, Norway is unusual. Because of its geographical isolation and the difficulties of travelling within the country, it has a long tradition of folk music of great variety peculiar to itself, whereas it came only recently into the realms of 'classical' music compared with other European countries. The folk music has had a major influence on Norwegian art music and is of some antiquity. Nils Grinde has said, 'A study of primitive cultures in our own time makes it tempting to assume that there had existed forms of primitive song . . . in our Stone Age',[2] but there is no absolute evidence for this.

A number of early writers and chroniclers, travelling in Scandinavia between the sixth and the eleventh centuries AD, mention (usually in disparaging terms) music being used at various events, so while it is certain that music of all sorts played a part at least in special occasions, the standard of performance frequently left much to be desired.[3] In *Beowulf* we read that all music was valued highly and there is a mention, at the court of King Hrothgar, of 'a fellow of the king's' whose singing 'gave gold to the language'.[4]

Songs and other music had a considerable place in Norse culture, although unfortunately we now have no way of knowing what it was like. As

1

in other European countries, the earliest extant examples are to be found amongst church music, while the secular melodies date from rather later. Certainly Norse literature regards singing as an entirely separate art form from instrumental playing, while singing and verse-making would appear to be one. Melodies to Skaldic verses were written down by J.E. Hartmann in 1762, as they were sung by a group of Icelanders visiting Copenhagen, and while Iceland was regarded as a major custodian of mediaeval Norse literature, it is scarcely probable that the melodies are of similar age to that of the verses they set.

As in other countries, many of the Norwegian secular tunes were adapted for sacred use with the coming of the Catholic church and here, perhaps for the first time, there is a strong influence from outside Scandinavia, for many of its scholars — especially Danes, but including some Norwegians and Swedes — began to study in Paris during the thirteenth century, where they cannot have failed to learn the part-singing of the Notre Dame school. However, as the participation of the lay congregation in services was minimal at that time, the degree of influence church music in Norway may have had on the majority of lay people or, conversely, how much the laity's music may have influenced the church is uncertain.

The Reformation brought more contacts with the cultural life of other European countries, although the break with the Catholic church did not necessarily mean a break with Catholic church music; Luther preferred to keep a number of Gregorian chants, while also introducing more opportunities for the use of the mother-tongue, until eventually Latin gave way more and more to hymns in the vernacular. Hymn-writing became and has remained an important part of Norway's literary output and still today many composers write new hymn-tunes and psalm settings. Grieg's own *Fire salme* (Four Psalms), op.74, are particularly splendid additions to the repertory. In some cases during the Reformation new words were put to existing secular melodies or new melodies were written to existing verses that had been, to borrow Nils Grinde's expression, 'converted to Christianity'.[5]

Most of what is known of early Norwegian secular music comes from references in literature rather than any extant music and, from these sources, it would seem that the ballad was very popular from mediaeval times. The chanting of these ballads, known as *kvedir*, is still a living tradition in the Faroe Islands and a particular feature of them, later to have some significance, is the *omkved*, the refrain at the end or between the lines of each stanza, which forms a type of coda, usually but not invariably drawing its material from the stanza melody. The song *Millom rosor* (Among roses), op.39 no.4 shows this feature and Grieg also reflects the idea to great effect in the coda of the Vinje setting *Langs ei å* (Beside a stream), op.33 no.5.

The ballad, relating as it does history and legend, is linked to the chanting of Skaldic verse in earlier centuries. However, although the compiling of collections of ballad verses in hand-written books was very fashionable in sixteenth-century court circles, once again it was much later that the traditional melodies were taken down in Norway. This collecting had begun in Sweden and Denmark, but was more avidly taken up all over Scandinavia during the nineteenth century. In Norway it was Ludvig Mathias Lindeman who laid the foundations for a study of his country's folk music. His reading during his youth of Asbjørnsen and Moe's collection of folk-tales led him to investigate the music too, and he travelled all over Norway, eventually amassing over one thousand melodies. His principal collection, *Ældre og nyere norske Fjeldmelodier* (Old and New Norwegian Mountain Tunes), appeared in three volumes between 1853 and 1867 and has provided valuable source material among its almost six hundred tunes, although purists have found fault with Lindeman's settings.

In order to appreciate their influence on the songs of Grieg and others, it is necessary to look more closely at the various forms of folk-song to be found in Norway. In spite of the extent of Lindeman's collection, it is still not possible to know just how these melodies would have been sung or played perhaps six or seven hundred years earlier. However, once again owing to its geographical isolation, which persists even today compared with most European countries, Norway still has a living tradition of folk music from which it is possible to glean some idea of the sound of the earlier music. Most of this music is linked to daily tasks and so where these tasks are still performed, the music persists; where the tasks have been superseded, so the musical tradition has also lapsed.

A great deal of folk-singing in Norway was associated with calling the farm animals, especially those that were sent out to graze for the summer months on the high mountain meadows, accompanied by their herd-girl or boy who lived during this period in a mountain chalet, the *seter* (or *sæter*). This practice has now been discontinued and so the associated songs and calls, the *lokk*, *laling* and *huving*, remain only as curiosities. Those melodies associated with continuing traditions – weddings, dances, soothing children, religious festivals and so on – remain, particularly in instrumental forms. No doubt in Norway, as in other countries where the colourful folk-traditions are a great tourist attraction, the forms will persist, albeit in a static condition.

While it is usual to divide folk music into either vocal or instrumental forms, these categories frequently overlap: a song may be echoed on, for example, the fiddle or the two performed together, and some instrumental pieces may be vocalised in the absence of a player, somewhat in the manner of Scottish 'mouth music'. It is the latter practice that Grieg imitates in *Kvålins halling*, the fourth of the songs in his *Album for Male-Voice Choir*, op.30.

The *seter*-melodies are all calls of one sort or another. The *lokk* was for animals, for example the *kulokk* or cow-call, while the *laling* and *huving* were for calling people, something akin to yodelling in Alpine regions, and more specifically the *huving* was often an individual cry which identified a particular herdsman. Musically the *lokk* is the most interesting, providing inspiration for later composers, and as the keeping of domestic animals in Norway goes back for some two thousand years, it is almost certainly the oldest. In some forms it demands from the singer a splendid degree of coloratura and great virtuosity in negotiating leaps of an octave or more in the vocal line. Not all *lokk* are so complicated, however, and obviously much would have depended on the skill of the individual singer to develop and embellish the calls. Grieg imitated the form several times in his songs, most obviously in *Lokk*, the third of the *Barnlige Sange* (Children's Songs), op.61 and in the *Haugtussa* cycle, op.67, both in *Killingdans* (Kids' dance), no.6, and in the unpublished *Kulokk*.[6]

Of the music associated with other domestic tasks, one of the forms still surviving in several areas is the *bånsull* or lullaby. As in the *lokk*, the simplicity or complexity of the melody is an individual matter, but usually the melodies are built up from small snatches, have a limited vocal range and, occasionally, a certain improvisatory element. Once again, an example can be found in Grieg's *Barnlige Sange*, in the fifth song, *Kveldsang for Blakken* (Evening song for Blakken).

*Stev* is another term frequently encountered in Norwegian music. This is a song to a traditional four-line stanza found in Norwegian folk poetry and is of some antiquity. Magnus Brostrup Landstad, whose collection of old Scandinavian ballads, *Norske folkeviser*, was published in 1853, divides *stev* into two groups, old and new, which differ in rhyme-scheme and in the number of stresses to each line.[7] The old form, *gammelstev*, used by Grieg only in *Den Bergtekne* (The Mountain Thrall), op.32, can be traced back at least to the sagas of the thirteenth century, while the more literary new form, *nystev*, has developed since the seventeenth century. The musical settings of the *nystev* form are frequently characterised by a three-note anacrusis and a number of examples exist in Grieg's vocal output.

The general heading *folkeviser* (folk-songs), as in many languages, covers a wide variety of forms from ancient to comparatively modern, but in Norway the term is usually used for the ballads which are rooted in the Middle Ages. The *viser* are divided according to their subject-matter and labelled accordingly: *kjempeviser* concern giants, *historiske viser* are historical tales, and so on.

Of instrumental music, mention must be made of the dances, the *slåtter*, the distinctive rhythms of which are sometimes found in Grieg's songs as well as in his instrumental pieces. Of the *slåtter* which were also sung, some had texts and some were sung wordlessly, and all fall into two main groups: those dances in triple time and those in duple time. The *slåtter* in $\frac{3}{4}$ are also called *springar* and have a strong rhythmic pulse and an accented second beat; of the duple time *slåtter*, the *halling* is generally in $\frac{2}{4}$ and the more stately *gangar* in $\frac{6}{8}$.

The last and most influential aspect of Norwegian folk music that must be investigated concerns harmony, and more especially the question of intervals which are peculiar to the Norwegian tradition. Natural intervals based on the scales produced by the *lur* and other wind instruments have played their part. The *lur*, for example, has three-quarter intervals rather than semitones and this feature has influenced other music, including that for the Hardanger fiddle (or *hardingfele*). In particular, the fourth degree of this scale lies between a perfect fourth and an augmented fourth, and the leading note is a little below the sharpened seventh of the major and harmonic minor scales. Eivind Groven, the stoutest champion of the view that Norwegian classical music should be based directly on the country's folk music, interpreted these intervals by dividing the first five notes of the scale into four equal intervals and devised a diagram to show their relationship with the intervals of the standard scales and modes, which may be simplified thus:

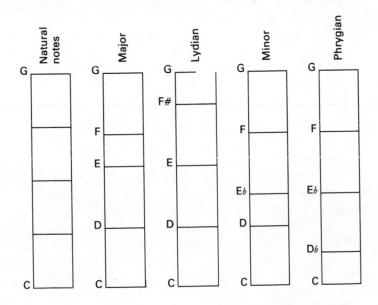

Of course, these three-quarter tones cannot accurately be reproduced in piano writing nor in songs accompanied by piano, but Grieg's occasional use of the sharpened fourth and the flattened seventh of a scale is an attempt to convey the idea. The Hardanger fiddle is also distinguished by its four sympathetic strings and the drone effect produced by them and by the short strings on the other popular stringed instrument, the *langeleik*, is also reflected in Grieg's frequent use of pedal notes, especially as these are not restricted to tonic and dominant, any more than they are on the instruments.

The collecting of folk music by Lindeman and others was one direction taken by that surge of national feeling and pride engendered by Norway's political independence from Denmark in 1814. All things truly Norwegian rather than Dano-Norwegian suddenly became very important, and these feelings continued to generate nationalist art forms until complete national independence was achieved in 1905. But as well as the folk music itself, the performance of it also became important and the better exponents were respected and fêted. The most famous of all the fiddle-players was Torgeir Augundson, known as Myllarguten (the Miller's Boy), whose playing was known and celebrated in many regions of Norway. The virtuoso violinist Ole Bull was a great admirer of Myllarguten and from 1849 arranged many concerts where they both played, and he supported him in other ways, too. Myllarguten had a great talent for improvisation and was said to be able to create quite large musical forms out of a small *slått* theme. He was, however, not unique and among a number of other talented fiddle-players was Knut Dale from Telemark, whose *slåtter* provided a source of material for other composers as well as Grieg.

Of the generation of classical composers who preceded Grieg, there were two to whom he was particularly indebted. The first was Ole Bull, who, as will be seen, played a significant part in organising Grieg's musical education. As a violinist Bull had a brilliant international career, both in Europe and in the United States of America, and besides the standard repertoire he played his own compositions, so beginning to show that Norway had a musical life of her own. Most of his music is no longer played, mainly because it was designed to show off his virtuosity (which reputedly rivalled Paganini's) and therefore it is almost totally associated with Bull's own performance. However, he will always be remembered in Norway for his rhapsody *Et Sæterbesøg* (A visit to the seter), which combines folk melodies with an original tune; the latter later had words put to it by Jørgen Moe and, as *Sæterjentens Søndag* (The seter-girl's Sunday), it has become as much a part of Norwegian hearts and tradition as any true folk-song. Grieg also loved the song and it is almost certainly that to which he refers in a letter to Bjørnson: 'How the Ole Bull song lives! Does it not spring forth from a bright fairy-tale morning high up?'[8]

Music, however, was not Bull's only interest. He was responsible for opening the Norwegian theatre, Den nationale Scene, in Bergen on 2 January 1850, a date now known as Ole Bull's Day. In Norway it is this theatre that is considered to be Bull's greatest achievement for native art, for he used Norwegian actors and writers, Norwegian composers and music, and in its early days both Ibsen and Bjørnson held posts there. Bull's life was restless and gave him little time to develop the inspiration he had gained from folk music. However, he began the task and, as Bjørnson said at his funeral, 'He gave us self-confidence, the greatest gift he could have given us at that time.' It was Lindeman, two years younger than Bull, with his collection of *Fjeldmelodier* and his adaptations of folk music for performance, who began to show the extent of the material. Although most of Lindeman's original compositions are in the realms of sacred music, including the book of hymn-tunes officially adopted by the Norwegian church, it was the *Fjeldmelodier* that were to ensure the indebtedness of later generations of musicians.

Grieg did not 'discover' folk music until the mid-1860s and his early music clearly reflects his studies in Leipzig and the influence of Mendelssohn and, particularly in the first published songs, opp.2 and 4, of Schumann. The Norwegian song-writing influence from the preceding generation was Halfdan Kjerulf, who lived right through that period known in Norway as 'the National-Romantic Break-through'. Kjerulf set a wide range of texts in his 126 known songs, by Norwegian, Danish, German and French poets, and even four Norwegian translations of Thomas Moore and one of Byron. He had a great respect for the German Romantics, especially Schumann and Mendelssohn, and his piano writing, like Grieg's shows much of their influence, not least in the use of preludes and postludes to his songs. Perhaps because he was the first song-composer to gain any wide currency in Norway, Kjerulf is often referred to as the 'Norwegian Schubert'.

Grieg acknowledged his own and succeeding composers' indebtedness to Kjerulf and Kjerulf's indebtedness to folk music. In an obituary in *Illustreret Tidende* in August 1868, he wrote that Kjerulf had taken the folk-song 'as his starting point and has chosen the *romanse* as his field of activity. Therefore, we should thank him, for in this it was given to him to find the national colour wherein our music is able to achieve its natural and healthy development.'[9] Like Grieg, Kjerulf also arranged a number of folk-tunes for piano and these were undoubtedly a model for Grieg's own arrangements later. Kjerulf's somewhat cosmopolitan style has earned him a genuine place in Norwegian musical history, a place won not just by being a 'nationalist' composer, and, as with Grieg and so many of their compatriots, it is only the lack of good translations that prevent his songs from having the wider currency outside Scandinavia that they deserve.

By the time Grieg and his contemporaries began to emerge as composers of talent, they were expected to be 'Norwegian'. This was not so difficult in songs, for besides having Kjerulf's *romanser* as models, songs have words and when those words were by the best Norwegian writers, the settings immediately acquired something of a national character. It was not so easily captured in abstract music; although piano transcriptions of folk music were abundant, there was no tradition in Norway of opera, symphony or other large-scale forms. Grieg's own attempt at a symphony was made at the instigation of the Danish composer Niels Gade, and is a joyful if unsophisti-cated work. It is certainly not poor enough to warrant his ban on performances after 1867, [10] even if the interest in it today is largely as a work of youthful promise. The early Piano Concerto, on the other hand, is the major work with which Grieg has achieved international fame. As is well known, its themes are very Norwegian in character and there is not just the natural feeling for piano writing one would expect from an accomplished pianist, but also for orchestration. The flowing melodies of many of his songs are foreshadowed in the second movement, but it was perhaps this very gift for melody that prevented Grieg from being able to handle the larger forms, where it is necessary to have the sort of thematic content that can be developed rather than that which is complete in itself and thus precludes development. Grieg's ideas are manifold and he blamed his training at the 'confounded' Leipzig Conservatory for his inability to work with them in any extended form.

It is interesting to note that the Piano Concerto was written before Grieg came to know Lindeman's collections. Once he had encountered the *Fjeldmelodier*, they were a source of great inspiration and from this time on his interest in the smaller musical forms became much more pronounced. He wrote to Henry Finck, his American biographer, in 1900: 'Norwegian country life, Norwegian sagas and history and above all Norwegian nature from my youth exerted a great influence on my creative work. However, the opportunity to engross myself in Norwegian folk-song I only acquired later.' [11] A letter to Gottfred Matthison-Hansen of October 1877 shows the beginnings of his realization of the importance of his conception of Norwegian nationalism with regard to his own music:

> For you must not say, because the old masters did not use national motifs more than occasionally, that we should not do so either; in other words, that we should not ally ourselves differently and more closely with our national folk music than they did, because *we do*. I do not believe, as Gade said, that one tires of the nationalistic, for if one could, it would not be an idea to fight for. But for myself I believe that I have kept on stagnating through lack of both composition-technique — mechanical skill on the whole — and lack of occupation with the large forms. But I can take a hint and in that you are right: no chasing after nationality. I will see that I throw out what is merely reflected and write straight from the shoulder; it will either be Norwegian or Chinese. [12]

Because of its almost direct development from folk-song without many of the major outside influences that affected other, less isolated European cultures, the song form in Scandinavia, the *romanse*, is as different from the German Lied as is the French *mélodie*. This particular type of lyric song is somewhat akin to the better quality nineteenth-century English ballad, characterised by its mainly strophic form, a straightforward melodic line, its rather formulated emotional content and the largely supportive role of the piano accompaniment. As John Horton has said, 'The composer of *romanser* relies on the poem and the interpreter to communicate subtle variations in rhythm and mood from stanza to stanza, against a musical background that remains constant, with little organic development and with the piano accompaniment subordinated to the declamation of the poem.'[13] The mainly strophic form of Grieg's songs suits both the lyric poetry he was happiest setting and his paramount concern with words. Where he was drawn to a through-composed form for larger-scale songs, for example, *Efteraarsstormen* (The autumn storm), op. 18 no. 4 and *Udfarten* (The outward journey), op. 9 no. 4, much use is made of thematic material to provide a cohesive whole, but the result is not entirely satisfactory.

It was Schumann who, in succession to Schubert, developed the art of Lieder-writing and achieved an almost perfect balance between the melodic expression of the words he set and the piano accompaniment. Later Brahms was to develop the more purely musical aspects of Lieder and Wolf the poetic ones. Grieg leans towards the Brahmsian side and his gift for melody makes his songs easily adaptable into abstract musical forms. He himself arranged many of them for piano solo and four, the two *Elegiac Melodies*, op. 34 and the two *Melodies*, op. 53, for string orchestra. Often, as for example in the second movement of his C minor Violin Sonata, the music lacks only a text to become a song, although many of his best melodies are built up from the innate music suggested by words.

Grieg frequently acknowledged Schumann as one of his mentors and wrote about him at length in an article, 'doubtless ghosted',[14] published in January 1894.[15] Much of what he says of Schumann's song-writing could equally well apply to himself; for example, 'With Schumann the poetic conception plays the leading part to such an extent that musical considerations technically important are subordinated, if not entirely neglected' and, more particularly, 'With Schubert the most of what is to be done is explicitly expressed; while with Schumann one must understand the art of reading between the lines – of interpreting a half-told tale.'. Perhaps it is the lack of explicit expression that has deterred singers from tackling more of Grieg's songs, for 'reading between the lines' and 'interpreting a half-told tale,' especially in the reiterated melodies of the many strophic settings, is essential and demands a great deal of interpretative ability. Neither, as will be seen, have the poor translations of so many of Grieg's songs helped the non-Scandinavian speaker towards this goal.

Grieg also writes of Schumann's 'great demand upon the compass of the voice' and continues, 'It is often no easy thing to determine whether the song is intended for a soprano or an alto, for he ranges frequently in the same song from the lowest to the highest register. Several of his most glorious songs begin in the deepest pitch and gradually rise to the highest, so that the same singer can rarely master both.' Grieg himself only occasionally presents a similar problem, predictably perhaps in an early song like *Eingehüllt in graue Wolken*, op. 2 no. 2, which also musically owes a good deal to Schumann's influence, to great dramatic effect in *Soldaten* (The soldier), op. post., and more unexpectedly in *Fiskervise* (Fisherman's song), the fourth of the *Barnlige Sange*, op.61.

Grieg's usual concern for the voice is apparent from some of his letters to Delius. He wrote of Delius's *Five Songs from the Norwegian*, which are dedicated to Nina, 'There are so many beautiful and deeply-felt things in them . . . And then again there are other things which I find difficult to accept . . . in the form and in the treatment of the voice. A Norwegian melody and a Wagnerian treatment of the voice are dangerous things indeed to try to reconcile. But we can discuss this. Perhaps I am too narrow-minded . . .'.[16] In another letter he discusses Delius's setting of *Paa Vidderne* (On the heights) for narrator and orchestra: 'You see, you have composed with an unbelievable lack of consideration for the declaimer.'.[17] He goes on to tell Delius of the difficulties he himself had with *Bergliot*, his melodrama for speaker and orchestra, and says of it, 'The battle between *voice* and *music* is frightfully unpleasant. And how *fantastically* little is needed to mask the voice.' He shows a similar consideration with all the piano accompaniments to his songs; the piano supports the voice and is a partner with it, but is never allowed to overwhelm it.

It is, in fact, often in the piano part that the true subtleties of the music are to be found and the accompaniments must never merely be dismissed. Once again what Grieg wrote about Schumann could equally refer to his own songs: 'I have no faith in a renderer of Schumann's songs who lacks appreciation of the fact that the piano has fully as great a claim upon interest and study as the voice of the singer',[18] a similar criterion being especially applicable to the great settings of Ibsen (op.25), Vinje (op.33) and Garborg (op.67).

In spite of his desire to be able to handle the larger musical forms, it was in the smaller forms, especially songs and piano music, that Grieg was to make his singular mark. His ability to write songs he attributed largely to the influence of his wife Nina, and it is significant that, as will be seen, he was unable to do so when things between them became particularly difficult. In the same long letter to Finck quoted above, however, the mature composer was able to write,

> I don't believe I have more talent for song-composition than for any other genre in music. From whence does it come then, that the song plays such a prominent role in my output? Quite simply for the reason that I, like other mortals, on one occasion in my life (to quote Goethe) was brilliant. The brilliance was: love. I fell in love with a young girl with a wonderful voice and similarly wonderful interpretation. This girl became my wife and life's partner right to this day. She has been for me — I may certainly say — the only true interpreter of my songs.[19]

Grieg's excellent feeling for the voice was no doubt indeed largely due to

Nina's influence and his songs offer the performer a wealth of diverse material from dramatic to lyrical, from emotional involvement, nostalgia and nature to travel, description and ironic observation. One of their main features is that so many are settings of poems by the great writers of the day, for Grieg's time was also a golden age for Norwegian literature, and the extent to which the quality of his music is directly influenced by the quality of the words he chose to set is not so surprising when one realises that he himself was more than a fair exponent of words, a fact attested to by his numerous letters and articles. His selection among the literary treasures of his time almost always had a personal connotation, sometimes perhaps subconsciously significant, and he told Finck, 'My choice of poet is always connected with what I have experienced.'[20]

Another major factor is the languages he set – principally German, Danish and the two forms of Norwegian – the choice of the language being directly affected by particular phases of his life. For example, as Astra Desmond has pointed out in *Grieg: A Symposium*, Grieg seems to have been drawn to the *landsmål* dialect whenever he was most depressed. This had started as early as 1866 with his setting of Kristofer Janson's *Vesle gut* (Little boy), published for the first time in the *GGA*, but occurred more specifically during 1880 with the Vinje settings, op.33, and again towards the end of his life with the song-cycle to Garborg's *Haugtussa*, op.67. It may be that he was particularly drawn because he associated the sound of *landsmål* with the lilting speech patterns of Bergen and the west coast of Norway, the speech of his home and childhood.

Grieg's settings of five major writers – Andersen, Bjørnson, Ibsen, Vinje and Garborg – correspond to five significant periods in his life and musical development. With these five writers, rather in the manner of Hugo Wolf, after devoting himself to a considerable number of their verses, he never returned to that poet again. With less important writers, for example his friends John Paulsen and Holger Drachmann, he returned once or twice, perhaps bowing to amicable pressure from the figures concerned.

Very receptive to poetry, even on some occasions to rather inferior poetry, Grieg always composed music to suit the intrinsic melody of the words, whatever the language. Norwegian speech patterns, particularly the rise at the end of a phrase or sentence (or even an individual word) may to a certain extent be discerned in his corresponding musical phrases. There is something in the Scandinavian psyche which appears to regard being happy as tempting fate and so often a darker feeling is to be detected behind the seemingly innocuous. In this Grieg is a true Scandinavian, and while the slighter poems frequently drew forth pleasing enough settings, it was to tragedy and real depth of emotion that he responded best. Thus he achieved his greatest melodic heights with the finest of his choice of verse: that of Ibsen and Bjørnson, and by Vinje and Garborg.

One of Grieg's main objections to translations was that the words then had to be made to fit the music, which was exactly opposite to the way he worked. In a further letter to Henry Finck written in 1903, he expressed his entire song-writing ethos thus:

> For me, it is important when I compose songs, not first and foremost to make music, but above all to give expression to the poet's innermost intentions. To let the poem reveal itself and to intensify it, that was my task. If this task is tackled, then the music is also successful. Not otherwise, no matter how celestially beautiful it may be. [21]

## Notes

1   Some have been discovered comparatively recently in Bergen, Oslo and elsewhere. Volume 15 of the *GGA* contains twenty-one previously unpublished songs and these are indicated in the main text.

2   Nils Grinde: *Norsk Musikkhistorie* (A History of Norwegian Music), 1971, p.9.

3   For a detailed discussion see Grinde: *Norsk Musikkhistorie* and John Horton: *Scandinavian Music*, 1963.

4   Lines 867 and 869 in the translation by Michael Alexander, Penguin Books 1973.

5   Grinde: *Norsk Musikkhistorie*, p.34.

6   Included in the *GGA*, Vol.15.

7   A fuller discussion of these forms and some of the instruments associated with the Norwegian folk music is to be found in Appendix D.

8   Grieg to Bjørnson, 1 February 1900 from Copenhagen.

9   Grieg's obituary of Kjerulf, reproduced in *Edvard Grieg: Artikler og Taler* (E.G.: Articles and Speeches), ed. Øystein Gaukstad, 1957, pp.72–74.

10   The ban was overridden in 1981 when the Symphony was performed at the Bergen Festival, having been 'scooped' in Moscow some months earlier.

11   Grieg to Finck, 17 July 1900; thirty-six sides written in German, for his supposedly poor use of which Grieg apologized: 'In the use of "der, die, das" I was always a fool'.

12   Grieg to Matthison-Hansen, 17 October 1877 from Lofthus.

13   Horton: *Scandinavian Music*, p. 108.

14   John Horton in a letter to the author.

15   *Century Illustrated Monthly Magazine*, January 1894, p.447.

16   Grieg to Delius, 23 September 1888 from Troldhaugen, quoted in Lionel Carley: *Delius, A Life in Letters*, ed. Lionel Carley, Vol.1, 1983, p.24.

17   Grieg to Delius, 9 December 1888 from Bergen, quoted in *Delius, A Life in Letters*, Vol.1, p.28.

18   *Century Illustrated Monthly Magazine*, p.447.

19   As note 11.

20   *Grieg. A Symposium*, ed. Gerald Abraham, 1948, p.86.

21   Grieg to Finck, (undated) 1903

# 2 Translation and Interpretation

Almost everyone who has written anything at all about Grieg's songs has bemoaned the lack of good translations, and most especially of translations into English. Dan Fog, the Danish musicologist, antiquary and publisher, in his catalogue of first and early editions of Grieg's music, writes: 'A number of the songs would, moreover, be served by new translations; among other things it can be seen that a number of English translations go back to less successful German translations . . .'[1] John Horton, at the end of his chapter on the solo songs in his biography of Grieg, speaks of 'the dearth of satisfactory translations' and goes on: 'Bad as many of the German ones are, the English published alongside them are often worse.'[2] The same author again comments that 'clumsy German translations have done the composer poor service . . . because of the false declamation they impose on the singer, and the actual mistranslations with which they baffle the hearer . . .'[3] The Norwegian composer and respected authority on Grieg, David Monrad Johansen (1888–1974), referring in his biography[4] to the op.33 songs, wrote about 'the dreadful translations which preclude the possibility of a full and complete appreciation and understanding.' Sergius Kagen, the Russian-American composer and musicologist, observes somewhat mildly: 'It is a great pity that most of Grieg's songs have been known in English-speaking countries practically exclusively in German versions, and that the available English versions are for the most part rather poor',[5] and Astra Desmond, the English contralto who specialised in performances of Grieg's songs, gave in her article some pertinent examples of what she called 'gems of the "translator's" art'.[6]

It is regrettable that Peters' *Grieg Gesamt-Ausgabe* retains the former German versions of the songs, but it is to be hoped that the much improved and frequently skilful new English translations by the Americans William Halverson and Rolf Stang will go a considerable way to abrogating what has gone before. However, as the earlier editions are, and undoubtedly will for some time remain, in circulation in music libraries and amongst non-specialist performers, it would seem pertinent to discuss the whole question of translation in this case and to indicate some of the more extreme vagaries of the older translations by which many singers may still be judging Grieg's songs.

Two questions immediately arise: first, why are translations needed at all and, second, why are there apparently such difficulties for the would-be translator?

The answer to the first question is that, apart from the twenty two German texts and one (unpublished) to an English poem, Grieg's songs are in minority European languages and most singers, while having at least a working knowledge of German, French and Italian, do not know Norwegian and Danish. This is a great pity, for the Scandinavian repertoire is vast and contains some most beautiful songs. It is also unfortunate that, while we now expect to hear Musorgsky and Rakhmaninov in the original Russian and Bartók and Kodály in Hungarian, outside Scandinavia Grieg is still largely sung in German. He may even be found in music festival syllabuses listed among those composers suitable for inclusion in a Lieder class, which does him a double injustice.

Grieg had little choice but to find a publisher outside Scandinavia if his music was to reach a wider public and it is those editions printed by C.F. Peters that have come into popular circulation, rather than those from the Danish sub-publisher, Wilhelm Hansen. It is also interesting to note that English translations of the songs began to be made over a hundred years ago; the British Library has a version by J. Goddard of *Taksigelse* (Thanksgiving), op. 10 no. 1, which dates from 1878. However, owing to the scarcity of Scandinavian language exponents in other European countries, existing English versions have largely been translated from the German rather than from Norwegian or Danish. Consequently, rather as in childhood games of 'Chinese whispers', by the time the English is arrived at, it often bears little resemblance to the original.

The nature of that original language can also be in doubt, with some translations stating they are 'from the Norwegian', when the poems are actually Danish — as R.H. Elkin does with regard to the op. 44 songs — and vice versa. Admittedly, the written languages at the time were very similar, but such inaccuracies do little to inspire confidence in the quality of the translation. Even the titles of songs can be confused, for instead of rendering the heading the poet or composer had used, some translators have felt it necessary to give a more detailed idea of the content; thus *Ved Rundarne* (At Rundarne), op. 33 no. 9, becomes 'Auf der Reise zer Heimat', 'On the way home'. Even more confusingly, two of Grieg's songs, *På skogstien* (On the woodland path), op. 26 no. 5 and *Når jeg vil dø* (When I shall die), op. 59 no. 1, are given the same title, 'Herbststimmung', in German.

There are many arguments, frequently repeated, both for and against using the original language in opera and song, and certainly an audience unfamiliar with the language it is hearing will miss a good deal. As Kirsten Flagstad said in her autobiography,

> It has been the same with my Norwegian songs, those beautiful settings of beautiful poems by the great poets of my country. Often there would be synopses or explanations in the printed programmes, but it was never the same thing as knowing, from word to word and phrase to phrase, just what the poet, and the composer after him, had in mind. I always regretted that so much of our beloved Grieg was lost on my audience because of the barrier of language.[7]

However, to sing inaccurate and clumsy English versions deprives an audience just as much and possibly more and, with inexpensive duplicating now readily available, it is not difficult to provide a separate sheet with accurate prose translations to supplement a programme.

Grieg himself placed great importance on the communication of meaning in his songs and in the already quoted letter to Finck of July 1900 he went into some detail about the problems of translation:

> That my songs . . . have found so little circulation abroad . . . lies without doubt partly in the difficulty of translation . . . If the Scandinavian poet, whose language the foreigner neither understands nor sings, is mutilated by the translation, not only he but also the composer suffers by this mutilation. Unfortunately, in my efforts to obtain good translations I have often had great bad luck. It is true that the task presupposes a versatility rarely to be found, since the translator must at the same time be poet, linguist and musically knowledgeable. In addition there is the sad fact that most publishers do not appreciate a *good* translation so much as — a cheap one. My Leipzig publisher, C.F. Peters, has certainly made an effort to obtain good ones. The result, however, is that even in favourable circumstances the translation is usually forced *to fit the music* and seems unnatural. I am a friend of good declamation. In my mother tongue I have always taken this into consideration. This is perhaps the main reason why my songs are sung all over Scandinavia. If, however, a rhythmically bad translation is also unpoetic and banal, then the poet's meaning is downright distorted, as is so often the case in the German, English and French translations of my songs . . .

It is not just the meaning, but the whole sound of a song that is important and Astra Desmond quotes a critic who once remarked, after hearing some of Grieg's songs sung in Norwegian, that 'the whole atmosphere of the songs changed from the fustiness of later nineteenth-century German romanticism to the bright, clear air of the fjords.'[8] As Grieg himself put it in a letter of 5 June 1894, agreeing with his French translator William Molard, 'the closest possible translation will be that which keeps the closest contact with the music'.[9]

That the English translator should go back to the original language would seem obvious and, in the case of the Scandinavian languages, more logical, for they are far closer to English than German in syntax and also in the softer sound, neither Danish, Norwegian nor Swedish having voiced sibilants. One might consider the opening line of *Saa du knøsen*, op.49 no.1, in the original and in two German versions. The original – actually in Danish, but as is the convention with Grieg's songs sung with Norwegian pronunciation – opens 'Saa du knøsen som strøg forbi? (Did you see the fellow who swept by?)', a line full of unvoiced sibilants and forward vowels. Wilhelm Henzen's German version for the first Peters' edition of 1889 renders the line: 'Sähst vorbei mit dem Gluthblick du?', improved only a little in the later version by Hans Schmidt: 'Sähst den seltsamen Burschen du?' Both require a greater variety of sounds and more labial movement than the original and both are rather difficult to enunciate at the 'allegro vivace' tempo Grieg requires.

With regard to the problems facing a translator, there are linguistically two main features of the Scandinavian languages that present particular difficulties. The first is that the indefinite article is attached to the end of the noun to make the definite form; for example, *en gutt* – a boy, becomes *gutten* – the boy; *et tre* – a tree, becomes *treet* – the tree. This is a major difference from other European languages and one that necessitates a change of accent or an anacrusis in translated versions. The second problematic feature is the large number of common disyllabic words whose English equivalents are mono-syllabic, for example *svane* – swan, which makes a satisfactory translation of that beautiful song almost impossible. In fact, the first phrase of *En svane*, op.25 no.2, is doubly difficult to render: 'min hvide svane' means 'my white swan', which leaves the English two syllables short, a problem not really resolved in any of the English editions: 'My swan, my pale one' (Frederick Corder), 'The swan is silent' (Dawson Freer), 'My swan, white-feathered' (Mary Dacre), 'My swan, my white one' (Astra Desmond) or Rolf Stang's 'How still, my white swan', both the last with unsatisfactory accents on 'white'. A similar problem is encountered in another of Grieg's most well-known songs, *Jeg elsker dig* (I love you), op.5 no.3. Again, various solutions are presented in English editions: 'I love but thee' and 'I love thee, sweet' (Laubach), 'I love thee, dear' (Lily David), 'I love thee now' (Elkin) and 'I worship you' (Astra Desmond). None is entirely satisfactory, but neither is the carrying of the monosyllable 'love' over both the dotted quaver and semiquaver.

A major feature of Grieg's song-writing style is the number of feminine cadences, engendered at least in part by the many disyllabic words in Norwegian and Danish. Once again this presents a problem for the translator, not least because so often these words occur in rhyming positions, for example at the end of every line in *Våren* (The Spring), op.33 no.2, and the carrying over of a single syllable, which is sometimes found in translations, distorts the character of the musical phrase.

The syntax of the Scandinavian languages is very similar to English, whereas German, with its strict placement of verb and participle, is not. It

is, therefore, surprising that so many difficulties apparently arise from it.
Corder's English version in the first Peters' edition of *Med en Vannlilje* (With
a waterlily), op. 25 no. 4, for example, contained the lines

> Like the stream thy bosom clear is
> And it dreams not danger near is.

The same translator opens the second stanza of *Et håb* (A hope), op. 26 no. 1,
with 'What strains of music my pulses sound me!' As well as being graceless
and awkward to sing, anomalous word-order can occasionally give rise to
ambiguity of meaning. In *Tytebæret* (The wild cranberry), op. 33 no. 4, a
berry is growing on a hillside, destined to be plucked and eaten by a young
boy, and the poet, Vinje, draws an analogy between the berry's sacrifice and
the privilege of giving one's life for one's friends. In R.H. Elkin's translation
for the Ashdown edition, these rather noble sentiments were completely
spoiled, as it ends with the berry's words to the boy rendered

> When to manhood you have ripened,
> You will pray the same as I:
> You will have no greater longing
> Than for those you love to die.

If it were not possible to rearrange the last line to read, 'Than to die for those
you love', with an appropriately altered preceding rhyme, then the meaning
might surely have been clarified by the use of a comma after the first word
and the fifth, although this would not be easy to observe in performance.

Misinterpretation of a different kind has occurred in several translations of
*Solveigs Vuggevise* (Solveig's Lullaby) from the music to Ibsen's *Peer Gynt*. The
song comes at the very end of the play when Peer, after all his wanderings
and now an old man, returns at last to the faithful Solveig. She cradles him in
her arms and, as the sun rises and the curtain falls, sings quietly. She
addresses him as 'gutt' – boy or lad – and refers to herself as 'mother'.
Translators, however, misled by the title and apparently not having read the
poem in the context of the play, have rendered 'gutt' as 'kind', 'child', 'son',
'laddie' and 'baby', all of which have a rather different connotation. Worst of
all was the early English version by Theo. Marzials[10] and Mrs J.P. Morgan
for the Pitt and Hatzfeld edition of 1888,[11] which began:

> Sleep, my sweet little baby dear!
> Mother watches her dainty darling.

This was not greatly improved by Corder for Peters:

> Sleep, my treasure, my baby boy,
> I will rock and watch over my darling;

nor by Elkin in the Ashdown edition:

> Sleep, my own little baby, sleep,
> I will watch as I rock the cradle.

Fashion in usage also plays its part in translation. It can never be possible to predict how language will change and a word or phrase which sounds well now can become dated in a comparatively short time. It is also difficult to retain the charm of an original in another language and colloquialisms rarely translate well. Neither do diminutives and it is no longer acceptable to use such terms as 'lambkin' or, worse still, 'kidling', which is to be found in English translations of the sixth song of the *Haugtussa* cycle. The terms 'thee' and 'thou' until recently seem to have been obligatory as the equivalent of the informal second person, as if their use could imbue the verse with the desired 'poetic' quality. However, that gives rise to such unwieldy phrases as 'O mindest thou last summer together how we went?', the opening line from Corder's translation of *På skogstien*, op.26 no.5.

It ought to be unnecessary to amplify Grieg's list of desirable qualities for the ideal translator to include the requirement that he or she should also be a singer, or at least work closely with a singer, for while it is possible to achieve an accurate translation which rhymes and scans, that unfortunately does not presuppose that the verse is singable. Pity the performer using Corder's translation of the beautiful song *Det første møte* (The first meeting), op.21 no.1, who is presented with the opening line 'The thrill of love's first eye-glance'! The placing of words and vowel sounds is also important in singing and stressing the second syllable of 'wonder' on a high A flat at the end of Marzials' and Morgan's version of *Det første møte* is incomprehensible:

Ex.1                                                                Det første Møte

Astra Desmond translated several songs by Grieg, none of which, unfortunately, is currently available. Frequently her translations, including *Jeg elsker dig*, *En svane* and *Våren*, sacrifice rhyme for scansion and sensible English; this is certainly preferable to rhyme for the sake of rhyme, however inane, but, except in *En svane*, one is left with a slight sense of something incomplete.

As seen in the letter to Finck quoted above, Grieg was always most anxious that translations of his songs, besides being accurate, should also follow the original declamation as closely as possible. It is unfortunate, then, that this stipulation has so often been ignored – although firmly adhered to in the *GGA* – especially when the composer has been careful to match the musical declamation to that of the poem. As an example, in *Stambogsrim* (Album verse), op.25 no.3, Ibsen describes his beloved as 'a messenger of happiness that went — went out' and Grieg placed a semiquaver rest to point this change of emphasis and meaning:

Ex.2                                       Stambogsrim

In the Peters' edition, Henzen gives the line in his German version as 'du täuschest mich', completely ignoring the rest and changing the rhythm, a practice followed in the English version by Corder:

Ex.3                                       Stambogsrim

Grieg was also very upset about the criticism of his declamation made by Gerhard Schjelderup in his study of Grieg and his work,[12] writing to Julius Steenberg in December 1903, '. . . he is a little unjust, I think. He talks about bad declamation. And I, who have always stressed the importance of declaiming naturally . . . I have a strong suspicion that Schjelderup has only had the German edition of the songs in his hands.[13]

In a long letter to William Molard, Grieg went into great detail about the translations into French on which Molard was working and, after thanking him for the latest versions, wrote that he would 'take the liberty of taking them one by one',[14] going on to list the points where he was not completely happy. In another letter Grieg said he was surprised to learn from Peters that only one of the three volumes of songs already translated into French was to be retranslated, that is the volume with versions by Tranchant on which Molard was now working; the others, by Victor Wilder, were to remain in use. Grieg told Molard, 'if he [Dr Abraham, proprietor of Peters] should want some of the songs in T's translation retained, I ask you to stand firm so that this cannot happen, because I have declared them all absolutely unusable.[15] It is interesting to note from a further letter to Molard that Grieg was most concerned about those songs he considered to be his better ones. Having made some points about emphases in 'Foi', the French version of *Trudom*, he added, 'But I don't care for this song, so it matters less. The main thing is that my best songs should be the best from your hand, too.'[16]

Again from the letter to Finck of 1900, it is apparent that it was not just for his own benefit that Grieg was so insistent on accurate translations, but also for the sake of the poet. In the letter to Molard in which he discusses 'Foi', Grieg also shows concern for the accuracy of 'Le Printemps' (*Våren*). He points out that by using 'endnu' and 'endnu ein gong (yet; yet once again)' at the beginning of so many lines in the poem, Vinje has 'achieved something lovely and tender', which Molard should try to emulate in the French.

It was on Bjørnson's behalf that Grieg expressed discontent with the first German translation by Emma Dahl of *Foran Sydens kloster* (Before the southern convent), op. 22, a cantata for soprano and contralto soloists, female choir and orchestra. The composer wrote to the poet from Leipzig in March 1875, 'Yesterday evening Foran Sydens kloster was presented in Euterpe[17] ... Emma Dahl's translation must be abandoned, since it was found by competent people here to be – dreadful; the well-known opera-writer – the composer Franz von Holstein – has now translated the poem[18] to everyone's satisfaction – also to mine, and I hope – to yours.'

The desire for accuracy was by no means a one-sided matter and Grieg showed the same consideration when requiring translations into Norwegian. In a letter of November 1876, he asked the Bergen writer John Paulsen if he could translate Schubert's *Gesang der Geister über den Wassern*. 'It is,' he wrote, 'an atmospheric, strange poem, so you will certainly take pleasure in it. But you must keep *exactly* to the metrical feet of the original for the sake of the music.'

Perhaps because of the demands of the *romanse* style, particularly the dependence on the performer to bring out the finer points of the different stanzas in the many strophic settings, Grieg was throughout his life greatly appreciative of what a musicianly singer could achieve and generous in his praise of those few who met his high standards. He objected vehemently to the practice of singers embellishing his songs, or adding and altering notes which the composer had so carefully written. To Finck he cited what he called 'the prima donna insolence' of singers who, at the end of a song, sing 'instead of 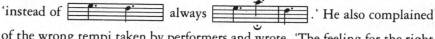 always .' He also complained of the wrong tempi taken by performers and wrote, 'The feeling for the right tempo should be in the blood.' He went on, 'Why has Mother Nature as a rule bestowed a voice only on those beings who possess neither the intelligence nor the deeper feelings to use the voice as a means to a higher end?'[19] So intent on accurate performance was he that, even in a fervent love-letter to Isabella Edwards, he was able to concern himself with the finer points of interpretation, instructing her that the phrase 'Hverken slag (neither throb)' in *En svane* 'must be a single pp, without any crescendo whatsoever'.[20]

Lack of musicianship annoyed and frustrated him. The soloist in a Leipzig performance of *Den Bergtekne* (The Mountain Thrall), op. 32, was described to his friend Frants Beyer as 'an unmusical fool'. Another letter describes a concert in London on 17 May (Norway's national day) in 1906, which the composer conducted: 'All the renderings in the programme were excellent, except the interpretation, or rather non-interpretation, of the songs. The orchestra sounded so lovely and the voice so absolutely insignificant. It was a daughter of T— who sang; she calls herself Dolores and by God it was dolorous in the worst sense.'[21] Again to Finck, he complained bitterly:

> I have certainly said that my songs are often sung in Scandinavia. I have not said anything about their being sung *well*. Far from it: I have become depressingly aware that true interpreters of my songs, as I myself envisage them, are not to be found among the present generation in Norway. Both the musical education and the musical understanding are lacking . . . Our vocal artists have neither the artistic conviction nor the courage to try anything not yet put to the test, for fear it should be over the public's head. . .[22]

Grieg in fact placed musicianship above sheer splendour of voice and accurate declamation above beauty of melodic line. Once more the letter to Finck of 17 July 1900 offers elucidation:

> . . . I have taken upon myself the task of improving declamation in the Wagnerian sense. At times I have composed in an almost recitative style . . . For the most part, however, it is contrary to my nature to go as far as the modern *German* Lieder composers. I do not wish to see the melodic element concentrated mainly on the piano and am no ally of the efforts to translate Wagnerian operatic style into song. The lyrical drama of a song must, to my mind, always be absolutely different from that of the music-drama.

Grieg was always grateful to Nina, whose interpretative powers were her greatest asset, and she remained the principal exponent of his songs for a large part of both their lives, but other singers did occasionally please him. In 1886 the young Anna Kriebel visited the composer at Troldhaugen; Grieg described her to Beyer as 'really a true singing talent, the best in this country. Big voice, which she has learnt to use and – a whole lot of fervour'. In another letter to Beyer he described a concert in Stockholm at which the Norwegian-born Dagmar Møller sang 'with the finest intelligence and understanding'. He continued, 'The voice is not beautiful, but that doesn't matter to me nor to the audience, for she had a storming success.'[23]

One of Grieg's favourite interpreters of his songs was Ellen Nordgren Gulbranson, and a number of letters to her, preserved in the Grieg Collection in Bergen, show his appreciation of her talents. Again to Beyer he wrote of the first time he heard her: 'a sweet young Swedish girl – Ellen Nordgren – remember the name.' . . . She sang among other things "Ragna" and "Ragnhild" from op. 44 absolutely beautifully. I dare say I have not met anyone so sympathetic to me with regard to song'.[24] John Horton has said of her that 'Grieg must have been satisfied that Gulbranson had the sensibility to distinguish between operatic and lyric song styles, for he welcomed the wider currency she gave a number of his Norwegian songs through her international recitals'.[25]

Grieg expected a great deal from all his performers, an attitude that could no doubt be daunting as well as inspiring. The songs are always considerately written for the voice; one cannot agree, however, with Sergius Kagen's assertion that they 'can hardly be considered either musically or vocally taxing',[26] for the full range of Grieg's artistic abilities is to be found in them. He was a man for whom self-expression and communication were very important. It is a great pity and no little cause for shame that even now, more than eighty years after his death, his ability to communicate through song is still so little understood or appreciated outside Scandinavia.

## Notes

1    Dan Fog: *Edvard Grieg – Værk Fortegnelse* (E.G. – A Catalogue of Works), 1966, Introduction p. III; typescripts in Bergen Public Library and Oslo University Music Library. (*Not* in the bound edition published by Fog, Copenhagen 1980, under the title *Grieg-Katalog*.)
2    John Horton: *Grieg*, 1974, p.195.
3    Horton: *Scandinavian Music*, 1963, p.107.
4    David Monrad Johansen: *Edvard Grieg*, 1934, p.259.
5    Sergius Kagen: *Music for the Voice*, Indiana University Press, 1968, p.613.
6    Astra Desmond in *Grieg. A Symposium*, ed. Gerald Abraham, 1948, pp.73–74.
7    Kirsten Flagstad: *The Flagstad Manuscript* 'as told to Louis Biancolli', Heinemann 1953, p.223.
8    Astra Desmond in *Grieg. A Symposium*, p.73. The critic is not named, but the remark may perhaps have been made in a review of one of her own concerts of Grieg's songs.
9    Grieg to Molard, 5 June 1894 from Grefsen Bad near Christiania.
10    Marzials also translated songs by Kjerulf; the British Library has four volumes published between 1883 and 1892. Mrs Morgan's translations are still retained in some volumes of Grieg's songs published in Kalmus Vocal Series (Belwin Mills, New York).
11    The publishing house of Hatzfeld was eventually acquired by Edwin Ashdown.
12    Gerhard Schjelderup: *Edvard Grieg og hans Verker* (E.G. and his Works), Copenhagen 1903.
13    Grieg to Steenberg, 22 December 1903 from Eidsvoll.
14    Grieg to Molard, 5 June 1894 from Grefsen Bad.
15    Grieg to Molard, 13 June 1894 from Grefsen Bad.
16    Grieg to Molard, 10 July 1894 from Troldhaugen.
17    An organization founded by Grieg, Nordraak and others for the promotion of contemporary Scandinavian music.
18    From Bjørnson's epic poem *Arnljot Gelline*, 1870.
19    Grieg to Finck, 17 July 1900.
20    Grieg to Bella Edwards, 1 December 1895 from Leipzig.
21    Grieg to Beyer, 22 May 1906 from London.
22    Grieg to Finck, 17 July 1900.

23  Grieg to Beyer, 5 November 1896 from Christiania.
24  Grieg to Beyer, 16 June 1888 from Copenhagen.
25  Horton: *Grieg*, p.168.
26  Kagen: *Music for the Voice*, p.613.

# 3 'Lillegrieg'

Edvard Grieg was born in Bergen on 15 June 1843 and all his life was to remain extremely fond of his birthplace, although in later years his delicate health could not withstand its climate for the whole of the year. His debt to Bergen, and the consequence of being a Bergen man, he extolled in a speech to the people of the city on the occasion of his sixtieth birthday: 'It is, you see, not only Bergen's art and Bergen's science I have drawn substance from; it is not only Holberg, Welhaven and Ole Bull I have learnt from . . . No, the whole of the Bergen environment which surrounds me has been my material. Bergen's nature, Bergen's exploits and enterprises of every kind have inspired me. . .'[1]

Grieg's musical talents seem to have come mostly from his mother's side of the family. She herself had studied singing, piano and theory in Hamburg and was well-known in Bergen as a pianist and poet. Grieg's sister Maren became a piano teacher and his elder brother John was an accomplished cellist who also studied in Leipzig for a time. Grieg's own early predilection was for the spoken word and his first ambition was to be a parson. In *Min første succes* (My First Success)[2] he tells how he used to improvise sermons and declaim them to his long-suffering family and, even though music was to become his life, the early love of words shows itself time and again in his attention to detail in the poems he set, and in his articles and vast correspondence. His introduction to music was no doubt hearing his mother play the piano. Her favourite composers were said to be Mozart, Beethoven, Weber and Chopin, and Grieg began to have lessons from her at the age of six. However, *Min første succes* describes his even earlier first encounter with the instrument: 'Why not begin by remembering the strange, mystical satisfaction of stretching my arms up towards the piano and discovering – not a melody. Far from it! No, it had to be harmony. First a third, then a triad, then a four-note chord. And finally, both hands helping – o joy! – a five-note chord, a ninth. When I had discovered that, my delight knew no bounds . . . I was at the time about five years old.' Strangely enough, the chord of the ninth was to play a significant part in Grieg's harmonic style.

That he should study music when he left school, however, was not at first considered and was only prompted by a sudden visit from Ole Bull in the summer of 1858. Bull was called 'onkel' by Grieg, although the relationship was a distant one by marriage,[3] and he was a popular if somewhat legendary figure in the Grieg family. Grieg vividly recalled the visit which was to seal his fate:

> . . . one summer day at Landås [now a suburb of Bergen, where Grieg's mother had inherited a house] a rider came rushing at an upright gallop down the road. He drew close, halted his worthy Arab and jumped down. It is him [sic], the fairy-tale god I had dreamed of but never seen before: it is Ole Bull . . . His violin, unfortunately, he did not have with him. But he could talk. And that he did in full measure. We listened speechless to his accounts of his travels in America. It was something of a child-like fantasy. Then, when he got to know that I was fond of composing and improvising, there was nothing else for it: I must go to the piano.
>
> 'I cannot understand what Ole Bull at that time could have perceived in my naive childish music, but he became very serious and talked quietly with my parents. What was discussed was not to my displeasure. For suddenly Ole Bull came over to me, shook hands in his distinctive way and said: "You shall go to Leipzig and become an artist!"
>
> 'Everyone looked fondly at me and I understood only this one thing, that a good fairy had touched my cheek and that I was lucky. And my parents! Not a moment's opposition or even consideration. Everything was settled. And I thought the whole matter was the most natural thing in the world . . .[4]

So in October 1858 the young Grieg was despatched to Leipzig, the musical centre of Europe at the time. There were a number of Norwegians there in the 1850s and 1860s, as well as would-be musicians from all over Europe and America. Grieg travelled under the supervision of an old friend of his father. Once more *Min første succes* tells of the experience: 'I was delivered to a boarding-house, father's old friend said goodbye, the last Norwegian word I heard for a long time, and there I stood as a fifteen-year-old boy, alone in that strange land among strange people. Homesickness gripped me, I went into my room, where I sat and wept without stopping until I was fetched to a meal with my hosts.'[5]

In spite of the homesickness and a serious illness in 1860, which forced him to return to Bergen to recuperate and left one lung permanently damaged, the effects of which were to plague him for the rest of his life, Grieg spent four years in Leipzig. His brother John came to study cello in 1860 and in a letter to Julius Röntgen of 3 May 1904 Grieg tells how the German students called them 'Grieg den første' and 'Grieg den annen' (Grieg the First and Grieg the Second), although among the Scandinavian students they were known as 'Storegrieg' and 'Lillegrieg' (Big Grieg and Little Grieg, or Grieg Major and Grieg Minor), not least because of the difference in their heights.

The Conservatory at Leipzig was founded only in 1843, although the city had a long tradition of music right from Bach's time, and must have come as something of a cultural shock to Grieg. In Bergen almost all music-making at the time was on an amateur scale, even the orchestra, Harmonien. However, he soon realised the opportunities he now had to hear music of all sorts – Conservatory students had free admission to Gewandhaus concerts – and he became an avid concert-goer, a habit that was to remain with him all his life. Wagner's *Tannhaüser*, for example, was produced in Leipzig late in 1858 and Grieg saw fourteen performances. His letters speak with enthusiasm and appreciation of many concerts and first performances he attended throughout his life and also illustrate his catholic tastes. To Beyer he described a performance of Boito's *Mefistofele* in April 1884: 'It is a brilliant work, novel, bold and inspired in many parts.' To Gottfred Matthison-Hansen he wrote from Christiania as l: .e as 1906, 'we hear Richard Strauss, Weingartner, Hugo Wolf, yes, even the Frenchman Debussy (a remarkable brilliance and audacity in his treatment of harmony), not to speak of the Finn Sibelius's beautiful music. . .'[6]

Grieg also stated, in *Min første succes*, that the concerts he heard as a student 'compensated for the teaching in composition technique I did not have at the Conservatory',[7] for he felt throughout his life that his studies in Leipzig had been somewhat lacking. He studied harmony with E.F. Richter, Robert Pappernitz and Moritz Hauptmann and his work-books, preserved in the Grieg Collection in Bergen Public Library, show some surprising trends towards extensive chromaticism. In his last year as a student he studied composition with Reinecke, who described his student in his final report as having 'a most highly significant musical talent, especially for composition.' Yet Grieg was to write to Aimar Grønvold, his first Norwegian biographer, in 1881, '. . . I left the Leipzig Conservatory just as stupid as when I arrived. I had certainly learnt a lot, but my own individuality was still a closed book to me.'[8] And to Röntgen he wrote in 1884, 'How I envy you a technique which every day I constantly miss more. It is certainly not just my own fault, but principally the confounded Leipzig Conservatory, where I learnt *absolutely nothing*.'[9] That this is an exaggeration is obvious from what he achieved later and even if his lessons in harmony and composition were not as rewarding as he might have wished, the Conservatory gave him the opportunity to study piano with Ignaz Moscheles, one of the leading virtuosi of the day. Grieg told how he studied Beethoven sonatas 'by the dozen', but that his greatest 'success' was an occasion on which he played one of Moscheles's own studies without once being stopped, and at the end Moscheles had turned to his other pupils and said, 'See here, gentlemen, that is musicianly piano playing'.[10]

Whatever the quality of teaching at Leipzig, it is hardly surprising that with all the German influence Grieg's early works should have reflected that, rather than at first showing any marked individuality. Hardly surprising either that his earliest known song should be a setting of a German poem. This was *Siehst du das Meer?* by Emanuel Geibel, and the song was written on

New Year's Eve 1859. It exists in sketches in Grieg's notebooks, but was reconstructed by Benestad and Schjelderup-Ebbe for inclusion on the record that accompanied their book on Grieg.[11] Marked 'Allegro molto', it is a short song, only thirty-four bars including the four-bar postlude, but it is not as insubstantial as some others of Grieg's early vocal compositions.

The song comprises the first two of Geibel's three stanzas. Grieg sets these two almost identically, the only difference being that the first strophe ends in the dominant key, while the second, extended by two bars to accommodate a repeat of the last phrase, 'Darüber hin', ends firmly in the tonic. The melody is rather static and the vocal range less than an octave, but there is already a feeling for the lyrical flow. Most of the interest, however, lies in the harmony and although the accompaniment right hand is in quavers almost through-out, the abundance of inner movement, frequently chromatic, holds the attention and is a foreshadowing of the composer's later style. As became his usual practice, Grieg sets the poem almost completely syllabically and it seems to have been the phrase 'In stolzen Wogen rollt mein wilder Sinn... (In majestic waves my wild spirit rolls)' in the second stanza that engendered the urgency of the music.

Grieg's next dated song is a far inferior product. *Den syngende menighed* (The singing congregation) is a setting for contralto and piano of a poem by the famous Danish writer N.F.S. Grundtvig, a hymn in which each of the three stanzas ends with the line 'Saa liflig lege vi for vor Herre (So gaily we play for our Lord)', and typifies Grundtvig's philosophy of 'glade Kristendom (happy Christianity)'. Grieg's setting of this line in the first stanza is remarkable only for the chromatically descending bass and the use, twice in three bars, of the tonic—leading-note—dominant motif, which was later to become so much associated with him. The song is very simple, not to say naive, and after the limited range and scope of the melody of *Siehst du das Meer?*, this song demands a range of almost two octaves from the G below middle C and the vocal line contains a number of wide intervals, some clumsy double-dotted rhythms and a good deal of unadroit chromatic writing.

*Den syngende Menighed* was performed together with the first and last of the op. 2 songs and *Ich denke dein* (no longer extant) by Wibecke Meyer, accompanied by the composer, at a concert in Bergen in May 1862. Dag Schjelderup-Ebbe comments that this song is not one of the works Grieg asked to be destroyed after his death and adds, 'Perhaps he should have, since of all his compositions this is the only one that properly deserves such a fate.'[12] It may be, however, that Grieg had already destroyed his own manuscript, for the one preserved in Bergen, dated July 1860, is not autograph; the signature at the bottom, although a little indistinct, looks like 'Wibecke Meyer'.[13] Although it is his earliest completed song, one could have wished that, even for the sake of curiosity, it would have remained unpublished. It will almost certainly remain unperformed, despite its inclusion in the *GGA*.

In Grieg's first published songs, the *Vier Lieder für Alt und Klavier*, op.2, which he accompanied at the *Hauptprüfung*, the final concert at Leipzig, there are more sure signs of things to come, not least in the harmonic adventurousness. Once again, unsurprisingly, he chose German texts and his library (preserved in the Grieg Collection in Bergen) shows that he had already acquired a collection of German verse; Chamisso's *Gedichte* is inscribed 'Edvard Grieg 1860' and Uhland's *Gedichte*, an edition published in 1860, 'Edvard H. Grieg. 15. juni 1862. *Fra Moer*' was apparently a nineteenth birthday present from his mother. The German press received the songs well and the famous musicologist Hugo Riemann later wrote in his obituary of Grieg in the *Frankfurter Zeitung* that they 'remind one of Schubert's best', praise that must now be considered over-enthusiastic. In his music encyclopaedia, however, he was to express regret that Grieg had limited himself to national characteristics, instead of writing works of permanent significance in the musical language of the (presumably German) world.

The *Vier Lieder* were written in 1861 and are efficiently prepared, although they show little real distinction and are rarely performed today. Together with the next group of German songs, op.4, they owe a good deal to Schubert and more especially to Schumann, understandably, as Grieg was extremely fond of Schumann's songs and piano music. His own songs, however, even here are more than 'the piano piece with words, which Schumann had shown both by precept and example to be how pianists wrote songs',[14] Grieg being not only a pianist but, as has already been illustrated, a talented user of words.

The first of the four, *Die Müllerin*, to a poem by Chamisso, opens with a figure in the right hand of the accompaniment, which on its own is reminiscent of Schubert in *Gretchen am Spinnrade*. Grieg's harmonization, however, immediately negates this impression:

Ex.4

Die Müllerin

There is a good deal of chromatic movement right from the beginning, not always used successfully as yet. The tonic key of B minor is not established until the voice enters in the fifth bar and there are a number of tempo changes that are unexpected in so early a song.

The vocal line is lyrical if undemanding and it seems that right from the first, with the exception of *Den syngende Menighed*, Grieg tried above all to express the text. There are one or two passages in *Die Müllerin* that show some special thought: for example, the lilting phrase for 'der Wind, der bleib mir treu' (bars 46 to 49) and the suspended C sharp in a chord of B minor on the word 'Schwüre' (bar 55), no less effective for being very Schumannesque. In the accompaniment the mill-wheels are only conjured up during the introduction and postlude, and the representation of the storm, while conventional, is left to the Allegro section, where the miller-girl's own words are heard. This reflects the imagery of the poem itself, with its use of pathetic fallacy, where the real storm is mirrored by the storm in the girl's heart caused by her unfaithful lover.

The second and third songs of the group are both to poems by Heine. *Eingehüllt in graue Wolken* is a vivid musical portrayal of a storm, with the lightning and thunder represented in the upward-sweeping arpeggios and staccato chords of the piano introduction. The vocal line is dramatic, with a wide range from low B to high G. It makes much use of ascending and descending arpeggios and the dramatic impact is aided by the number of voiced and sibilant consonants in the poem, words abounding in 's', 'sch', 'ch' and 'w', and the whole stormy sea is summed up in the phrase 'herrenlosen Wellen'.

The setting of the second stanza begins similarly to the first, but then changes and Grieg builds the tension by using a vocal phrase in the lower register, which gradually rises a semitone at a time (bars 44 to 48) and which is then immediately repeated an octave higher, a device unique to this song. Monrad Johansen's opinion that the song has a greatness in construction and that the strength of the portrayal of nature is worthy of a master[15] seems a little exaggerated, but the 'prestissimo' postlude certainly has suggestions of the one which was to end the last of the Vinje songs, op.33, almost twenty years later. The harmony is rather predictable, although Grieg was already making much use of pedal points, but the frequently changing character of the accompaniment, together with the shifting between the major and minor modes, helps to avoid monotony. Occasionally the vocal tessitura is high for the designated contralto, even though the high-lying passages are marked 'fortissimo', but the long-held high F sharp at the end, with its crescendo, demands a voice of dramatic proportions.

*Ich stand in dunkeln Träumen* is the best song of the group, which must to a large extent be due to the fact that the poem is also the best of the four Grieg chose here. Heine was the most gifted writer of his era and succeeded more than all his predecessors in making the German lyric a European medium. His talent was not only for words and bold imagery – he frequently takes his readers from reality to a world of enchantment and mystery — but also for form, where his apparent simplicity makes the imagery all the more effective. Heine was happiest in short stanzas and some of his verses, for example *Die Lorelei*, have passed into German folk-literature. Heine's early irony became intensity and bitterness in later life, producing the familiar twists at the end of innocuous-seeming verses, and caused in part by resentment at the progressive paralysis which gripped him and condemned him in his final years to what he called a 'mattress-grave'.

However good the poem, *Ich stand in dunkeln Träumen* is a strange choice for inclusion in an album of songs for female voice. Certainly there is nothing which definitely states that it concerns a man looking at a woman's picture, but that is the impression one has. That being said, the vocal line is much more expressive here than in the earlier songs and the range more truly contralto — A flat below middle C to high E flat. The harmony is more adventurous and the building up of phrases from 'um ihre Lippen' to 'ihr Augenpaar', with the transitions through F major, G flat major, A flat minor and A major, is particularly interesting and effective, even if the constant tremolo in the accompaniment is not very original. The unexpected use of a chord of the ninth to point 'Auch *meine* Thränen flossen' is very graphic and Schjelderup-Ebbe has also pointed out[16] the unusual use of the Neapolitan sixth in the second half of bar 25, which is approached chromatically in all parts:

Ex.5                                          Ich stand in dunkeln Träumen

The return to the first theme for the penultimate line lulls one into a false sense of security before the key-change and the unexpected last line, 'ich kann's nicht glauben, dass ich dich verloren hab'!' This time the short postlude over a pedal C is completely uncontrived, and the accompaniment throughout this song is better constructed than previously, now that Grieg seems to have given more thought to portraying the sense of the words. The whole is much more imaginative than Schubert's rather austere setting of the same poem.

In contrast the last song of the set, *Was soll ich sagen?*, is in many ways the weakest of the four. The vocal line is for the most part uninspired, although there are glimmers of Grieg's later soaring melodies in the second phrase, and the accompaniment is written in a tedious, almost continuous semi-quaver broken chord pattern. There is, however, some harmonic interest, particularly in the many transitions at the end of the first section. The poem by Chamisso — a comparison of the poet's age with his beloved's youth — is not one of the best-known from this French-born German writer, who is renowned to singers as the author of *Frauenliebe und -leben*. Here the feeling of understatement is reminiscent of Heine, but although Grieg points individual words with subtle dissonances and increases the tension of the second stanza, there is a sense of anticlimax at the end, which does nothing to underline the foreboding of the last phrase. 'Ich seh' dich so an und zittre so sehr (I gaze at you thus and tremble so much)'.

The *Vier Lieder* were dedicated to Wibecke Meyer and first published by Peters in 1863. They were reissued, also by Peters, in 1883, this time with English translations by Frederick Corder.

Whatever the contemporary praise for these songs, Grieg's immediate problem on completing his studies at Leipzig in April 1862 was to plan his career. His father was no longer prepared to support him and, as he wanted to travel more and broaden his experience, Grieg applied for a scholarship from the Norwegian government and accordingly sent a letter to the king. He enclosed testimonials and said, somewhat pretentiously, that he wanted the scholarship in order to 'achieve results, which could be significant, not only for me, but also for music in my native country, where it is my intention to remain'. [17] His eloquent request was unfortunately refused and he had to reconsider his position. He tried to establish himself as a piano teacher, but Bergen at that time was a fairly small town and pupils were few. With a view to embarking on a career as a performer and composer, he hired the Workers' Association hall in Bergen and gave a concert there on 21 May 1862. The programme included three of his piano pieces, op. 1, as well as the four songs already mentioned, Beethoven's 'Pathétique' sonata and some of Moscheles' studies. Grieg's own pieces were all well received by the local press. The critic in *Bergenposten* for 23 May wrote, 'His compositions were especially appealing, and as a composer Herr Grieg seems to have a great future in store' and such praise obviously encouraged him in his attempt to procure a scholarship.

Eventually Grieg spent a year in his home town, broken only by a long trip abroad in the summer of 1862 with his father and brother John, which included visits to London and Paris. In 1863 he obtained a loan from his father and went to Denmark, arriving in Copenhagen in April. Like so many

Norwegians, because of the long political and business ties as well as those of family and culture, which existed between the two countries, Grieg had connections in Denmark and he spent most of the next three years in and around Copenhagen, at that time the thriving cultural centre of Scandinavia.

Undoubtedly, he began to be drawn to Danish verse, although the first song from this period was a setting of a poem by the Norwegian-born Andreas Munch, *Solnedgang* (Sunset). Written in 1863, the song was not published until 1866, when it appeared with three other Munch settings as the album op.9. While of no great significance, the song is light and lyrical, and reminiscent of Schubert in songs like *Im Haine*. Although the setting is largely diatonic, there is some occasional interesting movement in the inner parts, which, together with the use in the accompaniment of the augmented fourth of the scale and bare fifths in the bass, saves the song from being merely commonplace. The uncharacteristic falling sevenths seem to depict the sinking sun. Perhaps because of the very immediacy of its appeal, the song has been dismissed by other writers: Benestad and Schjelderup-Ebbe say that 'the main impression one gets of the song is artificiality' and that 'many features result in a strong impression of monotony',[18] citing the number of times the dominant occurs in the vocal line and the repetition of the rhythmic pattern ♩ ♪. However, the song has a lyrical if undemanding melody and is pleasing to sing. The poem does not call for deep insight and Grieg has combined with Munch to give a fresh, unsophisticated view of a natural phenomenon in a folk-song style.

It is interesting to compare Grieg's setting with that of Delius, who included *Solnedgang* (to a German translation)[19] in his *Five Songs from the Norwegian* of 1888, which are dedicated to Nina Grieg. Delius's setting is much more lush in its chromatic harmony, and it has an atmosphere more akin to a sultry summer night than Grieg's spring-like music.

*Solnedgang* was originally the last of the *Fem Sange til min Ven Louis Hornbeck* (Five Songs to my Friend . . .), which Grieg prepared for publication in 1865, but which were never published in this form. In fact the manuscript of the *Fem Sange* was only discovered in 1971. Three of the other songs were also published later: no.1, *Kjælighed* (Love) and no.4, *Langelandsk folkemelodi* (A Langeland folksong), as part of the op.15 album, and no.2, *Soldaten* (The soldier), in a revised form posthumously. The third of the five songs, *Claras Sang* (Clara's song) was never printed.

The manuscript of *Solnedgang* as part of the *Fem Sange* has several differences from the song as it is printed in the op.9 album, principally in the coda. The first version shows a completely strophic setting; the end of the accompaniment is extended into a short coda for piano only after the final strophe, which begins like bars 14 and 15 of the printed song, but has no vocal line above. It is shorter than the later version, but has a most interesting cadential sequence: Ex. 6.

Ex.6  Solnedgang

Among the residents in Copenhagen in the early 1860s were two great Danish composers, J.P.E. Hartmann and Niels Gade. Grieg, however, associated with a group of younger Danish musicians, some of whom had been his fellow students in Leipzig, including Emil Hartmann (son of J.P.E.), C.F. Emil Horneman, August Winding and Gottfred Matthison-Hansen, and he also met Rikard Nordraak, who was to have a great influence on him. Grieg went to see Niels Gade with his first two published works, but was too shy to show them to the great man, who in any case considered such small-scale pieces as trifles. Gade's advice was to write a symphony, but Grieg first wrote several more songs.

This time in Denmark was among the most happy and productive periods in Grieg's life. He met his cousin, Nina Hagerup,[20] who had also been born in Bergen, but had lived in Denmark since childhood and who was studying singing with the well-known Danish teacher Carl Adolph Helsted. Grieg's next songs, the six German settings op.4, were dedicated to Nina, although they are again designated for contralto, whereas she was a soprano. In comparison with the op.2 settings, these songs begin to reveal something of a new maturity in Grieg's creative abilities. Most noticeable is the greater freedom with which the vocal lines are shaped, so that they become a real entity rather than being contrived from the harmonic progressions, which is the impression made by the melodies of the earlier songs. Perhaps Nina's influence as singer and interpreter was already making itself felt, an influence by no means occasioned only by their romantic attachment. Grieg wrote to Henry Finck that from the time they made their home in Christiania in 1866, all his songs were written for Nina.[21] In the periods when their relationship was very strained, once or twice almost to breaking-point, Grieg wrote no songs.

In the *Sex Digte* (Six Songs), op.4, to three further settings of Heine and two of Chamisso, Grieg adds a setting of a poem by Uhland. The first song, *Die Waise*, to a poem by Chamisso, is one of the best of the album. It owes something to Schubert, especially in the rhythmic figure in the accompaniment in the middle of the first and last sections: Ex.7.

But Schumann's influence is also to be seen, particularly in the bars between the first and second stanzas and in the postlude. The chromatic

Ex.7                                    Die Waise

writing is not so contrived as in the earlier songs and so now has much more effect. The melodic line finds a new freedom and Grieg has characterized the voices of the orphaned girl and her dead mother not in the melody, but in the accompaniment figures. Foreshadowing the composer's mature style is the absence of accompaniment at bar 19, 'viel geweinet hab', and the long series of dissonant chords, here sevenths and ninths, in bars 33 to 43. In the final stanza the apparently comforting words of the mother – that a young man will caress her daughter with tender words of love – are underlaid with yearning chromatic movement, as if the unspoken thought is one of sorrow that the mother will not be there to see it, and the sadness is continued into the postlude, with its dissonant suspensions, before the final resolution to the tonic major key:

Ex.8                                    Die Waise

Chamisso's joy in the simple things of life, his warmth and rather sentimental naiveté, was in spite of his birth not at all French, but wholly German. The gentle nature of the poet is rarely concealed, even when the themes of his ballads occasionally become gruesome, and it is the mellow quality that comes to the fore in *Morgenthau*. It also uses a favourite theme of the German romantics: the night, with its blessed relief from the worries of the day, the time of love. *Morgenthau* is a bright song with some of the most interesting piano writing so far seen in Grieg's songs, from the performing point of view if not the harmonic. The poem suggests a certain sadness at the passing of the night, but the composer has instilled into his setting a lighter, happier, even slightly mocking atmosphere. In the middle section the vocal line adds independently to the dissonances, not least in its sustained upper E, which forms an inverted pedal, underneath which the piano takes the music back from a suggestion of the Dorian mode to the tonic A major.

*Abschied*, the first of the three Heine settings, is one of the two least successful of the group. There is certainly a bold use of dissonant harmony and the sadness of the verse is well portrayed, but unfortunately, because of the almost completely strophic setting, the anguish of the final stanza does not really make itself felt. Where the dissonance could have been used here to great effect, its use throughout the first three strophes negates the natural climax in the words. Nor is the sense of monotony alleviated by the accompaniment, with its relentless rhythmic pattern.

Between *Abschied* and the last two songs, which again are settings of Heine, comes the Uhland setting, *Jägerlied*. Uhland was the acknowledged leader of the Swabian school of poets, an off-shoot of the German romantic movement which was dedicated to preserving the ideals of the romantic tradition during (as the group saw it) the barren age of the liberal movement, Jungdeutschland, and to hand them on to the generation which came after. Together with Eichendorff, Uhland brought the idiom of folk-poetry to a peak and he was a fine ballad writer, drawing inspiration from the Minnesänger, the Skalds and the Volkslied. Strong, bright tones predominate in his poetry and he has a worldly air, which is apparent in the only other of his poems set by Grieg, *Lauf der Welt*, op.48 no.3, but which is only superficially evident in the slight *Jägerlied*.

The description of the song by Monrad Johansen as 'fresh and cheerful'[22] sums it up and, except for the occasional unexpected use of chromatic movement, it is a lightweight piece rather reminiscent of Schubert. The hunting idea is conveyed by the key, E flat – the key of the natural horn – and the $\frac{6}{8}$ rhythm. One feature that looks forward to the later Grieg is the long-held B flat at the end of the vocal line, which is used as an inverted pedal. The optional note, one octave higher, in the Hansen edition is a little optimistic in a collection of songs for contralto! Like the third and fourth of the op.2 songs, this is a strange choice of poem to set for female voice.

The fifth song of the set, *Das alte Lied*, has rightly been judged to be the best of the six, for Grieg has now matched his music exactly to the verse. Heine's poem is written in a deceptively simple, folk-song style, which makes the shock of the ending – the death of the young queen and her page – so much more effective. Grieg complements the verse with an unadorned musical setting, something between a folk-song and a hymn, which, with the modal harmony, helps to conjure up the atmosphere of an old song. From the beginning the Schubertian dotted figure in the accompaniment left hand has a doom-laden feeling, which points towards the end of the story. It is especially effective when it is subtly altered, becoming more sprightly in order to depict the young pageboy in contrast to the old king, and amplified in the harmony by Grieg's use of the sharpened fifth to form an augmented triad (Ex.9). The avoidance of any contrived climax makes the end all the more poignant, while the chorale-like postlude continues and completes the sombre mood.

Ex.9

Das alte Lied

Together with *Abschied*, the last song of the set, *Wo sind sie hin?*, again to a poem by Heine, is the least successful. There is some remarkably daring chromatic and dissonant writing, but viewed overall the song is rather artificial. Grieg apparently had a special interest in the poem because it was 'tinged with nordic Romanticism,'[23] that is, the mention of the rune-stone and the concise but colourful description of the sea, that natural element so close to all Scandinavian hearts. Heine once told Hans Christian Andersen that, to him, 'Scandinavia seemed to be the mystical country in which the treasure of poetry was buried', and he stands apart from the German poets of the time in his love for the sea.[24]

Grieg's melody for *Wo sind sie hin?* is little more than workmanlike, but here for the first time there is an echoing of a vocal phrase by the piano, a trait which later was to feature in so many songs. The angularity of the vocal line helps to portray the blustering storm and the music swells and recedes like sea-waves, the restlessness further underlined by the lack of definite cadences. It is, with one slight variation, a strophic setting, quite over-balanced by the long postlude of twenty-two bars, which owes more to youthful enthusiasm than to anything suggested by the poetry, or even by the need to end the set of songs forcefully. Grieg's later songs, where they have a long postlude, usually show much more concentration of thought. The most interesting thing about this postlude is its foreshadowing of the Piano Sonata, which was to be composed just over a year later.

One of the most curious things about the album is the indifferent translation of the poems into Danish. There are no glaring inaccuracies, but occasionally the anonymous translator has lessened the impact of the original. For example, in the last line of the final stanza of *Abschied*, he renders 'du warst der sterbende Wald (you were the dying forest)' as 'du var det visnende Blad (you were the withering leaf)'. Again, at the end of *Das alte Lied*, for the original 'Sie müssten beide sterben, sie hatten sich viel zu lieb (They both had to die, they were too much in love)', the Danish version has 'De maate dø saa unge; hun var ham kun altfor huld (They had to die so young; she was just too fond of him)'.

The op.4 songs were first published by Horneman and Erslev in Copenhagen in December 1864. The dedication to 'Fräulein Nina Hagerup' was omitted in the subsequent Hansen edition.

By the summer of 1864 Grieg was back in Norway, staying with his parents. He gave a recital with his brother John in Bergen and also spent some time with Ole Bull on his estate at Osterøy. It was Bull's habit to play host to local Hardanger fiddle players at his home, and this visit may have been Grieg's introduction to the living folk music tradition. If so, that first taste was to be developed further on his return to Copenhagen in the autumn, when he became acquainted with Rikard Nordraak.

Nordraak was extremely enthusiastic about anything Norwegian, especially folk-song and dance. He was a cousin of Bjørnstjerne Bjørnson, whose patriotic poem *Ja, vi elsker dette landet* (Yes, we love this land), set to music by Nordraak, has become Norway's national anthem. Bjørnson considered his cousin the most gifted man he had ever met, while Ole Bull thought him talented but lazy. Nordraak had no time for the conventional methods of teaching and sought to work by intuition rather than by formal study. However, this attitude was probably responsible for his great harmonic adventurousness, although he also owed much to Norwegian folk music, in particular that for the Hardanger fiddle. Nordraak's friendship with Grieg developed and was strengthened by an agreement that they should make their main purpose in life to express in their music the essence of Norway, and so fulfil the task which Ole Bull had begun.

It was, however, a Danish friend, the author and music-teacher Benjamin Feddersen, who provided Grieg with the texts for two more songs during 1864. The first was a short verse by the Plattdeutsch poet Klaus Groth[25] ('Beim Kirchgang von Allen die Stillste ist sie') translated into Danish by Feddersen as *Til kirken hun vandrer*[26] (To the church she walks). The poem extols an unnamed 'she' and most particularly her eyes, 'as blue as the sky, as deep as the sea,' but is no more than pleasantly unassuming. The manuscript is dated February 1864 and shows many alterations, some of which in their turn have been further erased and altered. The song, which is through-composed, has been described by Schjelderup-Ebbe as being 'of small merit' and showing 'little imagination'. Certainly the vocal line is restricted and the rhythm of both it and the accompaniment, while perhaps trying to interpret the walking suggested in the first line, nevertheless becomes monotonous. The main interest is centred on a phrase in the second stanza (Ex. 10), which started out as:

Ex.10                                           Til Kirken hun vandrer

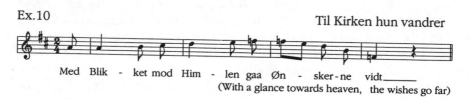

Med Blik - ket mod Him - len gaa Øn - sker-ne vidt____
(With a glance towards heaven,  the wishes go far)

but was altered to:

Ex.11                                           Til Kirken hun vandrer

Med Blik - ket mod Him - len gaa Øn - sker-ne vidt____

The apparent anticipation of the opening of *Solveigs Sang* is remarkable, although Grieg was later to admit that that was the only one of his songs where he was influenced by a Norwegian folk-song. However, it is not surprising that the song was never published in the composer's lifetime, although it is to be included in the *GGA*.

The second song was from a comedy, *Frieriet på Helgoland* (The Courtship on Heligoland), which had been 'freely adapted' by Feddersen from a farce by the German writer Ludvig Schneider. The play was very popular and was performed at the Casino Theatre in Copenhagen nineteen times between January 1865 and March 1867, and once at the Dagmar Theatre in 1868. This was Grieg's first venture into incidental music, but only *Claras Sang* still remains. This song, which was written in the autumn of 1864, is only known now because it was included among the *Fem Sange* dedicated to Louis Hornbeck, but there were no words written into the manuscript and it was never printed. It is, however, included in the *GGA* with the text restored.

*Claras Sang* has a jaunty simplicity belying the strength with which the sentiments — that love and happiness are to be prized above mere material possessions — are expressed. The harmony shows a few points of interest, especially in the middle bars of the strophe, where dissonances and chromatic chords are sounded over a dominant pedal in the dominant key:

Ex.12                                                                    Claras Sang

(Hvad) hjæl - per vel Rig - dom, naar Bar - men er fuld af

Angst og u - læ - ge-lig Smer - te, hvad

What use are riches, when the heart is full of anxiety and incurable pain

Although Feddersen referred to an overture in a letter to Grieg later, it is not now known what other music was written for the play, other than that it consisted of songs and choruses. Apparently, it was all well received by the press, although the composer was not named in the reviews.

The next published songs, the four op. 10, if viewed in chronological order of publication, would make it appear that the composer had taken a backward step in his development, but in fact these songs date from a few years earlier than opp. 5 and 9, and were written at much the same time as the *Seks Digt*, op. 4. Schjelderup-Ebbe has said that Abraham's and Grove's dating of these songs as 'before 1862' is untenable[27] and it is now accepted that they were written in 1864, even though their quality is inferior to other songs of the same period.

The op. 10 songs are settings of Danish verse and the marked difference in standard between these and the Hans Christian Andersen settings, op. 5, cannot entirely be attributed to Nina's later influence, but must also be due to the inferior quality of Winther's poetry compared with Andersen's. Christian Winther was born in 1796 in the Fensmark district in the south of

Zealand and throughout his life was spiritually bound to the area, which inspired his long descriptive poem *Sjælland*. The four poems Grieg chose to set are all trifles, and it is a pity that he did not select some of the better ones, as had other composers, notably Kjerulf and Winther's compatriot Peter Heise. The original title, *Lette Sange med Piano* (Easy Songs with Piano), sums up the unpretentious nature of these songs. The first of the four, *Taksigelse* (Thanksgiving), is typical of the whole group, with its lyrical melodic line, simple diatonic harmony and a folk-song-like innocence. The poet thanks his beloved for her support throughout his life, but these outwardly sincere sentiments are occasionally allowed to slip into the mundane; for example, in the first stanza, 'du . . . helbredede mit Hjerte, og fik min Kummer lagt i blund . . . (You . . . restored my heart and made my sorrow take a nap)'.

The song is strophic, a structure that works well except in the fourth stanza, where the sense carries over from the third line to the fourth, while the musical phrase stops and restarts. However, as the song might be thought too long for modern audiences, it would be possible to omit this stanza in performance, and in fact the English translation in the Ashdown edition uses only the first three stanzas. Musically the song is quite straightforward, with some small interest in the vocal line in bars 6 and 7, where the modulation to the dominant is accomplished by the pivot chord (II/V) under a chromatic melody, creating a dissonance between the E sharp in the vocal line and the E natural in the bass. Otherwise, the only individual feature is the postlude, the first two bars of which (Ex. 13) are melodically

Ex.13                                        Taksigelse

almost identical to one of the *Lyric Pieces, Ensom vandrer* (Lonely wanderer), op. 43 no. 2, written twenty-two years later (Ex. 14).

The next song, *Skovsang* (Woodland song), also shows one or two Griegian

Ex.14                                        Ensom vandrer

traits. The unassuming poem, with its nine four-line stanzas, is once more in the style of a folk-song and Grieg's setting immediately captures this by using a tonic pedal in the first seven bars. The lilting melody is well matched to the cheerfulness of this little picture of nature, with its rather obvious use of pathetic fallacy: the poet is happy and so, too, are the creatures of the natural world. The one unusual feature is again the postlude, which not only seems out of place after such a simple piece, but is also quite mannered musically, at least in its first five bars:

Ex.15

Skovsang

One might have expected to find such a postlude after a better song than *Skovsang* and its material is quite separate from what has gone before. In fact, its melancholy rise and fall seems to contradict the lightheartedness of the song itself. As with *Taksigelse*, for modern performance the song would be better shortened, but the choice of stanzas to omit would be an individual matter as for the most part each of them describes a particular creature.

It is difficult to see what Grieg saw in these poems, apart from a certain inherent singability. In *Blomsterne tale* (The flowers speak), however, the music is very monotonous, with its ♩♪♪♩♪♪ rhythm in both voice and accompaniment unbroken except for two bars at the final cadence of the strophe. Nor is much allowance made to accommodate the words in the strophic setting of the three stanzas, a rare exception with Grieg, who was normally so attentive to declamation. The imagery of the poem is also very uninspired. However, as in all the songs in this album, there is one touch of individuality in the setting. Here it is to be found in the harmonisation of the second half of the strophe, a passage abounding in seventh and ninth chords, some with added or chromatically altered notes, before the conventional Ic-V-I cadence.

To describe the final song of the op. 10 group, *Sang på fjeldet* (Song on the mountain), as the most original of the four is in this context faint praise. Once again there are glimpses of the composer's latent talent, but they are not enough to raise the song to any great degree. The vocal line is certainly the most inspired of the four songs, although the range of them all is very limited – a ninth, an octave, a ninth and a tenth, respectively.

The metre of the verse in *Sang på fjeldet* is not as four-square as in the other songs and Grieg accommodates the long first and third lines and the short second and fourth lines in what feel like three-bar phrases, but are in fact four bars long (Ex. 16). The use of a note held in the vocal line over changing harmonies in the accompaniment and the shifting between major and minor modes is also typical of the later Grieg. The five long stanzas might again be thought too many for modern performance and would benefit from a little

Ex. 16

Sang på Fjeldet

(In the glow of the evening, I wonder if the mountains' body will shine, and...)

judicious pruning. Grieg no doubt liked the poem for its last stanza: 'O! Nina, min unge Kvinne! Liflig og varm! (Oh! Nina, my young wife! Delightful and warm!)'. The album was published by C.E. Horneman in Copenhagen in 1866 and later by Wilhelm Hansen, but not by Peters (with German translations by W. Anger) until 1885. The composer himself later arranged *Taksigelse* for mixed choir.

There are in all his early songs things that point to the master of song-writing Grieg was to become and, with youthful enthusiasm helping to compensate for musical deficiencies, some of them stand comparison with the contrived and impersonal offerings that occasionally came from the mature composer's pen. The bones, one feels, were there, but Grieg needed something more in order to flesh them out. This was soon to come from two directions: his marriage to Nina Hagerup and his growing regard for her interpretative abilities, and his friendship with Rikard Nordraak, which was to stimulate his nationalistic instincts.

## Notes

1 Reproduced in *Artikler og Taler*, ed. Gaukstad, 1957, pp. 196–98.
2 Autobiographical article reproduced in *Artikler og Taler*, pp. 10–30.
3 A sister of Grieg's mother married Bull's brother Jens.
4 'Min første succes', *Artikler og Taler*, p. 18.
5 Ibid. p. 19.
6 Grieg to Matthison-Hansen, 19 December 1906 from Christiania.
7 'Min første succes', p. 26.
8 Grieg to A. Grønvold, 25 April 1881 from Bergen.
9 Grieg to Röntgen, 30 October 1884 from Lofthus.
10 'Min første succes', p. 23.
11 Finn Benestad and Dag Schjelderup-Ebbe, *Edvard Grieg, mennesket og kunstneren*, 1980; the song is also included in the *GGA*, Volume 15.
12 Dag Schjelderup-Ebbe: *Edvard Grieg: 1858–1867*, 1964, p. 54.
13 The composer Sverre Jordan in the 1959 supplement, p. 6, to his *Edvard Grieg. En oversikt over hans liv og verker* (A Survey of his Life and Works), 1954, says the name is 'Wibecke Aljer (or Aloger)' and adds: 'The composition is written in a childlike hand'.
14 Eric Sams: *Brahms' Songs*, BBC Music Guides 1972, p. 15.
15 David Monrad Johansen: *Edvard Grieg*, 1934, p. 53.
16 Schjelderup-Ebbe: *Edvard Grieg: 1858–1867*, p. 77.
17 Reproduced in *Artikler og Taler*, p. 233.
18 Benestad and Schjelderup-Ebbe: *Edvard Grieg, mennesket og kunstneren*, p. 57.
19 Translation by von Holstein, the same as in the first Peters' edition of Grieg's setting.
20 The daughter of his mother's brother, Herman Hagerup.
21 Grieg to Finck, 17 July 1900.
22 Monrad Johansen: *Edvard Grieg*, p. 65.
23 John Horton: *Grieg*, 1974, p. 168.
24 Quoted in Elias Bredsdorff: *Hans Christian Andersen*, 1975, p. 158.
25 Klaus Johann Groth (1819–99), perhaps best known as the author of 'O wüsst' ich doch den Weg zurück', set by Brahms as op. 63 no. 8.
26 Schjelderup-Ebbe in *Edvard Grieg: 1858–1867*, p. 189, entitles the song 'Til kirken hun *vandrede*' and says that Sverre Jordan (*En oversikt...*) is incorrect in using the title as in the text above. That, however, is the title that appears on Grieg's manuscript, and the first line of the poem.
27 Schjelderup-Ebbe: *Edvard Grieg: 1858–1867*, p. 201.

# 4 'Melodies of the Heart'

Early in 1865, together with Horneman, Hornbeck and Matthison-Hansen, Grieg and Nordraak founded Euterpe, a society dedicated to the promotion of contemporary Scandinavian music, borrowing the name from a similar organisation in Leipzig. Concerts were given between March 1865 and April 1867, though with less frequency towards the end, and in one of its early programmes, on 1 April 1865, the second and third movements of Grieg's symphony were performed. Being in frequent company with Nordraak helped to bring out Grieg's talents and led to the *Humoresker*, op.6, four piano pieces which were a major breakthrough for the composer's national style. Grieg wrote to Aimar Grønvold in 1881, 'Now there came a happy time of joy and productivity. This was in 1864–65. In a short time in Copenhagen, during daily company with Nordraak and the Scandinavian-inspired young people, I wrote many songs, the *Humoresker* op.6, Sonata op.7 [for piano] and Sonata op.8 [for violin] .'

As far as the songs are concerned, it was the four published as op.5 that really began to show signs of the maturing composer and in which Grieg succeeded for the first time in finding his true self and a personal form of expression. They come like a breath of spring sunshine, light of heart, melodically beautiful, and two of them may be counted amongst his best songs. The poems Grieg chose for these songs came from a collection of eight short love-poems by Hans Christian Andersen, *Hjertets Melodier* (Melodies of the Heart), written in 1830, which were the result of Andersen's love for Riborg Voigt. At the time of their meeting, she was unofficially engaged to someone else and, although obviously attracted to Andersen, she married her fiancé six months later. Andersen tried to comfort himself with the idea that Riborg had really loved him and married only out of duty, and during the next few months he wrote a large number of rather melancholy poems, the best of which were published in the collection. In January 1831 a new volume, *Fantasier og Skitser* (Fantasies and Sketches), was published, which included these and all his love-poems to Riborg Voigt.

Because of his recent attachment to Nina Hagerup, Grieg's choice of the happiest of these poems (actually numbers I, VI, IV and II in the order of the album) was understandable and, as Benestad and Schjelderup-Ebbe have observed, 'a more beautiful engagement present would be difficult to imagine'.[1] Grieg and Nina were in fact not engaged until Christmas 1864 and even then it had to be kept secret for some time, as both sets of parents were against it. Nina's mother was reported to have said of Grieg, 'He is nothing and has nothing, and he writes music which no-one is inclined to listen to.'[2] Nor were Grieg's parents overjoyed and they did not give their permission for the engagement to be made public until July 1865.

None of Andersen's poems has a complicated form or language; some have a brief allusion to mythology or history, but on the whole they are pictures of homely scenes and simple faith, and the unsophisticated rhymes and rhythms make them ideal for musical setting. Throughout his life Andersen himself was fond of singing. As a boy he had a beautiful voice and was known as the 'little Funen nightingale'.

The first song in the *Hjertets Melodier, To brune Øine* (Two brown eyes) is one of the best of the set. The lively melody is a delight to sing and never allowed to degenerate into banality, while the principal accompaniment figure has an impudent charm and is very similar to that in Hugo Wolf's song *In dem Schatten meiner Locken*.[3] The setting is largely diatonic, although with some shifting between major and minor modes, which was to become typical of Grieg. In contrast to most of his songs, the accompaniment here is almost completely independent and there is little chromatic writing, except at the climax of 'De glemmes aldrig i Evighed (They will never be forgotten in eternity)' and, as the poem has it, 'Jeg glemmer dem aldrig i Evighed (I will never forget them . . .)'. This alteration of the words is worth noting: the modified line is set in the relative minor key (E minor) over an intricate harmonic progression which uses suspensions and chromatically altered notes to bring the music back to the tonic G major:

Ex.17                                                        To brune Øine

Where Andersen's original words are used, there is an emphasis on the word 'Jeg' (I) and the affirmation is underlined by the major key, the whole passage being much more effective than a direct repetition would have been. However, this song is unusual in having undergone a number of revisions, apparently by the composer, for a later edition published by Hansen's in about 1890, revisions which are followed by the Peters' editions. The original notation, however, is found as late as the English edition published by Pitt and Hatzfeld in 1888. The main alteration is to the declamation of the vocal line from:

Ex.18a                                    To brune Øine

Fred,   Jeg glem-mer dem al - drig

to:

Ex.18b                                    To brune Øine

Fred,   Jeg glem-mer dem al - drig

so that the emphasis is now on the word 'glemmer' (forget), rather than 'Jeg' (I).

In the later editions also the flat sign in the right hand accompaniment in the ninth bar is omitted, so retaining the E natural throughout the bar and keeping 'the element of harmonic surprise'[4] until the end of the song. The rhythmic augmentation on 'Evighed (eternity)', which underlines its meaning, is another example of Grieg's attention to detail.

The ideas expressed in *En Digters Bryst* (A poet's heart), the second song of the op.5 album, are on the sentimental side to modern ears. If we cannot understand the wonders of nature, Andersen asks, then how can we hope to understand the poet? Grieg's setting, marked 'Allegro molto ed agitato', looks back to earlier songs such as *Eingehüllt in graue Wolken*, having, as David Monrad Johansen saw it, 'some of the Leipzig period's threatening passion about it',[5] although the vocal phrases here are longer and freer. The rapid semiquaver movement of the accompaniment gives a feeling of the turbulent thoughts behind the verse, but it is without the freshness of approach that marks out *To brune Øine*. Alongside bars of straightforward harmony are passages of more complexity; for example, the rising phrases in the middle of each strophe, where the vocal line is built up using a diminished seventh in arpeggio, but where, because the F sharp in the bass is sustained throughout by the pedal, the effect is of eleventh and thirteenth chords with a flattened ninth. An interesting false relation occurs in the penultimate vocal bar, occasioned by the G natural of the Neapolitan sixth – used here, as so often by Grieg, in the root position – and the G sharp of the succeeding dominant seventh and at the end of the postlude Grieg uses another feature that was to become more important to him later: a dissonant ending, here adding the sixth to the tonic F sharp minor triad.

The third song of the group is probably Grieg's best known, even though it is rarely sung as he intended. *Jeg elsker dig* (I love you), described by Benestad and Schjelderup-Ebbe as 'one of the romantic period's most treasured love-songs',[6] has a freshness and innocence which is so often spoiled in translation by clumsiness or over-enthusiasm and, even more, by the addition, first by Frank van der Stucken in the French version and followed by von Holstein in German, of a second stanza, which has since been translated into almost every other edition. This practice does both Andersen and Grieg the great injustice of assuming that a verse or song with only one stanza cannot be complete like that. To add more lines or, as is often the case in performances by Scandinavian singers, to repeat the single stanza, is to ruin the fine balance of words and music. It also provides a terrible anticlimax, especially, as Astra Desmond pointed out,[7] if the composer's making of 'Poco accelerando' is observed both times.

Schjelderup-Ebbe has described the musical structure of the song as 'varied strophic . . . two stanzas of unequal length, the first parts of which are similar, while the last part of the second stanza is subtly varied and extended',[8] an analysis which the present author finds incomprehensible. Very many melodies repeat their first musical phrase later in their structure, without that being taken as the beginning of a new strophe, and the four lines of Andersen's verse rhyme alternately, not in couplets which could possibly have suggested two stanzas.

Harmonically, *Jeg elsker dig* is more chromatic and more overtly 'romantic' than *To brune Øine*, but the chromaticism only underlines the tenderness and yearning of the melody and words, without in any way overwhelming them. The chromatic movement within otherwise regular chords and especially the lush introduction appears, to an English singer, to foreshadow Roger Quilter's style early in the next century, in such songs as *Now sleeps the crimson petal*: Exx. 19 and 20.

Ex.19                                                              Jeg elsker dig

Ex.20                                              Now sleeps the crimson petal*

Grieg's song has a youthful exuberance that is just held in check and is full of a sincerity which must have delighted Nina, both as singer and fiancée.

The bass of the accompaniment partly doubles the vocal line, a device Grieg was occasionally to make use of again. The build-up to the climax of the song, with sequentially rising phrases, is, even with the 'poco accelerando', always controlled, and it is made more effective and beautifully counteracted by the dying fall in the vocal line to the flattened submediant in the chord of the supertonic seventh. The subsequent cadence is one of Grieg's favourites — a perfect cadence, but with the dominant seventh in its second inversion. That he can end such a song quietly and then use the postlude to bring down the dynamic even further is a sure sign of a composer gaining in confidence.

As well as translations into many languages, including Dutch and Spanish, the song has had numerous arrangements made of it. Grieg himself transcribed it for piano solo in 1884, one of six such transcriptions published by Peters in 1885 as the *Piano Pieces*, op.41. There are also vocal duet versions, an orchestration by Max Reger and other arrangements for organ, for brass band and for cornet, euphonium or trombone solo.

Unusually in the final song of the op.5 album, *Min Tanke er et mægtigt Fjeld* (My thoughts are like a mighty mountain), Grieg sets the two short four-line stanzas in through-composed form. Marked 'Allegro molto', the accompaniment triplets sustain the feeling of unrest in the poem, while the vocal line at the beginning is angular, as if to portray the mighty crag towering to the sky. The last line of the stanza, 'Hvor dybe Brændinge laae (Where deep passions lie),' is repeated in shorter note-values, so that the song ends with a feeling of urgency, and this is further emphasised by the 'stringendo' marking in the postlude, with triplets in the right hand over quavers in the left.

Harmonically, the song is not extraordinary. The most interesting passage occurs between bars 8 and 14, where the tonality becomes blurred both by dissonances (for example, between the E flat in the vocal line and the D natural in the bass) and by the raising of A flat to A natural and E flat to E natural in the ascending bass line.

In his article *Fra Griegs ungdom* (From Grieg's youth) written in 1899,[9] Benjamin Feddersen relates that Grieg could not find anyone who would publish the *Hjertets Melodier* and the album was first printed in Copenhagen in 1865 at the composer's own expense: 'Grieg was in high spirits [staying with Feddersen in Rungsted for the summer] although no-one had wanted to print his *Hjertets Melodier*, and very few people had bought the album after he had paid for its publication. On his homeward journey to Bergen he presented me with 50 copies of this worthy composition, so little did he expect from the future.' In its review of 30 April 1865 the Copenhagen newspaper *Illustreret Tidende* described the songs as having 'tuneful melodies and lively accompaniments, which however are not free from sometimes having much too sudden changes of key, something which seems to be caused by a desire to imitate the great model Schumann. But there is a freshness in the construction which ensures that the compositions will be heard with interest.' In spite of these comments, the op.5 songs owe less to Schumann's influence than earlier ones and the 'sudden changes of key' were to become more startling as time went on.

When one considers that most of Andersen's poems are about love, it is perhaps remarkable that he never had a successful love-affair. Like other romantic writers before and since, it seems that he was more in love with the idea of being in love than with any one person and indeed he was a rather prudish man and sexually innocent.[10] It has been alleged that he was homosexual, such being the modern fate of sensitive, unmarried artists, although there is no evidence for it.

Grieg appears to have met Andersen in Copenhagen early in 1864, when the writer was enjoying considerable fame in many parts of Europe for his stories, novels and poetry. That the composer admired the writer is obvious from the fact that Andersen's collected works in twelve volumes appear on Grieg's list of necessities for his new home in Christiania after his marriage, a list which was enclosed in one of his mother's letters. Among the composer's effects, left to Bergen Public Library, are Andersen's complete works in twenty volumes, as published in Copenhagen between 1854 and 1863, and dated by the composer '1864'. Grieg's admiration was tempered with realism, however; in a letter dated 2 April 1905 he said of Andersen, 'He writes only to one child: to the child in himself'.[11] In October 1874, he wrote, 'I was recently with H.C. Andersen, who can now appropriately be called Nonsense Andersen – he is going back into childhood!'[12]

It was Andersen's poetry rather than his other writing that appealed to Grieg in that happy period of his life in the mid-1860s, and in his fifteen solo settings (one more, *Danmark*, was set as a choral piece) he has mostly chosen the best of the lyrics. In most cases he selected the concise poems, the five stanzas of *Poesien* (Poesy), op.18 no.5, being the longest, and it is some of the shorter settings that have come to be counted among the most popular of Grieg's songs. Both Andersen and Grieg have suffered outside Scandinavia from being regarded as innocent, childlike figures with little idea of the real world, although this is true of neither of them. As John Horton has pointed out, a wider knowledge of songs like *Soldaten* (The soldier) 'might do much to dispel the popular misconception'.[13] Andersen's 'fairy-tales' were, after all, designed to be read on two levels: by children, who could enjoy the stories *per se*, and by adults, who could appreciate the deeper philosophy behind them, and the words 'told for children' were deleted from the collections of stories published after November 1843.

Andersen was also involved to some extent in Euterpe, having been asked to write a prologue to be recited by the actor Alfred Finck at the society's first concert on 18 March 1865, at which the writer was also the guest of honour. The prologue lays out the aims of the society:

> ... That those who love music should hear
> For little payment, really good concerts
> By young powers with young hearts,
> Music by the best, the great masters! ...[14]

Dating from the same time as the *Hjertets Melodier* is another song to a poem by Andersen, *Min lille Fugl* (My little bird). It is a poem of almost unutterable despair, the absent bird being a metaphor for absent love. Grieg sets it strophically in a folk-song style with a very simple piano accompaniment and with a modal quality to the harmony. Although he retains the desolation of the words in its starkness, the vocal line is static and the song lacks the fluidity of Niels Gade's setting of the same poem written in 1850: Exx.21 and 22.

Grieg allows no lingering over the words, but his repetition of the last line of each stanza, first pianissimo, then fortissimo with an almost immediate diminuendo, underlines the poet's loneliness.

Three versions of the song exist in manuscript in Bergen Public Library. The (apparently) earliest of these is undated. The second is dated '12 August 65' and has an inscription at the end: 'Til Benjamin Feddersen at synge allene! (. . . to sing alone!)'. This manuscript shows some alterations from the first, principally a change of harmony in bar 9: Exx. 23a and 23b;

Ex.21

Grieg, Min lille Fugl

(My little bird, where are you flying amongst the green branches? Ah...)

Ex.23a          Min lille Fugl

Ex.23b          Min lille Fugl

although with the exception of the vocal rhythm, the former is nearer to what appears in the printed edition (Ex.23c). The third manuscript is dated simply '1865' and has no inscription. In this version too, the tonic fifth in the left hand and the dominant in the right are omitted in the very first bar, leaving just the semiquavers, and the left hand in bar 8 has some additional passing notes to give more inner movement, but this is not found in the printed edition.

Ex.23c    Min lille Fugl

*Min lille Fugl* was first printed in 1895 as the fourth of a series of *Nordiske Sange* (Scandinavian Songs), published by Det Nordiske Forlag in Copenhagen. It was also included in the first volume of *Posthumous Songs*, along with two other Andersen settings, *Taaren* (The tear) and *Soldaten* (The soldier), in the Peters edition of 1908, with a German translation by Hans Schmidt and English by John Bernhoff, but for some reason it was omitted from the Hansen edition of the same year.

*Taaren* and *Soldaten* were also written in 1865. In his setting of *Taaren* Grieg seems to be unsure of his own intentions. The poem extols tears, saying that as they contain all one's sorrow, then 'if you have wept your eyes weary, you will become light of heart'. Although the two stanzas are contrasted, Grieg, as so often with similar poems, sets them strophically. The vocal line, although largely diatonic, is angular and the accompaniment is mostly very chromatic, especially in the inner parts. This chromatic movement gives rise to false relations, while the climax of the strophe has a vocal line built up on diminished triads that are, with the accompaniment, the upper three notes of dominant sevenths in arpeggio, and with this more conventional harmony the atmosphere is lightened for a while. The manuscript shows only one change from the original to what was eventually printed and that is the alteration of the position of the repeat marks from bars 5 to 22 inclusive, to bars 4 to 25. Thus the final version incorporates the original postlude (identical to the introduction) into both stanzas. The song was not published separately. Originally to have been part of the *Fem Sange* to Louis Hornbeck, it did not actually appear in print until after Grieg's death.

*Soldaten* is probably Grieg's most remarkable song. The poem is said to be based on an actual event from Andersen's youth in Odense and describes a firing squad, one of whose members is the only friend of the condemned man. The other eight, trembling with grief, miss their target; only the narrator, out of friendship, shoots his comrade through the heart.

The history of the composition of *Soldaten* is not completely clear. Two manuscripts exist. One is exactly the same as the printed version of the song, which was first published among the *Posthumous Songs*; the other shows an earlier version, which while essentially the same, has some marked differences from the published edition. This earlier manuscript is part of the *Fem Sange* to Louis Hornbeck, which was acquired by Oslo University Library in 1971 and probably dates from 1865. Øystein Gaukstad expresses the opinion that the song was rewritten 'many years later when [Grieg] was both capable of and dared to express himself more boldly than in his youthful years'. [15] Yet the earlier version has almost all the daring chromatic writing of the later one and the manuscript of the later version, one of those kept at Troldhaugen, has at the end 'Komp. 9d Mai 1865 i Kjøbenhaven'. Also at Troldhaugen is a manuscript of *Taaren*, which, at the bottom of the second page, has the first three bars of *Soldaten* in its *first* version. (It is in the third bar where the difference between the two is first apparent.) Unfortunately, nothing more has been found of this manuscript in spite of enquiries by the present author, but it is possible that Grieg had planned another group of Andersen settings, perhaps before he included *Soldaten* and *Taaren* in the *Fem Sange*.

*Soldaten* in both versions is very dramatic, with chromaticism and dissonance used to underline the horror of the story. Apart from the last fourteen bars, the later version improves on the original only by making some of the ideas more concise, the main difference being the alteration of the time-signature of the vocal line, so that finally it is in $\frac{4}{4}$ throughout, over a $\frac{12}{8}$ accompaniment, instead of both parts being in the compound time for the first eight bars. The original 'Tempo di marcia' marking is expanded to 'Tempo di marcia funebre' in the later manuscript and the muffled drums of the firing-squad's procession are conjured up, as the voice enters, in the descending chromatic 'rumbles' in both hands of the accompaniment. In the first version the voice part is written an octave higher than in the printed edition, but the lower register aids the word-painting and also gives the vocal line room to grow, so that the final range is from low A to high F.

The tension begins to increase in the second stanza, created in the vocal line by a wider range and frequent changes in tessitura over the insistent triplets of the accompaniment. In the third stanza the vocal melody becomes even more angular, especially in the final version, but Grieg reserves his master-stroke for the last stanza. The first setting here has a vocal melody which is built up in minor triads, doubled an octave lower in the accompaniment.

Ex.24                                                            Soldaten

(At once all nine took aim. Eight shot right past him,)

In the final version Grieg sets the whole of the stanza in a recitative style, with the rifle shots depicted in the accompaniment. The vocal phrases descend in sequence and the dynamic marking is reduced from 'forte' to 'pianissimo', so that the words 'kun jeg . . . (only I . . .)' (with, in the second version, the high F extended to five beats instead of one and the A natural in the bass brought in almost a bar earlier) come as a terrible cry of anguish: Ex.25.

The postlude is similar in both versions of the song, although the later version is more dissonant. The starkness of the recitative, which extends the feeling of inevitability similarly created by Schubert at the end of *Der*

Ex.25                                                                          Soldaten

(Only I struck him right in his heart.)

*Erlkönig*, is far more dramatic and tragic than any melodic setting could have been, and Schjelderup-Ebbe has also compared Grieg's word-setting in this song to that of Musorgsky and Hugo Wolf.

Schumann's setting of the same poem, published as *Der Soldat*, op.40 no.3, is not as vivid as Grieg's. It was made to a German translation of Andersen's poem by Chamisso. The two poets met in Berlin in 1831 and Chamisso, who could read Danish, subsequently translated a number of Andersen's verses into German. It is Chamisso's version that Grieg has written into the Troldhaugen manuscript of the final version of his song, although it does not exactly fit his setting, but the Peters' edition in the *Posthumous Songs* has a German translation by Hans Schmidt. It would appear, however, that Grieg did know Schumann's setting. Schumann depicted the drum-rolls in his opening piano figure and the same figure is used throughout much of the accompaniment. Interestingly, he also set the final phrase as recitative, but pianissimo over tremolo chords.

Two further Andersen settings, *Kjærlighed* (Love) and *Langelandsk Folke-melodi* (A Langeland folk-song), also written in 1865, were included in the group of songs published as op.15, and will be dealt with in that context below. Also during 1865 Grieg made his only setting of a poem by the Danish artist and nun Caspara Preetzman, who wrote under the pseudonym 'Caralis'. This was *Dig elsker jeg!* (You I love!), written at Rungsted, apparently as a counterpart to *Jeg elsker dig*. This song is not of any especial interest, but is pleasing enough in its simplistic way, and scarcely 'among the most inferior of Grieg's compositions in all respects'.[16]

The vocal line is lyrical and almost entirely diatonic, but this is a more subdued if no less sincere affirmation of love than the Andersen setting. The chromatic writing is mostly confined to inner parts and some use is made of pedal points, notably the dominant pedal in the opening bars. The accompaniment is very simple, occasionally doubling the vocal line in octaves, with syncopation adding interest in the first two phrases, and the recitative style in the middle of the strophe anticipates what Grieg was to do more frequently in later songs. The interlude seems to bear no relationship to the rest of the song and ends oddly on a chord of the supertonic seventh with a flattened fifth, before the return to the beginning for the second strophe. *Dig elsker jeg!* remained unpublished until 1908, when it was included in the first album of *Posthumous Songs*.

During the prolific period of the spring and summer of 1865, besides the songs to texts by Andersen, Grieg also wrote *Efteraarsstormen* (The autumn storm), a setting of a poem by Christian Richardt which a year later was to provide thematic material for his Concert Overture, *I Høst* (In autumn). The song was the earliest written of those published as op. 18. Like *Udfarten* (The outward journey), op. 9 no. 4, composed the following year, it is a large-scale, through-composed song, 136 bars long, which, again like *Udfarten*, makes much use of motifs for cohesion. The poem has vivid descriptions of autumn, winter and spring and Grieg's setting is very dramatic.

The voice, with the principal motif

Ex. 26                                                        Efteraarsstormen

I Som-mer var Sko-ven saa  grøn, saa grøn, og  Kvid-de-ren gik saa  lunt i løn.

(In summer the wood was so green, so green, and the chirping goes on so cosily, secretly)

enters quietly as the poet remembers the greenness of summer, but suddenly (bar 15) the storm bursts forth for the first time, the accompaniment making much and not very original use of tremolo. First the trees shake in the wind, then the tops are taken off and finally all the leaves: 'All blev plyndret en Efteraarsnat (Everything was stripped one autumn night)'. As the winter makes its appearance, the melodic line becomes much more static, 'quasi recitando', and the accompaniment is confined to crotchet chords. Again making use of the opening motif, the music builds up before yielding to the inevitable: 'Somren er omme! (The summer is over)'. The German translation by von Holstein gives this line as 'Lenz [spring] ist vergangen', which does not fit the song at all; neither is the finality felt in Corder's corresponding 'Summer is waning'.

The next section also uses the opening motif, now in the relative major key, before a new passage in the tonic major describes the snow as it covers the wounds made by the storm. This leads to yet another passage, now with a wide-ranging theme in the vocal line, which is combined with elements of

the first motif in the accompaniment (Ex.27), as the poet speaks of the hope
of spring:

Ex.27                                                          Efteraarsstormen

(Every little seed knows)

and the song ends peacefully, yet confidently, in D major.

The use of a principal motif helps to link the sections together and to give
a feeling of unity to what is in some ways a lightweight and rather
fragmentary song. The harmonic structure is largely conventional, with little
chromatic movement except at the very end, although the later Grieg is to be
discerned in the occasional modal feeling and the extensive use of pedal
notes, which gives rise to a number of dissonances. In the F major section,
the phrases of the vocal line are frequently echoed in the piano left hand, the
first time that the feature has been used to this extent in one of his songs.
However, for all its drama, this is essentially a musical picture of a Danish
winter, in keeping with Richardt, rather than a much harsher Norwegian
one.

A slightly more Norwegian flavour is to be found in the op.9 songs to
texts by Andreas Munch, *Romancer og Ballade til Digte af A. Munch*, although
truly distinctive nationalist elements in the music are limited. Grieg had
already set two of Munch's poems, one as a solo song (*Solnedgang*) and one for
choir, before they met in Rome at the end of 1865, and during the early part
of the following year the two were to become better acquainted.

Grieg had planned to spend the autumn and winter of 1865–66 in Italy
with Nordraak, but delayed the journey because he was so happy at
Rungsted. Nordraak went on to Berlin where, in October, he contracted the
pulmonary consumption from which he was not to recover. Grieg's reaction
to his friend's illness was very strange. He was very annoyed that Nordraak
was not well enough to make their proposed trip when he came to fetch him
from Berlin and his letter to Hornbeck (of 22 October 1865) gives the

impression of a spoilt child who cannot have his own way, with little sympathy for Nordraak's condition: '. . . I come to Berlin to fetch Nordraak for our journey to Italy and the man is in bed and sick unto death! He has now been in bed for 14 days with the most severe pneumonia and would certainly have died if his fantastically strong constitution had not prevented him.' He goes on to describe Nordraak's symptoms, says that even if he goes on to Leipzig to wait, Nordraak cannot possibly make the trip before 1 December and complains that by then they will have all the hardships of a winter journey. However, off to Leipzig Grieg certainly went, to hear performances of his piano and violin sonatas, promising to return to Berlin to visit his sick friend. In spite of pleas from Nordraak, who must by this time have realised he was dying, Grieg went on saying he would come, but then wrote to say he had gone straight to Italy. In a letter dated 30 November 1865 Nordraak wrote that he could not understand such treatment, but that he still forgave his friend.

After Nordraak's death in March 1866, Grieg, perhaps through remorse, became more determined to go further towards the truly Norwegian music to which Ole Bull had first led him and which Nordraak's enthusiasm had encouraged. He wrote later to Grønvold, 'Without him [Nordraak] I should perhaps have had to struggle who knows how long without finding myself.' Modern scholarship has suggested that Nordraak's influence was not after all so great, but in a letter to Iver Holter in 1897 Grieg stated, 'Nordraak's significance for me is NOT exaggerated. It really was so: through him and only through him, a light dawned for me.'

In spite of his friend's death, Grieg's time in Italy was pleasant, useful and inspiring, the last being what Andersen had wished for him in the verse he wrote in Grieg's album on his departure:

> Flyv ungdomssund til den evige Stad,
> Kom Dig selv og begeistret tilbage,
> Lad Norden, med Dig, faae et Tone-Quad
> For Tusinde Aar og Dage!
> (Fly, youthfully fit, to the eternal city!/Come back yourself
> and inspired,/let Scandinavia with you acquire a song/for a
> thousand years and a day!)

He visited the usual sights – Rome, Naples, Caprì, Sorrento and Pompeii – during that winter, as well as going to concerts *en route*. In Rome, too, he met Ibsen. He also saw Liszt for the first time at a concert, 'making eyes at some young ladies', and attended a church concert, which he described in his notebooks as containing 'dreadful music . . . Bellini, Donizetti, Rossini. Two castrati, unnatural, loathsome'. Other church music by 'new Italian masters', who are not named, was described as 'deadly boring'.

In Rome, Grieg became a member of the Scandinavian Association and it was here that he furthered his acquaintance with Andreas Munch. Munch was born in 1811 and during the 1850s and 1860s was regarded as one of Norway's greatest poets. He was also recognised in Denmark, where he later lived, both for his elegiac poetry and for his plays. A number of these plays are in blank verse after the manner of Oehlenschläger, although some of the subject-matter was taken from Old Norse history, and in that they also owe something to the saga-dramas of Ibsen and Bjørnson. Munch's poetry-cycle *Kongedatterens Brudefart* (The Princess's Bridal Journey), written in 1850, was briefly considered by Grieg as an opera libretto, but nothing came of the idea. However, amongst the collection *Sorg og Trøst* (Sorrow and Comfort) of 1852, Grieg found two poems, *Harpen* (The harp) and *Vuggesang* (Cradle song), which he was to include in the group of songs composed between 1863 and 1866 and published as op.9.

*Harpen*, the first song of that group, was written on 4 April 1865. It is in no way a distinguished piece; Benestad and Schjelderup-Ebbe are of the opinion that it 'ought to be passed over in silence'[17] and consider the setting to be almost a parody of Grieg's true style, especially in the over-use of the tonic—leading-note—dominant sequence, which was to become known as the 'Grieg motif'. The uninspired poem drew, for the most part, equally uninspired music from the composer. The picture of a lady and her knight, bound together through the music of her harp, even though they are soon to part, is marked to be sung 'i Balladetone (in ballad style)' and the simplistic strophic setting was obviously an attempt to match the old-world tone of the words, as had been done so successfully in *Das alte Lied*, but so unsuccessfully here. For once chromaticism is not used to any telling effect; the introduction, for example, has some self-conscious chromatic contrary motion which leads nowhere and seems quite superfluous. The three repetitions necessary to accommodate all the stanzas do not enhance the song. The only glimpse of Grieg's true style or of anything remotely Norwegian occurs in the piano figure which begins in the last bar of the vocal line: Ex.28.

The next song, *Vuggesang* (Cradle song), is quite another matter, and yet according to Grieg's diary, was written the day after *Harpen*. Here the simple

Ex.28                                      Harpen

musical treatment of the poem is full of sincerity, rather than the sentimentality the subject might have engendered. The poem depicts a father speaking to his motherless infant son and was written from personal experience: Munch's own wife had died in 1850 giving birth to twin boys, one of whom was shortly to follow his mother. Grieg's setting is strophic and, after using the four eight-line stanzas, he repeats the first half of the first stanza and makes up a full strophe by using the third and fourth lines again, and then the fourth line once more, with the music altered to remain in the tonic key.

The song is basically in G sharp minor, although the flattened leading-notes of the melody do give a modal feeling. Benestad and Schjelderup-Ebbe go so far as to see the song as 'dominated' by the Aeolian mode and cite it as 'an early example of a sustained use of a modal style in nineteenth-century music', [18] and the latter earlier considered the song as an example of Grieg's originality in the use of modal scales 'combined with complex dissonant chords in unorthodox progressions'. [19] The accompaniment chords are divided between the hands, with quavers in the left and syncopated semiquavers in the right, in all but four bars of each of the first four strophes and almost totally throughout the last strophe, the restlessness aptly portraying the father's anxiety for his child which underlies the legato vocal line. The whole setting is slightly understated to great effect and the unusual progressions and the dissonance add to the picture of despair behind the words. Even the apparent resolution into E major (bar 17) soon disappears and there is no comfort of coming home to the tonic key at the end of the first four strophes. In the modified second half of the final strophe, with its reiterated words, there is a phrase in G sharp *major* (albeit with a non-diatonic accompaniment), but any sense of relief is soon negated by the dissonant chord, which so bleakly underlines the last repetition of the word 'kolde (cold):'

Ex.29                                              Vuggesang

(lies in the cold grave.)

Grieg considered *Vuggesang* to be among his best songs and he made a piano transcription of it, published in the *Piano Pieces*, op.41. In a letter written from Leipzig in January 1896, he described the effect on him of hearing the song again some thirty years after its composition: 'Yesterday evening Röntgen's friend, the excellent Dutch singer Messchaert, also sang my Vuggesang to Munch's "Søv, min Søn" [Sleep, my son – the first line of the poem] . . . absolutely beautifully, with a colour and a stillness exactly as it should be . . . I felt a great inner happiness and gratitude towards the artist who did not ruin my most intimate intentions, but exactly understood them and understood how to impart them to others.'[20] Another idea of the kind of performance Grieg wanted comes in a later letter from Paris, dated 26 December 1889: '. . . Mad. Colonne[21] sang with such a deep understanding and "noblesse", that both Nina and I were enchanted by it. She is neither young nor pretty and has no large voice. Her performance counts all the more. She sang in particular "Søv min Søn" (A. Munch) wonderfully prettily . . .'[22] The song was included amongst the music Grieg took to show Liszt when he visited him in Rome in 1870.

The third song of the op.9 album, *Solnedgang* (Sunset), was the earliest, written in 1863, and has already been discussed in Chapter 3. The last of the four, *Udfarten* (The outward journey), is one of Grieg's longest songs, 104 bars in length. The poem tells of a young couple travelling to Italy, of the hopes of the wife and of the sorrow soon to come with her early death. The opening of the song sets the scene of a summer night, with a ship ready to sail on the morning tide, portrayed in the lilting arpeggios in the accompaniment. The little triplet decoration in the eighth bar of the vocal line is characteristic of Norwegian folk music, perhaps to remind listener and performer where the journey begins. Preceded, as here, by a wide-ranging arpeggio of the major seventh, it is also typical of the later Grieg:

Ex.30                                                                    Udfarten

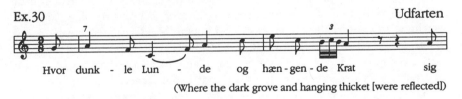

Hvor   dunk - le Lun - de   og   hæn - gen - de Krat        sig

(Where the dark grove and hanging thicket [were reflected])

The song is through-composed, although, as in *Efteraarsstormen* some of the motifs are used more than once to give an overall unity. The first real changes of mood occur as the poet speaks of the ship's imminent departure. The impending sadness is anticipated in the harmonisation, where in three successive bars (33 to 35) there is a diminished seventh on G flat, a D major triad, and an A flat major triad with an added sharpened sixth, all over a low C sustained by the pedal. From this last chord each note except the third moves by a semitone to resolve to the tonic C major on the word 'Hav (sea)'. For the description of the young wife the key changes to a warm A flat major and another significant change comes at bar 55 when the goal of the journey is revealed as Italy. Grieg's piano writing here in the tremolando chords is full of the lightness and warmth which all Scandinavians seem to associate with that country. The final high tremolo chord, after a two-bar pianissimo postlude, has been described by Monrad Johansen as 'illuminating . . . like a faint star-shimmer over death and the grave'.[23]

Grieg sets the poem in a very direct way, stopping only twice to reflect on the words; first, at 'Hun svævede ud paa den herlige Fart, som Dronningen i et Digt (She floated out on the splendid journey, like the queen in a poem)', where he repeats the first three words and echoes the arpeggio vocal figure in the accompaniment (bars 80 and 81), something which Monrad Johansen has described as being 'like a victory fanfare',[24] and, second, for the final line, 'under Mold med hviden Kind (under the earth with a white cheek)', which is repeated once.

Once again, as in *Vuggesang*, there are personal undertones in Munch's poem, for he and his wife made a journey to Italy in 1847, only three years before her untimely death. As the song was written in the autumn of 1866, Monrad Johansen and Schjelderup-Ebbe have also seen in it Nordraak's death and Grieg's own journey to Italy, and Grieg told Finck, 'my choice of poet is always connected with what I have experienced'. Whatever the case, the poem drew from the composer some of his most sensitive and beautiful music.

The first edition of the op.9 songs was published by Horneman/Erslev in Copenhagen in December 1866. The album is dedicated to Erika Lie (later Nissen), the Norwegian pianist who was to give the first performance in Christiania of Grieg's Piano Concerto.

Grieg's hectic social life in Rome gave him little time to write and he produced only four works during the spring of 1866: two of the Munch settings, the overture *I Høst* and a 'Funeral March for Nordraak'. The overture, based on material from *Efteraarsstormen*, has been lost in its original form; it survived in a popular version for piano duet and some years later the composer prepared a new orchestration with some revisions.

Grieg met Ibsen at the Scandinavian Association in Rome and got to know him well enough during the early months of 1866 to ask him for a reference later in the year. On 30 March the poet wrote in Grieg's album the lines entitled *I en komponists stambog* (In a composer's album):

> Orpheus slog med Toner rene
> Sjæl i Vilddyr, Ild af Stene.
> Stene har vort Norden nok af;
> Vilddyr har det og en Flok af.

Spil saa Stenen spruder Gnister;
Spil saa Dyrehammen brister!
(Orpheus with his pure notes struck/souls into wild animals, fire into stones./
Of stones our Scandinavia has enough,/we have wild animals, many of them./
Play, so the stones spark!/Play so the animal-hide cracks!)

In April Grieg travelled in Italy and Switzerland, arriving back in Leipzig on 26 April. By May he was back in the usual daily round in Copenhagen and once again seemed uncertain about his future, both professional and personal. Nina arrived after a six-month stay in Bergen, but from Grieg's diary the reunion seems to have been only luke-warm. A letter from Benjamin Feddersen written in August 1866 shows that matters between the couple were not all they might have been. Feddersen is frank about his own opinion of Nina: 'I regret that she does not understand her relationship to you . . . That is not the woman who deserves to support and encourage you in the development of your talents.' Neither did Feddersen think very highly of Nina's parents, and he told Grieg: 'You cannot flourish amongst them; you would perish like a plant that lacks air and sun.'[25] Grieg was obviously in conflict with himself: should he sacrifice his art, or sacrifice himself for it? One possible compromise was to become a church organist, so that he would have a regular income on which to support a family, and he began to have lessons with his friend Matthison-Hansen. This was not so unlikely a proposition as it may at first seem, for at the end of six weeks' tuition he was declared good enough to deputise for his teacher at St Frederik's church in Copenhagen, but such a career was not to be.

At the beginning of September Grieg returned to Bergen to visit the parents he had not seen for two years. He was there for five weeks. However, his home for the next ten years was to be in Christiania. At first his career was still undecided and it was then that he wrote to Ibsen asking for a reference for the post of musical director at the Christiania Theatre, at that time being run by Bjørnson. Bjørnson did not answer Grieg's application and Ibsen consoled him by commenting, perceptively, that his future was surely to be 'something more and better than a capellmeister's post'.[26]

On 15 October Grieg organised a concert at the Hotel du Nord in Christiania, with a programme entirely of Norwegian music. Nina sang songs by Kjerulf and Nordraak and the Hjertets Melodier, while Grieg himself played three of the Humoresker, all but the first movement of his Piano Sonata and the accompaniment for his Violin Sonata. The concert attracted some very favourable press reviews and left Grieg with a handsome profit.

At the end of 1866 he made his first setting of a landsmål poem, Vesle gut by Kristofer Janson. Grieg probably met Janson in Rome, where they were both members of the Scandinavian Association. He must certainly have acquired the poem from the poet, for Janson's collection of Norske dikt

(Norwegian Poetry), which contains the verse, was not published until 1867 and that is also the date in Grieg's copy of the book, now in the collection in Bergen Public Library. Janson (1841–1917) was a novelist as well as a poet and, although influenced by Bjørnson and a friend of Ibsen, from whom he borrowed money, he was an advocate of *landsmål*, the literary language based on Norwegian dialect. Michael Meyer tells of the Scandinavian Association's Christmas party in 1866, where Janson announced that he would read one of his stories in *landsmål*. Ibsen, who would have nothing to do with the new language, declared that if that happened, he would leave.[27] Ibsen seems to have had rather ambivalent feelings about Janson's abilities and saw him as something of a model for the character of Hjalmar Ekdal in *The Wild Duck*, suggesting in a letter (quoted by Meyer) to Hans Schrøder of the Christiania Theatre, who was to direct the play, that for the role he should think of Kristofer Janson, 'who still contrives to give an effect of beauty whatever drivel he may be uttering.'[28]

   *Vesle gut* (Little boy) is a sad little poem. A small boy is sitting on a hillock crying and wondering if he will always be so little and so the butt of everyone's bad temper, even that of the animals. Grieg linked Janson's seven four-line stanzas to form three long ones, set strophically, and a short final stanza set differently. The setting has a very simple texture which resembles Norwegian folk-song both in the melodic decorations and the modal feeling to the harmony. Although the manuscript shows some alterations from the first version, which do not have it following the vocal line so exactly, the accompaniment remains largely homophonic:

Ex.31                                                                Vesle Gut

(Little boy sits on the hillock with tears on his cheeks)

Most of the harmony is built on tonic and dominant pedals and there is also some use of the 'Grieg motif', both in its major and modal forms. Dated 12 December 1866, the song was never printed in Grieg's lifetime, but will be included in the *GGA*.

The success of his Christiania concert prompted an invitation to Grieg to become the conductor of the amateur orchestra Det philharmoniske Selskab, and this gave him an opportunity to perform more of his own music. The concert given on 23 March 1867 included three movements of the Symphony and, in the autumn of the same year, the society gave an all-Grieg programme, which included *I Høst* (in the piano-duet version), a Gavotte and Minuet for violin and piano, the G major Violin Sonata and some part-songs for male-voice choir.

The early publicity helped Grieg to obtain a number of piano pupils and in January 1867 he opened an 'academy' with Otto Winter-Hjelm, a venture which only lasted for one year. Grieg's teaching at the academy and at home left him with little time for composition, but by the end of 1866 he felt that his income would be enough to support a family. Neither he nor Nina was popular with the other's family. Nina's parents were not invited to the wedding and Grieg's father seemed not to know anything about it, but the ceremony took place – between concert seasons – at St John's church in Copenhagen on 11 June 1867. Grieg resigned from Euterpe and the couple moved to Christiania, where the composer became closely involved with his compatriots Svendsen and Kjerulf.

The autumn of 1867 saw Grieg's first setting of a poem by Bjørnson, *Den blonde pige* (The blonde girl), although the song was not published until 1908, when it appeared as the first of the *Posthumous Songs*. *Den blonde pige* is a lovely lyrical song to sing, if rather long, with the four eight-line stanzas set strophically. In both this setting and the second (see below) the first two lines of the poem are preceded by the third and fourth; the poem itself begins: 'Although *she* [not 'you' as in the song] will fade like an airy vision, if I dare to speak thus: I love you, you fair-haired girl . . .' The vocal line of the first setting is lyrical, but contains some wide intervals, for example both rising and falling major sevenths, that are not often encountered in Grieg's early songs. The opening of the accompaniment is similar to that of *Dig elsker jeg!*, with syncopated chords in the right hand and a descending chromatic line in the left, although there is much more variety in the piano writing in this song. Most of the chromatic movement occurs in the inner parts, occasionally giving rise to some striking dissonance, and there are also several typically Griegian features, not least the sounding of the dominant chord over the tonic. The interlude figure is marked 'Animato molto, scherz.' and the 'scherzando' aspect is strengthened by the syncopated chords and the chromatic sliding under the descending scale in the right hand: Ex.32.

The silent bar between this passage and the next strophe, and at the end before the final cadence, anticipates a similar device, which Grieg used to indicate a sense of fun in the Benzon settings, *Til min Dreng* (To my son), op.69 no.2, and *To a devil*, written in English, previously unpublished, but also included in the *GGA*.

Ex.32                                                              Den blonde Pige

Another setting of *Den blonde Pige* was discovered much later in Peters'
archives in Leipzig, the only time that Grieg made two completely separate
settings of the same poem. Written in 1874, this is a quite different song,
with a more yearning quality than the first. The vocal line is very chromatic
and unusually wide-ranging — from middle E to high G in less than three
bars — and is doubled almost throughout in the accompaniment, although
not always by the right hand. The sequences in the middle section foreshadow
later songs such as *Eros* (op.70 no.1) and other harmonic interest lies in the
dominant pedal at the beginning, in the descending bass and middle lines in
bars 15 to 17, the enharmonic change to D flat major at bar 18 (Ex.33) and in the
use of the dominant seventh in second inversion in the final cadence.

Ex.33                                                           Den blonde Pige (II)

and is reflected in the flow of thought and knows not what it has

*Den blonde Pige (II)* is published in the *GGA*, but recently similarities have been pointed out (by Audun Kayser, the present intendant at Troldhaugen) between this setting and the second of Grieg's *Albumblad*, op.28, also written in 1874. Nils Grinde is of the opinion that 'Grieg first wrote the song and then found he could use it as an Albumblad'.[29] It may be that the composer – or Nina, as a singer – realized that the first setting was the better; it is certainly the more vocally conceived.

The first of the *Lyric Pieces* for piano, which were to make Grieg known around the world, also date from this time and the first eight (of an eventual sixty-six) were published in Copenhagen in December 1867 as *Lyrisker Småstykker*, op.12. The following year he completed the second Violin Sonata, which was dedicated to Svendsen. This shows many elements of national music and Grieg seemed to be trying to show that folk music and classical music could be combined, as Svendsen himself was to do in a number of large-scale works.

On 10 April 1868 Nina gave birth to a daughter, Alexandra, and this event was the inspiration for Grieg's first setting of an Ibsen poem. *Margretes Vuggesang* (Margaret's cradle song), eventually designated as op.15 no.1, comes from the historical drama *Kongsemnerne* (The Pretenders), written in 1863, which tells of the struggle for sovereignty between King Håkon Håkonssøn and Earl Skule in the thirteenth century. Margrete is Skule's daughter and the king's wife and in the play the song occurs immediately following the death of Bishop Nikolas of Oslo. Ibsen, however, took some liberties with historical chronology, for in fact 'lille Håkon' was the king's second son and not born until seven years after the bishop's death.

Grieg matches the simplicity and sincerity of the verse with his straightforward setting. Although the accompaniment is completely homophonic, there is some harmonic interest in the suspensions and pedal notes, while the middle section is lightened by a change of tessitura and therefore colour in the piano writing. The melodic line here twice includes a descending augmented second, which gives an added poignancy to the words, as if the composer envied the baby its chance to glimpse heaven, a chance denied the parent. Retaining the A flat tonic fifth in the left hand at the recapitulation of the first section instead of moving to the second inversion of the dominant as before adds a new stability at this point: 'Guds Engle smaa de vaage for Vuggebarnets Fred (God's little angels, they watch over the cradle-child's peace)'. Some years later Delius also set Ibsen's poem as *Cradle Song*, the first of his *Seven Songs from the Norwegian*.

Op.15 no.2, *Kjærlighed* (Love), to a poem by Hans Andersen, is a light and airy song with a lyrical vocal line, which has been dismissed as being 'without interest, except that it shows the composer's altered state of mind towards the light, the optimistic'[30] and as 'an insignificant banality',[31] neither an opinion with which the present author is able to agree. The poem with its rather unoriginal imagery is certainly not one of Andersen's best and the music is better than the words deserve. The accompaniment, with its arpeggios and broken chords, is more obviously 'pianistic' than the previous song. The harmonic structure is largely straightforward, but there is once again an imaginative use of pedal notes, providing points of stability for the ever-changing harmony. There is a good deal of chromatic movement, especially in the two bars that form the introduction and postlude, and a number of chords are also chromatically altered to change the tone-colour, accomplished very effectively, for example, in bar 13, where the A flat of the dominant seventh chord on D flat is sharpened to A natural, and then the G flat of the next bar's resolution is anticipated by a quaver's length:

Ex.34                              Kjærlighed

(the wind, they [kiss])

Another Andersen poem was used for op. 15 no. 3, *Langelandsk Folkemelodi* (A Langeland folk-song), where both the words and the music keep the essence of folk music. The poem has four three-line stanzas, each of which is preceded by an identical two-line refrain:

> Hun har mig glemt, min Sorg hun ei see!
> Ung Elskovs Død gjør Hjertet saa Vee!
> (She has forgotten me, she doesn't see my sorrow!/the death of young love makes my heart so sore!)

Grieg's music owes more to Norwegian folk-song than to Danish in its use of pedal notes. The vocal line is simple and with a small range until the last phrase, which comes as something of a surprise and which lifts the song out of the ordinary: Ex. 35.

The agitation of the jilted lover is conveyed in the syncopated rhythm of the accompaniment at the beginning and Grieg also sets the refrain in a minor key. He then modulates to the relative major for the more prosaic

Ex.35                                      Langelandsk Folkemelodi

(The thrush flutes his song)

stanzas, where the poet talks of going on his way to new countries where he may forget his sorrow, although something of the agitation is kept in the continued use of semiquavers in the right hand and a dotted rhythm in the left. In spite of his apparent optimism, the poet says that 'the heart's sorrow becomes a song' and the final phrase is altered to end on the lower dominant. The short postlude seems rather too romantic for so slight a song and by sharpening the D and the F in the altered final phrase, Grieg effectively ends in the dominant key and, by further retaining the D sharp in the triplet decoration of the last bar, makes the song sound unfinished.

The last of the op. 15 album again has a text by the Danish poet, Christian Richardt. *Modersorg* (A mother's sorrow) was composed in 1868, the same year as *Margretes Vuggesang*, and a year before Grieg himself was to know the sorrow of losing his only child. Where the minor key was poignant in the former song, here it is deeply tragic and the stark simplicity of the vocal line is full of emptiness, its understatement exactly matching the words, where the simple imagery is more heart-rending than any histrionic outburst would have been. Particularly moving is the last line, 'o hjælp mig til at græde! (O help me to weep!).' The accompaniment for the first part of each of the two strophes portrays the rocking of the cradle, but this ceases at the words 'Ak, saa tom staar nu hans lille vugge (Oh, so empty his little cradle now stands)' and becomes more homophonic and almost hymn-like in character. The rocking figure is not resumed until the interlude, which interestingly comprises the accompaniment to bars 3, 4, 5, 9 and 10 of the strophe, a passage only slightly altered to form the postlude.

The first three songs of the op. 15 album were all previously printed elsewhere. *Margretes Vuggesang* was published in October 1868 in Copenhagen in Volume 2, Number 2 of Horneman & Erslev's *Album for Sang*. *Kjærlighed* and *Langelandsk Folkemelodi* were both included in the *Fem Sange* to

Louis Hornbeck, although they were never printed in this form. *Kjærlighed* was first printed in the *Album for Sang* in December 1867 and *Langelandsk Folkemelodi* in the same publishers' *Musikalisk Museum* in January of the same year. The manuscript of the *Fem Sange* shows some minor differences from the printed versions of the songs, but nothing of any musical significance. It seems that both the songs were first intended to be part of a group of five *Sange og Romancer* to be published as op.9, and the manuscript of this group, which also contains the first three Munch settings, is preserved in Copenhagen.[32] In November 1866, however, Grieg decided that his op.9 album should consist only of Munch settings and instructed his publisher, Erslev, accordingly.

The four songs that now comprise op.15 were first published together by Horneman & Erslev in Copenhagen in December 1868 under the title *Romancer af H. Ibsen, H.C. Andersen og Chr. Richardt*. They were never published as a separate album by Peters, although each of the songs appears in one of the five volumes of the Grieg-Album, which appeared between 1874 and 1885.


Life in Christiania was unfortunately not all that Grieg had hoped it would be. He had acquired a good deal of teaching, but this was poorly paid, and he was frustrated by the poor standards that prevailed in Det philharmoniske Selskab. Also for the press and public, the novelty of his appearance amongst them was waning and he began to find himself considered as an outsider who was impudent enough to want to reform the capital's musical life. To relieve some of the frustration, the family went back to Denmark for the summer of 1868 and while there, Grieg wrote the work that was to ensure his lasting world-wide fame, the Piano Concerto in A minor. They returned to Christiania in the autumn and, apart from a short cantata for the unveiling of the statue of W.F.K. Christie,[33] Grieg composed nothing more that year. He had little time to do so with his teaching and conducting commitments and although the period from the winter of 1868 to the summer of 1870 was a time of change in many ways for both him and for Nina, his compositions from this time, comprising only songs and some arrangements of folk music, show little originality.

In the autumn of 1868 Grieg again applied for a travelling scholarship and asked various friends for help by giving him references. Moscheles, Gade and Hartmann all obliged and, through his friend Ravnkilde in Rome, Grieg also obtained a glowing testimonial from Liszt. The Norwegian government granted his request six months later. Tragedy struck, however, when Alexandra died suddenly on 21 May 1869, shortly after the family had arrived to spend the summer with Grieg's parents at Landås. The distraught Grieg buried himself in his work, producing the twenty-five *Norske folkeviser og danser* (Norwegian folk-songs and Dances) for piano, op. 17. During the remainder of the summer he also completed another group of songs, which were published in two albums, containing numbers 1 to 4 and 5 to 9 respectively, in Copenhagen in December 1869 as op. 18. Dedicated to Nina, they were entitled, rather verbosely, *Romancer og Sange af danske og norske Digtere componerede for Mezzo-sopran eller Baryton* (Romances and Songs by Danish and Norwegian poets composed for Mezzo-soprano or Baritone).

The final song of the op. 18 collection, the *Serenade til Welhaven* (Serenade to Welhaven), and the fourth, *Efterårsstormen* (Autumn storm), were both written earlier than the rest. The *Serenade* was originally composed for baritone solo and male-voice quartet and was first published in Johan D. Behren's *Samling af flerstemmige Mandssange* (Collection of Part Songs for Male Voices), as no. 474 in the fifth series. As one of the op. 18 songs, it may be used as originally intended or with the quartet parts played as a piano accompaniment to a solo voice. The poem is by Bjørnson and the piece was written and set to music for a Norwegian students' parade in honour of the great poet Welhaven in 1868. Johan Sebastian Welhaven (1807–73) is one of the greatest figures in Norwegian literature and later poets have acknowledged their debt to him. Unlike his contemporary and great rival, Wergeland (and indeed Bjørnson himself), Welhaven considered that Norway's own traditions were not enough to build on without the cultural influence of Denmark. His own poetry shows him as vulnerable, melancholy and rather narrow-minded, but it is always elegant. Grieg did not complete a song to any of Welhaven's poetry, unlike his compatriots Kjerulf (who set twenty-two poems) and Agathe Backer Grøndahl, although sketches in his notebooks show that he began a setting of *Dyre Vaa*.

This is a humorous poem about Dyre from Vaa, the 'most gifted yeoman in the Vinje district', who had the strength of twelve men and who is incited, after a good deal of ale, to pit that strength against a troll. The very brief sketches show a main theme in a march rhythm, with accompaniment chords accenting the first and third beats of the bar. The humor is felt in the trills, low in the piano's register, and in the chromatic movement of vocal line and accompaniment at the words 'with trolls and mountain giants', but the tremolando in the accompaniment and the wide intervals in the vocal line are reminiscent of some of Grieg's weaker settings.

Bjørnson's praise of Welhaven in the *Serenade* is, appropriately, elegantly phrased, describing the older man as a 'brilliant singer' and one 'who in winter cradled the spring's words'. Even the structure of his verse, with the rhythms and the alliteration reminiscent of Old Norse literature, reflects Welhaven's own use of these elements. Grieg's music, in spite of consideration for the non-expert forces originally intended to perform the piece, still conveys the sincerity of the poem. The solo vocal line is immensely singable and its first rising phrase is reminiscent of Schumann's song *Flutenreicher*

*Ebro.* It is very lyrical and the more static, chordal male-quartet writing, the rhythm of which reminds one of early Verdi, works well as a piano accompaniment, using the optional extra notes written in for this purpose. The harmony holds no surprises, probably because of the intended student singers, although there is some chromatic movement in the inner parts, and the initial six-bar phrase is unusual for early Grieg.

Of the remaining songs published as op. 18, no fewer than six are to poems by Hans Andersen. The first, *Vandring i Skoven* (Walking in the woods), is a joyous love-song in a fresh-sounding style akin to the *Hjertets Melodier*. Folk-song elements are to be found in the decorations in the vocal line and in the extensive use of pedal notes, and almost the whole of the first section of the song, after the introduction, is built over a pedal tonic fifth. The rhythm of the accompaniment, ♩♩𝄽 ♩│♩♩𝄽 ♩, underlines the jaunty feeling of the song as well as the obvious walking movement. The vocal line is a good deal more flexible than in some of the early songs and the triplet decorations add to the cheerful atmosphere. The triplets are also used in the descending phrases of the introduction and these phrases are then played in ascending order to form the postlude, so that the song ends on a happy upward note.

As well as being a love-song, Andersen's poem is a delightful picture of the Danish countryside, with its beech-woods, nightingales and peace, all of which Grieg loved too. The first line of the first stanza, 'Min søde Brud, min unge Viv, min Kjærlighed, mit Liv (My sweet bride, my young wife, my love, my life)', is also the last line of the other two, although this feature and the internal rhyme of each half line have not proved easy to retain in translation and therefore most often ignored, thereby unfortunately losing the unity given by Andersen to the original.

According to Monrad Johansen, Andersen's *Hun er saa hvid* (She is so pale) was a rewriting of a Russian poem and although there is a very un-Danish melancholy about it, the symmetry of the opposing ideas in the two stanzas is yet typical of Scandinavian poetry and thought. The bareness and simplicity of expression in the words drew a very delicate setting from Grieg and while the melody is the same for both stanzas, the change of harmonisation adds a poignancy to the second that a strictly strophic setting would not have had. Although the time-signature is $\frac{6}{8}$, there is a waltz-like feeling to the rhythm, emphasised by the wistful semi-quaver figure which ends each stanza: Ex. 36.

There is also an expressive change of accent, in the music in the second stanza, from 'Nu *er* hun død (Now she *is* dead)' in the first line to '*Nu* er hun død (*Now . . .*)' in the third.

The third song of the group, also an Andersen setting, is *En Digters sidste Sang* (A poet's last song). It is a rather pious view of the poet's gift, not easily reconciled with Andersen's own bitterness at certain aspects of his life, although he may well have looked forwad to 'en evig Somer (an eternal

Ex.36                              Hun er saa hvid

summer)' for himself. Neither does the obedient acceptance of one's lot fit
with the ambitious side of Andersen, who wrote in his diary for 20
November 1825, '. . read Byron's biography, oh! he was just like me, right
down to his fondness for scandal, my soul is ambitious like his, happy only
when admired by everybody . . .'[34] Grieg set the poem in, for him, an
unusual, largely homophonic style in two identical strophes with unremarkable harmonies. There is an eloquent introduction/postlude, which does not
detract from the almost reverent atmosphere of the song. If Andersen's poem
has something slightly ironic about it ('I went the way God bade me, forward
with an uplifted brow'), Grieg appears to set it in all seriousness and the song
was written before he might have seen shades of his own life in the words and
reflected any irony in the music.

For the fifth song of the album, Grieg again chooses Andersen, whose
*Poesien* is an exuberant panegyric to the 'land called Poesy'. The vocal line is
much freer and more interesting than in many of the earlier songs, perhaps
owing to Nina's influence, and has a range of an octave and a half. It flows
over the rippling arpeggios of the accompaniment, the semi-quavers of
which are variously grouped into fives, sixes and sevens, with some demi-
semiquaver groups. The bass note of each group is frequently accented and
the harmonic structure is more adventurous here than earlier in the
collection. The postlude is most beautiful and owes something to Schumann,
although as John Horton has pointed out, 'Schumann would hardly have
marred the effectiveness of a carefully constructed stanza by repeating it
twice in identical form.'[35]

The sixth song, *Ungbirken* (The young birch), is one of only two in the
album to words by a Norwegian poet, here Jørgen Moe. It is also the only
one of Moe's poems that Grieg set as a solo song (he set two more for male-
voice choir) and the only Norwegian song he wrote during the summer of
1869 at Landås. *Ungbirken* is a portrayal of a birch tree growing on the bank
of a fjord, from whose acceptance of its fate the poet hopes to learn humility.
Indeed 'Humility' was the rather pious title given to the song in the English

version by Marzials and Morgan. The poem is set strophically, with some slight alterations in the accompaniment to the second stanza. In the third phrase of the first stanza the vocal melody is doubled in the inner part of the left hand, giving a particularly sonorous effect, an unusual practice for Grieg, but which he also uses in *Den blonde Pige (II)*. The opening bars provide most of the thematic material for the song, in a way similar to *Efteraarsstormen*, although on a smaller scale, and, typically, Grieg uses a number of keys besides the tonic B flat major. The song is pleasing in its directness.

The seventh and eighth songs are once again settings of Andersen. *Hytten* (The cottage) is another of the writer's happy love-songs, as well as a description of a natural scene. The idyllic sentiments of a couple needing only each other are epitomised in the Hatzfeld and Ashdown editions' English title, 'Love in a cottage'. Grieg matches the mood with a folksong-like melody, which makes use of arpeggios and decorations, and the accompaniment is built over the pedal tonic fifth for more than half of each of the two strophes. The rhythmic figures of the accompaniment are also reminiscent of Norwegian folk-dance and similar figures are found in some of Grieg's folk music arrangements for piano:

Ex.37                                                                      Hytten

(Where waves beat high against the coast)

The vocal melody is more graceful than that of *Ungbirken* and there is a tender lingering over the word 'Kjærlighed (love)' at the end of each stanza.

*Rosenknoppen* (The rose-bud) is another cheerful song, with an engaging light-heartedness, the principal sentiments of which are summed up in the final stanza (the fourth; the third is omitted only in the Ashdown edition):

> Danmarks Døttre ved min Grav
> Sige for hver Sang jeg gav:
> 'Han just havde Kys fortjent!'
> Herligt sagt, men lidt for sent;
> (Denmark's daughters by my grave/will say for every song I gave:/'He really deserved kisses!'/Grandly said, but a little too late;)

While the poem may be accepted at face value, it also hints at the sadder and more bitter side of Andersen's character: unlucky in love and late to find fame. The song is marked 'leggero' and the impudent quality is emphasised from the very beginning in the semiquaver B natural to C in the introduction, a figure continued in the accompaniment of the first eight bars. The tonality of A flat major is further challenged in the fourth bar by the G flat in the vocal line and the A natural in the piano. Far more subtle, however, is what John Horton calls the 'magical glide'[36] in the middle of each strophe from the tonic to the key of the flattened submediant, a modulation often used to great effect by Schubert and one that was to become more important to Grieg.

None of the op. 18 songs is a masterpiece, but there is a new freedom of writing evident in them, at least in the vocal melodies, even while the harmonic structure for the most part remains conventional. Grieg, however, was soon to move forward from the purely attractive and easily accessible song to a more mature style of vocal writing, building on the ideal of a faithful interpretation of the poet's intention above mere beauty of musical setting, as he had begun to do in *Soldaten*.

## Notes

1   Finn Benestad and Dag Schjelderup-Ebbe: *Edvard Grieg, mennesket og kunstneren*, 1980, p.66.
2   Gerhard Schjelderup, quoted ibid., p.66.
3   From the *Spanisches Liederbuch*, composed during the winter of 1889–90.
4   Dag Schjelderup-Ebbe: *Edvard Grieg: 1858–1867*, 1964, p.206.
5   David Monrad Johansen: *Edvard Grieg*, 1934, p.66.
6   Benestad and Schjelderup-Ebbe: *Edvard Grieg, mennesket og kunstneren*, p.66.
7   Astra Desmond in *Grieg. A Symposium*, ed. Gerald Abraham, 1948, p.75.
8   Schjelderup-Ebbe: *Edvard Grieg: 1858–1867*, p.208.
9   Benjamin Feddersen: 'Fra Griegs Ungdom' in *Illustreret Tidende*, no.13, Copenhagen, 24 December 1899, pp.212–13.
10   Elias Bredsdorff: *Hans Christian Andersen*, 1975, particularly Chapter 13.
11   Grieg to Georg Brandes, 2 April 1905.
12   Grieg to Bjørnson, 1 October 1874 from Copenhagen.
13   John Horton: *Grieg*, 1974, p.174.
14   The programme of this concert is preserved in Bergen Public Library.
15   Gaukstad, footnote to the Norwegian edition of Horton: *Grieg*, 1978, p.163.
16   Schjelderup-Ebbe: *Edvard Grieg: 1858–1867*, p.211.
17   Benestad and Schjelderup-Ebbe: *Edvard Grieg, mennesket og kunstneren*, p.90.
18   Ibid, p.91.
19   Schjelderup-Ebbe: *Edvard Grieg: 1858–1867* p.300.
20   Grieg to Beyer, 24 January 1896 from Leipzig.
21   Wife of Edouard Colonne (1838–1910), a well-known conductor in Paris and capellmeister to the Paris Opéra.
22   Grieg to Beyer, 26 December 1889 from Paris.

23    Monrad Johansen: *Edvard Grieg*, p.91.
24    Ibid, p.91.
25    Feddersen to Grieg, 10 August 1866.
26    Ibsen to Grieg, 24 August 1866 from Frascati.
27    Recounted by Michael Meyer: *Ibsen*, 1974, p.274–75.
28    Ibid, p.559.
29    Nils Grinde in a letter to the author.
30    Monrad Johansen: *Edvard Grieg*, p.67.
31    Benestad and Schjelderup-Ebbe: *Edvard Grieg, mennesket og kunstneren*, p.64.
32    In the Musikhistorisk Museum, Copenhagen.
33    W.F.K. Christie was one of the signatories to the Norwegian Constitution in 1814; his statue in Bergen was unveiled on 17 May (Norway's national day) 1868. He was also a cousin of Grieg's and Nina's grandfather, Edvard Hagerup.
34    Quoted in Bredsdorff: *Hans Christian Andersen*, p.57.
35    Horton: *Grieg*, p.171.
36    Ibid, p.170.

# 5 'A balanced mind, a spiritual vitality...'

After the mostly happy, lyrical years, Grieg's world had been shattered by the sudden death of his daughter from 'inflammation of the brain'[1] and it was undoubtedly this tragic event that inspired the song *Millom rosor* (Among roses), which although written in 1869, was not published until 1884, when it was included in the op.39 group, the *Romancer Ældre og Nyere* (Songs Old and New). The poem, by Kristofer Janson, was written soon after the death of *his* only child. This and *Vesle gut* were the only settings Grieg made of Janson's verse, although a letter from the poet, dated 12 November 1900, states that he is sending Grieg a poem 'which came to me here one night' and which he intended as a text for a religious piece. The poem is not mentioned by title, however, and the copy of it is no longer with the letter, which itself is preserved in Bergen Library.

There is a restraint about both the words and the music of *Millom rosor* that makes the song all the more moving. The poem uses the literary convention of contrast in its two stanzas. The first is a happy picture of a young mother sitting in the garden, playing with her child, and she asks that she may always see him resting 'among roses'; in the second stanza, that wish is tragically granted. Grieg sets the song strophically and in a minor key, so that the sorrow is felt right from the beginning. The setting is typical of the composer's maturing style, where there is often something fateful and inevitable created by stark simplicity. The melody makes much use of sequence and the ends of the first two phrases are echoed by the piano an octave higher than the voice, to ethereal effect, after the previous sonorous accompaniment chords. In fact, the lower register of the piano is used each time the words 'millom rosor' occur. The harmony is unremarkable, as if the composer did not want anything to detract from the tragic simplicity of the setting, but there is a telling use of the subdominant minor key in the second half of the strophe.

Another fateful song which exists in sketches in Bergen may also date from around this time. This is the beginning of a setting of Ibsen's *Bergmanden* (The miner), a poem first written in 1850 and later twice revised; Grieg's sketches show the text of the later revision and must have been written after

1863, in Nils Grinde's opinion 'probably around 1870'.[2] The poem is typical of Ibsen: a simple image providing an allegory for the poet's deeper thoughts, here his doubts about the direction of his life. 'Have I erred?' he asks and concludes, 'Into the depths I must go', sentiments which may well have found an echo with the composer at this time. The setting is for bass voice and the piano's octaves and tremolandos in the Maestoso introduction together with the angular opening vocal phrase set the dramatic atmosphere, which is continued in the succeeding Allegro section. Here the vocal tessitura is very low, the chromatic melody slowly rising, doubled in both hands of the accompaniment and with the right hand triplets underlining the agitation of the words. With this imposing beginning and the strength of Ibsen's text, it is a pity that Grieg did not complete the song.

Two important things happened to Grieg before his next group of songs was published, the Bjørnson settings from *Fiskerjenten* (The Fisher-girl), op. 21. During the summer of 1869 at Landås he came across Lundeman's collection of *Fjeldmelodier*, and began for the first time to realize the wealth and range of Norway's folk music. He also admired Lindeman's arrangements, in which the accompaniments were not allowed to obscure the original melodies. Grieg derived harmonic inspiration from folk music, as he explained to Finck in 1900: 'I have found that the dark depth in our folk music has its basis in its unsuspected harmonic possibilities . . . I have been particularly attracted by the chromatic progressions in the harmonic texture.' He goes on to speak of 'an especial feature in our folk music I have always had sympathy for: the treatment of the leading-note and in particular, when the leading-note falls to the fifth.'[3] This feature, preceded by the tonic, was what became known as the 'Grieg motif' and is as much a part of his melodies as rising thirds and falling sevenths are of Elgar's. From the time of his 'discovery' of Lindeman's collections, Grieg's interest in the classical forms of music waned and, although he still dreamed of large-scale works in the form of dramatic stage presentations and works for chorus and orchestra, it was in the smaller forms, especially songs and piano pieces, that he was now to make his mark.

The second important occurrence was that he eventually received a second state grant and was able to spend another four months in Italy, from the end of November 1869 to April 1870. Although no actual compositions date from this time, the journey was of great significance to him. As he wrote in his formal report to the government, 'On the journey itself and during my stay in Italy the impressions were so numerous and overwhelming, that the one, so to speak, destroyed the other . . . I have certainly noted down a series of sketches and written various lyrical trifles, but have not had the peace to sink myself in the larger forms. But I have material in abundance in my memory and this must be presumed to be the main thing.' Grieg also felt very strongly that such travel was essential to broaden the outlook of a

Scandinavian artist and he goes on in the report to say that the most positive outcome is that

> the life here has filled me with an unending series of impressions . . . In Rome I found what I needed . . . peace to immerse myself in myself and in the greatness around me, a daily influence of a world of beauty. And it is of the greatest significance to a Scandinavian musician who had his elementary education in Germany, through a later stay in Italy to have his ideas clarified and purified of that one-sided-ness which only immerses itself in the German. A Scandinavian has in his national character so much that is heavy and reflective, which in truth is not counterbalanced by the *exclusive* study of German art. In order to serve the national cause, one needs a balanced mind, a spiritual vitality, which is acquired only when one has one's eyes opened to what can be learnt there in the south.[4]

During this visit to Italy, Grieg at last met Liszt, meetings which were a high-point of his journey. The pieces that he took to show the internationally acclaimed composer were played by Liszt with great enthusiasm, not least, as Grieg was to note later, the pieces that showed distinctive nationalist traits.

It was anything but nationalist traits, however, that characterized one of his songs from 1870, *Odalisken synger* (The odalisque sings), a setting of a poem by the Danish historical writer Carl Bruun. Bruun (1846–99) was also staying in Rome in 1869; from then until 1871, he was secretary to the Danish consul there. He later worked for the newspaper *Berlingske Tidende* in Copenhagen, but is particularly remembered for his massive illustrated history of that city.

His poem gives an idealized picture of the sultan's palace near the Bosphorus, with the roses, the sun sinking behind the mountains, the dancing-girls and the moon and stars shimmering, and the odalisque who is longing to be the one to enjoy Suliman's favours. Although not one of Grieg's great songs, *Odalisken synger* is notable for conjuring up in music a view, albeit a romantic view, of the exotic before such things became fashionable. The elusive quality of the poem, where nothing is stated but only hinted at, is matched by a similar 'veiled' feeling in Grieg's music, not least in the shifting tonalities.

Bruun apparently liked Grieg's setting: a long letter to him, written in a very flowery style and beautiful copperplate, is preserved in Bergen Public Library, in which he says, 'I am pleased that the young Norwegian ladies blush over "Soliman". If I dared to believe it was my accomplishment, I would be proud, but there is twenty thousand times more passion in your music than in my words.'

The opening rhythmic figure in the accompaniment is found throughout much of the first half of the song and suggests both the lapping of the waves and the swaying of the dancers: Ex.38.

Ex.38            Odalisken synger

Grieg also uses his predilection for chromaticism to underline the oriental flavour, although even here the chromatic movement gives rise to some dissonance, for example, the C sharp and B sharp in the same chord in the seventh bar. After a high tessitura for the opening and early accompaniment, giving an ethereal effect, depth and warmth are added in the fifth bar with a low bass line. A further 'oriental' touch is to be found in the use of the harmonic minor scale in the vocal melody and an occasional diminished interval. Otherwise, the harmonic structure is simple and the accompaniment largely homophonic, with the right hand doubling the voice and echoing the ends of the vocal phrases for the first half of each strophe. When the accompaniment figuration changes to semiquaver arpeggios in the middle, the right hand echoes overlap the vocal phrases at half a bar's distance.

*Odalisken synger* was first published in *Nordiske Musikblade* (Scandinavian Music Paper) in July 1872 and although Grieg edited the periodical together with the Dane Horneman and the Swede August Söderman, this was the only song of his to appear in it. Hansen's published the song separately in 1876 and later included it in the third volume of the collected *Romanser og Sanger*.

It was Italy, rather than anywhere further east, that inspired another song from Grieg in 1870. Bjørnson's poem *Fra Monte Pincio* (From Monte Pincio) was in its turn inspired by the writer's visit to Rome at the time of the city's liberation from the French and the unification of Italy. Grieg's music was written in the same year as the first two of the Bjørnson settings, op.21, and owes its existence to the composer's first visit to Italy, rather than the later one. However, the song was not published until it was included in the op.39 group of 1884. Grieg uses only the first and last of Bjørnson's four stanzas in his setting and transposes the last two lines of Bjørnson's second stanza to the end of the first in place of the original lines.

The poem ostensibly describes Monte Pincio, a favourite haunt of the citizens of Rome, where there is music and dancing every evening. Always enthusiastic for a cause, however, Bjørnson also sees in the happy gatherings the joy of forthcoming freedom for Italy and her people, especially in the last stanza:

Himmelen våger og venter opunder
Fortid som blunder
og Fremtid som stunder, . . .
(The sky stirs and waits under/the past which dozes/and the future which draws near . . .)

Throughout the poem there are musical references: horn music, a saltarello, a mandoline, singing and the playing of zither and flute. Each stanza falls into two sections, the first comprising eight long lines, the second four short and two long, and Grieg's music is also in two main sections in each strophe.

The opening bars are remarkable in anticipating the famous opening chords of the slow movement of Dvořák's ninth symphony, 'From the New World', written some twenty-three years later:

Ex.39                                                          Fra Monte Pincio

The first vocal melody is very broad and ranges over an octave and a half in its first three bars. It is full of the warmth of Italy, beloved by so many Scandinavians, and a feeling of freedom, although all is kept in check by the use of the pedal tonic fifth in the first six bars. The poem is also full of Bjørnson's favourite open vowels, which lend their own feeling of spaciousness. The echoing of the end of the vocal phrase by the accompaniment, so often found in Grieg's songs, here occurs in the left hand and the lower register of the piano.

The climax of the first section is built up over a pedal B flat, which leads to an interesting chord sequence, especially the clash on 'borte (away)' in bar 15, with the B flat of the vocal line sounded against an A natural in the accompaniment right hand. There are chromatic changes in every chord and one of Grieg's rare chromatic melodies (over transitions through A flat and D flat major) before the return to the tonic G flat major. The G flat is then altered enharmonically to F sharp, the mediant of the new key, D major.

This section, in $\frac{3}{4}$ and marked 'Vivo', is in a dancing rhythm, which seeks musically to match Bjørnson's change of rhythm and more earth-bound content: here it is the people who are being described, not the scenery or ideals, and the lines are short and brisk instead of long and soaring, both in the poem and the music. The mood of the Vivo section is broken by the intrusion of a B sharp into the melody, chromatically altering the submediant seventh chord (bars 29 and 30). This is made to lead back to the original G flat major, with the B sharp altered enharmonically to C natural and all the other notes of the chord slide up a semitone to form a chromatic supertonic seventh, which in turn resolves to the second inversion of the tonic triad at bar 32. All these convolutions are handled now with great subtlety.

The final Presto section is really a long postlude to the strophe as the music dies away into the night. (In the Scandinavian edition the song is subtitled 'Nocturne'). This is very effectively managed, but the return to the opening chord sequence for the second strophe comes as something of a surprise, and one cannot help feeling that a through-composed rather than a strophic setting here might have been preferable. However, the splendid matching of words to music has ensured this impressionistic song a popular place in the repertory of Scandinavian concert singers. Grieg also orchestrated *Fra Monte Pincio* in November 1894 in Copenhagen.

Settings of Bjørnson's verse were to play a large part in Grieg's output during the next few years and the major feature of his last years in Christiania was his collaboration with the two greatest figures of contemporary Norwegian literature, Bjørnson and Ibsen. The music Grieg wrote between 1870 and 1875 was also marked by his interest in the stage and drama, culminating in the incidental music to Ibsen's *Peer Gynt*.

It is strange nowadays, when Bjørnson is hardly read outside Scandinavia, to realize that in the 1860s and 1870s his role in contemporary life was such as to put Ibsen quite in the shade, and it was he who, in 1903, received the Nobel Prize. Bjørnson was often the more adventurous of the two writers and the one who first tried out new ideas. Even if he had not been a writer, he would still have been one of Norway's heroes, because of his unending support for the nationalist cause and his powers as an orator.

Bjørnstjerne Bjørnson was born on 8 December 1832 at Kvikne, in the North Hedmark district some sixty miles south of Trondhjem, where his father was a parson. By the mid-1850s he was attacking the late romantics, including Welhaven, and predicting a revolution in literature. He declared himself a follower of Wergeland, who stood for Norwegian nationalism, and throughout his life was to combine writing with politics. His early work was in the area of peasant tales, such as *Synnøve Solbakken*, and saga-dramas. He considered that rural life in the nineteenth century was not so far removed from that of the people in saga times and that, therefore, 'our people's life should be built up on our history and now the peasantry should be the foundation'. *De nygifte* (The Newly-Weds), written in 1865, was the first middle-class 'problem drama' in Scandinavian literature, a genre that most non-Scandinavians more readily associate with Ibsen, although the real introduction to realistic contemporary drama came in 1875 with *En fallit* (A Bankrupt) and *Redaktøren* (The Editor). Throughout his life Bjørnson remained a religious man, albeit in an unconventional way, but was very disappointed that the Christian establishment was not going to lead the way to political and spiritual freedom as he thought it should. These ideas came to full fruition in his most powerful play, the first part of *Over ævne* (Beyond human power), written in 1883, in which the priest, Sang, turns all his aspirations to the religious and awaits divine confirmation of the Christianity he preaches in a miracle. The miracle however, according to Bjørnson, is like the claim of Christianity on mankind: beyond human power.

Grieg first met Bjørnson during what he called his 'empty years' in Christiania, 1868 to 1872, and they became good friends. They wanted to find something on which they could work together, and from 1870 they discussed such a project, although nothing was achieved until the spring of 1871 when Grieg set a scene from Bjørnson's poem-cycle *Arnljot Gelline*. This work contains many of his best poems, among them the one Grieg chose, *Foran Sydens kloster* (Before a Southern Convent), and the whole work shows Bjørnson's commanding grasp of his art, with simple but strong imagery, rhythmic variation, and a richness and power of expression. Grieg set *Foran Sydens kloster* for soprano and contralto soloists, as, respectively, the young woman seeking admission and the nun at the convent gate, a female choir as the chorus of nuns, and orchestra, and he finished the work the same summer. It was published as op. 20 in a piano edition in December 1871 and was dedicated to Liszt. Bjørnson was delighted with the music and began work on the next projected collaboration, *Bergljot*, a melodrama, which was completed in sketches during the same summer as *Foran Sydens kloster*. Grieg envisaged it for full orchestra with declamation, but it was impossible to get such a work published in the climate of the time – incredibly, he was even having trouble in publishing the Piano Concerto, until Svendsen intervened – and so the piece lay dormant until 1885, when it was finally completed.

In September 1870 the Griegs went back to Christiania and the composer picked up the reins of the teaching and conducting that took so much of his time and energy. He was worried by his lack of productivity and wrote to Ravnkilde: 'I have done nothing; either I am an unmusical beast, or else all my creative talent is going into conducting concerts.' At one of these concerts, in April 1871, Grieg conducted the first performance in Christiania of his Piano Concerto, with Erika Lie as soloist, and it was very well received by the press. The summer of the year, however, saw him once more in Bergen, and here he found new zest for composition. The most important work from that time was the *Folkslivsbilder* (Scenes of country life), op. 19, three substantial pieces for piano, which became favourites for Grieg himself to include in his recitals. Back in Christiania once again, in December 1871 he formed the Musikforening (Music Society), the forerunner of the present day Oslo Philharmonic, with an orchestra of sixty players, largely from the theatre orchestra with the addition of some good amateurs, and a mixed choir of some hundred and fifty voices. Among the choir members was one of Grieg's piano pupils, Frants Beyer, with whom the composer was to have a very long and close friendship.

In the summer of 1872 the Griegs again escaped from the capital, this time to Denmark, but the holiday did not inspire Grieg to any great heights and in September they had to return to Christiania, to the eternal round of concerts and teaching. The Musikforening's concert on 30 November included a performance of *Foran Sydens kloster* with Nina as one of the soloists.

During the whole of the period from 1870 to 1874 Grieg was working closely with Bjørnson and had their proposed music-drama as a main interest. In 1872 the now well-known incidental music to Bjørnson's play *Sigurd Jorsalfar* was performed for the first time, although it was not published until 1874. A month later, on 17 May, the first performance of *Landkjenning* (Sighting of land) was given. This work, for baritone solo, two male-voice choirs, wind orchestra and organ, was written to raise money for the restoration of the Nidaros Cathedral in Trondhjem. It saw a number of revisions, including the replacement of the wind band by full symphony orchestra, before its eventual publication in 1881. The text is from the play *Olav Trygvason*, which for a number of years was planned as an opera by Bjørnson and Grieg. However, before making a start on that, Grieg went back to his friend's shorter verse.

Bjørnson's poetry is extremely musical and it is significant that his collection of *Digte og Sange* (Poems and songs), first published in 1870, was originally to be called just *Sange*. Some of the verses were from the prose works, as in the case of two of the three poems Grieg was to set in 1870 on his return from Italy: *Det første møte* (The first meeting) and *God morgen* (Good morning), which both come from the novel *Fiskerjenten* (The Fisher-girl). These poems, together with the love-poetry, nature lyrics and similar verses, form the largest part of Bjørnson's output. He also wrote a number of poems in praise of his homeland, notably *Fedrelandssang* (Song to the Fatherland) and *Ja, vi elsker dette landet* (Yes, we love this land), now the Norwegian national anthem. Other poems are occasional or political verse.

The originally conceived title, *Sange*, stresses the inherent musicality of Bjørnson's poetry; much of it was intended to be sung, unlike Ibsen's *Digte*, which were primarily for reading, and Bjørnson occasionally hints to the composer the sort of music he had in mind, by repeating lines or echoing phrases. Francis Bull, the editor of an edition of *Digte og Sange*,[5] has pointed out how many of the poems refer to singing; for example, *En sangers kall profetens er* (A singer's calling is as the prophet's) and the verse beginning 'Syng når du alene går, Syng når fler skal sammen bindes (Sing when you walk alone, sing when many are gathered together)'. Music was certainly important to Bjørnson; a number of the characters in his stories are musicians and he counted Ole Bull and Nordraak as well as Grieg among his friends. He liked to listen to music and his sense of rhythm was especially well developed. Also his use of words to express sounds is to be found everywhere in his writing and he employed euphonic vowels, especially the long Norwegian 'a', which is frequently found in the names of main characters in his plays and novels. He also used that sound for brightness and hope – '*Ja, vi elsker*' – and the tighter sounds, 'ø', 'e' and 'å', to express softness, darkness or loneliness.

Two of the songs out of the four from the novel *Fiskerjenten*, which Grieg set as op.21, were written in 1870, and in 1872 he added the second two. The novel, written in 1868, is a happy and in parts very amusing story about an imaginative girl, Petra, who, after various trials and tribulations, becomes an actress, and the book is a transition between Bjørnson's earlier peasant tales and the more realistic stories and plays of the 1870s and 1880s.

The first of the *Fiskerjenten* songs, *Det første møte* (The first meeting), written in the summer of 1870 at Landås, is also one of Grieg's very finest songs, where understatement reigns supreme. The song is the earliest in the novel of the four he set, occurring at the end of the fourth chapter. Petra and Hans Ødegård, the pastor's son, have just realized their love for each other: 'Then they felt, then they said, as they sat amongst the trees, with fjord and mountain in the evening sun before them, while a horn sounded in the distance and singing, that this was joy. The sweetness of first meeting...' The poem has eight short lines and an abundance of onomatopoeic sounds, especially the unvoiced 's', and euphonious vowel alliteration in the best tradition of Old Norse verse. Like most of Bjørnson's youthful verse, there are very few adjectives, in fact only three here in the whole poem.

Grieg's setting has something of the simplicity of folk music, but is by far the most sophisticated song he had yet written. Here the tonic pedal is concealed inside a melody in the right hand of the accompaniment, which shadows the first vocal phrase one third lower, while the bass has a long-held tonic chord. The decorations in the vocal line have a flavour of Norwegian folk music, but also add to the 'langsomt og drømmende (slow and dreamy)' quality Grieg required for the music. The vocal range here is a wide one for Grieg, from middle C to high A flat, and the melodic writing is most beautiful.

Harmonically, the song is quite straightforward, basically using the tonic, subdominant, dominant and submediant chords, but with subtle chromatic movement, which is used to telling effect by building up the tension towards the glorious culmination, and chromatically altered chords used to give a particular colour, for example, the F flat instead of F natural on the word 'sidste (last)' in bar 10. There is a lovely key-change from the tonic D flat major to B flat major in the twelfth and thirteenth bars, a passage which is then repeated in B flat *minor*, exactly capturing the haunting quality of the horn-call echoing amongst the crags which Bjørnson describes. The accompaniment also adds to the echo effect by taking part of the melody up an octave in both hands.

When the opening vocal melody returns at the beginning of the last section, it is heard over a dominant rather than a tonic pedal and the increased chromatic movement seems to hint at something to come. Unusually, but here to magical effect, Grieg repeats Bjørnson's last phrase, 'i et under (in wonder)', three times, each repetition set to a soaring melody that rises first a fifth, then a seventh and finally an octave to the crowning high A flat before sinking to end on the lower tonic, creating a wonderfully ecstatic culmination. As in his early songs, the melody here grows out from the harmonic structure, but now with a new independence and freedom. The postlude has mordent-like decorations and quietly disappears heavenward to end this sublime song in awesome silence.

Bjørnson's concise poem is almost impossible to translate if one wishes to retain the onomatopoeia of the original. Corder's rendition of the first line, 'The thrill of love's first eye-glance', has already been cited as one of the most inelegant in all the translations of Grieg's songs. R.H. Elkin's version, 'The joy of love's first meeting', was much more mellow and accurate. Schmidt, whose translation for Peters is loose in the extreme, also completely changes the end of the song by rendering the last line, 'forenes i et under (united in wonder)' as 'mit sehnsuchtvollem Drange (with wistful longing)'. Incredibly, Grieg himself, in his own orchestrated arrangement of the song, has a repeat from the second bar of the postlude back to bar 2, which even more than in *Jeg elsker dig* ruins the tension and the beautiful 'pianissimo' ending.

This particular poem of Bjørnson's is built up on sound pictures and was obviously intended for musical setting. At the time of its creation, it was considered by the Norwegian public to be something completely new and incomprehensible, and there exists a parodied version from the late 1860s under the title *Sæterjenten* (The seter girl), which condenses the original to just three lines:

> Det første møtes sødme
> i solens sidste rødme,
> det er som horn i uren.

(The sweetness of first meeting/in the sun's last redness,/is like a horn in the crags).

*God morgen* (Good morning), the second of Grieg's songs from *Fiskerjenten*, was also written in the summer of 1870, but is as different from the first as could be imagined. This is a cheerful song, as uncomplicated as *Det første møte* is sophisticated, perhaps because in the book it is played and sung by Petra herself. Overtones of folk-song are here, too, in the jaunty rhythm, the simple through-composed construction with a good deal of repetition and above all in the use of vocal decorations, with trills and mordents reminiscent of *lokk* all used here more than ever before in Grieg's songs to date.

Bjørnson's seven-line verse falls into two sections, one of four lines and one of three, and the last three lines are repeated in the setting to make a longer song. Harmonically it is much simpler than *Det første møte*, with almost no chromatic movement. There is, however, an interesting use of the supertonic seventh chord in arpeggio in the vocal melody at bar 15 and this exuberant song exactly reflects the lively atmosphere of the novel.

The third and fourth songs of the op.21 group were completed in 1872, when Grieg was very much involved in setting Bjørnson's works. The third song, *Jeg giver mit digt til våren* (I will give my song to the spring), has a lovely freshness about it and is the best song in the group after *Det første møte*. The poem occurs late in the novel, at the end of the tenth chapter, and in a somewhat incongruous setting: Ødegård is at the window watching some visitors make their way home over the mountain, trudging through the deep snow with no signposts but the trees. 'But inside from the living-room came a few introductory trills and then: "I will give my song to the spring . . ."'

The poem's twelve lines are set as a single strophe, the only repetition of words being Bjørnson's own reiteration of the first line as the last. Once again there is some beautiful vocal writing, with soaring phrases and a wide range (middle C sharp to high G) and Grieg is considerate enough to the singer to increase the dynamic markings as he moves the phrases ever higher towards the climax. The only decorations here are to be found in the piano introduction and postlude. The urgency of the longing for spring to come is felt in the chromatic movement right from the opening and in the syncopation in the accompaniment.

Harmonically the interest is in the modulations, from the tonic B major, through G sharp minor to the distant key of E flat major. Grieg again uses a repetition of a musical phrase first in the major key, then in the minor, as in *Det første møte*, to underline a contrast in the words, 'At lokke på sol med liste, så vinteren nød må friste (To lure the sun with cunning, so that winter must be tempted)'. The dominant B flat is then altered enharmonically to become the leading-note of the original tonic key and the music reverts to B major for the final section. The song builds to its climax with threats of what a combination of poetry and springtime will do to drive winter away, and a lovely release of tension comes at bar 28, which underlines the words 'med idelig blomsterduften (with the incessant scent of flowers)', before the final rising phrase. John Horton has seen in the 'gliding chromatic harmonies beneath fresh, diatonic melody'[6] anticipations of Grieg's great Vinje setting, *Våren* (The spring) written ten years later. Once again the German version of the song by Hans Schmidt is very generalized and he took the liberty of adding a second stanza, dedicated to love instead of springtime.

The final song of the four, *Tak for dit råd* (Thanks for your advice), is the most dramatic song Grieg had written since *Soldaten*, not least from the singer's point of view. The end especially demands vocal power to sustain the long phrases and the fortissimo. The poem has undertones of Viking journeys of exploration in the poet's determination to launch his craft. In the novel the song is sung by Petra immediately after she has sung *God morgen*: 'Then the piano was driven into a storm, and out of it broke forth the following song: "Thanks for your advice . . ."'.

The song is through-composed, although it makes use of similar rhythmic motifs throughout, and there is no relief from the '*meget hurtig og livfullt* (very fast and animated)' marking. The impetuosity which suggests the turbulent sea is established right from the beginning in the dotted rhythm and is maintained in the vocal line until the note of doubt creeps in – 'Om end rejsen skal blive den sidste jeg gjør (Even if this journey should be the last I make)' – when the melody becomes smoother. The syncopation in the accompaniment, however, keeps up the tension. The dotted rhythm of the opening is resumed for the second stanza, with the poet's renewed determination to set sail and Astra Desmond, who described *Tak for dit råd* as 'one of the finest songs Grieg ever wrote',[7] drew attention to unsatisfactory translations which require a one-note anacrusis and thus dissipate the strength of the rhythm. Harmonically there are some interesting modulations, particularly at bar 37 where the tonic F sharp minor dissolves into C minor, and the inner part of the right hand accompaniment frequently moves chromatically. However, the triumphant end, firmly in the major key, points to the hope of a successful voyage.

The four songs from *Fiskerjenten* op.21, were first published by Horneman in Copenhagen in 1873 and were dedicated to Grieg's friend August Winding, the Danish composer, and his wife Clara. *Det første møte* was also later arranged by the composer for piano solo with underlaid text, and by the Norwegian composer Eyvind Alnæs for violin and piano, both arrangements published by Wilhelm Hansen. The songs were not published in a separate edition by Peters,[8] but they were printed in Germany in an unauthorized version, which annoyed their composer intensely. He wrote to Bjørnson in 1875, 'To my great anger (I am suffering financial loss through it) in recent days a contemptible reprint of my songs from Fiskerjenten has come out in Berlin. The poems are even translated into German. I can do nothing, for the original edition came out in Copenhagen, from where they have had permission to reprint all the music that has been published there – but if only you as the poet *could* take steps, you would do me and my German publishers an eternal service by doing so.'[9] The songs are a splendid result early in the long collaboration between Grieg and Bjørnson. They come, in the words of Monrad Johansen, 'like a glowing streak of spring, like an inkling, like a portent of coming riches',[10] and show the composer's reaction to the first great Norwegian writer whose works he was to set. Some years later Grieg wrote to Bjørnson thanking him for 'what all your hideous poetry has been to me' and ended the letter with a much-quoted line from a poem in *Synnøve Solbakken*, famous in Norway in a wonderful setting by Kjerulf, 'Nu tak for alt ifra vi var små (Now thanks for everything since we were small)'. [11]

Several other songs to Bjørnson's verse also date from the early 1870s. One is *Dulgt kjærlighed* (Hidden love), which, like *Fra Monte Pincio*, was eventually published amongst the op.39 album in 1884. This sad little poem, written in stanzas of three couplets each, inspired one of Grieg's most beautiful songs. The theme of the verse is similar to the same poet's *O vidste du bare* (Oh, if only you knew), set with such effective simplicity by Kjerulf. The opening bars of *dulgt kjærlighed* are reminiscent of *Solveigs Sang*, although the former was written a year earlier, in 1873. Here are all the elements taken from Norwegian folk music: tonic fifth pedals, short phrases with vocal decorations, echoes in the accompaniment and contrasts between the major and minor modes. The last feature is especially effective in the ascending phrases at the end of each strophe to the same words: 'Men det var der ingen som vidste (But there was no-one there who knew)'. The gentle lilt of these bars makes it a pity that the German edition should alter the phrase so drastically and, in the present author's opinion, unnecessarily:

Ex.40                                                    Dulgt Kjærlighed

men,   det   var der in - gen som vid - ste.

doch das hat nie - mand er - fah - ren.

The simplicity of the first stanza is retained in the melody of the second, but the piano accompaniment is developed after the first couplet to underline the girl's grief at the prospect of losing her beloved, even though neither of them has admitted any attachment to the other. The harmonic device is straightforward: broken chords descending in the left hand, ascending in the right, but Grieg also uses syncopation to increase the tension. There are also some telling dissonances between the vocal melody and the accompaniment in the closing bars of this part of the stanza, an F sharp against an E sharp, for example, to stress the repetition of 'miste (lost)'. This time in the last line the rhythm is broken by rests in the vocal line, expressing the sobs of the girl. Unfortunately, the German edition again changes the note-values so that the effect is quite lost.

The third stanza is, musically, a reiteration of the first for the first two lines. Then, at 'Hun havde det godt, hun Fred havde fåt, hun tænkte på ham i det Sidste (She was well, she had found peace, she had been thinking about him with her last breath)', Grieg marks the music 'tranquillo' and we feel that the girl has indeed found peace. The melody ceases to be as angular as before and the harmonic impression is of D major rather than B minor. The minor key, however, reappears for the final phrase and we are left with the sadness that their unhappy misunderstanding remained forever unresolved. It is remarkable that Monrad Johansen could have written that 'Bjørnson's poem does not seem to have appeared especially inspiring to Grieg' and that he found the reiterated phrases 'weakening to the result', for both poem and music have about them a most effective understatement, which is typical of Norwegian restraint.

Both Grieg and Kjerulf, whose setting Grieg considered amongst that composer's most beautiful, keep the artlessness of the mediaeval picture created in Bjørnson's *Prinsessen* (The princess). The princess, in her room in the castle, hears a horn from below and cannot understand the feelings that the sound engenders in her. Grieg's setting begins with a folksong-like melody played in octaves by the piano as an introduction, a theme which is also used between the three strophes and as a postlude. This melody is taken up by the voice and is echoed and expanded in the accompaniment, imitating a horn-call, built on the E major arpeggio, but over an arpeggio in the left hand which is largely A major. The decorations are again typically Norwegian. In the middle of the second stanza in this almost totally strophic setting, Grieg imitates the horn-call in a different way – unexpectedly, as this is the stanza where the princess questions its silence. Harmonically the song makes good use of chromatic movement to underline the girl's longings.

Kjerulf's setting is absolutely strophic, with no introduction and no interludes, and, like Grieg, he keeps the folksong-like simplicity. This setting was made between 1861 and 1865, the first of his *Fem Sange af Bjørnstjerne Bjørnson* (Five Songs by . . .), published by Hirsch in Stockholm in 1865 under the title *Aftenstemning* (Evening Mood). It was an English composer, however, who made the most imaginative setting of *Prinsessen*. Delius's song entitled *Twilight Fancies* was written in 1892 as the third of his *Seven Songs from the Norwegian* dedicated to Nina Grieg. The horn-call is evoked from the very beginning with the haunting juxtaposition of the tonic and dominant fifths, played alternately in the accompaniment, but blended by use of the sustaining pedal, before their magical dissolution to the supertonic chord with a flattened fifth: Ex.41.

Melodically, Delius's setting retains the simplicity of both its predecessors, but here the princess's longings really do soar in the much freer vocal line.

Ex.41                                                    Delius, Twilight Fancies

Delius's voluptuous sounds worried Nina Grieg. She wrote to him about the *Seven Songs*: 'I am very fond of them, the last one [a setting of Ibsen's *En fuglevise* – A Bird Song] especially appeals to me. Only it's a pity to me that they are so *highly* erotic and it just doesn't work, to transpose love ...'[12] As Grieg set all but one of the poems included in the seven, it must be Delius's music to which Nina refers.[13] It is uncertain whether Delius made his setting of *Prinsessen* to the original words or, as he did elsewhere, to a German translation. The English version by F.S. Copeland, which now appears in the edition published by Oxford University Press, is far superior to that by Ethel Smyth which was printed in an old Peters' edition of the Grieg setting, with its 'My heart, why so heavy, Ah, well well-aday.' Most unfortunately it is this translation that is retained in the edition of Grieg's song published in 1981 by J.W. Chester in Book Two of their *Celebrated Songs*.

Another Grieg setting, of Bjørnson's *Den hvide, røde rose* (The white, red rose), creates a similar atmosphere to *dulgt kjærlighed*, if not so successfully, with a style again akin to Norwegian folk-song. The song was never published in the composer's lifetime, although it will now appear in the *GGA*. The manuscript is dated '1873 Sandvigen'. The poem tells the story of two sisters, one white 'rose', one red, who change character when the time of courtship arrives, for then the white one is flushed with happiness, while the red one pales at her father's rejection of her suitor. Like most such tales, it ends happily and Bjørnson captures the folk style with the simple contrast, repeated phrases, the 'yes' at the end of some lines and a straightforward structure and rhyme-scheme.

Grieg's setting reflects this style, certainly in the first part of each strophe, with a simple though angular melody and a mostly chordal accompaniment: Ex.42.

The second half is more complex; the piano echoes the end of two of the vocal phrases, the vocal line becomes much more angular and the accompaniment chords very chromatic. The basic jauntiness of the verse is well captured. The three stanzas are set strophically and the introduction (and identical postlude) is a decorated version of the first vocal phrase.

One more setting of a Bjørnson poem, *suk* (Sighs), was also written in the

Ex.42

Den hvide, røde Rose

(The white, red rose, so were called two sisters, yes two)

summer of 1873, but not published until 1908, when it appeared amongst the *Posthumous Songs*. This is a strange little song. The poem contrasts the brightness of the morning sun with the gentleness of the evening sun, neither of which can reach the writer's window, and the essence of it is contained in the last line of the first stanza, 'her er altid Skygge (here there is always shadow)'.

The setting is in A minor, each strophe just thirteen bars long, and the unadorned vocal line is purely diatonic. The harmony, however, contains a few surprises, not least in the ninth bar where Grieg has a transition to F major, creating a false relation with the F sharp in the right hand. The effect is somewhat to lighten the atmosphere, which is the opposite of what the poem suggests, where the repeated last line of each stanza is one of sadness or resignation.

The harmonization of the end of the vocal line is also unexpected, when the anticipated perfect cadence in the tonic A minor is contradicted by the bass and the D sharp in the right hand:

Ex.43

Suk

(Here there is always shadow)

Even the two bars of the postlude contain chromatic movement and consecutive sevenths in the bass. The semiquaver figure is used throughout, perhaps to illustrate the sigh of the title, but the song remains uninspired and any initial surprises lose their impact in the six repetitions necessitated by the strophic form.

Two more songs also came into being during the latter part of 1873, both of which were occasional pieces written for friends of Grieg's. The first is dated September 1st 1873 and celebrates the silver wedding anniversary of Lindeman and his wife. *Til L.M. Lindemans Sølvbryllup* was not printed at the time and the manuscript has no text apart from the 'tra-la-la' of the refrain. However, the song will now be published in the *GGA* with the text (by V. Nikolajsen) restored. The setting was designed for a soloist, with others joining in a unison refrain and Grieg has written '(Fru Wolf)'[14] at the beginning of the song and the refrain, and '(Alle)' at the repetition of the final two phrases before the refrain. The accompaniment also becomes fuller at the chorus points, with the right hand doubling the melody in octaves, where previously it comprised two chords to a bar.

The song opens with a genial $\frac{6}{8}$ melody in E minor, originally marked 'Allegretto', but altered to read 'Ikke for hurtig, i folketon (Not too fast, in folk-song style)'. It is, however, the refrain of the song, in E major and common time, that is of particular interest now, as it appears to anticipate the second, major-key section of *Solveigs Sang*, both in the melody – even to the long-held high E that begins it, and the upward octave at the end – and in the harmonization, with the pedal tonic fifth in the first phrases: Ex.44.

As it was only just over a year later that Grieg worked on the music to *Peer Gynt*, it may well be that he still had the idea of this phrase in his head.

The other song from late 1873 was a setting of a poem by Johan Bøgh, *Til generalkonsul Chr. Tønsberg på hans 60-årige fødselsdag* (To Consul-General Chr. Tønsberg on his 60th birthday), on 7 December. Oslo University Music Library has the manuscript of the song, together with a copy of the poem, presumably in Bøgh's handwriting, which shows alterations to the last three lines of the final stanza. Once again, this song will be published for the first time in the *GGA*. The long poem comprises five stanzas of seven lines and is naturally very complimentary to Tønsberg, referring to his work *Norges Historie* (History of Norway) and the way in which he stood firm for his country. Grieg's setting is strophic and, like the song for Lindeman, is divided between a solo voice and a unison chorus. Although not a great piece, it must have pleased its dedicatee.

It opens with a twelve-bar introduction marked 'Allegro vivace', but the song itself is marked 'Andantino' and is in a lively folk-song style. There is some small harmonic interest when a modulation to the dominant is effected by an unexpected C natural (the flattened submediant) in the bass of the

Ex.44                                          Til L.M. Lindemans Sølvbryllup

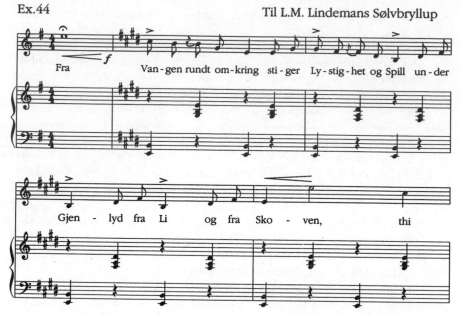

(From the meadow round about rises merriment and play amid
echoes from hillside and forest)

approach chord, and a suspension of the new dominant chord over the new
tonic:

Ex.45            Til generalkonsul Chr. Tønsberg

(Now you can gather the vanished [times])

Finally also dating from 1873 is *Ved en ung hustrus båre* (Beside a young wife's
bier), Grieg's only setting of a poem by O.P. Monrad, which was eventually
published as the third of the *Romanser*, op.39. The song is a very bleak one,
concerning the untimely death of a young woman, and Grieg emphasizes the
sorrow with an angular and wide-ranging vocal melody, which matches the
broken phrases of the poem. The accompaniment is largely chordal and the
music moves very slowly, although the manuscript has a red line through the

original time-signature, C, a correction also followed in the printed editions.

At the end of the first stanza, when Monrad asks if hope can be found in the sighs of longing, Grieg emphasizes the word 'Håb' (hope) and the question by sounding a low octave A flat under a chord of the tonic C minor. After the second stanza the three-bar postlude ends in the tonic major key, as if to underline the poet's assurance that those left behind will find hope. Monrad Johansen describes the song, together with *Modersorg* (op.15 no.4), as 'inspired and deeply felt'.[15] Unfortunately, the deep feeling it certainly possesses does not preclude a certain torpor in the setting and the song is not even mentioned by Benestad and Schjelderup-Ebbe, nor by John Horton.

Performances of the song are rare and any popularity it might have gained in English-speaking countries cannot have been helped by the appalling opening lines in Corder's translation:

> Rigid, rigid, she that ne'er looked for death!
> Frigid, frigid! She of the glowing breath!

The song was later arranged by the composer under the title *Blegnet, segnet!* (Pale, blessed) for unaccompanied eight-part choir, as the first of *To religiøse kor* (Two sacred choruses); the other was *Ave maris stella*. The pieces were dedicated to the Madrigal Choir of the Cæciliaforening (St Cecilia Society) of Copenhagen and its conductor, Frederik Rung, who gave the first performance in November 1899.

While the Andersen settings had produced some fine songs, the best of his early years as a song-writer, the Bjørnson settings are musically superior and the climax of Grieg's first mature period as a composer: the 'first meeting' between his music and great poetry. Andersen had inspired him in his youth and the first months of his relationship with Nina and apart from *Soldaten* – a unique song in his output – Grieg's music reflects the happiness and excitement of those years. In the late 1860s and early 1870s, with the exception of the tragedy of Alexandra's untimely death, the general contentment of his early married life is evident in his choice of some of Bjørnson's most euphonious verse, most particularly *Det første møte* and *Jeg giver mit digt til våren*, where he seems to have responded to the sheer sound of the words. Later, as deeper thoughts began to trouble him, it was the 'dark forces' behind Ibsen's terse poetry that came to appeal.

## Notes

1 Grieg's own description in a letter to Nils Ravnkilde, 29 July 1869.
2 Nils Grinde in a letter to the author.
3 Grieg to Finck, 17 July 1900.
4 Reproduced in *Edvard Grieg: Artikler og Taler*, ed. Gaukstad, 1957, p.235–37.
5 Bjørnson: *Digte og Sange*, edition published by Gyldendal Norsk Forlag, 1957.

6    John Horton: *Grieg*, 1974, p.177.

7    Astra Desmond in *Grieg. A Symposium*, ed. Gerald Abraham, 1948, p.81.

8    They are included in Vols 1 and 2 (as nos 2,3,4 and 1 respectively) of the Grieg-Album; *Tak for dit Råd* was also published separately by Peters, EP 2454.

9    Grieg to Bjørnson, 17 March 1875 from Leipzig.

10   David Monrad Johansen: *Edvard Grieg*, 1934, p.166.

11   Grieg to Bjørnson, 25 August 1890 from Bergen.

12   Nina Grieg to Delius, 29 June 1892 from Troldhaugen; reproduced in *Delius, A Life in Letters*, ed. Lionel Carley, 1983, pp.63–64.

13   The voluptuousness was apparently incompatible with Norwegian restraint: according to Wilhelm Kielhau: *Det norske folks liv og historie* (The Norwegian People's Life and History), Vol.10, p.297, Grieg called Richard Strauss's *Salome* 'forfallets evangelium (the gospel of decadence)'.

14   According to Sverre Jordan: *Edvard Grieg. En oversikt* . . . , p.28, this was 'presumably' the actress Lucie Wolff.

15   David Monrad Johansen: *Edvard Grieg*, p.166.

# 6 'The claim of the ideal'[1]

If, for Grieg, the early 1870s were largely concerned with solo songs, the next few years were to be dominated by music for the stage, and in the event it was not Bjørnson who was to provide the longed-for opportunity, but Ibsen.

The friendship between Grieg and Bjørnson was close, if not without its ups and downs, and the poet's admiration for the composer was expressed in a verse he wrote in 1899:

> Han gikk her ved min side,
> den store toneskald,
> jeg hørte elven glide
> med en skjønnere fall . . .

(He walked here by my side,/that great tone-poet,/I heard the river glide/ with a more beautiful cadence . . .)

In spite of the number of Bjørnson's poems he set, Grieg remained more excited by the prospect of collaborating with him on a music-drama. He had first considered *Arnljot Gelline* the cycle of poems from which he had taken the text of *Foran Sydens kloster* (Before the Southern Convent), with its theme that through suffering a proud man can be brought to service and sacrifice, if he finds something worth fighting and dying for, and this might well have suited Grieg's mixture of the romantic and the realistic. However, after discussion, they decided to use Bjørnson's play *Olav Trygvason*, written in 1861 while the author was in Italy. The history of this collaboration is long and involved and may be followed through the correspondence, frequently fiery, between the two.

Bjørnson sent Grieg the first three scenes on 10 July 1873 and in the accompanying letter promised that 'the whole act will follow shortly'. He was expecting the work to be ready for production in the autumn and gave Grieg instructions for the sort of music he wanted: '[It] must have a devilish speed! That is no joke . . . Now comes a hellish hullabaloo for the miracle, and then more miracle, wild possession, dance, delirium, whee!' Grieg replied a week later that he liked the scenes very much and he told Bjørnson that a friend, Rasmus Rolfsen, had a small summer-house on his estate Elsero at Sandviken, Bergen, which he had lent the composer to work in.[2] Bjørnson wanted Grieg to follow him to Italy to continue the collaboration at close quarters and to this end he persuaded some citizens of Bergen to put up 300 specie-dollars, without Grieg's knowledge of his involvement. Grieg felt that this was not enough for both himself and Nina to travel on and in any case he had commitments in Christiania in the autumn, and when Bjørnson left Bergen the two were destined not to meet again for seven years. The correspondence, however, went on.

In 1874 Grieg and Svendsen were awarded government grants of 400 specie-dollars (about £110) each per annum,[3] and in June Grieg received a letter from Bjørnson congratulating him. Grieg wrote back on 5 July: he was still waiting for further scenes from *Olav Trygvason* and had meanwhile made a choral setting of Bjørnson's *Oppsang for frihetsfolket i Norden* (Battle hymn for freedom-lovers in Scandinavia). He went on to say that he had not replied to Bjørnson before, 'because I was angry with you. For now I am sitting composing music to "Peer Gynt" instead of "Olav Trygvason". There you have the matter. But how can I bear a grudge against someone now, when I feel so fortunate, and least of all against you, whom I am extremely fond of, both for what you are yourself and what you awaken in me!'

Bjørnson's reaction to the news of *Peer Gynt* was swift and not exactly encouraging. He complained of the 'loss of time and money in writing opera-libretti', threw his earlier attempts at obtaining financial backing into the composer's face, and went on in an aggrieved way: 'Now you are into Peer Gynt! You are welcome to it! It has *some* parts for poetic music, but the whole is a flight away from it, and that frequently because of comic, dry passages which you will not conquer. Again you are throwing away time and strength. I will not refrain from sending you this, my warning, even if it jars. Possibly one day as an *older man* you will be able to overcome such material . . .' Although one may understand Bjørnson's annoyance at being passed over for Ibsen, especially as he thought at the time Grieg was setting *Peer Gynt* as an opera, it is ironic that the music to *Peer Gynt* was to find its place amongst Grieg's most famous and popular works.

Grieg did not reply to this last letter for two months. He then wrote to Bjørnson to thank him for his help in obtaining the grant from Bergen, but explaining that it really was not enough for him to do as Bjørnson wished. 'The truth is,' he continued, 'that had I had your text, I would have said No to Ibsen and avoided Peer Gynt with its many reefs. I hope this autumn to be finished with this task . . . and will then be ready with enthusiasm for "Olav Trygvason"'.[4] Unfortunately, Grieg's estimate of a completion date for the *Peer Gynt* music was far too optimistic. By the autumn he was writing to Bjørnson that he hoped to be finished by Christmas, so that he could have some money to travel south to meet him, but the music was still unfinished the following April and once again the journey was postponed. However, Grieg was still working on parts of *Olav Trygvason* and in May 1875 he wrote to Bjørnson about one or two points: ' . . . there is much I can see you have conceived as melodrama, not as opera. The beautiful monologue, especially, is too long and the chorus that follows it, too . . .'[5] Whether or not Bjørnson was offended by this criticism we do not know, but he would not come to Leipzig to meet Grieg, as the composer had suggested.

That, effectively, was the end of the collaboration, for Bjørnson felt that either Grieg should be prepared to spend a good deal of time with him (but not, incidentally, the other way round) to work on *Olav Trygvason*, or he would have no more to do with it. In the event, it was twelve years before Grieg returned to the project, when in 1889 he revised his sketches to form a cantata and then prepared an orchestral score from the piano edition, which was published in 1890 as his op. 50.

Popular as it has become, the music to *Peer Gynt* was to give Grieg many headaches, both in its composition and its eventual performance. Ibsen had been impressed by Grieg's musical talents from their first meetings in Rome in 1866, and also by the young composer's perception of literature. Ibsen was quite a different character from his great contemporary Bjørnson. He was born in 1828 in Skien, south of Oslo, where his father had a business. Unfortunately, owing to some ill-advised speculation, the business failed when Ibsen was eight. Ibsen senior was forced to sell or mortgage most of his possessions and the family moved to a farm outside the town. The subsequent loss of status is often blamed for the writer's later introspection. He was sent to Grimstad, further down the east coast, as a pharmacist's apprentice, instead of being able to study art as he had wished, and here he wrote poetry inspired by his own loneliness and by the 'revolutionary' ideals of Henrik Wergeland. He arrived in Christiania in 1850 where, amongst other things, he published poetry and critical articles, and in the autumn of 1851 he was appointed by Ole Bull to be resident author and instructor at Det norske Teater in Bergen. Here he was fortunate enough to have the opportunity to learn stagecraft, to try out his own plays, and he was also sent to learn stage technique in Denmark and Germany. Ibsen held this post for over five years and then moved to the Christiania Theatre, until that failed in 1862.

He left Norway in 1864 and, helped by a government grant from 1866, lived first in Italy and then in Germany, feeling that he had to get away in order to find freedom to write. His feelings of constraint were later reflected in *A Doll's House*, where Dr Thorvald represents Norway with its moral and religious narrow-mindedness, and Nora represents the author's desire to escape. The south of Europe appealed to him, as it has to so many Scandinavians, and it was with *Brand*, written in 1866, that he first achieved fame. It was Grieg's perceptive comments on *Brand* – that people could take the truth wrapped up in poetic form, but not in prose – that first attracted Ibsen to him.

*Peer Gynt*, Ibsen's last play in verse, was written in 1867 during the author's stay on Ischia and Sorrento. The rhyme-scheme varies, sometimes using couplets, sometimes quatrains, and although the metric feet vary in length, there are four stresses in each line. The rhyming words are frequently of two or three syllables and it is impossible to render their ingenuity in any translation. Although *Peer Gynt* is a dramatic poem in five acts, it needed some revision to prepare it for a stage production. The scene-changes are numerous and complicated to engineer and this, no doubt, was one good reason why Ibsen felt the need for incidental music. Another was that, to an audience used mainly to vaudeville and comic opera, five acts of unrelieved drama were unthinkable.

Ibsen wrote to Grieg from Dresden in January 1874 to ask him to compose the necessary music, and at the same time gave the composer detailed instructions about what he required:

> The first act is to be retained complete, with only some foreshortening of the dialogue! Peer Gynt's monologue . . . I wish to be treated either as a melodrama or partly as recitative. The scene where the wedding takes place . . . must be made more of than it is in the book, with the help of ballet. A special dance tune must be composed for this.
>
> In the second act, the three *sæterjenter* . . . may be treated musically at the composer's discretion, but there must be some devilry in it! The monologue . . . I have envisaged accompanied by chords, just like melodrama. The same applies to the scene between Peer and the green-clad woman . . . Likewise, there should be a similar accompaniment to the episode in the Dovregubb's[6] hall . . . Also the scene with the Bøyg[7] . . . must be accompanied by music; the bird voices must be sung; bell-ringing and hymn-singing are heard in the distance.
>
> In the third act I need chords, but sparingly, for the scene between Peer, the woman and the troll-child . . .
>
> In place [of Act Four] I have envisaged a great musical tone-picture, which will suggest Peer Gynt's roaming through the wide world; American, English and French melodies could be used . . . Anitra and the girls' chorus will be heard behind the curtain together with the orchestra. During this, the curtain will rise and one will be able to see, like a distant vision . . . a tableau, in which Solveig, as a middle-aged woman, is sitting singing in the sunshine outside her house. After her song the curtain rolls slowly down again, the music is continued in the orchestra and goes on to portray the storm at sea, with which the fifth act begins.
>
> The fifth act . . . is to be significantly shortened . . . The churchgoers are singing on the woodland path; the bell-ringing and distant hymn-singing are suggested in the music . . . until Solveig's song [actually *Solveigs Vuggevise*, the Cradle Song] closes the play, after which the curtain falls, while the hymn-singing sounds again, nearer and louder.[8]

Even after receiving all these details, Grieg still seems to have thought that the music would involve only 'fragments here and there', as he wrote to Bjørnson in September 1874. Less than one month later, in spite of his admiration for it as a work of literature, he was describing the play as 'that most unmusical of all subjects' and as an 'incubus', and the music actually took him until the autumn of 1875 to complete. In a letter to Beyer, written from the pavilion at Sandviken in August 1874, he wrote, 'Peer Gynt is going very slowly and for it to be finished this autumn is out of the question. It is a frightfully unmanageable subject, apart from a few places, such as for example where Solveig sings, which I have already completely finished. And I have also done something for the Dovregubb's hall, which I literally cannot bear to hear, it hums so much of cowpats, of ultra-Norwegianism and sufficient-unto-thyselfness![9] But I expect that the irony will also be able to be felt.'[10] Grieg was delighted to be told that *Peer Gynt* would not be produced before New Year 1875 for, as he wrote to Ludvig Josephson, the manager of the Christiania Theatre, 'the task is far greater than I had imagined, and in places I am encountering difficulties which bring me to a standstill.'[11] To Ibsen he wrote, 'there is much more music than I had imagined.'[12]

Some of the difficulties were due to the rather poor standard of musicianship prevailing at the Christiania Theatre and Grieg was obviously troubled and somewhat disheartened. He wrote to his friend August Winding, 'I am still hanging around with the music to Peer Gynt which doesn't interest me.'[13] Once the music was completed and rehearsals were to begin, Grieg was as concerned with detail as Ibsen had been initially. He was unable to be at the first rehearsals because both his parents were ill in Bergen and, after their deaths in the autumn of 1975, he stayed on there. In December he sent a letter of twenty-eight sides to Johan Hennum, capellmeister of the theatre, who was to conduct the performances. The letter goes into specific detail about the various pieces and makes it clear that it is not to be regarded merely as music for its own sake, except in a very few cases, but that it should be 'a question of making the effect so that the audience will understand the meaning'.[14]

Some of the music is well-known throughout the world through the two suites arranged from it by the composer, but it was only in 1978 that a recording of the complete music was released. There is material for soprano, mezzo-soprano, tenor and baritone soloists, chorus and orchestra, but the concern of this book is with those items which stand as solo vocal pieces, one of which, *Solveigs Sang* (Solveig's song), is one of Grieg's best known songs.

The first major solo vocal item is *Peer Gynt's Serenade*, which occurs in Act Four, when Peer is entranced by the Arabian girl Anitra. Some of the flavour of the east is imitated in the music, especially the accented chromatic appoggiaturas in the introduction, similar to the effect created in *Odalisken synger*. It is also felt in the acciaccaturas of the ritornello, which comes after each of the first two stanzas and at the end. The orchestral score adds oboes and a triangle to the strings in these ritornello passages to heighten the exotic atmosphere, but elsewhere the orchestral accompaniment is largely confined to strings playing pizzicato. There is, however, more than a little of Norwegian folk music about the E major section which sets the fourth stanza, not least in the pedal tonic fifth, sounded under dominant and supertonic chords.

The song is sung by Peer, supposedly accompanying himself on an Arabian lute. The simplicity of the accompaniment and the largely strophic setting is very much in the tradition of *Singspiel*, with which the Norwegian audiences were familiar and of which they approved. Grieg, in his letter to Hennum, says of the song, 'It must sound half sensually impassioned, half ironic. In the interludes and postludes, Peer must play his instrument with a certain passion'. This 'passion' is also to be found in the music, in the increased tempi of these passages and in the richer harmony.

The words of the *Serenade* are more than 'half ironic', telling of Peer's journey to the south in his usual exaggerated fashion. The lively rhythm catches the humour in the words very well and it is surprising that the song, unlike the other two solo songs from *Peer Gynt*, is rarely performed in England.

*Solveigs Sang*, together with *Jeg elsker dig* (I love you) and perhaps *En svane* (A swan) from the Ibsen settings, op.25 and *Våren* (The spring) from the Vinje settings, op.33, is one of Grieg's best known songs and it certainly has one of his loveliest melodies. Although the setting owes a good deal to Norwegian folk music, and in spite of what is often thought and written, Grieg never actually used a folk-song except in his acknowledged arrangements. He wrote to Finck, 'As far as my songs are concerned I do not myself believe that in general they are influenced by the folk-song to any essential degree. This is still the case even where local colour *had* to play a major part as, for example, in Solveig's song. But this is perhaps the only one of my songs where an echo of the folk-song may be detected.'[15] He was pleased when Finck, in his biography, included a chapter entitled 'Norwegian Folk-Music – Grieg's Originality', which as he told Beyer 'at last gives me a sort of compensation for the incorrect and uncomprehending criticism I have been exposed to by a number of German and Anglo-American journalists'.[16] The folk-song Grieg may have had in mind when he wrote *Solveigs sang* has never definitely been identified; the most likely would seem to be *Jeg lagde mig saa sildig* (I lay down so late), which is to be found in Lindeman's famous collection and which Grieg was to use as the first item in his *Album of Songs for Male-Voice Choir*, songs written between 1877 and 1878 and published as op.30: Ex.46.

However, as has been seen, other recent songs also contained hints of the song which was to emerge as Solveig's.

Whatever the influences, conscious or unconscious, the folk-song character is to be seen in the basically simple accompaniment, a good deal of which is built on the pedal tonic fifth and is also apparent in the second, humming

Ex.46                                      Jeg lagde mig saa sildig

Jeg lag - de mig saa sil - dig alt sent    om en kveld,

(I lay down so late, all late one evening)

section of each strophe, where the vocal line, with its decorations and repeated snatches, is very like a *lokk*. The rhythm here, too, with its accented second beat, is similar to the *springar*. This section is also thought to owe something to Kjerulf's *Synnøves Sang* from Bjørnson's novel *Synnøve Solbakken*, which has a hummed introduction and postlude, although Kjerulf's melody is much more melancholy than Grieg's and has more in common with the instrumental introduction and postlude in *Solveigs Sang* than with the vocal line (Ex.47). Harmonically, Grieg's setting becomes more interesting in the

Ex.47                                      Kjerulf, Synnøves Sang

second half of each strophe, where the chordal accompaniment gives way to very chromatic writing, perhaps reflecting the longing in Solveig's heart.

The melody of the song is heard earlier in the incidental music, played by the orchestra. The sung version occurs as the brief scene in Act Four – Ibsen's imagined 'distant vision', before he was persuaded not to replace the rest of the act with a tone-poem – and comes after Peer and Anitra have parted company, she having robbed him of most of his possessions, and Peer is wondering what new adventure awaits him. The song is the essence of Solveig's character, which epitomizes faithfulness and love. Grieg told Hennum, 'This song must be made the best of by the actress concerned, for it characterizes Solveig. At one time in a weak moment I noted in the score that if the actress was not able to perform the humming section, a solo clarinet could take it over.'[17] However, he changed his mind about that solution and decided that the actress would have to work at her singing. Fortunately, the Solveig in the first performance, Oda Nielsen, was well able to cope; Grieg wrote to her, 'Free and graceful as you are yourself, so too was your Solveig. I do not know if it was Ibsen's Solveig, but I do know that there was fragrance and music, purity and clarity about the character and the song. Thank you for that . . .' and he signed the letter, 'Your old admirer'.[18]

*Solveigs Sang* like *Jeg elsker dig* must be one of the most frequently transcribed of Grieg's songs, with several arrangements made for two-and three-part female choir and others for oboe and piano, and violin and piano, as well as an 'easily arranged' version for piano solo. Grieg, to his disgust, was also some years later to hear it played on a zither.

*Solveigs Vuggevise* (Solveig's Cradle Song) is the last of the three solo items and perhaps because it was the last piece in the incidental music, Grieg was very explicit about the effect he wished it to create. The introduction, played in the orchestral version by the strings, has a good deal of chromatic movement underneath the melody. By the time the voice enters, the accompaniment has become diatonic and has a rocking rhythm to suit the words. The melody is very simple and the last notes of almost every vocal phrase are echoed in the accompaniment. Grieg, in his instructions to Hennum, said he hoped for 'a poetic effect' at this point of the play and the song is to be sung while the sun rises and the curtain falls '*very* slowly, just as Solveig is sitting, bending over Peer Gynt'. The actress is to sing 'quietly and sincerely, later at the end louder and fuller' and Grieg made much of the contrast between the 'poco animato' passages and the alternating 'tranquillo'. Towards the end, he instructed that 'the strings must always emphasize the beginning of the bar and then go straight to "pp", so that the whole is almost in a dream state'. [19] In the original score, the orchestra and chorus were heard again (after bar 44 of the printed solo version) with the hymn-tune that Peer, on his way to Solveig's hut, heard the villagers singing, but in later productions this section was omitted. Grieg seemed to think that the passage might be thought over-sentimental, but the resumption of Solveig's melody makes more impact when the section is retained, for then the 'forte' and the chromatic accompaniment are emphasized.

Musically, it is the chromatic writing in an otherwise tranquil cradle song that makes the most effect. Where it begins in earnest, Grieg wrote, 'where it changes to D minor, it must be sung and played with sincerity and each of the following "sov!"'s [sleep] must have its definition. Ever fainter and fainter. . .':[20] Ex.48. As a postlude, the orchestra repeats the last four bars of the vocal melody, once again over chromatically changing chords, as if to remind the audience of all that has happened before peace is finally attained, although the ultimate end of the drama, as so often in Ibsen's later plays, is left to the imagination. As Monrad Johansen wrote, '*Solveigs Vuggevise* gives the Peer Gynt music a sublime ending.'[21]

In spite of the many difficulties, the first performance of *Peer Gynt* with Grieg's music took place at the Christiania Theatre on 24 February 1876, and it was very well received. Today its four-hour duration, as advertised on the programme, would be rather daunting, but the Christiania press greeted it enthusiastically and the public equally so. Josephson, the theatre manager, later recalled it as having been 'an unassailable victory'[22] and the drama was

(Sleep, my dearest boy! Sleep! Sleep!)

given no less than thirty-six more performances during that spring. Neither Ibsen nor Grieg was present at the first night; Grieg was in Bergen following the death of his parents the previous autumn, and Ibsen was still living abroad.

Modern opinions of Grieg's music to *Peer Gynt* have varied a good deal. As Benestad and Schjelderup-Ebbe have said, it has been fashionable in some circles to turn up one's nose a little and make derogatory remarks about its popular romanticism. Most of the major Norwegian musicologists have considered it more than worthy of Grieg. Nils Grinde, for example, has written that it has 'all of the melodic charm and freshness of the youthful works',[23] although he agrees that the best music is to be found in the more lyrical numbers. Other critics, particularly and perhaps significantly literary critics, have found the music too sentimental for its subject. Peter Watts, in the introduction to his English translation of the play, says that Grieg was possibly 'the wrong person to set an astringent play like *Peer Gynt*',[24] although he does attribute much of this criticism to over-familiarity. It is no doubt also due to the unfortunately widespread conception that Grieg was incapable of writing 'astringent' music. This idea is upheld by Michael Meyer who states that 'few musical scores can have so softened an author's intentions as Grieg's *Peer Gynt* suite [sic], which turns the play into a jolly Hans Andersen fairy tale'.[25] It is certainly difficult to dissociate the play from Grieg's music, even though in later times some producers have tried to do so.

In 1948 Hans Jacob Nielsen wanted a realistic production for Det norske Teater in Bergen and decided that Grieg's music did not fit his conception of the drama. He felt that, although lovely in itself, it does not match the play and in fact 'distorts' it, and in this, the first anti-romantic production, Solveig became a simple peasant girl and not a 'glossy picture'.[26] In 1967 Nielsen wrote his opinion of Grieg's music:

Solveig's song is a pearl in Norwegian music and in a way fits well, but in performance the song is a concert item and demands a singer who can master its great technical difficulties. It is eternally distant from how one can imagine Solveig – the forty-year-old plain peasantwoman – sitting and humming in isolation up in the Gudbrandsdal.

As a concert-number, the final cradle-song is also marvellously beautiful, but almost ludicrous when it comes in the context of the stage performance, where "sov, du dyreste gutten min" is played by a sixty-piece orchestra and sung by a woman of sixty–seventy years old with a light soprano – a cradle song which could awaken the dead![27]

(To be fair, Grieg actually wrote to Ibsen in March 1876 that he believed, 'because of a highly mangled musical performance', this last item had made 'a poor impression' and it was altered in later productions).[28]

For his own production, which was translated into New Norwegian by Henrik Rytter, Nielsen (who also played the title role) asked the composer Harald Sæverud to provide new music, which he wanted to be very different from Grieg's. Sæverud did so and also arranged his music into a concert suite, *Tolv orkesterstykker fra musikken til Henrik Ibsens Peer Gynt* (Twelve orchestral pieces from the music to...), and other modern Norwegian composers, including Finn Ludt, Arne Nordheim and Håkon Berge, have also written music for the play. The German composer Werner Egk wrote his opera *Peer Gynt* in 1938, and ten years previously the Austrian Viktor Ullmann had also composed an opera on the same subject.

Far less well-known is that music to *Peer Gynt* existed *before* Grieg's, by the Swedish composer August Söderman. His series of pieces for voice and piano was written in the late 1860s and is thought to have been used for a production of the play in Stockholm in 1871. The music apparently could not be found after Söderman's death in 1876, but, according to Benestad and Schjelderup-Ebbe, there was a performance of it in Stockholm in 1892, and nine of the pieces were published in 1895. Whether Ibsen or Grieg knew of the existence of Söderman's music is unknown, but Josephson, in his memoirs, related how he went through the music with Söderman scene by scene. He also said the music could not be found at the composer's death, 'so it fell to Edvard Grieg to set his great compatriot's ideas to music.'[29] This implies that Ibsen and Grieg did indeed know of Söderman's pieces, but Michael Meyer considers that, had this music been available, Josephson would have used it, even though Ibsen offered the idea of a stage production on the basis of Grieg's promise to provide incidental music. It is interesting to speculate that such world-wide favourites as *Solveigs Sang* and *Morgenstemning* might easily never have been written.

Grieg did not see a performance of *Peer Gynt* until November 1876 and after the success of the first season must have thought himself finished with the music. This, however, was not to be. The Christiania run was halted by a fire at the theatre in January 1877, which destroyed all the sets and costumes, but in 1886 the play was produced at the Dagmar Theatre in Copenhagen. It was shortened for this revival and Grieg, who was not completely satisfied with some of his earlier orchestration, took the opportunity to revise the music. Even this production was not without its performance difficulties, however, as Grieg told Beyer:

> This afternoon I have had my first rehearsal with the vocal forces for "Peer Gynt". When I came up the stairs at the Dagmar Theatre, I heard the Sæterjenter crowing at the tops of their voices, naturally in a raving mad tempo, just for once too slowly, so I was very pleased that I was there. But the voices are good and the girls seem to have some life in them, so I didn't give up on the scene, which is now much better orchestrated than before. Then I rehearsed Solveig's songs with Fru Oda P.,[30] but since Solveig has the misfortune to be expecting a baby, the illusion suffers significant damage. Apart from that, she set to work quite well and shows a musical temperament.[31]

In 1892 Bjørnson's son Bjørn, who was by then manager of the Christiania Theatre, wanted to revise *Peer Gynt* in the Norwegian capital with himself in the title role and Grieg was asked to contribute some new music. The composer was most indignant at this and insisted that he was 'finished with that period'. He was told, however, that if he would not provide the music, another composer would be asked to do so. Grieg felt he was being 'blackmailed', as he said to Max Abraham,[32] but he duly expanded the music for the scene with the Bøyg.

Printed excerpts from the *Peer Gynt* music had appeared as early as March 1876, when piano arrangements of *Anitras Dans*, *Solveigs Sang* and *Peer Gynts Serenade* were published in Copenhagen, and these pieces were soon followed by several others. Grieg himself arranged the two orchestral suites, the first as op.46 in 1887 and the second as op.55 between 1890 and 1892, and their popularity was such that in 1891 Peters was able to report performances as far afield as Asia, Africa and Australia. However, a complete score was not published until after Grieg's death, when one was prepared by Halvorsen. In spite of all this, Grieg was to remain convinced that the music 'belongs only in the theatre and not in the concert hall', as he wrote to Röntgen in 1893.[33] Benestad and Schjelderup-Ebbe quote Hanslick's opinion that 'Ibsen's "Peer Gynt" will only live further through Grieg's music, for I feel that it contains in each of its movements more poetry and artistic sense than in all Ibsen's five-act monster'.[34] The music is uneven in quality; very successful in the parts where Ibsen set Grieg's mind 'aglow', but in other places not so inspired. His doubts about the required expertise of the theatre orchestra must have inhibited him to some extent, but it is this music more than anything else he wrote which was to make him a household name.

Before the consideration of Grieg's next, great settings of poems by Ibsen, there is a little song written in 1875 which should be mentioned. This is *Morgenbønn på skolen* (Morning prayer at school) to words by Frederik Gjertsen. It is exactly what its title suggests, a school hymn, which asks that the work of the day shall be done to Jesus's honour and that His teaching shall be the guiding light to heaven. Accordingly, the song has a bright diatonic melody in D major and a straightforward harmonization, with the right hand mostly in thirds and sixths, built over the tonic fifth for the first three bars. It is not totally without harmonic interest, however, and there is effective use of suspensions in the penultimate bar. The song was published in Copenhagen in the *Nordisk illustreret Børneblad* (Scandinavian Illustrated Children's Journal) in December 1875 and is now to be found in the *GGA*.

After the success of the first season of *Peer Gynt*, it is hardly surprising that Grieg should have looked at Ibsen's poetry for song texts. The shorter verse, however, is quite different from Ibsen's verse-plays and different from almost all his drama. Grieg had said about *Brand* that the truth wrapped up in rhyme is easier to accept than when it is told in prose and it seems that Ibsen was more able to give direct expression to his thoughts in verse than in prose. In *Rimbrev til Fru Heiberg* (Rhyming letter to Fru Heiberg)[35] he sums up his idea: 'Prosa stil er for ideer, vers for syner (Prose is the style for ideas, verse for visions)'. Certainly his most significant poems were written during the times of crisis in his life. Parallels may be drawn here with the composer: perhaps the truth is also easier to express if wrapped up in music and certainly Grieg's most significant songs were written as a result of crises, real or imaginary, in his life and musical development.

Ibsen's collection of *Digte* (Poems), which contained all his poetry except most of the purely occasional verse, was published in 1871 and was into a second edition by 1875. He wrote to Brandes, 'There are things both old and new in it and there is much that I do not consider to be of any great importance; nevertheless it all belongs to the story of my development.'[36] Brandes later confirmed the last opinion when he wrote that the *Digte* 'mirror in microcosm the whole development of Ibsen's life'.[37] Again, a parallel may be drawn with Grieg's songs.

Ibsen revised many of his earlier poems for publication. His poetry, like that of Bjørnson, shows a wide diversity, from the purely elegiac, which owes something to Welhaven in its verse-forms, imagery and expression, to songs from the plays, like *Margretes Vuggesang*; from narrative poems like *Terje Vigen* (filmed in 1917 by a Swedish company) to political and occasional verse, such as the poem on Abraham Lincoln's assassination. Almost all are marked by their concentration of content and Ibsen, again like Bjørnson, most often uses nouns and verbs with few accompanying adjectives or adverbs. As in Old Norse poetry, he makes use of contrast and antithesis, often within one line of a poem as well as in the poem as a whole. The concentration is not just of ideas, frequently taken to their limits throughout a poem, but is also to be found in the imagery and vocabulary he chooses. His rhymes regularly occur on stressed words, or else important words are placed in a rhyming position to give them emphasis, a practice which, in conjunction with the terse imagery, creates tremendous problems for the would-be translator. Unlike Bjørnson, Ibsen was not very musically minded, but his sense of rhythm was strong and although many longer poems show great variety of line length and rhyme-scheme, his lines are usually short, once again allowing little leeway for a translator to change word order to capture the meaning.

Grieg found that Ibsen's shorter, more fateful poetry best matched his own state of mind during 1876. He had lost both his parents within a short time the previous autumn and his marriage was going through a very unsettled period. This crisis, according to Frants Beyer's wife, Marie, also made itself felt in some of Grieg's later works, for example the String Quartet, op.27, and *Den Bergtekne* (The mountain thrall), op.32. As he had after Alexandra's death, Grieg poured himself into his music, first and foremost the *Ballade* in G minor for piano. This work takes the form of variations on a Norwegian folk-tune, *Den nordlandske bondestand* (The Nordland peasant life), to be found in Lindeman's collection, the melody of which exactly matched Grieg's very melancholy mood. He described it as written 'with my heart's blood in days of sorrow and despair',[38] and indeed the thoughts behind it were so deeply felt that the composer himself could never play it in public.

This prevailing mood of despair drove Grieg to Ibsen's verse for the last time and almost all the six poems set in the op.25 album *Seks Digte af Henrik Ibsen* convey his melancholy in a most inspired way. The understatement rife in the poetry, the restraint of the emotion and the concentration of ideas are all mirrored in the music.

The first song of the six, *Spillemænd* (Minstrels), is based on a familiar Norwegian legend of a musician who is taught great powers of interpretation by a water-sprite, a *fossegrim*, only to find himself having to repay the debt with his own happiness. (The famous statue of Ole Bull in Bergen shows him being taught his art by such a sprite.) It is easy to see in Grieg's choice of this poem a reflection of the state of his own life at the time. In a letter to Iver Holter in 1897 he quoted* the first two stanzas of the poem, adding that 'as *you* will understand' it was 'a piece of life's history'. As the letters from 1866 show, Grieg's friend Benjamin Feddersen, as well as the composer himself, had had doubts about his attachment to Nina and whether or not art would have to be sacrificed for marriage, or vice versa. Ibsen too, first in the long narrative poem *Paa Vidderne*, and in many of his later poems, questioned whether the claims of art and vocation should be greater than those of life in

---

*or rather misquoted: he replaces 'somerlys (summer-light)' with 'månelys (moon-light)'.

general. Philip Wicksteed[39] has also seen in *Spillemænd* a view of Ibsen as a haunted man who, although 'he was always seeking to break through to the light, was often beset by a doubt whether darkness might not after all be the natural abode of men,' a description which could on occasion be applied equally to Grieg and many other Scandinavians.

The main problem at this particular time seems to have been caused by Grieg's desire (now that he had his stipend and no longer needed to remain in Christiania) to live in the Hardanger area, where he found the peace to compose, but which would be very lonely indeed for Nina. He later used the melody of *Spillemænd* as the main motif in his String Quartet, and Benestad and Schjelderup-Ebbe suggest that the song had become 'an unveiling of an extremely sensitive point in the relationship with Nina'.[40] However, the situation was not yet so desperate as to affect his song-writing abilities.

*Spillemænd*, whatever its instigation, is one of Grieg's finest songs. The poem, described by Wicksteed as 'mysterious and fascinating', is a youthful one, written in 1851 and later revised. The simple opening of the song is reminiscent of *Das alte Lied* and has the same 'old world' atmosphere. The accompaniment is straightforward, too, with the vocal melody played in octaves and a tonic pedal maintained in the inner part. At bar 5 the opening phrase is heard again, but now in A flat major, the key of the flattened submediant, a transition which Grieg so often used to marvellous effect, here accompanying the words which tell of the minstrel being lured to the river.

The middle section consists largely of recitative-like declamation for the singer over tremolando chords in the accompaniment, and this development of the music goes with the development of the story after the static statement of the situation at the opening. The poem here tells how the musician asks the sprite to teach him to play well enough to enchant the lady he loves, and the music makes much use of sequence, moving up a minor third at a time, and with chromatic movement in the inner parts of both hands in the accompaniment, building up gradually in pitch and dynamic to the final climax: 'men da jeg var bleven hans mester, var hun min broders brud (but by the time I had become his [the sprite's] master, she was my brother's bride)'. Throughout this passage, which in the present author's opinion is neither 'trivial' nor 'weak',[41] Grieg pays great attention to annotating the correct declamation of the words, and he builds up the tension by the use of diminished intervals, both in the vocal line and in the accompaniment chords.

The 'tempo primo' has a similar melody to the beginning, as the minstrel accepts his fate — to play alone, but never to forget the terror and the song he has learnt — but the dissonances in both vocal line and accompaniment, frequently created by suspensions, imply that the story is far from over. This applies especially to the word 'aldrig (never)' in the repeat of the last line, which, significantly, is the only repetition in the whole song: Ex.49.

Ex.49
Spillemænd

veg al - drig fra mit Sind,   veg   al - drig   fra   mit   Sind.

(go never from my mind)

The infrequency of performances of this song has been attributed by Benestad and Schjelderup-Ebbe to its wide range (A below middle C to high E),[42] but as most of it lies in the middle register and the higher notes are marked 'forte' or 'fortissimo', this seems unlikely. Far more tenable is Monrad Johansen's theory that the song requires a good deal of musicianship from the singer to make its effect and gives little opportunity for mere vocal display.[43]

The balance of Ibsen's poem and the contrast of the beginning with the end, as well as the inner contrast in the first line of the second stanza between 'gru (terror)' and 'sange, (songs)', has often been ignored in translations. Henzen keeps something of the latter with 'Gesang und Schauern', but Corder's 'song of magic' had nothing of the impending horror. Fortunately, William Halverson's new translation in the *GGA* retains much of the sinister atmosphere of the original.

The second song of the op.25 group, *En svane* (A swan), is one of Grieg's greatest and best known, although unfortunately, like *Jeg elsker dig*, it is rarely sung or heard outside Scandinavia as Grieg wrote it. As with *Spillemænd*, the poem seemed to the composer to be something of a reflection of his own situation. It was certainly symbolic to Ibsen, for at the time of writing it he is supposed to have been in love with a young girl who seemed unresponsive, but who, as he later discovered, had merely been too shy to reveal her affection for him.

The swan is an image often found in Norse mythology and literature and also in Celtic writing. In Celtic mythology the motif of swans linked by a silver chain is the symbol of divine beings in metamorphosis, and in the fifth of Samuel Barber's *Hermit Songs*, 'The Crucifixion', a setting of an anonymous twelfth-century Irish text, it is Christ who is referred to as 'Thou Swan'. To Scandinavians, the swan is a symbol of the soul and, as Wickstead has said, typifies the Norse belief in the 'dark, unknown passions and haunting obsessions above which life must be raised and against which it must be defended'.[44]

*En svane* is a fine example of Ibsen's most elusive and aphoristic writing. It dates from 1865, but some years earlier, in *I Billedgalleriet* (In the picture gallery) part III, he had explored the same theme:

> Taus svømmer svanen til den dør, – men klangfull
> blir stemmen når den skal sin sjæl utånde;
> akk ja! hva mekter ikke dødens vånde!
> (Silently swims the swan to that death, – but full of sound/its voice becomes
> when its soul shall expire;/ah, yes! what is death's anguish not capable of!)

The concentration of the later poem, however, is much more powerful.

Grieg marks his setting 'langsomt og tilbakeholdt (slowly and held back, restrained)' and the atmosphere of stillness is apparent from the very first bars. The basic harmonic structure is simple, but the accompaniment chords frequently have added or altered notes and there is a good deal of chromatic 'gliding', which mirrors the swan's movement. A particularly effective example of note alteration occurs in the third bar, where the D natural of the subdominant seventh chord becomes D flat, while the vocal phrase remains essentially the same. The now familiar echoing of the vocal line by the accompaniment is used in this song to wonderful effect; in the orchestrated version, prepared in Mentone and dated '1/4/94', Grieg scores these echoes for the plaintive sound of a solo oboe. The chords gradually build up from triads to sevenths and ninths in a way that anticipates the Impressionists, culminating in a particularly translucent passage (bars 17 to 19), where similar vocal phrases are harmonized by a chord of the ninth on the sharpened subdominant and, as in the preceding eight bars, over a dominant pedal.

The fortissimo climax is augmented by a marvellous descending chromatic phrase in the bass. Unfortunately, the crescendo marking which follows was blatantly altered in the German edition to a diminuendo, thus destroying the whole carefully constructed effect. This inexplicable practice has subsequently been followed in almost every edition, a notable exception being that published by Augener in 1961, with a new English translation by Astra Desmond, and it has now also been rectified in Nils Grinde's edition for the *GGA*. Grieg was always most particular that his dynamic markings be observed exactly, as the Swedish singer Dagmar Møller was to recall in her memoirs,[45] and in his long letter to Henry Finck, Grieg specifically draws attention to the climax of *En svane*: '. . . the words "Ja da, – da sangst du!" should be performed *ff*, if possible even increasing. Consequently, no diminuendo and piano.'[46] In a letter to Isabella Edwards of December 1895 he also gives instructions that the phrase 'hverken Slag eller Trille (neither throb nor trill)' in bars 5 and 6 'must be a single *pp* without any crescendo whatsoever'.[47]

The return to the opening melody (bar 22), although marked 'tranquillo' and 'pianissimo', is accompanied by fuller chords and once more Grieg uses that eloquent transition to the flattened submediant (bar 26) – 'du sang i døden (you sang in death)', – which makes the move back to the tonic F[48] for the conclusion – 'du var dog en svane (you were truly a swan)' – so much more awesome:

Ex.50

En Svane

(You ended your course. You sang in death; you were truly a swan!)

Grieg is always at his best when, as here, he is understating. The 'tilbakeholdt' marking in *En svane* refers to natural Norwegian restraint, that which John Horton calls the 'reticent emotion'[49] in the poem, and which is felt in Grieg's setting until the fortissimo climax. More significantly, as Astra Desmond has pointed out, the adjective is also the one used in Norwegian for 'bated' breath.[50] In his letter to Finck, Grieg tells of a performance of the orchestrated version of the song, which he conducted with the Belgian singer Grimand, who performed 'wonderfully well, with great dramatic accent'. He goes on to comment that no Norwegian would have dared give such an interpretation, because 'our nature would have to struggle with our national shyness'.

Some of the problems of translating this song have already been discussed in Chapter 2. It presents innumerable difficulties, from the disyllabic title to the conciseness, which, again to quote Wicksteed, 'forces the translator to give a definite interpretation to what the original leaves as an open challenge'.[51] The poem is in four short stanzas; each has four lines and each of these (with one exception) has only five or six syllables, reminiscent of Old Norse verse. The lines are rhymed ABBA in the first and third stanzas and alternately in the second and fourth. It is difficult in any other language to do justice to Ibsen's use of sounds, perhaps more so in this poem than anywhere else, and Sergius Kagen remarks, 'I have found no satisfactory English translation of this celebrated song'.[52] Apparently he did not know Astra Desmond's version, which is the most accurate and singable of all. In order to be so, however, it abandons rhyme, although such is the construction of the song that this omission is scarcely noticed.

Grieg had a good deal of correspondence with William Molard on the subject of the latter's translation into French and he pointed out a few incorrect declamations in 'Un cygne'. He was more unhappy with the translation of the penultimate line, which Molard gives as 'T' inspire au chant triste': 'But the word "triste" doesn't at all answer the poet's meaning. I wrote the music to the words "du sang i døden" and you will notice that they likewise light up in the music by the transition to D flat major. I hope you might be able to find a different, less dark word instead, with which to characterize the swan's song.'[53]

The next Ibsen setting, *Stambogsrim* (Album verse), is one of the most concise, both in terms of poetry and of music. At twelve bars long it is Grieg's shortest art song,[54] yet within this brief space he has constructed a lyrical piece in ABA form. Bars 5 to 12 are sometimes repeated, although as in other songs where such repetition has become the practice, it does destroy the balance and the dynamic construction of Grieg's music. Even more than in *En svane*, Ibsen's sparseness of expression in *Stambogsrim* makes the meaning nebulous; the reader is aware only of a beloved, a 'messenger of joy', a 'star' that is no more. Grieg matches the utter despair with a sighing, broken melody in F minor, all but two bars of which begin after a crotchet rest, and with syncopated chords in the right hand accompaniment, and the song is marked 'meget langsomt, talende (very slowly, eloquently)'.

The melody makes much use of augmented and diminished fourths and is largely built up in sequences. Once again, as in *Spillemænd*, Grieg is more concerned with accurate declamation than with beauty of vocal line and *Stambogsrim*, like the earlier song and perhaps for the same reason, is rarely performed. The elusive quality of the verse, a scene merely glimpsed rather than seen properly, an episode without beginning or end, is also conveyed in the way Grieg ends his setting, with the retention to the last of the syncopated right hand chords and with the plagal cadence blurred by the use of a sharpened third in the subdominant chord followed by a diminished seventh on G, over a tonic pedal, each note of which resolves up or down a semitone to the tonic chord: Ex.51.

The unexpected lyricism of the left hand of the accompaniment in bars 5 and 6 is immediately repudiated by the stark dissonance of bar 8, where the first chord, the submediant seventh, is sounded over G in the bass. Grieg also sets this bar very subtly, with the semiquaver rest just long enough a hesitation to point Ibsen's contrast, 'gikk — gikk ud (went — went out)', a subtlety frequently ignored in translation.

With the fourth song of this group, *Med en vandlilje* (With a water-lily), the atmosphere is partially but not totally lightened. Grieg marks this setting 'Hurtig og med skælmeri (Fast and with roguishness)', but under-

Ex.51                                                    Stambogsrim

der    sluk - ned   i   det Fjer   -   ne.

(extinguished there in the distance)

neath the playfulness in both poem and music there is a hint of darker forces
and the symbol of the water-sprite is used once again. The accompaniment,
which owes a good deal to Schumann, is the most consciously pianistic for
some time. The voice part is doubled in both hands for the whole song, the
only time this occurs in one of Grieg's songs, but found elsewhere in
Norwegian song literature, yet with the inner syncopation and the minims in
the bass the accompaniment has, also unusually for Grieg, a true independence. Astra Desmond described it further as racing off 'like thoughts ahead of
the spoken word . . . to be brought back to heel by the voice'.[55] As well as
the doubling of the melodic line, the last bar of almost every phrase is echoed
by the piano an octave higher. There are also a number of three-bar phrases in
the song, occasionally effected by the one-bar echo of a two-bar vocal phrase.

Ibsen's poem was written in 1863 and the usual printed first line, 'Se, min
beste, hvad jeg bringer (See, my best one, what I am bringing)' is altered in
the version used in Grieg's setting to 'Se, Marie, hvad jeg bringer'.
Accordingly, the first couplet of the second stanza, 'Vil du den til hjemmet
feste,/fest du på ditt bryst, min beste (Will you then secure it to its home,
firmly on your breast, my best one)', is also altered so that the lines end
'hjemmet vie (dedicate it to its home)' and 'Marie', and this practice has been
followed in Backer Lunde's setting and in all the translations of Grieg's.

In the third stanza of the poem the supernatural makes its appearance, the
danger represented by the water-sprite being used as an analogy for the
dangers of love, and the music accordingly begins to develop from the
charming, basically major key melody of the first two stanzas into the darker
minor. By use of sequences the melody is taken in downward chromatic
phrases through many transitions, until ultimate release comes with a
reiteration of the first stanza back in the tonic key. Thus the song, unlike the
poem, ends with a feeling of happiness and security, while the pianissimo
ending also has more than a touch of 'skælmeri' about it. There is a great deal

of interplay between the voice and the piano and it is essential that the performers observe all the 'crescendo-diminuendo' and 'poco tenuto' markings which Grieg has scrupulously indicated.

Ibsen's love of antithesis in adjacent lines is very apparent in the menace of 'Nøkken lader som han sover (The sprite idles as if asleep)' beside the innocuous 'liljer leger ovenover (lilies play above)'. Also notable is the contrast between the beginning of the third stanza, 'Vogt dig, barn, for tjernets strømme (Beware child, of the lake's currents)' and the beginning of the fourth, with its increased sense of warning, 'Barn, din barm er tjernets strømme (Child, your bosom is the lake's current)'. The word 'Nøkken (the water-sprite)' is translated by Henzen as a proper name, 'Neck', derived presumably from the German verb 'necken', to tease or chaff. This, however, makes no sense when transferred directly to English as 'Neck, the water-sprite', as given by L. Swinyard in his translation for the Novello edition of the song, published in 1958.

The fifth song, *Borte!* (Gone!), returns to the strange, elusive world of *Stambogsrim* with another brief episode, this time a seemingly commonplace one of guests departing. However, the desolation of house and garden obviously mirrors that of the poet and the essence is encapsulated in the last two lines: 'hun var en gæst kun, – og nu er hun borte (She was just a guest, – and now she has gone)'. As in *En svane* the lines are short, with four of five or six syllables in each of the three stanzas. It is one of Ibsen's most concise poems, described by Edvard Beyer as the 'finest and most delicate of all',[56] and Wicksteed suggests it shows that Ibsen could rival Heine in conveying vivid impressions with great simplicity.[57] It was written in the summer of 1864 and is generally assumed to concern Thea Bruun, a young woman Ibsen met in Italy, who was to die soon afterwards of tuberculosis. No doubt because of the quality of the poem, surely one of the finest in Scandinavian literature, Grieg's setting, in only thirteen bars, is also one of his masterpieces.

He captures the haunting quality once more in short phrases, every bar of the vocal melody beginning after a quaver rest. The style is like recitative, and the melody, although somewhat less angular than that of *Stambogsrim*, again makes use of downward intervals, here perfect and diminished fifths. The piano accompaniment moves slowly (the song, like *Stambogsrim*, is marked 'langsomt, talende'), mostly in crotchets and minims, while the harmony contains a good deal of chromatic movement, the many dissonances used to underline the words, for example 'øde (desolation)', and to mirror the despair of the poem as a whole, from the very first bar. The final echo in the piano must surely be Grieg's most despairing and haunting use of this device: Ex.52. Interestingly, Eyvind Alnæs in his setting of the poem (op. 1 no. 1, written in 1892) uses a similar recitative style to Grieg's and at the end has a most effective half bar's silence before the piano echoes the last two notes: Ex.53.

Ex.52                                                     Grieg, Borte!

(she was just a guest, and now she has gone.)

Ex.53                                                     Alnæs, Borte!

Alnæs' downward phrase, however, has a finality about it, while Grieg's upward interval, like Ibsen's poem, leaves the situation unresolved.

In his letters to Finck, Grieg names his 'teachers' in the use of chromaticism as Bach, Mozart and Wagner, who employed the technique to underline the 'deepest, most intimate things'.[58] Grieg developed his own ideas for the significant use of chromatic elements and cited *En svane* and 'especially' *Borte!* as examples of how he was progressing.

No translation can do justice to the original, and the title and final word, like 'svane', is one of those disyllables so frequent in Norwegian and so lacking in English. 'Departed' does not have the emptiness of 'borte', any more than does the German 'geschieden', and Grieg in his correspondence with Molard said he preferred the French title 'L'Hôte' to 'Disparue'. He also suggested the final words be 'Hôte apparue En ce soir de fête! Tu t'es enfuie Au fond des ténèbres',[59] which Molard adopted. William Halverson, in his translation in the *GGA*, has captured the opening atmosphere very well with 'The last farewells spoken, the mirth suspended . . .'

The final song of the six Ibsen settings, *En fuglevise* (A bird-song), is in the truly playful mood that is so rarely found in the poet's output. The poem tells of two lovers meeting under the trees, while the birds watch and sing around them, and was written in the 1850s during Ibsen's time at the Bergen theatre, when he was in love with the sixteen-year-old Rikke Holst. Unfortunately, it does not find Grieg at his most inspired and was omitted from the German edition of the op.25 songs. It comes as something of a relief, however, after the despair and fatefulness of the other five songs in the album; 'spring', as Monrad Johansen saw it, 'after a dark and hard winter'. [60] The whole tone of the song is much more cheerful than the earlier ones, indeed almost impudent, and Benestad and Schjelderup-Ebbe describe it as having 'something of the innocence of a good children's song'. [61]

The music opens with peacefully moving triplets in the left hand accompaniment, and the vocal melody is almost exactly echoed at half a bar's distance in the right hand. In the fourth bar the music is lifted from the tonic A flat to a bright C major, the opposite direction to Grieg's usual favourite modulation. The echo of the second phrase is repeated until it becomes like a bird-song and the new chirping motif, first heard in the eighth bar, is later used a good deal throughout the song: Ex.54.

The music is so essentially cheerful that it is impossible even to take the lovers' 'smukt farvel (sweet farewell)' with any seriousness, especially as the song increases in tempo throughout. The opening motifs are used in sequence all through the song, but the inspiration does fade and the key changes in the last third of the song become a little trite.

With the exception of *En fuglevise*, all the op.25 songs may be seen to portray the musician whose extraordinary ability is only achieved through considerable personal suffering and who finds that the ambitions he has cherished are after all beyond reach. This is most obvious in *Spillemænd*, but in *Stambogsrim* and *Borte!* the unattainability of desires – personal or musical – could be seen to reflect the composer's own situation. The swan is unable to express his innermost feelings except, finally, in song and even the water-sprite lurking below the surface of the stream in *Med en vandlilje* is seen to represent the dangers of love, particularly perhaps for the artist. One should not be misled, however, into thinking these songs excessively doom-laden. While not having the ecstatic vocal lines of *Jeg elsker dig* or *Det første møte*, they are nevertheless full of deep emotion and an inherent empathy for the voice. In four of them Grieg has pared down the musical idiom to its barest minimum, superbly matching the verse. He has often been censured as a miniaturist, but if this is miniaturism, he shows it here to be a fine craft indeed.

The six Ibsen settings were published in December 1876 by C.C. Lose in

Ex.54

En Fuglevise

(for) - bud - ne Sted.

(the forbidden place)

Copenhagen and are dedicated to Julius Steenberg, the Dutch singer whom Grieg described as 'a song-poet and a poetic singer, by the grace of God'.[62] These qualities are essential for this album where, more than anywhere else, it is the singer's ability to interpret deeper meanings that is vitally important, while sheer beauty of sound could take second place. In a letter to Frants Beyer from Rome written in March 1884, Grieg showed that Ibsen also appreciated this: at a party at the home of the Norwegian artist Kristian Ross, at which Ibsen, not noted for his affability, was also present, Grieg relates that

> Nina sang a great deal, including almost all my songs to Ibsen's poetry and, imagine, after lille Håkon [*Margretes Vuggesang*] and especially after *Jeg kaldte Dig mit Lykkebud* [*Stambogsrim*] and *Svanen* (!) the ice-berg melted and with tears in his eyes he came over to the piano, where we were, shook our hands, almost without being *able* to say anything. He mumbled something about this being understanding, and I don't have to tell you that Nina on this occasion did not sing any less intelligently than she always does.[63]

Whatever the problems that drove Grieg to Ibsen's verse, they were temporarily resolved and it is largely the light-heartedness of the last of the op.25 settings that is carried over into his next songs.

# Notes

1    Ibsen: *The Wild Duck*, Act 3; that is, the ideal of truth before beauty.
2    The pavilion may still be seen; it is one of the buildings in the Gamle Bergen (Old Bergen) Museum at Sandviken.
3    It is noteworthy that a country that had come so recently into the mainstream of European culture should have had such funds for artists and scholars.
4    Grieg to Bjørnson, 12 September 1874 from Kristiansand.
5    Grieg to Bjørnson, 14 May 1875 from Leipzig.
6    A troll-king in the Dovre mountains, usually called the Mountain King in English.
7    A large, invisible, serpent-like creature.
8    Ibsen to Grieg, 23 January 1874 from Dresden.
9    An interesting parallel may be drawn between Grieg's description here and that of Elisabeth Lutyens, who disparagingly termed the pseudo-folk music of twentieth-century England (by which she meant Vaughan Williams et al.) 'cowpat music'.
10    Grieg to Beyer, 27 August 1874 from Sandviken.
11    Grieg to Josephson, 28 August 1874 from Sandviken.
12    Grieg to Ibsen, 25 October 1874 from Leipzig.
13    Grieg to Winding, 5 April 1875.
14    Grieg to Hennum, 14 December 1875 from Bergen.
15    Grieg to Finck, 17 July 1900.
16    Grieg to Beyer, 20 December 1905 from Christiania.
17    Grieg to Hennum, 14 December 1875.
18    Grieg to Oda Nielsen, 7 May 1902.
19    Grieg to Hennum, 14 December 1875.
20    Ibid.
21    David Monrad Johansen: *Edvard Grieg*, 1934, p.204.
22    Josephson's memoirs, quoted in Benestad and Schjelderup-Ebbe: *Edvard Grieg, mennesket og kunstneren*, 1980, p.159.
23    Nils Grinde: *Norsk Musikkhistorie*, 1971, p.169.
24    Peter Watts, introduction to *Peer Gynt*, Penguin Books 1966, p.16.
25    Michael Meyer: *Ibsen*, 1974, p.426.
26    H.J. Nielsen: *Omkring Peer Gynt* (About Peer Gynt), p.120; quoted in Willy Dahl: *Ibsen*, 1974.
27    Ibid.
28    Grieg to Ibsen, 15 March 1876 from Bergen.
29    Josephson's memoirs quoted by Meyer: *Ibsen*, p.406.
30    Oda Petersen, later Nielsen (1851–1936). She married Jens Petersen in 1871, and after his death married Martinius Nielsen in 1884. In Marie Beyer's edition of Grieg's letters to her husband, the actress is referred to as 'Fru N.N.', but a letter from Grieg to Beyer of 21 January 1886 has 'Oda Nielsen'.
31    Grieg to Beyer, 22 December 1885 from Copenhagen.
32    Grieg to Max Abraham, 12 February 1892 from Troldhaugen.
33    Grieg to Röntgen, 19 February 1893 from Leipzig.
34    Eduard Hanslick, quoted in Benestad and Schjelderup-Ebbe: *Edvard Grieg, mennesket og kunstneren*, p.163.
35    Johanne Luise Heiberg (1812–90), Danish actress who directed the first Copenhagen production of *The League of Youth*.
36    Ibsen to Georg Brandes, 18 May 1871 from Dresden.

37   Georg Brandes, quoted by Meyer: *Ibsen*, p.364.
38   Grieg, quoted in *Edvard Grieg, mennesket og kunstneren*, p.175.
39   Philip Wicksteed: Introduction to F.E. Garrett's *Lyrics and Poems from Ibsen*, 1912, p.xvi.
40   *Edvard Grieg, mennesket og kunstneren*, pp.189–90.
41   Ibid., p.180.
42   As in key C published by Hansen; in the first edition by C.C. Lose the key was E.
43   David Monrad Johansen: *Edvard Grieg*, p.207.
44   Wicksteed: Introduction to *Lyrics and Poems from Ibsen*, p.xi.
45   Dagmar Møller: *Griegminne*, 1940; quoted in *Edvard Grieg, mennesket og kunstneren*, p.259.
46   Grieg to Finck, 17 July 1900; the letter is written in German and all song titles and quotations are given in German.
47   Grieg to Bella Edwards, 1 December 1895 from Leipzig.
48   Like *Spillemænd* the song was originally published by C.C. Lose in a higher key, G.
49   John Horton: *Grieg*, 1974, p.179.
50   Astra Desmond in *Grieg: A Symposium*, ed Gerald Abraham, 1948, p.83.
51   Wicksteed: Introduction to *Lyrics and Poems from Ibsen*, p.xii.
52   Sergius Kagen: *Music for the Voice*, Indiana University Press, 1968, p.614.
53   Grieg to Molard, 13 June 1894 from Christiania.
54   The melody for each strophe of *Morgenbønn på skolen* is only eight bars long, but scarcely qualifies as art song.
55   Desmond in *Grieg: A Symposium*, p.84.
56   Edvard Beyer: *Ibsen: The Man and his Work* (trans. Marie Wells), 1978, p.89.
57   Wicksteed: Introduction to *Lyrics and Poems from Ibsen*, p.xii.
58   Grieg to Finck, 17 July 1900.
59   Grieg to Molard, 5 June 1894 from Grefsen Bad, nr. Christiania.
60   Monrad Johansen: *Edvard Grieg*, p.209.
61   *Edvard Grieg, mennesket og kunstneren*, p.180.
62   Grieg in a letter of recommendation, 24 October 1900 from Voksenkollen Sanitorium.
63   Grieg to Beyer, 19 March 1884 from Rome.

# 7 '... Awakened from a long, long trance'

Grieg set more poems of John Paulsen than of any other poet as solo songs – seventeen, two more than either Andersen or Vinje, three more than Bjørnson or Garborg and six more than Ibsen.[1] Paulsen was born in 1851 and is regarded as a minor poet, frequently not even mentioned in books on Norwegian literature. He was a friend of Grieg's from their early days in Bergen, the recipient of many letters from the composer and the author of several volumes of memoirs. Grieg and Paulsen spent the summer of 1876 together, travelling first to Bavaria for the first Wagner festival in Bayreuth, where they heard performances of the complete *Ring* cycle, described by Grieg to Bjørnson as 'the most remarkable work of our whole cultural history'. The two then went to the Tyrol at Ibsen's invitation, to visit the writer at Gossensass. That Grieg regarded Paulsen as a close friend may be seen from a letter to the poet of 1876: 'There is nothing nicer than a friend's letter! My imagination is rarely in such a stir as when I write to a friend! And you are such a one to me, I feel that while I sit here writing. Not because I start the letter with: Dear friend! – but because you are what you are.'[2]

Paulsen was a native of Bergen and in his youth was admired by Ibsen as a poet and dramatist. His poetry, however, is weak and sentimental and lacks 'the authentic stamp of personal experience'[3] which had so marked the Ibsen poems. On occasion, more so in the op.58 album than in the op.26, one cannot help but feel that Grieg chose Paulsen's poems for the sake of their friendship rather than from any artistic motives. He obviously sensed something of Paulsen's weaknesses, however, for just after he had completed the op.26 songs, Grieg wrote to him: 'In you I see so much of myself from earlier days. Therefore I can say to you: acquire steel, steel, steel! And now you ask: where do I get it from? There is just one terrible answer: It is bought with the heart's blood. God knows that I speak from experience.'[4] And in 1881, after seeing a new book of Paulsen's, he wrote, 'You have so much in both your personality and your talent that reminds me of H.C. Andersen. Your fund of *naiveté* will only come into its own in the world of fairy tales. Beware!' But Paulsen was never to attain the heights that might have been expected from his early poetry and plays, and he is now chiefly known through Grieg's settings and for his memoirs, which contain some entertaining anecdotes of contemporary figures.

In a letter to Bjørnson at the beginning of 1876 Grieg described his transition from Ibsen to Paulsen as coming out of a 'dark and melancholy' winter — both figuratively and in fact, we are led to suppose — and as being 'awakened from a long, long trance'. Paulsen's verse, while containing some of the same emotions as Ibsen's, is clothed in much more tangible imagery and more easily accessible language and has little if any of Ibsen's elusive and haunted qualities, although some of the shadows of the op. 25 songs may still be felt in the first three settings of op. 26, *Fem Digte af John Paulsen* (Five Poems by . . .).

The first of the op. 26 album, *Et Håb* (A hope), is bright and cheerful, a joyful song of the hope the poet sees in the coming of spring. Grieg's music is not without its hints of doubt, however, and there are some interesting modulations throughout the song. He underlines the words 'min Glæde . . . vil man den forstå? (my joy . . . will anyone understand it?)' with a downward diminished seventh in the vocal line and a hint of the minor key, as well as a ritardando.

As usual, it is in the second half of the strophe that the harmony becomes

Ex. 55                                                                      Et Håb

(My heart burns, it trembles, beats in time,)

more interesting. Grieg hints at things to come by changing his harmonization of a thrice-repeated vocal phrase and, with a chromatic sliding from B flat to C flat, the tonality becomes F flat major: Ex.55.

A similar chromatic movement takes the music into F major and yet another back to the tonic E flat major. The whole is effective, if a little self-conscious. The vocal line is pleasantly varied and has a comfortable range of a tenth. The climax to high G is managed painlessly: Grieg is once again considerate enough to ask for his high notes fortissimo, and gives the singer room for breath before the final phrase. The song is strophic and here the end of the vocal line is well suited to the culmination of both stanzas. Each strophe is followed by a lengthy postlude, which is written almost entirely over a tonic pedal, for the low E flats in the bass are held with the sustaining pedal in most of the instances where a higher tonic is not being sounded.

The poem is exuberant and the two moments of doubt — 'Will anyone understand it?' in the first stanza and 'If I dared believe it' in the second — are not allowed to interrupt the overall feeling of joy and hope. The expression of the emotion and the imagery, however, are conventional. Henzen's German translation for the Peters edition is very accurate and one only regrets that he could not fit that first question within the original phrasing, for that gives part of the key to Grieg's setting. In a letter to William Molard of June 1894 Grieg discusses the French translation and mentions a few points 'where the declamation might be improved'[5] and gives examples: Exx.56a–c.

In the second Paulsen setting, *Jeg reiste en deilig sommerkvæld* (I went one lovely summer evening), we are back in the realms of Norwegian folk music, with a drone bass on the tonic fifth, a simple vocal line with delicate

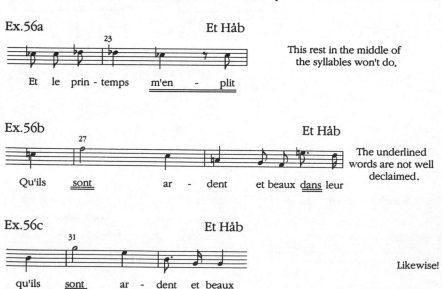

Ex.56a — Et Håb

Et    le   prin - temps    m'en - plit

This rest in the middle of the syllables won't do.

Ex.56b — Et Håb

Qu'ils    sont    ar - dent    et beaux dans leur

The underlined words are not well declaimed.

Ex.56c — Et Håb

qu'ils    sont    ar - dent    et beaux

Likewise!

decorations and a wavering between minor and major modes. The song is written almost entirely over the tonic pedal and there is the now familiar sounding of the leading note, as well as the minor seventh, against the tonic. The accompaniment in the middle section, which is in the tonic major, makes much use of acciaccaturas, which fill out the right hand chords and strengthen the folksong-like atmosphere.

The poem begins as a straightforward description of a Norwegian valley, with the fjord and the birch trees, the herd-girl with her goats, but in the third stanza a hint of sadness creeps in, as the poet wonders what the girl thinks about, 'alone, lonely in the narrow valley', and we feel something of the atmosphere of *Prinsessen* in the last four lines:

> Mon længslen ej over Fjeld sig svang?
>   Tys, luren svarer!
>   Mod Fjeldet farer
>   en Vedmodsklang.

(I wonder if her longing ranged out over the mountain?/Hush, the horn answers!/Towards the mountain travels/a sound of melancholy.)

The poem has a seven-line verse form, with four long lines followed by three short ones. Paulsen occasionally used stanzas with five or seven lines, some of them of unequal length (for example, in *Farvel*, op.59 no.5) and more unusual rhyme-schemes, but even though his poems are pleasing enough, the imagery is rarely more than commonplace. They never surprise or startle, as do those of Ibsen, Vinje or Garborg.

There is an interesting letter from Grieg to Paulsen which concerns *Jeg reiste*:

> . . . I now have many of your poems well translated into German. First Feddersen tried, but that was madness, so an attempt was made by a local doctor who writes and who has been in Norway. That was – if not madness – then certainly not poetry. Then at last I made the acquaintance of a young man of letters, Henzen,[6] who is the editor of every other drama-criticism paper and this man to be sure has no Norwegian, but is poetically gifted and earlier even spent ½ year at the Leipzig Music Conservatory. It's a rich find, for the musical declamation plays a major part.

Grieg then quotes the first stanza of Henzen's version of *Jeg reiste*, which now appears in the Peters edition:

> Am schönsten Sommerabend war's
> Ich ging durch ein einsam Thal,
> Der Fels stand licht und die Sonne schwand,
> Der Fjord war blau und grün der Strand –
>   Und Sommerlüfte
>   Und Birkendüfte
>   Und still das Land.

and adds, 'Remember how many difficulties and consider – and you have to admit, it is successful. The Norwegian mountain music quite certainly is not there, but that might also be impossible. Besides, one gets that in the music.'[7] Henzen's version is, in fact, very accurate and retains most of the spirit as well as the form of the original.

The middle song of the op. 26 album was omitted from the Peters edition, both in the first and subsequent printings, and neither did it appear in any of the collections with German or French translations, although it is restored in the GGA. *Den Ærgjerrige* (The ambitious one) is a strange song in some ways and not really typical of Grieg, in that it is very much more pianistically conceived than vocally inspired. It does not have the sincerity of the deeply felt Ibsen settings, the emotion here comes from the outside, both in the words and in the music. The idea behind the poem – of someone achieving ambitions at the expense of happiness – may once again have struck a chord with Grieg at this particular time, although here the poem is written from the point of view of the one left behind, whose position is summarized in the last two lines:

> Vel tabte jeg min Lykke;
> men du har tabt sig selv!
> (I certainly lost my happiness; but you have lost yourself!)

However, Grieg's repetitions of the final line lessens its impact and in any case the point is rather laboured in the poem.

The vocal line makes much use of sequence, and apart from the big climax to a high G at the end, offers the singer little chance for either vocal display or intellectual interpretation. The piano accompaniment, on the other hand, is very complex, and after the introductory chords becomes almost a *perpetuum mobile*. The 'allegro agitato' marking epitomizes the whole song, which unfortunately fails to convince.

*Med en primula veris* (With a primrose), on the other hand, is quite a different matter and is by far the best of the op. 26 songs. It is one of Grieg's most popular songs, rightly so, and is something of a companion-piece to *Med en Vandlilje*. The poems may not be of comparable quality, but the music to the Paulsen verse has something of the 'skælmeri' the composer asked for in the Ibsen setting. Grieg always responded best to the really fine poetry, but this is one example of a lovely song that rises above the mediocre verse. The poem advocates the enjoyment of spring; summer and autumn may have their joys, but spring is the loveliest time, and the poet asks his love not to scorn the spring's first flowers just because the roses are still to come.

The song has a beautiful, gently lilting melody with delicate decorations and the vocal line is doubled throughout by the right hand of the accompaniment. The middle section makes use of a chromatic scale passage, an infrequent occurrence in the vocal line of a Grieg song, but which exactly captures the charm and slight archness of the poem. The accompaniment is simple but expressive and the harmonic interest lies in the chromatically altered notes and the seventh chords, especially in the clash of the leading-note against the tonic, which Grieg absorbed from Norwegian folk music. The Hansen edition gives a repeat from bar 16 to the beginning, which is not found in the German edition. It is rarely observed and does rather spoil the ABA structure.

The last of the Paulsen settings in this group returns to the somewhat artificial style of *Den Ærgjerrige*. *På Skogstien* (On the woodland path) is another strange song, again chromatically involved, but this time without the impetuosity or the complex accompaniment of the former. Paulsen compares the changing of the season from summer to autumn with the changing of his beloved's mind. The introduction has a chromatic melody and counterpoint (Ex.57) and the right hand melody is taken over and extended by the voice.

Ex.57                                                                          På Skogstein

Some unusual dissonances are caused by the sounding of the tonic and the dominant in the accompaniment left hand against a descending chromatic phrase in the vocal melody and a rising melodic minor scale in the right hand, a complex arrangement which occurs several times. The brief postlude seems rather superfluous, and in its diatonic harmony has little in common with what has gone before.

In the poem Paulsen remembers summer, when 'every leaf was green with hope', and reflects sadly that now the leaves and flowers are gone. A repeat of the middle and last sections of the song (setting the second and third stanzas) given in some editions, including Hansen, detracts from the ironic twist at the end, where the poet discloses that it is not just the season that has 'changed its mind', but also his beloved.

This song was originally translated into German by Benjamin Feddersen, despite Grieg's comments in the letter to Paulsen quoted above, and in the first Peters edition the song is ascribed to him, although Henzen is named as the translator at the beginning of the album. The later Peters editions have a translation by Schmidt, headed 'Hans Schmidt nach [after] Paulsen', although his version is rather loose, especially in the first stanza, and Feddersen's is actually nearer to the original. The German versions are entitled 'Herbststimmung', the title confusingly also given to the German translation of *Når jeg vil dø*, op.59 no.1, also a poem by Paulsen.

The op.26 songs *Fem Digte af John Paulsen* were published in December 1876 by C.C. Lose in Copenhagen and were dedicated to the poet. The best of them, *Med en Primula veris* and *Jeg reiste en deilig Sommerkvæld*, cannot be compared with those in the Ibsen album, nor are they indicative of the music Grieg was to produce to Norwegian poetry just five years later.

## Notes

1    Grieg considered a total of twenty poems by Garborg, but six settings exist only as brief sketches.
2    Grieg to Paulsen, 8 September 1876 from Christiania.
3    Benestad and Schjelderup-Ebbe: *Edvard Grieg, mennesket og kunstneren*, 1980, p.180.
4    Grieg to Paulsen, 27 June 1876.
5    Grieg to Molard, 5 June 1894 from Christiania.
6    Wilhelm Henzen, author of many German translations for the Peters' editions.
7    Grieg to Paulsen, 7 March 1879 from Leipzig.

# 8 'The Mountain Thrall'

After his holiday with Paulsen in Bayreuth and the Tyrol, and concerts in Sweden with Nina to earn some money, Grieg returned to Christiania early in 1877. His unhappiness with life in the capital was becoming unbearable. He spent all his time there teaching and rehearsing and, as he said in a letter to Max Abraham of Peters, looking forward to the summer when he could 'go away to the country and work'. Abraham invited Grieg to Leipzig and August Winding asked him to Copenhagen, but he needed more than short periods away. What he wanted was the peace and quiet of a home on Norway's west coast and he was particularly attracted by the emptiness of the Hardanger area.

Towards the end of June the Griegs went to Ullensvang, near the head of the Sørfjord, the Hardanger fjord's southern arm, to a farm at Øvre (Upper) Børve which Grieg loved. The thought that he had left Christiania for good delighted him. He rented the little school-house to work in, but realized that because of the weather it would be impossible to use it or indeed to stay up in Øvre Børve during the winter. Accordingly the Griegs moved to Lofthus, a little further north along the Sørfjord, where the composer had built a small hut in which he could write.

In September and October 1877 Grieg gave two concerts in Bergen which provided enough money to enable him to spend the winter at Lofthus. The music coming from the hut – called 'Komposten', a pun on the words for 'tune' and 'compost' – began to attract some attention, so Grieg arranged for it to be moved to a site nearer the edge of the fjord, where he had more privacy. This was done in the traditional way, called in dialect *dugnad*, complete, on rollers moved by about fifty of the local people, a day-long task, which involved supplying the workers with suitable refreshment and even musical entertainment from the composer. Grieg's friend, the artist Wilhelm Peters, wrote and illustrated an amusing account of the operation. The hut was sold by Grieg in 1880 and was put to a number of uses until, in 1949, it was bought back by the Lofthus community, and it is now kept as a miniature Grieg museum.

In spite of attaining the longed-for peace and quiet, Grieg at first could not settle to work. He wrote to Matthison-Hansen that he had to do something towards his art, although nothing he did gave him any satisfaction. He was, however, still willing to 'battle through the larger forms, cost what it will'.[1] In October 1877 he wrote to Winding that he had had to go to Ullensvang if he was not to 'go under' as an artist, and went on: 'You will be surprised, perhaps, but you should know what inner struggles I have borne these last years and you will understand me. All possible external circumstances have hindered me in following my calling . . . I have lost the talent for the large forms – and if one loses that after having had it, which at one time I really did – then farewell future! . . . I am again in the process of steeping myself in my art and with God's help, something will come.'[2]

Grieg's artistic problems were compounded by those in his relationship with Nina and the complaints about his work were probably a way of covering up the more personal difficulties. David Monrad Johansen has said that this period shows the most intimate connection between Grieg's life and his art, and that 'hand in hand with the artistic crises he is going through at this time, are also personal experiences, which seem to have a great bearing on the whole of his destiny.'[3] Monrad Johansen, however, was writing during Nina Grieg's lifetime and he did not feel able to say all he might about the situation. Nina's feelings of loneliness, living out in the Hardanger area, were natural enough and a letter from Grieg's sister to their brother speaks of sadness that Edvard and Nina have 'distanced themselves so much from each other'.[4] Grieg, as has been seen, had earlier had doubts about combining marriage and art and in September 1879 he wrote to Paulsen, 'A woman has never comprehended and never learns to comprehend the great, wild, unlimited things in a man's – in an artist's love. And I am right in this, as I am certain at the same time that an artist should never marry . . .'[5]

Several years of tense relationships were to pass before the couple found a new peace. Nevertheless, the period produced a number of notable, albeit mostly instrumental compositions, written in short, hectic bursts: the String Quartet, a movement for Piano Trio, the last of the four *Albumblad*, op.28, the *Improvisations on Norwegian Folk-songs*, op.29, the *Album* for male-voice choir, op.30, and *Den Bergtekne* (The mountain thrall).

Still hankering after the larger forms he felt he had to master, Grieg had plans for a large-scale work for solo baritone, choir and orchestra, based on material from Norwegian folk-song, but he could find no suitable text. He read a collection of folk ballads by M.B. Landstad, which had been published in 1853, and in this found some Old Norwegian verses which related the legend of *Den Bergtekne*, 'the one taken into the mountain' or, to use John Horton's English title, 'The Mountain Thrall'.[6] The story is of a young man who wanders in the forest near an enchanted rune-stone, where he is bewitched by the daughter of a *jotul*, a mountain giant, so that he is unable ever to find his way back to a normal life. Grieg seems to have felt a similar affinity with this text as he had a year earlier with Ibsen's *Spillemænd* and although it did not provide the material for the large-scale work he had at first envisaged, the composer put a great deal of himself into the resulting setting.

The fragment consists of seven four-line stanzas in the *gammelstev* form and indeed Grieg sometimes referred to the work as a *stev*, first as a subtitle on the manuscript score, then in a letter to Beyer of the same time, 8 April 1878, and also in later letters, demonstrating that he envisaged his setting as being very much in keeping with the Old Norse tradition in that verse form. The seven stanzas fall into three groups of two (the seventh is a reiteration of the first) and each pair is closely related. Indeed, in each of the first two pairs, the first and the third lines are identical, while the second and fourth change only a little. The sixth stanza has an identical first line to the fifth, but otherwise is different, although the content is similar. The first two stanzas tell of the young man losing his way, the second two how he was chased by the jotul and bewitched by the jotul's daughter, and the third pair describes how everything in nature has its kith and kin, while he has no-one.

The unity in the poem created by these pairings is increased by a certain amount of both vowel and consonant alliteration after the style of Old Norse poetry, and Grieg took pains to underline these characteristics in his music. He described his methods to Finck: 'The concise brevity of style, which is so strongly expressed in Old Norwegian poetry, I have also striven after here in my music, and what I understand of it I have perhaps shown best in this little piece.'[7]

The work is scored for solo baritone, two horns and strings. It is more a miniature cantata than a song and falls into three main sections, which correspond to the poem's three pairs of stanzas, and Grieg's use of thematic material is much more cogent here than in the earlier extended songs, *Udfarten*, op.9 no.4 and *Efteraarsstormen*, op.18 no.4. The fourteen-bar introduction sets the scene with an atmosphere of foreboding. The first chord, despite a key-signature of one sharp, is G minor, which gives rise to a false relation as it moves to the dominant seventh chord of the tonic E minor. The horns' opening theme and the accompanying descending chromatic scale in the bass recall the opening of the G minor *Ballade*:

Ex.58　　　　　　　　　　　　　　　　　　　　　　Den Bergtekne

This theme is taken over by the upper strings and then the voice. The innocent-seeming opening statement, 'Eg for vilt i veduskogin (I was lost in the dark forest)', is belied by the ominous descending chromatic scales in the lower strings. The second stanza is set to one of Grieg's rare chromatic melodies, rhythmically almost identical with the first theme, which rises in agitation and then falls in despair to the line, 'eg hev inkji vegin funnid (I have not found the path)'. The interlude between this and the next section is built on material from the opening, but with a B flat and then an E flat introduced in the bass, which soon takes the key to G minor, instead of, as might have been expected, the relative major key. The agitated accompanying chords here in the upper strings, especially the A sharp and A natural clash with the horns' B natural (bar 37), are particularly effective in underlining the feeling of despair:

Ex.59

Den Bergtekne

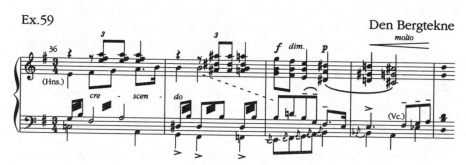

The new section, in G minor, marked 'Allegro agitato' and with a change of time-signature from $\frac{3}{4}$ to $\frac{6}{8}$, sets the second pair of stanzas. The agitation of the young man pursued by the jøtul is immediately apparent from the violin rhythm and the horns' sforzandi, and the horns also anticipate the vocal melody, which is now full of the young man's desperation at being unable to find or see the jøtul's daughters, although he tries to lure them out. For the fourth stanza the vocal melody, after beginning as before, moves down to form a sequence a minor third lower, while the string chords move upwards. The lower vocal tessitura also underlines the young man's resignation to his fate. A dominant chord of E minor leads back to a reiteration of the opening horn melody, once again in $\frac{3}{4}$, but the B flat which is heard three times in the bass is always hinting at the key of G minor and the harmony is even more chromatic than before.

The ensuing passage in C major has a slow *springdans* rhythm that lulls one into a false sense of security as the words describe seemingly guileless scenes of nature. A new horn figure adds to the calm and peaceful atmosphere, although the rhythm remains similar to the first theme. For the second half of the stanza the string accompaniment becomes fuller, with a counter-melody in sixths in the violins and violas. The second half of this third pair of stanzas shows more agitation in the overlapping of the vocal and string lines and a strange, almost unearthly effect is created by the low pedal F and the inverted pedal Gs, sounded together, and particularly by the use of the falsetto voice for the top G at bar 97:

Ex.60                                                                Den Bergtekne
                                                                        (Falset)

(Fis - kin ut - i fag - ran vat - ni,          og      i - konn up i tre___)

(The fish out in the beautiful water, and the squirrel up in the tree)

John Horton has suggested that this also depicts the young man's rising hysteria.[8]

The peace of the earlier bars has now been shattered and the ballad reaches its climax with repeated top Fs for the baritone and an abrupt change to a chord of the Neapolitan sixth in the accompaniment at the words 'men ingin så heve eg! (but I have no-one!)'. This melody makes use of the 'Grieg motif' (F, E, C), although the notes are not tonic–leading-note–dominant in this key, and it may be that the composer used his familiar motif with dissonant harmony to illustrate, consciously or sub-consciously, his own feeling of having no-one. Certainly the despair of the repeated line is deeply felt, and heavy string chords lead back to E minor for a recapitulation of the opening section. The string writing throughout, as so often with Grieg in this medium, is excellent and the *divisi* chords in these bars (104 to 109) are particularly effective.

*Den Bergtekne* was written during the winter of 1877 to 1878 at Ullensvang, and the completed manuscript is dated April 1878. However, the work was not published until 1882, when Hansen's produced both the score and a piano edition, each with Old Norwegian, Danish and German texts. The piano score was prepared by Holger Dahl, who also provided the Danish translation.

*Den Bergtekne* is often performed in Norway, but is nowhere nearly as well-known outside Scandinavia as it deserves to be, and for this, once again, poor translations must be in part to blame. Even the Danish does not have the flow and colour of the original, nor is it completely accurate, and unfortunately the German, French and English translations followed it.

The piece is dedicated 'To my friend Gottfred Matthison-Hansen', to whom Grieg wrote in September 1881, 'I know no-one better to dedicate it to'.[9] He also describes the piece as having 'marks and splashes of pure and simple heart's blood'. The first performance was given in Copenhagen on 5 April 1879, with Thorvald Lammers as soloist and the composer conducting. Nine years later, by which time Lammers was forty-seven, it seems that he was finding the tessitura of the work rather high and asked Grieg if it could be transposed. The composer replied in no uncertain terms:

> To transpose Den Bergtekne down to D would be as wrong in your interests as in mine. The piece would lose all its character, not to mention that the double basses, which, with their low E, contribute to the melancholy colour, *do not go lower* than E. You see then that there can therefore be no talk of it. But how can you say that the last part of the work doesn't suit you? It sounded splendid in Christiania, you know. The little passage in C major is after all sung with half voice and the only high G *is* taken falsetto. [10]

Grieg was very fond of *Den Bergtekne* and performances during his lifetime were very well received. In a letter to Beyer he described a performance in Christiania as sounding 'much better than I had ever heard it before . . . Lammers was at his height'. He went on: 'The story of the giant was of such a glittering demonic effect that even I was completely captivated.' [11] He then described the reception after the concert, held in the hall of the Arts Society, where two painters, Munthe and Bloch, had produced a mural based on *Den Bergtekne*, with the vocal line in huge notes over the whole and depicting, amongst the scenes illustrated, the composer himself on his knees in front of the jotul's daughter, while the jotul, depicted as the sculptor Bergslien, chases him! A further letter to Beyer in December of the same year describes another performance in Copenhagen, which was encored. Here the soloist was the Danish opera-singer Niels Juel Simonsen, and the work was presumably then sung in Danish, for Grieg quotes a line to Beyer in this language and not the original Old Norwegian.

The work is unique in Grieg's output, both in its scope and scoring and in its embodiment of the composer's feelings for Norwegian folklore. Although the nationalistic symbolism may not appeal to non-Scandinavians, it is nevertheless a pity that such a piece should be so little known abroad. Even with piano accompaniment, the song makes a strong impression and, although then admittedly lacking the idiomatic horn and string writing, it should certainly still appeal to any baritone with a predilection for dramatic interpretation. It contains some of Grieg's best and most personal writing and was described by the composer Sverre Jordan as 'perhaps his most brilliant work'. [12]

## Notes

1   Grieg to Matthison-Hansen, 13 August 1877 from Lofthus.
2   Grieg to Winding, 28 October 1877.
3   David Monrad Johansen: *Edvard Grieg*, 1934, pp.242–3.
4   Quoted in Benestad and Schjelderup-Ebbe: *Edvard Grieg, mennesket og kunstner-en*, 1980, p.188.
5   Grieg to Paulsen, 8 September 1879.
6   John Horton: *Grieg*, 1974, pp.158–61.
7   Grieg to Finck, 17 July 1900.
8   Horton: *Grieg*, p.159.
9   Grieg to MNatthison-Hansen, 18 September 1881.
10   Grieg to Thorvald Lammers, 20 May 1888 from London.
11   Grieg to Beyer, 25 October 1885 from Christiania.
12   Sverre Jordan: *Edvard Grieg. En oversikt . . .*, 1954, p.31.

# 9 'The Goal'

A few months after completing *Den Bergtekne*, Grieg set off on his travels once more. He had applied for another travelling scholarship in April 1877, which was at first turned down and then eventually granted one year later. The journeying began in October 1878, when he went to Cologne for a performance of his String Quartet, and this was followed by other concerts in Germany. The winter was spent in Leipzig where, for the first time, Grieg met Brahms, with whom he got on well. In the spring of 1879 he gave two concerts during a number of weeks he spent in Copenhagen and by the end of may he was back, by himself, in Hardanger. Here for the first time, as he wrote to Beyer, he felt lonely after all the social activity of the previous months. He gave two recitals in Bergen in the October of that year and was the soloist in a performance of his Piano Concerto in Leipzig. In February 1880 he went back to Copenhagen for more concerts and, after four recitals in Christiania, the journeying ended in mid-April. He then went back to Bergen, where on 28 April he made a setting of a poem by Vinje, *Tytebæret* (The wild cranberry).

*Den Bergtekne* had been Grieg's first major exploration amongst the non-standard forms of Norwegian, and with the poetry of Vinje and later Garborg he was to achieve great musical heights in songs using the literary form of country dialect, *landsmål*. It is difficult, living in a country which has many dialects and accents but only one official language, to appreciate the amount of strong feeling engendered by the language struggle, the *målstrid*, which took place in Norway in the mid-nineteenth century. The standard written language used at that time was almost purely Danish, although the pronunciation was not the same as that used in Denmark. Some writers, including Ibsen and Bjørnson, wanted to 'Norwegianize' this existing language by making the written form correspond to the spoken sounds. Knud Knudsen (1812–95), a headmaster, furthering the work begun by Henrik Wergeland towards this end, also suggested Norwegian equivalents for many foreign words. Gradually Dano-Norwegian began to lose its Danish elements and, from Knudsen's groundwork, developed into the present day *riksmål* (state language), also called *bokmål* (book language), as the standard and official form. Others, however, hoped to create a truly Norwegian language based on those dialects which stemmed from Old Norse, and the

136

first writer to demonstrate such a language was Ivar Aasen.

Aasen (1813–96) wanted to give the people a language they could recognize as their own and, as the son of a smallholder and a self-taught man, he probably more than most realized the importance of such a language. He spent four years travelling around Norway researching the dialects, work which resulted in two books of his 'people's language': a grammar, *Det norske Folkesprogs Grammatik* (1845) and a dictionary, *Ordbog over det norske Folkesprog* (1850). In a later book, *Prøver af Landsmålet i Norge* (Examples of Landsmål in Norway), written in 1853, Aasen laid out, as he said, 'for closer scrutiny, a suggested form for a Norwegian common language',[1] which he had built up especially on the dialects of western Norway, which had kept most closely to the old forms. *Landsmål*, the 'country' or 'rural' language, has since 1929 been known officially as *nynorsk* (new Norwegian) and today exists side by side with *bokmål*. Schoolchildren learn both forms, books, newspapers and magazines are available in both, and a certain proportion of all radio and television programmes are given in *nynorsk*. Thus, as Edvard Beyer has said, 'while Norway before 1840 did not have any language of its own, fifteen years later it had two',[2] and a way was open to establish an independent Norwegian literature.

Grieg was sympathetic towards those who wanted to use *landsmål*; writers were struggling to create a national language in the same way as he was trying to create a basis for national music. The extent to which this 'people's language' could be used by a writer of talent can be seen in the work of Aasmund Olafsson Vinje, who was an enthusiast for the language from the outset. The son of a crofter, he was born in 1818 at Vinje in the Telemark region and became a teacher at an elementary school. At the age of thirty-two he began to study law at the university in Christiania, but he did not graduate and for the rest of his life supported himself rather poorly by journalism, lecturing and an occasional minor clerkship in a government department. He died from cancer in 1870. Vinje was of a very different character from Aasen; where Aasen was a painstaking researcher and scholar, Vinje was always occupied with a myriad of subjects, perpetually hungry for all sorts of knowledge, an extrovert and a brilliant journalist and speaker. He was also full of self-doubt and, like Heine, tended to hide his inmost feelings behind irony and scorn.

Vinje was a very complex man, the epitome of the contemporary conflict between romanticism and realism, a conflict of which Grieg was also aware, but which he was better able to reconcile. In a letter to Paulsen written in June 1881 the composer wrote of the political climate in Norway: '. . . The older I get, I say to myself: not conservative, not liberal — but both. Not subjective, not objective, but both. Not realist, not idealist, but both. The one must accept the other in itself.'[3] Unlike Grieg, however, Vinje also fell between classes socially and culturally: as the son of a crofter, educated to a certain extent, but never a townsman; a non-graduate, yet thirsty for knowledge and at home in intellectual company; a working writer, but not an accepted literary figure. He was also unlucky in love, not marrying until middle age and then having to suffer his wife's death within the year. His self-contradictory character was difficult to understand even to those close to him, and he remained something of an outsider all his life.

Vinje's writing career was mainly as a journalist, first with the satirical magazine *Andhrimner*,[4] which he, Ibsen and others produced in Christiania between January and September 1851, and next as a correspondent for a newspaper in Drammen from 1851 to 1858. During all this time he was developing stylistically, but his talent only came to real fruition when he founded his own periodical, *Dølen* (The Dalesman), in which he wrote in *landsmål*. The journal lasted from 1858 to 1870 and Vinje regarded it, as he said, as 'a person and not some dead paper'. He addressed his readers directly – a number of poems are entitled *Dølen til Lesaren* (The Dalesman to the Reader) – and used the familiar form 'du', writing about any and every subject that interested him. Every edition contained at least one poem, some of those appearing here reckoned amongst his very best. The conflicts in Vinje's personality are also reflected in his use of language; his native dialect was *dølemål*, an upland dialect of eastern Norway, but he began to write first in the traditional Dano-Norwegian. Some fifty of his poems date from this period, but Vinje felt he had no room to manoeuvre in this language, and also that Danish could not flourish in Norway, because its roots were not there. In his transitional style, he moved away from the Danish influence and its literary clichés and eventually arrived at his own form of *landsmål*, a language which he said gave him 'tøyg' – elasticity. Vinje never minded borrowing words from dialects, making up words or giving existing ones new meanings, when that served his purpose.

His best work was achieved in poetry, where *landsmål* came to be most significant for him, and the main strength of his verse is to be found in the accord between form and content. The word must be appropriate to the thought, he said, or else it was a case of 'large staircases to small houses'. Like Grieg, he was happier in the small forms; he was strongly attracted by the simple and original and had little patience with what he called 'poetic harp-strumming'. The forms he used were quite strict and unusual for Norwegian poetry of the time. An avid reader from his youth, he was familiar with European poetry from Homer to Heine and with the many verse-forms used, for example, by Byron and Goethe. He used both the hexameter (as in *Våren* – The spring) and the octave (as in *Ved Rundarne* – At Rundarne), insisting that in order to have character, poetry must have rhyme. He gave the classical hexameter a new form by, in effect, dividing each line into two, putting a monosyllabic rhyme into the fourth foot and a rhyming trochee into the sixth, and this is the form used in *Guten* (The youth), *Våren* and *Det fyrste* (The first thing), set by Grieg in op.33. Vinje's poetry is often reminiscent of folk-song or *stev* in its use of everyday language and simple imagery, but his real gift was for concentrated and eloquent expression, and his personal ideas come through in his verse as nowhere else.

Having written nothing during his two years of travelling, Grieg, on his return to Bergen in April 1880, found new inspiration in Vinje's poetry and composed ten songs within a very few days. The Grieg Collection in Bergen Public Library contains the composer's own copy of Vinje's *Diktsamling* (Collected Verse), published in 1864, which has a number of poems marked in pencil, including the ones he eventually set. Besides these fifteen, he apparently also considered a further eight. It was as if he found similarities of character between himself and the poet, for they were both able to reach the greater heights only after personal suffering. As Vinje had found his true expression in *landsmål*, so Grieg too was striving for something purely Norwegian in his music, and the Vinje settings are the most truly Norwegian he had yet composed, distilling elements of folk music into a harmonious art form.

Of fifteen settings, twelve were published as *Tolv Melodier til Digte af A.O. Vinje* (Twelve Melodies to Poems by . . .), op.33, the first of which is *Guten* (The youth).[5] The poem was published in *Dølen* on 5 December 1858 and is in the form of a warning of what to expect from the wider world to the youth who finds his present life 'between the mountains' too restricting. All Vinje's experiences of faded hopes and lost loves are here, and his philosophy of life is summed up in the last two lines of the penultimate stanza:

> Du på ruinane må stå af livet dit,
> først riktig då du ret kan sjå ikring deg vidt.
>
> (You must stand on the ruins of your life,/only then can you properly see all around you).

Grieg sets only the fourth, sixth and eighth stanzas of the original nine, but his choice encapsulates all the main elements in the poem and means that the above lines end his song. Some of the bitterness of his current personal situation has found its way into the setting, for the music is rather more dissonant than might have been suggested by the resigned acceptance of the poem. Musically, too, at this time Grieg felt that his life might be in ruins and while Vinje sees good coming from the bad times, Grieg seems unable to do so.

The bitterness in Grieg's setting is established right from the opening supertonic seventh chord; some of the later dissonances are caused by suspensions, both in the melody and the accompaniment, as much as by any chromatic movement. His characteristic motif occurs several times in *Guten* and in other songs of the Vinje group. The vocal line is marked to be 'freely declaimed' and, with the phrases each beginning on the half-beat after a chord, this suggests a recitative style. However, the song builds up in sequences to a soaring melody and has a range from middle B to high F sharp, while the darkness of the poem is conveyed in the accompaniment chords, which are almost totally in the lower register of the keyboard. The music hovers between the tonic B minor and its dominant minor key, and the alternate long and short phrases match Vinje's divided hexameter, here with monosyllabic rhymes throughout.

In short strophes, only twelve bars long, Grieg has created a strong opening to this set of songs. Monrad Johansen described the stanzas as 'solid, as if they were carved in stone . . . concentrated and chiselled'.[6] and Grieg's friend and fellow-composer Johan Svendsen said that he did not know 'any counterparts to it in the whole of song-literature'.[7]

Throughout the manuscript of the Vinje songs, Grieg has written in passages in Danish, some of which appear in the published Danish translation. He also occasionally altered Vinje's original *landsmål* for various musical reasons. At the end of the last stanza of *Guten*, however, the printed Danish version is quite different from the original and from Grieg's suggested translation: 'Kun døbt i Sorgens bittre Ve du ånder frit . . . (Only baptised by sorrow's bitter woe will you breathe freely . . .)' which has none of the strength or weight of Vinje's lines. The German by Hans Schmidt (who changed the title from Lobedanz's 'Der Bursch' to the inexplicable 'Dichterlos', although the former is restored in the *GGA*) tends to condense the meaning of each stanza, and the final two lines here change places with the first two, once again losing the impact of the original.

*Våren* has been described as quite the most beautiful melody Grieg ever wrote. It seems all the more exquisite coming, as it does, immediately after and in such contrast to *Guten*. A Danish critic, writing in *Dagbladet* on 29 November 1885, even considered that the melody 'was worth a better creation than to be illustrating the words "Enno ein gong . . . [yet once again]"'.[8] The poem, written for the issue of *Dølen* of 3 June 1860, is again in divided hexameter form and Vinje considered it to be amongst the best, if not actually the best, of all his verse. This time Grieg treats each line as one melodic phrase rather than two and although each phrase has an almost identical rhythm, there is never any sense of monotony. Far from it. Even with the strophic construction, the melody, and especially the climax of the last line, cries out to be sung. This climax makes the vocal line feel more wide-ranging than it is (in fact only a tenth) and Grieg keeps us in suspense by centring the preceding phrases between C sharp and E sharp, until the culmination finally and triumphantly reaches the high tonic F sharp.

Two of Grieg's now familiar traits are also to be found in *Våren* (The spring): the 'Grieg motif' and the echoing of the ends of vocal phrases. The accompaniment is quite sparse, largely in minims, but with much chromatic movement from the very beginning. The use of tone-colour is very well developed here; for example, the placing of the piano part in the higher register of the keyboard at bars 12 to 15, which, together with the sharp key (F sharp major), has the effect of filling the music with a sense of the clear mountain air and vast emptiness of Norway, which Grieg loved. Spring is very special to Norwegians, for it is such a short season, often taking only two or three weeks for the landscape to change from unending snow to green growth and, as with the short summer nights, there is both sadness and wonder in the transition. This feeling comes through strongly in Vinje's poem, where he is grateful for being allowed to see this phenomenon 'yet once again', perhaps for the last time, and it is as if all Grieg's love for Norwegian nature is poured into the music.

The song may be thought rather too long for all but Scandinavian-speaking audiences and although Grieg has all four stanzas in his manuscript, the second is omitted in all the printed editions. Arne Runar Svendsen[9] is of the opinion that 'Grieg found the poem too long for song-performance', but later, for example in the Drachmann and Benzon settings, he was to set longer verse. Some writers have also criticized Grieg's use of the strophic form, but here it positively helps to maintain the unity created in the poem by Vinje's repeated use of the phrase 'enno ein gong'. Sigurd Skard, in a doctoral thesis on Vinje dating from 1938 (quoted by A.R. Svendsen), comments on the intimate interaction of content and form in the poem and says that Grieg's music has given it 'a wistfully longing violin melody, which erases the structure', and Svendsen himself has said that he would have liked 'a development in the music's intensity of mood towards the poem's climax, "Alt dette vaarliv . . ." [all this spring life]' in the third stanza. Conversely, the Danish critic quoted above considered Grieg's music too good for a poem in 'that unappetizing language', landsmål.

What Grieg certainly has done is at last to create a melody that lends itself to the performer's individual interpretation in each stanza, rather than one so closely knitted to one stanza that it cannot satisfactorily fit the others. Even the end of the melody, as it falls to the lower tonic, can create a thoughtful atmosphere and so is suited to the final words of the fourth stanza, 'meg tyktest å gråta (it seemed to me to weep)' as much as to the contentment at the end of the first, 'mot sol og mot sumar (to sun and to summer)'.

The German version by Hans Schmidt gives the title as 'Letzter Frühling', which neither Lobedanz, the first German translator, nor Corder (in the English) used, and this is also the title translated by Rolf Stang in the GGA. Certainly the poet asks in the third stanza whether this might not be his last spring, but in connection with the song Grieg always used the title Våren. In his long letter to Finck of 17 July 1900 Grieg says that he wanted 'to clarify the contents [of the songs] through expressive titles' when he arranged Våren and Den Særde (The wounded one) for string orchestra as Two Elegiac Melodies, op. 34, [10] and refers to them as Siste vår (Last Spring) and Hjertesår (Wounded heart), although *Våren* retains its one-word title in the score. John Horton, in the introduction to his edition of the *Elegiac Melodies*, says that 'later the content of the poem was made clearer to non-Norwegian audiences by calling the piece "Letzter Frühling"',[11] but the present author considers it a practice that tends to sentimentalize a most unsentimental song.

Schmidt's translation, made for the later Peters edition of 1911–12 and reprinted in the *GGA*, as with others by this writer, is so loose that it scarcely deserves the description. At the end of the first stanza, for example, he describes the nightingale singing at night, where the original has 'the spring bird sang to sun and to summer'. Schmidt's German version lacks all the wonder and mystery of the original poem. Leclercq, in the French translation, piously replaced Vinje's 'enno ein gong' with 'Dieu m'permis' and, like Astra Desmond in her otherwise excellent version for Augener's in 1961, he abandoned all attempts at rhyme. Rolf Stang's English translation in the *GGA* is accurate, but not always smoothly flowing; his phrase 'their ice-crusts extinguish', for example, is not easy to articulate in singing.

From his correspondence with Molard, it can be seen that Grieg was again most concerned with accuracy and correct declamation. In his letter dated 13 June 1894 he criticises Molard's use of the words '*quand* les oiseaux (sic)' at 'the big forte on F sharp' and asks for 'a more telling word to be brought in'. He continues, 'Remember that it is a big musical accent. The translation's last word: *heureuses* I would ask [to be] replaced by one that is more in keeping with the poet's thoughts', and he quotes Vinje's last line. In a later letter Grieg is still critical of the way Molard has sought to rewrite the first stanza after taking account of his earlier comments:

> . . . that in "Le Printemps" you have changed around two lines in the 1st verse is unfortunate. For with that the poetic embroidery is lost. The main point must be: "Once again I heard the spring bird that sang to sun and to summer". Vinje has repeated the word "endnu" and with it has achieved something lovely and tender in the result. Why not do the same in French, e.g:
>
> > J'ai de nouveau contemplé dans les près
> > Les fleurs printemières,
> > *J'ai de nouveau entendu dans les bois*
> > Les chantes d'espérance.[12]

> Certainly here the word 'ois[s]eaux' is missing, but the meaning is there and you can no doubt bring it in easily if you think so. But both poetically and musically it is best as I have suggested. Then you must just see to it that it is also French.[13]

The third song of the Vinje settings, *Den Særde* (The wounded one), presents a very different picture of spring from *Våren*. Here the season is unwelcome to the poet, for it reopens the wounds that life has inflicted on him. However, just as the spring represents new life after the winter, so hope also blooms again. This, then, is really the sequel to *Guten*, for now the poet has won his victory over pain and, as the poem has it, 'flowers grow in the wound'. Grieg wrote to Finck of 'the deep melancholy of the poetry', referring to *Våren* and *Den særde*, which 'explains the serious sounds of the music.' Vinje's poem, which appeared in *Dølen* on 23 January 1859, has three stanzas of five lines each; the first three lines of each stanza concern the bitter experience of life, which is then resolved in the hope expressed in the last two lines. Grieg uses the whole poem, set strophically, and repeats the last line of each stanza, so emphasizing the hope and creating a better musical balance.

The bitterness and melancholy of the first part of each stanza is apparent from the opening dissonance in the music and the song continues with many chromatically altered notes which form augmented and diminished chords. The modulation in the middle of the strophe is effected by a Neapolitan sixth in the eighth bar and chromatically moving inner parts, which in bar 9 give an impression of the dominant seventh of D major. The C sharp, however, becomes D flat, and with the other parts moving up or down a semitone, the chord at the beginning of bar 10 is not D major but the second inversion of D *flat* major. As Nils Grinde has observed, this use of a chromatically altered pivot chord, 'with its possibilities for enharmonic redesignation', is something that Grieg 'exploits often and with sophisticated results'. [14] The enharmonic change in *Den særde* marvellously underlines the hope contained in the second part of each strophe: Ex.61. The familiar 'Grieg motif' is also here, and although the harmony is anything but diatonic, there is a sense of triumph about the end of the strophe.

*Den særde*, together with *Våren*, as transcribed for string orchestra 'found a wide circulation outside my homeland', as Grieg wrote to Finck. The composer conducted the *Elegiac Melodies* frequently at concerts both at home and abroad, performances that usually affected him deeply, and his comments on some of these occasions offer illumination to the performer of the songs. He wrote to Beyer from Leipzig in October 1883, 'You should have heard "Den særde" and "Våren" yesterday evening. It was really marvellous to hear how they played it. Beautiful crescendos, pianissimos such as you never dreamt of and fortissimos like a world of sound.' From London in 1888, again to Beyer, he wrote, 'Then I stood and conducted "Våren" and it sounded as if the whole of nature there at home would embrace me; yes, then I was very proud and happy to be a Norwegian'; and he continued later in the same letter, 'If only you had heard "Den særde" and "Våren"! How I thought of you! There were things in it to weep over...' [15]

The next Vinje setting in the op.33 album, *Tytebæret* (The wild cranberry), was also to a poem which made its first appearance in *Dølen*, on 17 April 1859. Once again it is a picture of good coming from bad, a parable of self-sacrifice for friends, [16] told in simple four-line stanzas and using

Ex.61                                                                    Den særde

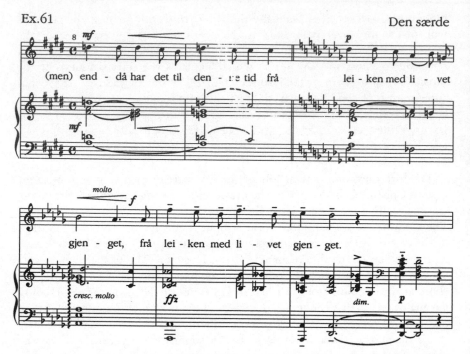

(Yet by this time it had withdrawn from the contest with life)

natural imagery with which the journal's readers would have been familiar. For the first time in this group the song is not strophic but in ABA form. That at least is true of the vocal line; harmonically it is through-composed. the 'Grieg motif' appears at the very beginning in the piano introduction and the melody makes much use of sequence. The vocal line, which trips along neatly, suddenly blossoms in the middle of the song with octave leaps, a new *springar*-like rhythm and arpeggio figures, which over the tonic pedals (minor and relative major) actually form fresh-sounding major sevenths. The tension builds with the berry's command to the boy to drink its 'blood' and when the opening melody returns, it is against descending chromatic scales in the right hand and a syncopated low A, providing a dominant pedal, in the left. Grieg repeats the last line of the poem three times, twice taking the phrase progressively higher at the end, but finally closing more pensively on the lower tonic.

Two of the settings that comprise the op. 33 album were written some years before the rest. One of these is the fifth song of the published twelve, *Langs ei å* (Beside a stream), the manuscript of which is dated Børve, 8 July 1877, and it was one of the 'gullkorn' (grains of gold) that Grieg felt he produced during that first season in Hardanger. The poem was not written for an edition of *Dølen*, but comes from Vinje's most significant work,

*Ferdaminni fraa Sumaren 1860* (Travel memories from the summer of 1860), which Edvard Beyer describes as 'a subjective and whimsical travel picture ... akin to Sterne's *A Sentimental Journey* ... and Heine's *Reisebilder'*.[17] During that summer Vinje travelled, partly on foot, to Trondhjem for the coronation in Norway of Carl XV, and the *Ferdaminni* describe all the things he saw and experienced *en route*. The work includes a number of lyrical poems, among them *Langs ei å* and *Ved Rundarne*.

In *Langs ei å*, as in *Tytebæret*, Vinje uses a natural phenomenon to illustrate human behaviour and likens the stream gnawing at the trees' roots to the man who kisses the hand that deals the severest blow. The single eight-line stanza is set as a through-composed song and Grieg matches the simplicity of Vinje's nature-picture with musical restraint, at least at first, and uses some traits derived from folk-song, for example the little vocal decorations and the sounding of the dominant chord against the tonic, the latter frequently used to haunting effect.

The accompaniment has a quaver figure which continues through much of the song, perhaps to illustrate the stream's inexorable erosion of the trees' roots, although it is not particularly expressive of water. It gradually develops with echoes of the vocal line in the right hand and a chromatically descending bass, and the melody and harmony undergo a number of transitions in major and minor keys, so that the whole song has an ambiguity of mode and even a modal final cadence. The contrast between the words 'he kissed the hand' and 'that dealt his worst heart's wound' is underlined (bars 17 to 20) by a change from major to minor and the song is thus given an atmosphere of sad resignation at the harshness of life.

The coda is an inspiration on Grieg's part, for, as John Horton has pointed out, the poem gives no justification for it. The piano first takes the vocal melody from the beginning of the song, over a tonic pedal as before and using the same quaver figure, but with more chromatic movement in the inner parts. The voice has four iterations of 'du skog (you wood)', the first two phrases echoed by the piano, but harmonized differently:

Ex.62

Langs ei å

In the new *GGA* English translation, Rolf Stang repeats his opening words, 'Still woods' here, but unfortunately the loveliness of this coda has not always been reflected in translations. Elkin's 'Ah, me!' for the first 'du skog' gave an artificial quality which is quite absent from Vinje's poem, while Hans Schmidt's German version for Peters simply repeats the whole of the poem's last line, giving a disjointed effect and not at all what Grieg must have intended. Schmidt and Corder also altered the original 'du skog' to the singular 'o Baum' and 'Poor tree' respectively, thus destroying the universality of Vinje's image.

The sixth song, and the last in the first album, is *Eit syn* (A vision), prosaically entitled 'Was ich sah' by Kalbeck in the Peters translation. Vinje's poem was first published in *Dølen* on 11 September 1859 and in setting only the first four stanzas, Grieg has chosen the best. The remaining three stanzas continue and extend the sentiments already expressed: sorrow that the beautiful girl is only a dream that cannot be recaptured.

Here the music is more lively than in the earlier settings, although the song is not without its reflective moments. The first section is in a fast triple time in the style of a *springar*, with its vigorous dancing movement and strong accents, a choice of style which has puzzled some writers. A.R. Svendsen comments that 'Grieg's lively dance-rhythm to the poem can at first encounter appear somewhat misplaced',[18] and he goes on to quote Sigurd Skard, who called the melody 'absolutely bewildering'. Yet the energetic setting, with its infectious principal melody, suits the breathless quality of the poet's account of his vision of a girl so beautiful he cannot adequately describe her. The song was the one most frequently performed in the first years after publication, finding favour with audiences and critics alike, and is still one of the most popular of the op.33 songs.

The first two stanzas are set strophically and each has a 'piu tranquillo' or a 'ritardando' over the second half as the poet reflects on his vision, and where the yearning chromatic phrase in the bass is echoed in the off-beat chords in the right hand. For the middle section of the song the music becomes more dream-like, accomplished by augmentation of the melody rather than by slowing the tempo, and the last stanza is then set to the same music as the first two. Harmonically, the music develops most in the middle section and once more there is some ambiguity of mode. The melody in bars 37 to 40, for example, is effectively in C sharp major, while over a dominant pedal the right hand has chromatically altered chords which convey the uncertainty in the words as the poet speaks of the features of the girl, which he can see in his mind but not describe.

The Danish version of this stanza is much more defined than Vinje's original and describes those features which the poet says he cannot put into words. Similarly in the other stanzas, the Danish is less elusive than the *landsmål*, and this tends to spoil the dream-like atmosphere Vinje created. As in *Guten*, Grieg's manuscript has a number of pencilled annotations of a Danish translation, which are not the same as the eventual printed version. Also in the manuscript the second beat of each of the first two bars is further accented by having a four-note chord in the left hand resolving to a bare octave on the third beat, but in the printed editions (Hansen, Peters and Ashdown) the middle notes of the chord are given as minims, thus filling out the third-beat chord, too.

No translator has rendered the last line satisfactorily; Vinje has written 'men borte og borte og borte (but gone . . .)' and the disyllable defies the translator here as it does in the Ibsen setting, op.25 no.5. In the second line of the first stanza of his translation, Corder presented the singer with quite a task with the phrase, 'In loving toils I long'd to net her', but he effected a solution to the last line of the song with ''tis vanished, 'tis vanished, 'tis vanished!' and similarly, Rolf Stang in the *GGA* has 'but vanished'.

The seventh song, and the first of the second album, *Gamle mor* (Old mother), was also the first of the Vinje settings to be composed, having been written in Sandviken in 1873. Astra Desmond described it as one of the few *un*sentimental songs about a mother, but not, as she also observed, in the English version, nor in the Danish on which this is based. [19] The poem was published in *Dølen* on 9 December 1860 and its sincerity must have appealed to Grieg, who appreciated the same qualities in his own mother's character as Vinje extols. The song was not, however, written soon after Gesine Grieg's death, as Paulsen had stated in an article written for the Christiania newspaper *Verdens Gang* in 1905. Grieg wrote to Paulsen in June of that year to correct the statement: 'She was still living in Sandviken, where I brought her the song, which had arisen from thoughts of her, as with her relentless energy and sense of duty she guided and toiled until she dropped . . .' [20]

Grieg's setting is strophic and has something of the folk-song in its simple melody and, in fact, his second manuscript of the song is marked 'i folketone (in folk-song style)'. There is some chromatic movement, particularly in the second half of each stanza, and the song again makes use of sequence. The four-bar postlude after each strophe is an elaboration of the vocal melody from bars 7 to 10, with much more chromatic movement, which, however, does not detract from the inherent sincerity.

Vinje's poem is a tribute to the way his mother toiled to bring him up, wiping his tears and inspiring him to success. The first two lines, 'Du gamle mor! du sliter arm, so sveitten er som blod (Old mother! you toil impoverished, so that your sweat is like blood)', are replaced in the Danish version by the mannered 'Du gamle mor i hytte lav, du svæder Trældoms Blod (Old mother in your humble cottage, you sweated the blood of slavery)', and few mothers, however old and frail, would have appreciated being called 'feeble' by R.H. Elkin. Grieg warned Molard in his letter of 5 June 1894 not to use the Danish edition as a basis for his translation, but added that '"La vielle mère" is very good'. He criticised only the words 'Un bras puissant Et l'interpidité', in the first stanza, which, he said, 'could appear too vague. I would prefer, for example: "Mon bras puissant, mon interpidité".' The manuscript again has some pencilled annotations for a Danish translation, although some of these have been crossed out again.

It is interesting, considering that *Gamle mor* and *Langs ei å* were written some time before the rest of the Vinje settings, that the intervening years did not lessen their impact. The later songs are equal to, but no better than, these and it is as if Grieg set himself a standard with Vinje that was maintained all through the years of composition.

The poem *Det fyrste* (The first [or only] thing) was first published in *Dølen* on 18 September 1859. It is written in four stanzas, each comprising two long lines, and each line is a divided hexameter with monosyllabic rhymes in each part. Grieg sets the stanzas in pairs, so making two long strophes set identically, and he also follows Vinje's line division in the musical phrasing, as he had in *Guten*. The music itself, however, is much more stark here than in the first song of the group, with the melody doubled in the accompaniment for most of its length. In the few bars in the second half of each strophe where this is not so, the voice is accompanied by a long-held chord.

There is a now familiar ambiguity of mode throughout the whole song; for example, in the second half of each strophe where, in the cadence in F major, the dominant chord retains its *minor* third. The song also ends in the tonic minor key, with the plagal cadence approached by a chord of E flat minor, all with an inverted tonic pedal in the vocal line and the accompaniment:

Ex.63                                                                    Det fyrste

(it is ashes.)

Grieg also made much use of the echoing of the vocal line in the accompaniment and with this and the divided hexameter matched by two musical half-phrases, the song is constructed in four six-bar phrases. The unsophisticated folksong-like melody reflects Vinje's simple message, that if one can no longer love then the only thing to do is to die, and the poem is also sometimes entitled 'Når ikki lenger du elska kann (When you can no longer love)', the third line of the first stanza. As in *Guten, Tytebæret* and *Langs ei å*, in fact all the serious songs of the group, the music begins simply and gradually becomes more complicated as the poem unfolds.

The ninth song, *Ved Rundarne* (At Rundarne), is a great favourite with Norwegians and, like Bull's *Sæterjentens Søndag*, is almost a folk-song in its popularity and wide appeal. Like *Eit syn*, public opinion has thus outweighed that of the 'experts'; A.R. Svendsen again quotes a Danish critic, writing in December 1881, who opined, '. . . one must wonder that such an experienced song-composer as Grieg allows himself passages that sound most strange, not to say bad',[21] citing the sixth bar of *Ved Rundarne*, with its beautiful transition from the tonic D flat to F major:

Ex.64                                                              Ved Rundarne

(som) deim eg i min før-ste ung-dom såg,_____ og sa-ma

(as I saw them in my earliest youth)

The manuscripts of both this song and *Det fyrste* are dated 4 May 1880 and as the preceding day is the date on the manuscripts of *Den Særde, Trudom* and *Attegløyma*, it may be seen that Grieg at this time was having a very energetic and productive period. *Ved Rundarne*, like *Langs ei å*, comes from Vinje's book *Ferdaminni fraa Sumaren 1860* and it consists of four octaves, with the rather restrictive rhyme-scheme ABABABCC. Grieg sets the first two of the four stanzas and the whole poem describes a nostalgic revisiting by the poet of the scenes of his childhood, with all the memories which that visit awakens. As in *Våren*, Grieg here constructs a beautiful but unsentimental melody and once again, the song begins simply and builds up melodically and harmonically in the second half of each strophe. The second half of the melody is counter-balanced by a chromatically descending melody in the right hand of the accompaniment: Ex.65.

Ex.65　　　　　　　　　　　　　　　　　　　　　　　Ved Rundarne

(There is a childhood language, which speaks to me)

Like *Våren*, the song builds to a triumphant, soaring climax, here introduced by a series of chromatically altered chords, and then dies away to end on the lower tonic. The chromatic movement in the middle section also subsides along with the melodic line to almost completely diatonic harmony. The nostalgia does not tempt Grieg to dwell on words or phrases and the song gains strength from being set syllabically.

Both Lobedanz and Schmidt used the unnecessarily explanatory title 'Auf der Reise zur Heimat', subsequently followed by all the earlier English translations: 'Homeward' (Marzials and Morgan), 'On the Way Home' (Corder) and 'The Wanderer's Return' (Elkin). Rolf Stang in the *GGA* fortunately retains Vinje's title 'At Rondane'. Schmidt's version (reprinted in the *GGA*, but now retitled 'Bei Rondane') is far more sentimental than vinje's poem, especially in the concluding couplet of the first stanza. Vinje wrote:

> Med ungdomsminne er den tala blandad:
> Det strøymer på meg so eg knapt kan anda.
> (With childhood memories the speech is mingled: It streams over me, so I can scarcely breathe.)

which Schmidt renders:

> Ich sink an ihrem Mutterbusen nieder,
> und fühl in ihrem Schoss als Kind mich wieder.
> (I sink down on her mother's breast, and in her bosom feel myself a child again.)

while his second stanza bears little resemblance to Vinje at all. Molard once again had to make some alterations in his French translation to please the composer, but on 5 June 1894 was rewarded with a letter from Grieg to say that he was 'very moved by the changes of declamation in "Ved Rundarne"'.

Grieg seems to have poured much of his love for his homeland into this song and the sincerity of his feelings shines through, which is no doubt why it has remained so popular in Norway, where a large part of the Rondane (as it is now spelled) area is preserved as a national park. The composer also arranged the song for unaccompanied three-part female choir, dedicated to 'Hanchens Damechor', a ladies' choir founded by A.M. Hanche, a version which was printed for the first time in volume 17 of the *GGA*. Delius included a setting of *Ved Rundarne*, known in English as 'The Homeward Way', as the second of his *Seven Songs from the Norwegian* of 1892. His strophic setting is much more voluptuous than Grieg's, but the English composer's love for the Norwegian mountains is apparent in the music's soaring vocal phrases and the chromatic harmony.

With *Eit vennestykke* (A broken friendship) we return to the feeling of bitterness at one's fate encountered earlier in these settings. The poem is not one of Vinje's best; it was written in 1857 and is printed in the *Diktsamling* of 1864. Vinje was always unlucky in love and one can understand the resentment here of the older man outmatched by a young rival, whilst at the same time wishing that the sourness had not been allowed to take precedence over literary values. Grieg constructs an angular melody, frequently in uneven two- and three-bar phrases, which has all of the poem's resignation, and the accompaniment is very dissonant right from the beginning, with much use made of eleventh chords. The sharpened subdominant is also much in evidence in this song. The melody builds up in each of the two strophes to a longer penultimate phrase and is counterbalanced by the brief final phrase, which with its change of rhythm is tossed away like the bitter words it sets: 'og tog sigte på (and took aim)' and 'uden ro og rist (without peace or rest)'. Grieg emphasised the opening words of each stanza with a long-held note: in most printed editions this is a dotted minim tied to a minim, but in the manuscript and the first Scandinavian edition the note is a minim only.

*Trudom* (Faith) is one of the earliest written of the Vinje poems Grieg set. It was printed in *Dølen* on 30 January 1859 and is in four six-line stanzas, rhymed ABABCC, of which Grieg sets the first and last. The poem is an ironic indictment of the hypocrisy of Christianity, a religion which claims to stand for peace, yet which causes so much strife in the search for truth, and a God who, according to Vinje, knows that if a man kills his brother, it is only for His sake and in order to attain heaven. Grieg's hymn-like setting has been considered by some writers to be a misinterpretation of the poem. However, Grieg may well have employed his literary and musical acumen to underline Vinje's irony, for what could be more derisive than to set these scornful words to a pious hymn-tune?[22] Grieg may also have felt sympathy with Vinje, as his own religious views were not those of the orthodox Christian. He never doubted the existence of God and saw the Creator's hand in nature and art, but he was not convinced of the divinity of Christ. A kind and generous man, he eventually found a philosophy that suited him both spiritually and intellectually in the Unitarian movement.

However, if he were guilty of mis-interpretation in *Trudom*, he is not alone. There are several choral versions of the song, including two apparently intended for church use: one, arranged for solo and chorus, is published amongst Novello's series *Collection of Anthems*, and the other, arranged by Henry Coleman and published by Oxford University Press in 1959, uses as text a real hymn, 'Lo, God is here', a translation by John Wesley of words by Teersteegen (1697–1769). Grieg himself, however, made no choral arrangements, as he might well have done if he really had misunderstood Vinje's poem.[23]

The melody and accompaniment of *Trudom* move in slow note-values, the vocal line mostly doubled by the piano. The harmony, as befits a song 'i salmetone (in hymn style)', is largely homophonic, with little chromatic movement, and the modulation to the dominant in the eighth bar is also typical of the conventional hymn tune. A more individual touch is the sequence in bars 9 and 10, 11 and 12, which is built over a tonic pedal. The only non-hymn-like characteristic is the wide range of the vocal line – middle D to high G flat – although performance by a congregation, in spite of the later arrangements, was not what Grieg had in mind. There is an interesting dissonance at the very end of the setting, where the voice holds the tonic G flat, while the accompaniment moves to the concluding plagal cadence by way of the second inversion of the tonic seventh chord, so that the F in the piano right hand clashes directly with the vocal line, perhaps to emphasise the dissonance of the thoughts in Vinje's poem.

The final song of the group, *Fyremål* (The goal), is a splendidly vigorous one to end the cycle and all the earlier bitterness and dissonance are resolved in its liveliness. Here Grieg, on his own admission, really did set the words under a misapprehension. If he had read the poem in *Dølen*, where it appeared under one of Vinje's favourite titles, *Til Lesaren* (To the reader), rather than in the Collected Poems, he would not have missed the point so easily. He wrote to Finck, 'I believed that the energetic poem was directed to a friend or even to the poet's wife',[24] for he supposed that the poem extolled companionship. In fact Vinje wrote it to encourage all good Norwegians to use *landsmål* and, appropriately, it was printed in the first issue of the second volume of *Dølen*, published on 23 October 1859, by which time he must indeed have felt that the language was 'trygt og trufast (safe and sure)'. The 'goal' of the title is the country-wide acceptance of *landsmål* and Vinje uses a verse-form akin to Old Norse poetry, with short lines each containing only two stresses, and a wealth of alliteration both of vowels and consonants:

> Vegen vita
> på villstig venda,
> fram å fara
> og ferdi enda . . .

The manuscript of *Fyremål* is dated 7 May 1880, making the song the last of the Vinje settings to be written. Grieg's bold, march-like melody is, for-

tunately, just as appropriate to the poem's real meaning as to the one the
composer imagined. The strong rhythm, reminiscent of a *halling*, is established from the very opening bars and maintained in the vocal line too. Much
use is made of sequence and of decorated repeats of phrases to strengthen the
folk music feeling, especially in the middle section. With the ends of vocal
phrases echoed in the accompaniment, the effect is frequently of three-bar
phrase lengths.

The long first section is repeated after the lyrical middle section, making
the song at 158 bars one of Grieg's longest. The harmony is largely diatonic,
perhaps to underline the poem's command to 'pull together', and the
accompaniment requires a virtuoso pianist, especially in the middle of the
first section, where the words are beautifully reflected in the music:

Ex.66                                                                Fyremål

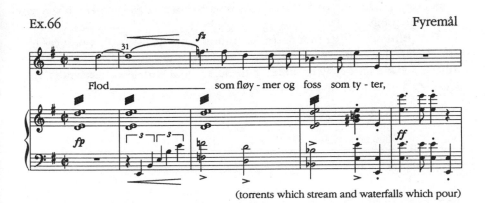

(torrents which stream and waterfalls which pour)

and in the long postlude, which is built over a tonic pedal. At the very end of
the outer sections there is an interesting use of the flattened submediant in
the major key so typical of Norwegian folk music and an unusual third
inversion of the dominant seventh chord at the final cadence. The vocal line
builds to a powerful climax, but, considerate as always, Grieg marks the
higher-lying phrases 'fortissimo' or louder and he leaves plenty of room for
breath, so that the song, although demanding, is a delight to perform.

The middle section is marked 'tranquillamente' and, with the transition to
the minor key, becomes something of a Trio section to the original March.
The new relaxed atmosphere is also accomplished, as in *Eit syn*, by an
augmentation of the rhythm. The section is introduced by the tonic chord of
E flat major, followed by the dominant chord of the same key, but which
contains the sharpened fifth, before the key of G minor is established by the
vocal line. Vinje made a number of alterations to his original words in this
section and, although both versions use alliteration, the final one is the more
accomplished:

Kom daa kjere!  
Vi kjæmpe saman;  
naar vi vinna  
vi njota Gaman.  
Stor var Skammi  
vi skulde bera,  
naar vi neitta  
at Norske vera.

(Come then, dear ones! we'll fight together; when we win, we'll taste delight. Great would be the shame we should bear if we refuse to be Norwegian).

Kom daa, Snille!  
vi slita saman.  
For den Gilde  
er Gant og Gaman.  
Trygt og trufast  
vaar Norsk vi tala  
Med det sama  
slags Maal vi mala.

(Come then, dear ones! we'll pull together. For the daring, there is joy and delight. Safe and sure is this Norwegian we speak; we work away at the same goal).

Grieg repeats the first four lines of this part of the poem to complete his middle section before the first section is repeated to give an energetic finale to the Vinje songs.

The alliteration of the poem is almost impossible to reproduce in translation. Lobedanz, who made the German translations for the first Peters edition, made an excellent attempt to do so, followed less successfully by Corder's English in the same edition:

Wegeskundig, vom Weg sich wenden,  
vorwärts fahrend, die Fahrt doch enden . . .  
Zangen, Zacken und hohe Halden!  
Fels und Fluten und wilde Wogen,  
Schwall, sich schwingend in Wasserbogen . . .

Rocks and reefs with their jaws all jagged!  
Shore and sea with the waves that wallow  
Rocking, rearing like caverns hollow . . .

Schmidt's translation for the later German editions unfortunately uses a large number of words containing the consonant 'ch', which makes the overall sound of the song much harsher than when it is sung in *landsmål*. He also repeats the word 'vorwärts' tiresomely often in the outer sections and, in spite of the title 'Mein Ziel', nowhere does he mention what the goal is. Elkin also obscured the point of the poem by giving, in the middle section:

Proud of the northern tongue we're speaking,  
Truth the goal that we all are seeking.

Lobedanz marred his earlier commended efforts by writing 'Lass denn, *Liebste* [author's italics], uns wandern beide' in this section, which was followed by Corder with 'Let us, *love*, then together wander', and later with 'With us, *darling*, oh wilt thou wander'. Vinje used the word 'snille', which like 'kjere' in his first version is a mild endearment and the Hansen edition actually gives 'kjære (dear)' in an explanatory footnote. Both Elkin for the Ashdown edition and Marzials and Morgan for Pitt and Hatzfeld used the word in the Danish sense, meaning talent or ingenuity, and both versions render it as 'wisdom', a translation that Grieg described to Finck as 'false' and 'risible', adding that an accurate translation would be 'Come then, dear, we'll bear the load together.'[25]

The twelve songs of op.33, dedicated to 'fru Agathe Grøndahl, født [née] Backer', were published in two volumes, each containing six songs, by Wilhelm Hansen in December 1881, although their imminent publication had been heralded in *Bergenposten* as early as 22 September. Originally, as we have seen, there were to have been fifteen songs, but three of them were taken out by the composer before publication, two remained in manuscript only until their publication in the *GGA* and the other, *På Hamars ruiner* (On Hamar's ruins), was published in 1908 as one of the *Posthumous Songs*. The reason for omitting these three songs from the printed edition is not clear. It may be that the publishers felt twelve to be a more acceptable number, for none of the three deserves omission on the grounds of quality, and the present author is unable to agree with the opinion of Benestad and Schjelderup-Ebbe that *På Hamars ruiner* is 'by far the weakest of the fifteen'.[26]

This poem, written in Danish, dates from pre-*Dølen* days and was an occasional verse composed for a conference of schoolteachers which took place at Hamar in July 1857. It describes the ruined cathedral, where the arches still stand, reminding visitors of the greatness which was once there. Vinje compares these arches to the bones of the huge clay man made by the giant Hrungnir, or Rungne, to frighten Thor before their battle. The second and third stanzas describe the area around Hamar and mention a number of local places and features.

Grieg sets the poem strophically and the song has a number of folk music characteristics, which later give way to a more sophisticated melodic and harmonic structure. The first six bars are written over a pedal tonic fifth, a feature which once again leads to the familiar Griegian sound of dominant chord against tonic. The composer here actually uses the dominant ninth chord and an interesting effect is created in the sixth bar, when the fifth of this chord, F, is chromatically altered to F sharp, anticipating the key of G minor found in the succeeding phrase.

The second half of the strophe becomes more art-song than folk-song and the bare fourths, fifths and octaves in the left hand now give way to a triplet arpeggio figure. This passage begins in D flat major, a key far removed from the tonic E flat, and the vocal line towards the end of each strophe is particularly wide-ranging and melodious. The harmony becomes more adventurous, using suspended notes, chords of the ninth and a good deal of chromatic movement, which delays a return to the tonic key until the final cadence. The ritornello after each strophe contains in its lingering triplets something of a foreshadowing of the postlude to Wolf's song *Anakreons Grab* written nine years later:

Ex.67                                                      På Hamars ruiner

The other two songs omitted from the op.33 collection are *Atte(r)gløyma*[27] (The old maid) and *Jenta* (The girl), the manuscripts of which are part of the Grieg Collection in Bergen. Both are marked 'går ud (take out)' in pencil by the composer. Benestad and Schjelderup-Ebbe have suggested that Grieg chose to omit these two because, as they concern women, they are not integral to the cycle, which as a whole deals with Man or the universal.[28]

In *Dølen*, where the poem was first published on 20 February 1859, *Attegløyma* is entitled *Møykerting-Vise* (The old maid's song). It is a humorous verse, in which the old maid regrets that she did not 'take the first bait', but missed her chance of marriage, in spite of being a pretty girl who 'blossomed like the fresh flower', and Grieg uses the first, third and ninth stanzas of the original fifteen. The manuscript is dated 3 May 1880 and the poem is set to an angular melody, which makes use of the harmonic minor scale, and the sardonic humour is further indicated by the dotted figures in the accompaniment. The first two vocal phrases are doubled in octaves by the piano, alternating with a dotted tune, inverted from the introduction,

Ex.68                                                      Attegløyma

(Hard to bear up)

but at bar 11 the voice takes over the dotted rhythm, which is then rather comically divided between the hands in the accompaniment. There are traces of the influence of folk music to be found in the frequent use of the sharpened subdominant, in the tonic pedal through bars 18 to 20, in the rhythmic hints of the *springar* and in the ambiguity of key, where major and minor are further mixed with the Aeolian mode.

*Jenta* is entitled *Til jenta mi!* ('To my girl!') in *Dølen*, where it appeared on 28 November 1858, and it is the earliest of the poems set by Grieg which originated in that publication. The song was written on 30 April 1880, the day before *Guten*. In a way it is the counterpart to *Attegløyma* — here the girl says that it is more important to find oneself than to find a man — and Grieg uses all but the second stanza of the original five. Once again the setting owes something to the *springar*, particularly in the accompaniment's ♩ ♩ rhythm at the beginning. The transition from the tonic C major through the dominant seventh of B minor in bar 7 to the dominant seventh of A minor is rather abrupt, though fresh-sounding, and the sevenths in the chords and in arpeggio in the vocal melody are typical of Grieg in folk-song style:

Ex.69

(You need not wait long for the boy, with eyes burning bright)

With the exception of *Gamle mor* and *Langs ei å*, the Vinje songs were completed in less than two weeks, from *Tytebæret* on 28 April to *Fyremål* on 7 May, with *Den særde*, *Trudom* and *Attegløyma* all dated 3 May. As Grieg wrote to Paulsen, they came 'thick and fast in my childhood home in Strandgaten in the spring of 1880. It is quite certain, as you say, that besides the purely spiritual aspect, the nature of Hardanger is also concealed in these songs. In a few years, it took me completely and set its mark on everything I wrote at that time. Its influence, moreover, has extended right to this very day.'[29]

Some of the Vinje settings are amongst Grieg's best songs, and performances of them were popular throughout his lifetime. However, in the early years after publication it was individual songs that were sung and not the collection as a whole. Those most frequently mentioned by name in programmes and letters are *Eit syn, Guten, Gamle mor, Ved Rundarne, Våren* and *Langs ei å*. Many of the performances are described in the composer's letters to friends and they were not all formal occasions, but sometimes given by popular request. A letter to Beyer from Christiania dated 25 October 1885 tells of a concert and a reception afterwards: 'Then came toasts and speeches and a laurel wreath, then at 1 o'clock I had to go to the piano and play folk dances and then Lammers [who had earlier performed *Den Bergtekne*] sang "Gamle mor", "Det Første", "Ved Rondarne" and "Guten" . . .'[30] Lammers gave the first performances of many of Grieg's songs and became particularly well-known for his interpretations of the Vinje settings.

Besides the two *Elegiac Melodies*, a number of other arrangements of the Vinje songs exist. The choral versions of *Trudom* and Grieg's own SSA arrangement of *Ved Rundarne* have already been mentioned, and there are also choral versions of *Våren* (for SSATB by Lionel Lethbridge)[31] and of *Gamle mor* (for SATB by Margrethe Hokanson).[32]

It is extremely unjust that these songs are so little known outside Norway. Vinje is very difficult to translate, and even in Scandinavia the publishers considered that a complete Danish version would be necessary, rather than just an explanation of individual words, as Grieg had apparently thought sufficient.[33] However, it is inexcusable to dismiss the songs cursorily on this basis alone, as did Kurt Pahlen, referring to all the Vinje and Garborg settings: 'They are based on peasant texts, are therefore hardly translatable, and for this reason have been reserved mostly for home consumption.'[34] The edition published by Hansen's in 1881 contained a full Danish text, although the translator is not named. A.R. Svendsen is of the opinion that Grieg himself worked towards a fuller Danish version, as the manuscripts of several of the songs have long passages in Danish in his handwriting. It may be, however, that the composer collaborated with someone else on the final Danish texts, as he was to do with John Paulsen with regard to the *Haugtussa* songs. Certainly he appreciated that it was the difficulty of obtaining good translations that so often prevented many of his songs from acquiring a wider currency. As Monrad Johansen wrote, 'If abroad the Vinje songs still belong to the least known of Grieg's things, the blame should certainly fall to a large extent on the awful translations, which preclude the possibility of a full and complete appreciation and understanding.'[35] Rolf Stang's new translations in the *GGA*, although rather wordy and occasionally awkwardly accented for singing, are accurate and should go some way to illuminating the quality and diverse content of Vinje's verse, and with that give a new lease of life to some of Grieg's most important songs.

# Notes

1  Quoted by Edvard Beyer: *Utsyn over norsk litteratur*, 1971, p.70.
2  Ibid.
3  Grieg to Paulsen, 3 June 1881 from Carlsbad.
4  No exact translation of the title is possible. The name may derive from 'Hrimr' (Sooty), the name of the cook in Valhalla.
5  Oddly entitled 'The Sorrowful Minstrel' in the English edition published by Pitt and Hatzfeld in 1888.
6  David Monrad Johansen: *Edvard Grieg*, 1934, p.254.
7  Johan Svendsen to Grieg, 22 June 1882 from Christiania.
8  Quoted by A.R. Svendsen: *Edvard Griegs Vinjesanger*, 1971, p.60.
9  Ibid., p.102.
10  Published by Peters, 1881.
11  Eulenberg miniature score no.1373, 1978.
12  This is exactly what appears in the Peters edition attributed to J. Leclercq.
13  Grieg to Molard, 10 July 1894 from Troldhaugen.
14  Nils Grinde: *Norsk Musikkhistorie*, 1971, p.174.
15  Grieg to Beyer, 4 May 1888 from London.
16  In their translations for Peters both Lobedanz and Corder give 'my' ('people' and 'country') rather than Vinje's more impersonal pronoun.
17  Beyer: *Utsyn over norsk litteratur*, p.76.
18  Svendsen: *Edvard Griegs Vinjesanger*, p.104.
19  Astra Desmond in *Grieg: A Symposium*, ed. Gerald Abraham, 1948, p.88.
20  Grieg to Paulsen, 4 June 1905.
21  Svendsen: *Edvard Griegs Vinjesanger*, p.59 quoting the critic in the *Berlingske Tidende*, 24 December 1881.
22  Grieg's enthusiastic but not very discerning American biographer, Finck, had no doubts, writing in an article 'Grieg's influence on the musical world' published in *The Musician*, July 1898, p.191, 'Though an agnostic, I felt the magic of religious devotion when listening to "Faith".'
23  A parallel might be drawn with Parry's noble setting of Blake's *Jerusalem*, sung in Britain as a hymn, but intended ironically by the poet.
24  Grieg to Finck, 17 July 1900.
25  Ibid.
26  Benestad and Schjelderup-Ebbe; *Edvard Grieg, mennesket og kunstneren*, 1980, p.204.
27  Literally 'forgotten again'. Grieg spells the word without the 'r', but it does appear in the title as it is printed in the *Diktsamling*.
28  *Edvard Grieg, mennesket og kunstneren*, p.208.
29  Grieg to Paulsen, 4 June 1905 from Christiania.
30  Presumably sung in Danish, as that is the form of the titles Grieg uses here.
31  *The Last Springtime*, Elkin and Co., London 1961.
32  *My Mother*, J. Fischer & Bro., New York 1954.
33  Wilhelm Hansen to Grieg, 15 August 1881 from Copenhagen.
34  Kurt Pahlen: *Music of the World* (trans. James A. Galston), Crown Publishers, New York 1949, p.218.
35  Johansen: *Edvard Grieg*, p.259.

# 10 Travels and 'Travel Memories'

The early 1880s were to prove another difficult period in Grieg's life, both on an artistic and a personal level. He was not even really happy in Lofthus any more, feeling, as he recalled in a letter to Schjelderup in September 1903, that 'the mountains had nothing more to tell me'[1] and that the area as a permanent place to live was too confining. Neither was Bergen's musical life much better than Christiania's had been; the same petty problems of administration cropped up and there were even arguments over his salary as director of Harmonien. He conducted the orchestra from the autumn of 1880 to the spring of 1882 and once again used up almost all his energies in the process, so that he had neither the strength nor the inclination, let alone the time, to teach and compose.

Always anxious to turn the blame for lack of compositions on outside factors, Grieg wrote to Max Abraham in August 1881 that, perhaps, if he had a stipend, he would feel obliged to compose to justify it. Abraham promptly replied offering three thousand marks for a series of works over the ensuing twelve months. Grieg hastily wrote again to say that he had meant the idea as a joke and although an informal contract was established, the first of the promised pieces, the Cello Sonata, was not despatched to Abraham until the spring of 1883.

It has been suggested that Grieg needed outside inspiration and initiative in order to compose.[2] Certainly he was a romantic composer in times that were turning against romanticism and he was too unsure of himself to follow his own inclinations. Therefore the non-productive patches continued to occur periodically and to depress him, and he tended to blame these times on all sorts of things — Leipzig's supposedly poor training, his personal relationships, his working conditions. Benestad and Schjelderup-Ebbe have noted the lack of reference to Nina in Grieg's letters to Beyer until later in his life, when he frequently expressed his gratitude to her as a wife and as an interpreter of and ambassadress for his songs. It is significant that in the years 1880 to 1883, when the relationship between them was at its lowest ebb, Grieg wrote no songs. In fact the only compositions from this period are the *Norwegian Dances*, op.35, for piano duet.

From a letter he wrote to Paulsen at the end of April 1881, Grieg apparently thought this particular non-productive phase might be permanent: 'You are living in a productive period which every true artist has. Yes, it is a lovely time. *My* productive time was so short. I have waited and still wait constantly for it to return. But the fine weaving of circumstances must be in order before this will happen.'[3]

The year 1882 was one of health problems for Grieg, which must have compounded his lack of inspiration for composition, and 1883 was a year of travelling. He went first to Bayreuth, where he heard *Parsifal*, then to various other German cities and finally to Holland, arriving in Amsterdam in the New Year of 1884. He had also been learning French 'one hour every day', as he wrote to Beyer, but in the event was too exhausted to go to Paris as he had intended.

During all this time Grieg had been very unhappy with his married state. His frustrations of the late 1870s had not been resolved and he still felt that Nina and the sort of life she wanted put a barrier between him and his art. Much of his unhappiness was conveyed in letters to Beyer, but Beyer destroyed a number of them before his own death and Marie Beyer's tactful selection, published in 1923, contains no letters at all between August 1874 and June 1882.

Nina recognized that artists are frequently attracted to their admirers, and Benestad and Schjelderup-Ebbe mention a woman who appeared on the scene early in the 1880s. This was Elise ('Leis') Schjelderup, the twenty-six-year-old artist daughter of a Bergen magistrate and sister of the composer Gerhard Schjelderup, Grieg's first Norwegian biographer. Leis lived at this time in Paris, the incentive, no doubt, for Grieg's lessons in French and his intended visit there, and there exists (again according to Benestad and Schjelderup-Ebbe) a collection of letters to her from Grieg, which are not publicly available. It certainly seems that, because he associated his songs primarily with Nina even when not expressly written for her to sing, Grieg was unable to compose songs when his life with her was unhappy. This had happened between 1878 and 1880, although apparently without the agency of a third party, and was to happen again in late 1895, preventing him from finishing the *Haugtussa* song-cycle for almost three years. The attraction to Leis Schjelderup caused him to leave home in the summer of 1883 and it is not clear whether or not he intended this to be a permanent break from Nina.

In a letter to Beyer from Rudolstadt Grieg wrote, 'Your letter fell like balm on a sick soul' and continued with a long discussion on whether one should subjugate the personality to the general good. He ends: 'I repeat, to come home now would be my ruin . . . it would be to tear myself away from my development, that fermentation I can only go through out here.'[4] Although another letter to his friend, from Leipzig in October of the same year, states that he has 'just written a page to Nina', yet a letter to her for her birthday was enclosed in one to Beyer rather than sent directly. Admittedly, Nina was staying with the Beyers at the time and Grieg was concerned that his friends should do all they could to make the day a happy one for her. This letter goes on:

> I think and think, so I could go mad, but will not even try to root around in the anthill of feelings, moods and impressions, which really make me feel that I am best where I am . . . On the 25th I go to Breslau and from that day on it will be a travelling life until Christmas. Only I know that I must find Norway again one day and with that find pleasure by thoughts of home . . . But happiness for me is to be found nowhere if I can't find it — within myself.[5]

It was Frants Beyer, good friend to both the Griegs, who eventually tried to heal the breach and the couple were reconciled early in 1884, when all four met in Leipzig and journeyed on to Italy. Grieg wrote to Beyer from Amsterdam on 29 December 1883 to thank him for his friendship: 'As unhappy as I was when I left and later that first part of the summer, and so much less unhappy as I now feel — no, I would not have believed it possible! Happy!'

The period of turmoil saw no songs and those from the next few years were for the most part not amongst the composer's most inspired. In fact, to furnish the next album, the *Romancer Ældre og Nyere* (Songs old and new), op. 39, Grieg wrote only two new songs to add to four earlier ones.[6] The first of these two was *I Liden højt deroppe* (In the meadow high above), the only solo setting Grieg made to a poem by Jonas Lie.[7] Lie (1833–1908) was trained as a lawyer but, after his bankruptcy following some dubious speculation in timber, he decided to try and earn his living by writing. He is known first and foremost as a novelist and was hailed by Bjørnson early in his career. Very generously, in 1905 Lie declined the Nobel Prize for literature, because it had not yet been awarded to Ibsen. Although he was a great novelist, his two volumes of poetry, published in 1866 and 1889, uphold his reputation as an unremarkable poet.

*I Liden højt deroppe* is a rather tongue-in-cheek poem, describing the writer who, whether he is up in the mountain pastures, beside a river or amongst a crowd, can still, like a sharp-eyed hunter, see the blue of the sky above the trees or in someone's eyes. The three stanzas are interrelated by content, for example in the lines that appear identically or only slightly changed in a type of refrain before the last line of each stanza:

> . . . Himlen
> blå, o, så blå,
> evig, herlig blå!
> ( . . . the sky, blue, oh, so blue, eternal, glorious blue!)

Grieg sets the song strophically to a beautiful, flowing and wide-ranging melody that almost sings itself. The piano accompaniment is more varied than in many of his songs and makes use of a wide range of piano 'colour', both in tessitura and in rhythmic figures. The two-bar introduction, which is the accompaniment to the third and fourth bars an octave higher, was, as may be seen from the manuscript, added later. This is a 'hunting horn' theme and, together with the rhythm of voice and piano at bars 13 to 16, is very reminiscent of Schubert (Ex. 70).

The feminine cadences in the first part of each strophe have a softening effect and even the dissonance caused by the melodic sequence in bars 5 to 8, where the B sharp to C sharp in the left hand is sounded against the B natural in the vocal line, thrills rather than jars. A beautiful modulation occurs at the word 'blå (blue)', when the tonic E becomes the leading-note of F major and suddenly the breadth of the sky stretching overhead can be felt, and the music broadens for one bar from $\frac{6}{8}$ to $\frac{2}{4}$. Each chord in this bar undergoes a chromatic alteration, finally resolving to a Ic-V-I cadence in the tonic E major:

Ex.70                                      I Liden højt deroppe

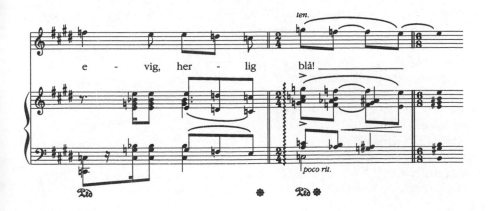

There is a freshness and clarity about this song, and although the period in which Grieg wrote it is not amongst his most inspirational, it is nevertheless difficult to understand how Benestad and Schjelderup-Ebbe could dismiss it as being 'like a routine exercise'.[8]

The second of the two 'nyere' songs written in 1884 was to provide the final song of the op.39 album. However, *Hører jeg Sangen klinger* (When I hear the song resound) is scarcely comparable to *I Liden højt deroppe*. The poem is a translation by Nordahl Rolfsen of Heine's 'Hör' ich das Liedchen klingen', which was also set by Schumann in the *Dichterliebe* cycle. Grieg's setting has a simple vocal melody over a busy accompaniment which, although pianistically written, has a rhythmic figure that is repeated throughout the song until it loses its impact. The song is through-composed and has a very long postlude of eighteen bars.

Harmonically, there is nothing truly adventurous until towards the end, when (bars 41 to 45) the bass ascends chromatically, ending in the subdominant chord, broken in the right hand and sounded over the dominant in the left. The anticipated cadence is delayed as both melody and the left hand of the accompaniment move downwards in semitones, finally resolving to the tonic *major* key, all to the words 'min grændselose Kval (my boundless pain)'. Apart from this passage, the song is largely uninspired.

The op.39 songs were published by Wilhelm Hansen in December 1884 and were dedicated to 'Hr. Professor Niels Ravnkilde in Rome'. They were not published as a separate album by Peters, but all but the third of the six, *I Liden højt deroppe*, were included in the fifth volume of the *Grieg Album*.

The Griegs remained in Italy for four months, spending Norway's national day, 17 May, beside Lake Maggiore. A letter to Beyer of that date relates that Grieg left Rome and Florence, and to a certain extent Milan too, 'sick and sad', but that as he travelled further north, he began to feel a new strength and hope for the future. The mountains and lakes reminded him of the Sørfjord and the letter ends: 'That first evening, and especially next morning when I awoke, I was moved to tears at seeing the snow and the mountains, those things so long, long missed.' This yearning for Norway and the fact that the Beyers were at this time in the process of building a house, Næsset, on the fjord a little south of Bergen motivated the Griegs to make plans for a permanent home of their own. Consequently, in the following months Troldhaugen (Troll Hill) took shape and, by the spring of 1885, Grieg was supervising his own building work. Troldhaugen was on the opposite promontory to Næsset and the Beyers and their new neighbours frequently crossed the fjord by boat. The Griegs moved into Troldhaugen in April 1885 and, although the composer was beginning to win recognition in Christiania as well as abroad, he was not particularly well-off and the house eventually cost 12,500 kroner. Perhaps it was not totally in jest that Grieg had written to Röntgen referring to the op.39 songs: 'I have completed an album of songs and with it hope at least to be able to obtain money for the windows in the basement.'[9]

Nordahl Rolfsen, the translator of *Hører jeg sangen klinger*, also provided the Norwegian translations of the German poems set by Grieg in the *Seks Sange*, op.48, the first two of which, *Gruss* and *Dereinst, Gedanke mein*, were also composed in 1884. Less successful was Rolfsen's own text for the only song Grieg wrote in 1885. This was *Under Juletræet* (Under the Christmas tree), which is simpler and rather more sentimental than Krohn's *Sang til Juletræet* (Song to the Christmas tree), which Grieg was to set as one of the *Barnlige Sange* (Children's songs), op.61, and it bears little comparison to the later song in either literary or musical value. The song was published as a supplement in an edition of a children's paper, *Illustreret Tidende for Børn*, in Bergen in 1885–86, and Oslo University Library also possesses a photocopy of another edition of the song, published by Fr. G. Knudtzon's in Copenhagen.

The vocal melody of *Under Juletræet* is built largely on a descending sequential phrase over a chordal accompaniment, which has some interest in the string of plagal cadences and in the flattened fifth in the first inversion of the supertonic seventh, which precedes the perfect cadence:

Ex.71                                                                Under Juletræet

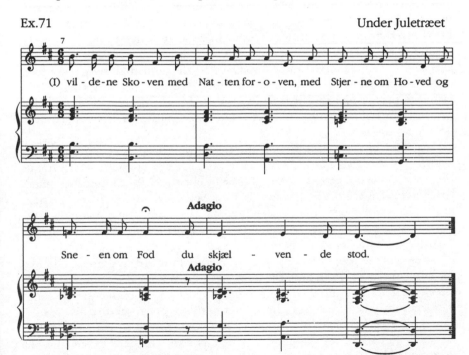

(I) vil - de - ne Sko - ven med Nat - ten for - o - ven, med Stjer - ne om Ho - ved og

Sne - en om Fod du skjæl - ven - de stod.

(In the wild wood with the night above, with a star at your head and snow at your feet,
you stood trembling)

The year 1885 was a comparatively static one for Grieg and Nina, with no travelling except for concerts in Christiania and in Copenhagen, where they stayed into the spring of 1886. Before leaving, Grieg gave a series of recitals in Danish cities and it was during this time that he met Holger Drachmann. As Drachmann was as much influenced by music as Grieg was by poetry, the two soon became firm friends.

Drachmann was the son of a naval doctor and he had a special association with the sea right from childhood, graduating from the Academy of Art in Copenhagen in 1865 with special honours in marine painting. His complex character affected his writing, which shows elements of both revolution from and a concern for folk traditions. His three marriages marked different periods in his life, which were also reflected in his writing, and he produced several collections of poetry throughout his lifetime, as well as novels, plays and melodramas. Interestingly, like Grieg, he also went to Italy and gained a great deal from the light and warmth he found there, and Paul V. Rubow has commented, 'When late in the year 1875 Drachmann travelled south to Italy, he instilled into Danish poetry a new spring.'[10] His verse shows a wide variety of style, meter, rhyme-schemes and subject-matter and it is unfortunate that Grieg did not set the best examples.

The first group of poems he did use were inspired by a tour the two made in the Hardanger area and up to Jotunheim in the summer of 1886. Drachmann proposed to depict the tour in verse for Grieg to set. However, instead of the portrayals of the natural surroundings which might have been expected, Drachmann was more impressed by the human 'scenery', and four of the six poems have female names as titles. Deprived of descriptions of his favourite part of Norway, it is little wonder that the poems did not inspire greatness in the composer, and both words and music are little more than occasional pieces.

The most interesting feature of the songs, published as op.44 under the title *Reiseminder fra Fjeld og Fjord*, is the prologue and epilogue which frame the four female portraits. The *Prolog*, subtitled 'På Skineggen, mod Jotunheim (On the Skinegg, towards Jotunheim)', is not so much a picture of the place or the view, but rather a personal communing with nature by the poet, who wants to enter the womb of the mountain like an embryo and to become one with his surroundings.

Grieg sets the poem's three stanzas in ternary form, in an unusual, almost recitative style, which in both the form and the harmony have suggestions of later songs, for example *Eros*, op.70 no.1. The *Prolog* is marked to be sung 'not too slowly and freely declaimed, but with the given rhythm as a basis'. The quality of declamation was important to Grieg, who wrote in one of his letters to Finck, 'to come completely into its own, this bold poem must if possible be declaimed in the original language'.[11] The four-bar introduction and the first three bars of the vocal melody are based on the chord of the dominant ninth of the tonic C major; the eleventh is added in the eighth bar and the use of these chords has the flavour of early impressionism. In fact, almost the whole of the first section is built over the dominant pedal. The anticipated cadence in the tonic key does not materialize. In the recapitulation, the chord superimposed on the dominant pedal is first a tonic triad with an augmented fifth, that is a G sharp, which clashes with the dominant G natural before proceeding as before. The middle section is built on another unusual chord sequence, which falls into two halves; first, four bars which contain one chord each: E minor, F sharp major, F major and C major, and then four bars which alternate chords of A major and C major, with a chromatic passing note in the third of them.

Grieg paid a great deal of attention to the notation of the vocal melody in order to achieve the correct declamation he required and the line rises sequentially to a joyful high G at the end of the stanza. The whole song is quietly impressive and quite different from anything he had written so far, even though free declamation had been used in earlier songs.

The second song, *Johanne*, is much less inspired, in spite of one or two pleasing touches in the music. While on their walking tour, Grieg and Drachmann called a number of times on the sculptor Nils Bergslien, who had a studio at Eidfjord. Johanne was Bergslien's wife and Ragna, the subject of the fifth song of the set, his daughter. *Johanne* seems to aspire to a folk-song style without actually achieving its aim, except in the major key section from bar 17, where suddenly we seem to hear the true Grieg. The mists, however, clear only briefly and even the movement from the tonic chord to the chord of the flattened submediant in the introduction and postlude, a device which elsewhere is used to great effect, here seems merely contrived.

Interestingly, Grieg, who was usually content to leave the subtleties of interpretation to the performer, here makes sure of the correct stressing of the ironic final lines of each stanza by underlining the important words and noting that 'The underlined syllables in this bar should be lingered over a little longer, the non-underlined ones a little less, than their true values.' The poem is a saccharine account of how Johanne, who had no possessions or dowry apart from her 'fresh and healthy' self, offered her love to Bergslien, in spite of the scorn of the local people.

The next song, *Ragnhild*, is much superior from the musical point of view if not the poetic. The Ragnhild of the title was a pretty girl seen on board the fjord steamer, who made such a deep impression on Drachmann that, even after her departure, he still saw her everywhere he looked. Musically, the song has a folk-dance character and much use is made of the pedal tonic fifth and the alternation of the major and minor modes. The ends of a number of the vocal phrases are echoed in decorated form in the accompaniment to lovely effect: Ex.72.

Ex.72                                                                      Ragnhild

Everything began to sing,

There is also a freshness in the reiteration of this phrase in F major and the first phrases of the outer sections are saved from mediocrity by the chromatic harmony, beginning with the subdominant chord instead of the anticipated tonic.

The middle section opens over a dominant pedal, but with a hint in the A flat of the tonic minor key. The tonality eventually settles into the dominant, C major, with the B natural of the vocal line sounding against the chromatically altered mediant of the new key, and then the dominant ninth chord, bringing a breath of fresh air and beautifully conveying the regret of the end of the voyage and Ragnhild's departure. More melancholy creeps into the second half of this section, as the poet can no longer see any beauty in his surroundings. Here the piano leads and the voice echoes and, with more chromatically altered notes, the music glides back to the tonic F major for the recapitulation of the opening section.

Although Drachmann was not quite so sentimental here as elsewhere in these poems, the music is far better than the poem deserves and the published edition is in fact the second version of the song. Grieg wrote to Beyer in September 1886 that he could not choose between two versions of some songs: 'Do you remember Ragnhild? I have composed it completely anew. Also Julesne [op.49, no.5]. There are also things where my self-criticism says stop. And there is no-one to be found here besides you, neither musician nor enthusiast, whose judgement carries any weight with me.'[12] This was just a week after the letter to tell Beyer that the op.44 cycle, 'in spite of everything, is now finished'.[13]

Bergen Public Library contains the manuscript of the first version of *Ragnhild* as well as the later one, which was the version eventually published. The first manuscript has many of the elements of the later version, for example the piano echoes of the vocal phrases: Ex.73.

Ex.73                                                    Ragnhild (first version)

(Everything began to sing, fjords and mountains in a cluster)

but it lacks the polish of the finished song (Ex.72). The rhythmic figures are
frequently found in augmented form in the final version, both in the outer
and middle sections, so giving a more peaceful atmosphere to the song, and
the tonality of the later setting in F *major*, with transitions into F minor, is
certainly more subtle. The middle section is similar in both manuscripts
except in some details of rhythm, although the piano writing was refined in
the later version.

It is surprising, when his unusually well-developed sense of self-criticism
caused him to rewrite *Ragnhild*, that Grieg did not do the same with other
songs in this album. The fourth song, *Ingebjørg*, for example, is very weak,
and Drachmann's verse even more trite than elsewhere in the set. The four
lines at the beginning of the second stanza are of almost unsurpassed inanity:

> Dit Bryst er hvælvet, Ingebjørg,
> lig Bræens høje Sne,
> men ingen Fjeldbestiger
> få Underet at se . . .

(Your breast is domed, Ingebjørg,/like the glacier's high snow,/but no
mountain-climber/is allowed to see the wonder...)

It is hardly unexpected, then, that Grieg's setting of this poem lacks any
originality. The simple, folksong-like melody and equally straightforward
accompaniment here have none of the charm of such simplicity elsewhere. As
Benestad and Schjelderup-Ebbe put it so well, 'there is no fresh mountain
water in his melodic veins.'[14] There is little harmonic interest even in the
occasional chromatic movement and the resultant dissonances between
accompaniment and melody. The three stanzas are set strophically and in
almost the entire second half of each strophe, the accompaniment right hand
doubles the vocal line. The use here of a transition to the subdominant
instead of the expected tonic has no freshness about it and the short vivace

postlude serves no real purpose, except perhaps to suggest that the song should not – and indeed cannot – be taken seriously.

Inspiration returns to some extent in the fifth song, *Ragna*. The poem begins promisingly, with regret that time passes and children grow up, but becomes rather sentimental later, as the poet compares the girl growing to womanhood with a mountain lake fed by a 'restless river'. A lovely flowing vocal melody, with an effective ascending chromatic passage, is accompanied by rippling broken chords that create a gentle atmosphere:

Ex.74

(Oh, Ragna, how the time goes: the other day you were four years old)

Grieg sets the first two stanzas strophically and repeats the first of Drachmann's three stanzas for his recapitulation. The third stanza, where the girl speaks of her growing up, is set in a recitative style over a dominant pedal, with alternate G major and G sharp minor chords, each resolving to the dominant seventh. The contrast of the minor key of the vocal phrases with the major key for the final climactic line, 'til sidst en Huldre for dig står (Until at last an alluring woman stands before you)', is effectively managed and gives a certain melancholy to the return of the first stanza. A nostalgic coda is built on the final words of that stanza, set to a phrase which falls sequentially over a chromatically descending bass, and the song ends with a modal cadence. The music once more surpasses the quality of the poem and *Ragna* certainly deserves some consideration by singers.

The *Epilog* is in a similar recitative style to the *Prolog*. The poem here is subtitled 'Farvel til Tvindehaugen (Farewell to Tvindehaugen' – Drachmann's mountain cottage in Jotunheim), but as with the *Prolog* there is little scenic description; instead a pious wish that, from the mountains, one could learn the way to purity and the unity brought by devotion to nature. Each of the two stanzas, set strophically with minor variations, ends with a quotation from a folk-song from Kährnten: 'Auf der Alm da giebt's ka' Sünd'! (On the Alm there is no sin)', a Tyrolean yodelling song which, so John Horton has related, 'Drachmann was fond of giving vent to when in the mountains'.[15] Grieg was obviously not entirely convinced of the wisdom of using the quotation, and wrote to Finck that 'the Epilog has failed on account of that banal phrase . . . The poet sang this phrase for me as he had heard it in the Tyrol and in a way suggested its use to me. Perhaps I'll come to *eliminate* it in an eventual new edition.'

The recitative style builds up, both in tempo and texture, for the second part of each strophe, although the vocal line remains more declamation than melody, and the triplet chords in the accompaniment increase the agitation. The key of this section, D flat major, is altered enharmonically to C sharp minor, and the yodelling song is eventually introduced in what one expects to be the dominant of C major, the tonic key. However, as in the *Prolog*, the anticipated resolution is unforthcoming, Grieg using the same modal cadences at the end of each strophe as he had at the end of the outer sections of the first song.

The album was at first to be called, at Drachmann's suggestion, 'From Troldhaugen to Tvindehaugen', described in a letter to Grieg as 'lyrical, musical collegial tramps in three sections: 1) The End, 2) The Beginning, 3) The Continuation, which thus implies the work's undying, i.e. immortal character'.[16] However, Grieg did not seem to think that the resulting poems justified this title, probably because of the lack of any description of the journey. He wrote to Beyer, 'I would have no objection, if he would write some more poems, which could form a bridge over the Løvstakk to Eidfjord. If he doesn't do so, I have thought of calling the collection *Reiseminder fra Fjeld og Fjord* [Travel Memories from Mountain and Fjord]',[17] the title under which the songs were in fact eventually published in December 1886 by Wilhelm Hansen. They were dedicated to the poet and appeared in this first edition only in Danish. The later Peters edition, published in 1899, had translations into French by Victor Wilder and into German, 'aus dem Norwegischen' (sic) by Wilhelm Henzen.

If the *Reiseminder* are little more than album sketches, we should at least be grateful that Grieg enjoyed the trip and that it gave him new heart for composing again, for 1886 also saw the inception of his third and last violin Sonata, which was completed the following year. However, the next two years were to prove very busy ones, involving concerts all over Europe, and between the autumn of 1887 and the spring of 1890, Grieg was in Norway for only a total of nine months. He visited England, Germany and France, and had invitations from Vienna, Prague and St Petersburg amongst others. All the travelling meant very little composing and, although he was still determined on a large-scale work, the only music published during this time was two more books of songs.

The first of these was the *Seks Sange* (Six Songs), op.48. The most interesting thing about these songs is that they are to German texts, the first time Grieg had used the language since the op.4 songs of 1864. The songs also had Norwegian words by Nordahl Rolfsen and, contrary to the usual practice, are more often sung – when they are sung at all – in Norwegian than in German. Monrad Johansen felt that with the return to German poetry Grieg also returned to earlier values and that all his fine work with the poetry of Ibsen, Bjørnson and Vinje had been in vain. The op.48 songs, however, are much more mature than the early German settings and if they do not rank amongst the greatest of the composer's songs and if they are more in the Lieder tradition than *romanser*, they are nevertheless deserving of inclusion in many a recital programme.

According to the dates on the manuscripts, the first two songs were written earlier than the other four, on 16 and 17 September 1884, while Grieg was staying in Lofthus. The first song, *Gruss* (Greeting), is an exuberant setting of a poem by Heine and the cheerful atmosphere is evident right from the start in the opening bars for the piano, a figure which then serves as an accompaniment to the vocal line. Although quite a short song at fifty-six bars long, it is through-composed and falls into two sections. The second is the more adventurous in harmonic structure, with transitions to come already hinted at by the C natural in bar 24. The ensuing vocal line rises chromatically, resulting in a number of dissonances between voice and accompaniment, before finally resolving to the tonic:

Ex.75                                                                         Gruss

(If you see a rose there, say that I send her greetings)

A return of the opening upward arpeggio figures (similar to bars 45 and 46 above) in the accompaniment, which disappear brightly, ever higher, forms the short postlude. In style, *Gruss* is more German than Norwegian, but the maturity of the adventurous harmony and chromatic vocal line of the second section makes it difficult to agree with Monrad Johansen that 'it would not be surprising if it had been found in the op.2 songs'.[18]

The second song, *Dereinst, Gedanke mein* (One day, my thoughts), is quite opposite in feeling to *Gruss*. The poem, also set very differently by Hugo Wolf, is by Emanuel Geibel (1815–84), the author of the words of Grieg's very first song, *Siehst du das Meer?*. He published several volumes of poetry in the 1840s and eventually became an honorary professor at Munich University and the centre of that city's literary circle. Grieg sets this poem strophically, in a slow molto andante, hymn-like style. The vocal range is very small, less than an octave, and the melody is broken by a number of rests. It is quite beautiful, with some lovely wide upward and downward intervals, which occur at the end of each half of the strophe, and the tonic to dominant fall especially underlines the words 'wirst ruhig sein'.

The song opens in B major, with some suggestion of the relative minor, but modulates by the end of each strophe to the key of the mediant, D sharp major. The accompaniment is very sustained, moving largely in minims, and occasionally there is some striking chromatic movement within an otherwise uncomplicated harmonic structure:

Ex.76            Dereinst, Gedanke mein

(if love's glow will not let you be still, in cool earth)

There is a restraint about the setting which suits the poem without illuminating it in any fresh or original way, and Monrad Johansen observed that the emotions are seen at second hand, rather than personally experienced by the composer. There is certainly little of the searing grief of Wolf's setting in the *Spanisches Liederbuch*.

The remaining four songs of the op.48 group were written five years later than the first two, all between 15 and 20 August 1889. *Lauf der Welt* (The way of the world), however, seems immediately to recapture the lighthearted atmosphere of *Gruss*, and there are many elements from folk-song, which suit the happy innocence of the poem. The pedal tonic fifth of the accompaniment left hand throughout the first fourteen bars leads to the familiar Griegian sound of the dominant chord over the tonic. Also, between bars 7 and 10, the subdominant chord is sounded over the tonic, which is reminiscent of the folksong-like music of Mahler and in a way bridges the gap between the countries of the poet and the composer. The supertonic ninth chord which precedes the perfect cadence, however, is pure Grieg.

The three stanzas of Uhland's poem are set in ABA form and, as usual, it is the middle section that contains the most interesting harmonic progressions. From the relative minor key, B minor, with echoes of the vocal line in the right hand of the accompaniment, the melodic sequence moves the tonality to C sharp minor, while the pedal B is retained in the left hand. Then the chromatic shifting begins: first to the dominant seventh chord of A flat, then to the dominant seventh of D and back again, before the latter on the second occasion resolves to the tonic D major for the recapitulation of the first section, which sets the third stanza. The wistful ending, 'doch keines sagt: ich liebe dich!', is underlined by Grieg's carefully placed marking of 'senza cresc.' over the last phrase. As in *Gruss*, the opening accompaniment figure is used as the short postlude and once again the music fades into silence. Because of the folk music elements, this song is rather more typical of its composer than the previous two, but is still a long way from the originality of the Vinje settings.

*Die verschwiegene Nachtigall* (The discreet nightingale), the fourth of the six songs, is much more in the tradition of Lieder than *romanser*. Although there are some familiar Griegian elements in this strophic setting, for example the decorations in the vocal line and the way the piano doubles the voice throughout, the style is more reminiscent of German folk-song settings than anything Norwegian. Also the harmonic structure, for example in bars 13 and 14, is very like Brahms, especially in the way the phrases end on the third beat of a $\frac{3}{4}$ bar: Ex.77. Unusually, Grieg set the word 'brachen' over two bars of the vocal melody (a sequence one tone lower than bars 12 and 13 below) and it appears as if, even more unusually, he had placed the musical considerations of continuing the sequence above those of declamation. Even more awkwardly declaimed is the corresponding passage in the third strophe: Ex.78.

The end of each strophe is broadened out to $\frac{4}{4}$ and the extended use of a descending sequential phrase, here shared between piano and voice, is also very unusual for Grieg, although this whole section is written over a dominant pedal, which is not. The accompaniment figure of the opening bars serves at the end of each stanza to imitate the nightingale's song and also provides the link between each strophe and as the brief postlude.

Ex.77                        Die verschwiegene Nachtigall

da mögt ihr fin - den, wie___ wir Bei - de die (Blumen brachen)

(there you might find the two of us picking flowers)

Ex.78                        Die verschwiegene Nachtigall

Kei - ner er - fah - - - re das, als er___ und ich;

(no-one knows it except him and me)

The poem, by Walther von der Vogelweide, has an impudent charm which is not unlike that to be found in some of Andersen's verses, for example *Rosenknoppen*. Von der Vogelweide (c. 1170–1230) was the great lyric poet of the Middle Ages in Germany. Little is known of his origins, but he was at the court of Duke Leopold V in Vienna at the end of the twelfth century, and then a 'fahrender Sanger' for the next twenty years. According to tradition, he spent his last few years in Würzburg and is buried there. His courtly love-lyrics are his best and *Unter den Linden* — the original title of this poem — is considered to be the pearl of them. The poem was written in Middle High German and whoever translated it into the modern form of the language omitted the third of the original four stanzas. The modern version has also been somewhat 'refined', omitting references to the lovers' bed of flowers and giving instead 'wo ich mit meinem Trauten *sass*'. In the last stanza, the reference to the girl's lover lying with her is modified to 'wie ich da *ruhte*' in the German, but is omitted altogether in the Norwegian! Grieg directs his setting to be sung 'mezza voce' throughout and if, once again, he offers us no original thoughts, he has created a pleasant enough song.

After a great poet of the Middle Ages, the next song is a setting of a poem by a great poet of the romantic era, Goethe. *Zur Rosenzeit* (At rose-time) is very far removed from folk-song. The syncopated chords in the right hand accompaniment indicate from the very beginning that 'Rose-time' is not a happy time and the piano part is full of languishing dissonances. The song has an angular vocal line with many rising and falling intervals, often augmented, and as in *Stambogsrim* (op. 25 no. 3) the composer underlines the anguish of the words by having every phrase begin on the second beat of the bar:

Ex.79                                                                          Zur Rosenzeit

(blossom, ah! for the hopeless one, whose soul is broken by grief!)

The left hand doubles the vocal line for the outer sections and for part of the longer middle section and it is, as usual, this middle section which has the harmonic development.

The F minor tonality of the opening modulates to C flat major within eight bars. The dominant of this new key, G flat, undergoes an enharmonic alteration to F sharp and the opening phrases of the section are repeated a semitone higher than before, to take the tonality to the distant key of C major. For the next eight bars the C major triad is retained in the syncopated chords of the right hand, while the voice, now doubled in octaves in both hands of the accompaniment, has a melody in C *minor*. This passage is then reiterated sequentially in F major/minor. The vocal line throughout moves stepwise and it is the dissonant harmonies in the accompaniment that point the sorrow of the words. Nevertheless, as with other songs from this period, the emotion appears rather contrived and not from the composer's personal experience.

The final song of the op. 48 set, *Ein Traum* (A dream), is considered to be the most significant and certainly has more immediacy of feeling to it than the others. This time the dream, unlike *Eit syn* (op. 33 no. 6), is a happy one, for it becomes reality, and the urgency felt in the triplet arpeggios of the accompaniment stems from passion not despair. The vocal line is less angular than in the preceding song, but there are rising and falling intervals of fifths, sixths and sevenths. Here, however, they underline hope and contentment instead of anguish and are marked by the composer to be sung 'sehr weich' (Ex. 80).

Harmonically, the song is much more serene than *Zur Rosenzeit*, with a conventional modulation from the tonic D flat major to the dominant in the first section. The vocal phrases in *Ein Traum*, as in the previous song, each begin after a rest, here of a quaver's instead of a crotchet's duration, and the shorter hesitation is no longer a long-drawn sigh of anguish, but rather a quick catching of the breath with joy. Interestingly, the songs were written on consecutive days, *Ein Traum* on 19 August and *Zur Rosenzeit* on 20 August. The more settled feeling about *Ein Traum* does not exclude some chromatically altered chords, nor the occasional dissonance, for example the G flat in the accompaniment against an F natural in the vocal line in bar 5. The little accompaniment figure in bar 10 is reminiscent of some of the folk music characteristics used elsewhere, especially in the G natural sounded against the A flat major triad:

Ex. 80                                                                                      Ein Traum

Mir träum - te einst ein schö - ner Traum: mich lieb - te ei - ne

blon - de Maid, es war am grün - en Wal - des - saum,

es war zur war - men    Früh - lings-zeit:

(I once dreamt a lovely dream; a fair maid loved me; it was at the edge of the green wood,
it was in the warm springtime)

The song builds to a fine climax as the poet speaks of his joy that his dream is
reality. *Ein Traum* is a big song with a vocal range from middle C to high A
flat and very rewarding to sing, which no doubt accounts for its popularity
despite its otherwise conventional character.

The poem is the only one Grieg set by Friedrich Bodenstedt (1819–92),
who, after Geibel, was the most popular lyric poet of the Munich literary
group. He spent some time in the east and, in 1851, published a volume of
imitations of oriental verse, *Die Lieder des Mirza Schaffy*, which proved
enormously popular, but which rather overshadowed his later work.

The *Seks Sange* were first published by Peters in 1889 and then by Hansen
in 1894. They are dedicated to the Swedish-born Wagnerian soprano, Ellen
Nordgren Gulbranson. The Norwegian versions by Nordahl Rolfsen are for
the most part very accurate and Grieg was well pleased with them. A later
edition published by Peters in 1890 had French translations by Victor
Wilder; the same edition's English versions are not attributed, but are
probably by Corder. There is also a good translation of *Ein Traum* by Astra
Desmond, published by Augener of London in 1961, but unfortunately no
longer in print, and various other arrangements of the same song exist,
including a duet version and one for male-voice choir.

The second book of songs from this period consisted of more settings of
poems by Holger Drachmann and was published as *Seks Sange*, op.49. Most
of the poems are long and elaborate in style and they drew from Grieg a
larger-scale response than the *Reiseminder*. The poems are similar to some to
be found in the German romantic tradition and totally unlike the concentrated style of, for example, Ibsen. Grieg's musical effects thus tend to be
made in an extravagant manner, rather than in the fine attention to detail of
which he was capable.

The first of the six settings, *Saa du Knøsen, som strøg forbi* (Did you see the
lad who swept by), is a big song both in vocal and pianistic terms. The vocal
range is from the A below middle C to high F sharp, and the full range of the

keyboard is also exploited. The very first bar has a familiar Grieg-like ring, with the dominant chord sounded against the pedal tonic fifth, and the numerous transitions are created both by chromatic movement and by some sequential writing. The opening melody is built largely on the tonic triad and the notes of the various other triads used provide much of the thematic material for the rest of the song. In the second phrase the melody, now in the relative minor key sounded over the open fifth of the supertonic chord of the original A major, creates a chord of the ninth to lovely effect.

It is interesting that in many of the songs in this set effects are created by what Grieg does *not* write, as well as by what he does; for example, the first vocal phrases of this song are accompanied by the left hand only. The song is set strophically, with minor alterations in each strophe to accommodate the changes of rhythm of the words. All the effects are created on a large canvas and John Horton has described the song as 'overpowering in its hearty rhetoric'.[19] Certainly four long stanzas are rather overwhelming, especially for modern audiences who might also find the late nineteenth-century moral tone of not judging people by their appearances rather hard to take seriously.

The second song, *Vug, o Vove* (Rock, oh waves), again makes full use of both voice and piano, with a vocal range here from middle C sharp to high F sharp. Although each strophe ends pianissimo, in the penultimate phrase

Ex.81                                                                                    Vug, o Vove

(Rock, oh waves, with your gentle hand the boat in which we glide,)

Grieg asks the singer to sustain a high F sharp, marked 'fortissimo' and with a crescendo, for seven bars — that is, fourteen allegro beats — before it falls to the lower octave. In the final strophe an optional top A is written over the sustained F sharp!

The song opens with a pianistic evocation of water, and the internal shifting chromatic notes are also to be found in the first two bars of the vocal melody: Ex.81.

This melody is much more legato than in the previous song, gently gliding up and down as befits the watery imagery of, at least, the first stanza, and of the slightly erotic nature of the rest. The eroticism was unintentionally carried into the first stanza, too, in the English translation by Corder, which reads

> Waft, o waters, with wavelets bland
> Lightly our vessel gliding,
> Stroke us, stream, with thy cooling hand
> Over our quarter sliding.

As in the first song, parts of the vocal line are accompanied only by sustained chords, and the poet's musings about the girl in the boat are given an airy, thoughtful quality in the music too. Some lovely effects are created here — and even more so in the third stanza, where this section is extended — by a series of eleventh chords built up in arpeggio over a pedal bass note in the left hand, a characteristic to be found more frequently in Grieg's later songs. The second stanza is set identically to the first and could, as Astra Desmond has pointed out, successfully be omitted if the song were felt to be too long for modern performance. One is also tempted to wonder whether the suggestion was made because this is the stanza where, more than the others, 'modesty sleeps'?

The third strophe has a modified middle section, which begins as an extension of the musing part of the first two. This time there is a change to allegro vivace, as, beginning pianissimo, the song builds up with a 'hunting-horn' theme, which anticipates the last line and its allusion to Diana, the goddess of hunting. The strophe ends similarly to the other two and the song concludes quietly, with the 'water' theme of the opening used as a short postlude.

With *Vær hilset, I Damer* (Greetings, ladies), Grieg returned to the bravura style of the first song and to rather contrived effects. Once again, there are declaimed vocal phrases over sustained chords in the accompaniment and some abrupt changes of key. The transition in the sixth bar from C major to A flat major, for example, is not very subtle: Ex.82. The song falls into two sections, a narrative first half and an allegro vivace second, which, after a cadenza-like passage for the piano, has some elements of a folk music style to underline the words 'Saa væver vi Vadmel og lægger det sammen (So we weave homespun and put it together)'. This part, with the tonic fifth in

Ex.82                 Vær hilset, I Damer

(What will my foot venture to,)

the accompaniment left hand, is very like the opening of *Saa du Knøsen*. The ♩ ♩♩ rhythm of the vocal melody retained throughout this section, perhaps to portray the incessant movement of the weaving shuttle, does become rather wearisome, and once again the key changes are very contrived. The rapid, wide-ranging arpeggios and chords in the accompaniment at the end would have had more effect if the whole song were not then repeated for the second strophe. As in the first song of the set, a contrast is drawn between the honest, unfettered country boy and the ladies of the title.

The fourth song, *Nu er Aftnen lys og lang* (Now the evening is light and long), is much more typical of Grieg in his lighter moments. The thought of the light summer nights, more valued in the northern parts of Scandinavia than in Denmark, perhaps, always drew lovely music from the composer, even where, as in *Lys Nat* (op. 70 no. 3), the shortness of the night provokes melancholy rather than happiness. As in the earlier songs of the op. 49 album, the balance between accompanied and unaccompanied passages, as well as the alternation of passages for accompaniment and for voice, is very important. The jauntiness of the opening in both words and music echoes in feeling *Lauf der Welt*, op. 48 no. 3, and anticipates *Mens jeg venter*, op. 60 no. 3.

The key changes are much better managed here and the tonality moves from A flat major by way of C major to E major in eight bars, an unusual progression through intervals of a major third each time, which creates a freshness to match the light-heartedness of the poem. The alternating piano and vocal phrases also disguise what might otherwise have seemed a contrived chromatic descent from E major to E flat.

*Nu er Aftnen* is set strophically, and the introductory bars with the addition of four tonic chords serve as the quiet postlude. Each strophe falls, musically, into two halves, not engendered by the form of the poem in this instance, but although the second half is more like recitative in style, the jauntiness is still felt in the accompaniment figures between each vocal phrase.

*Julesne* (Christmas snow) is quite different again and, at the very least, this op.49 album is interesting for its variety of settings. The poem here is full of contrasting thoughts generated in the poet by snow, and Grieg follows suit with a diversity of musical ideas. The song opens with a slow, hymn-like melody, doubled at first in octaves by the piano, with the chords filled out at the cadence points, and then accompanied by semibreve and minim chords played alternately in the middle of the keyboard and an octave lower, all adding to the atmosphere of stillness and silence. Even the dissonances, like the falling snow, have an inevitability about them and the augmented seconds in the chords and the vocal line created by the minor key add to the starkness of this opening section. Suddenly the mood changes as the poet sees on his hand not a snowflake but a frozen tear, and memories well up. But, says the poet, 'the Christmas snow is mankind's friend; it hides his deepest mysteries', and Grieg matches this new idea with another hymn-like melody, now in consoling E major. The vocal line here is especially beautiful, with its rise of an octave and fall of a seventh at the end of the phrase:

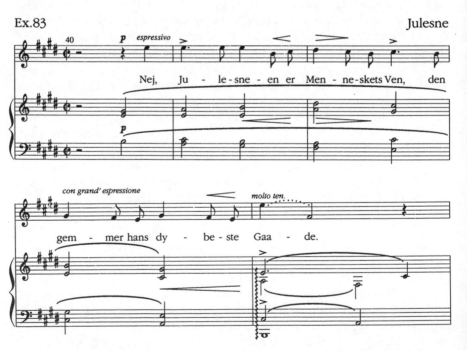

Ex.83                                                                    Julesne

*Julesne* was the first song of the op.49 album to be composed, having been written at the same time as the *Reiseminder* in 1886. The final song of the six was also composed some time before the others, in September 1887, and is the best of them all in many ways. *Foraarsregn* (Spring rain) is a very impressionistic piece of music and here, even more than in the other songs of the set, it is the rests and silences that are so important.

The song is in varied strophic form, with a more lyrical vocal line than some of the others in the album, and with a very delicate accompaniment conceived entirely in pianistic terms. Drachmann's poem uses musical images to describe the gentle rain of springtime, which brings happiness to the young, but which is tinged with sadness as one grows older. In the second stanza the poet speaks of a 'cascade of pearly notes' shaken from the bush, and it is this image that seems to be the key to Grieg's setting, for the cascade of raindrops is found in the semiquaver figures of the accompaniment from the beginning and it is left to the vocal line to link these groups together into a cohesive whole.

For anyone who doubts Grieg's influence on French composers, this song should serve to show whence the influence comes. It is quite as impressionist as some of Debussy's Preludes with its subtle shifting of keys and 'blurred dissonances',[20] created by the use of the sustaining pedal throughout the groups of semiquavers, even when the chords move chromatically:

Ex.84           Foraarsregn

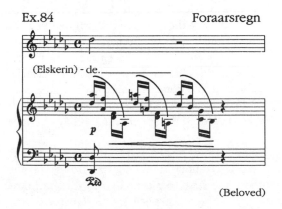

The vocal range of the song is quite wide, from middle D to high G flat, and the melody again has its share of wide intervals, while the ecstatic outbursts in the second half of each stanza are matched by a more declamatory vocal line, accompanied by forte semibreve chords. There is a breathless quality to the rests in both melody and accompaniment at the end of the first stanza which exactly reflects that line in the poem: 'og lytende stod Busk og Blomst og Blad (and listening stood bush and flower and leaf)', and even more underlines the respective phrase in the second stanza: 'om end en Vemod dirrer i det Kvad (even if a sadness quivers in the song)': Ex.85.

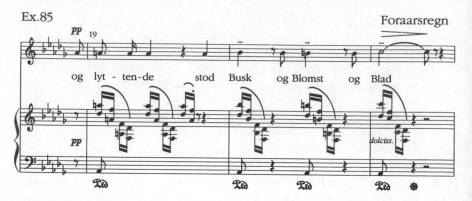

*Foraarsregn* stands alone, not just in this collection, but in Grieg's vocal output to this time, and if, elsewhere, it is Drachmann's poetry rather than Grieg's music which is a little difficult for modern performances and audiences, this poem is quite beautiful and has accordingly inspired some of the composer's most original ideas, both in the vocal and the piano writing.

The six songs were published by Peters in 1889 as *Sechs Gedichte von Holger Drachmann*, with both Danish and German texts; the Scandinavian edition did not appear until 1894. The album is dedicated to Grieg's friend, the singer Thorvald Lammers, although most of the songs in the original keys lie too high for baritone. The German translations of the first edition were by Wilhelm Henzen, but when the songs were published separately by Peters, new versions by Hans Schmidt were used. Schmidt gave each of them a title, regardless of whether or not Drachmann had done so, and thus *Saa du Knøsen* is called 'Der Vagrant', *Vug, o Vove* becomes 'Der Sänger', *Vær hilset, I Damer*, 'Der Fahrende' and *Nu er Aftnen*, 'Der Spielmann', all with little justification.

During these years, perhaps because of extensive travelling, Grieg felt that he was beginning to become more cosmopolitan and, regardless of the varying quality displayed in them, the best thing about the three albums opp.44, 48 and 49 is that he was composing once more. However, the originality and promise of so many of the earlier songs, especially the Vinje settings, is not present except in brief flashes; neither is there much feeling of personal experience behind the music, in spite of what might have been expected. Fortunately, the mediocrity was to prove a temporary trait and even greater achievements than the op.33 songs lay less than a decade ahead.

**Notes**

1   Grieg to G. Schjelderup, 18 September 1903.
2   Wilhelm Kielhau: *Det norske folks liv og historie*, Vol. 10, p.296.

3  Grieg to Paulsen, 28 April 1881 from Bergen.
4  Grieg to Beyer, 29 July 1883 from Rudolstadt.
5  Grieg to Beyer, 15 November 1883 from Leipzig.
6  *Millom rosor, Fra Monte Pincio, Dulgt Kjærlighed* and *Ved en ung Hustrus Båre* — see Chapter 5.
7  Another poem by Lie was set for baritone solo and male-voice choir in 1896, under the title *Kristianiensernes Sangerhilsen*, also known by its first line, 'Nu Pinsens klokker ringer' (Now Whitsun's bells are ringing)', a hand-written copy of which is preserved in the Grieg Collection in Bergen.
8  Benestad and Schjelderup-Ebbe: *Edvard Grieg, mennesket og kunstneren*, 1980, p.221.
9  Grieg to Röntgen, 26 August 1884.
10  Amongst a number of quotations on the back cover of *Dansk lyrik*, ed. Carl Bergstrøm-Nielsen, Gyldendals Tranebøger, Copenhagen 1966, undoubtedly taken from one of Rubow's several books about Drachmann.
11  Grieg to Finck, 17 July 1900.
12  Grieg to Beyer, 6 September 1886 from Troldhaugen.
13  Grieg to Beyer, 27 August 1886 from Troldhaugen.
14  *Edvard Grieg, mennesket og kunstneren*, p.239.
15  John Horton: *Grieg*, 1974, p.78.
16  Drachmann to Grieg, 19 August 1886.
17  Grieg to Beyer, 27 August 1886 from Troldhaugen.
18  David Monrad Johansen: *Edvard Grieg*, 1934, p.331.
19  Horton: *Grieg*, p.185.
20  *Edvard Grieg, mennesket og kunstneren*, p.255.

# 11 'Homecoming'

However weak the Drachmann settings, Grieg was certainly in the midst of a new creative period and in the next five or six years was to produce more music than for some time. Few songs date from the turn of the decade, however, and none of those that do is a significant contribution to his development as a song composer. Not surprisingly, only one of them appeared in print during Grieg's lifetime.

This was *Osterlied* (Easter song), written on 7 June 1889 to a poem by Adolf Böttger, which was published by Peters in 1904. The Grieg Collection has Grieg's copy (a present from Edvardine Kühle) of *Dichtergarben*, an anthology of poetry by Goethe, Heine, Rückert and others; *Osterlied* is the first poem by Böttger appearing in the book. It describes the Easter bells, which ring out heralding not just the festival, but also the coming of spring and an earth which bustles with new life and light. Grieg repeats the first of Böttger's three stanzas again at the end of his setting and he matches the simple imagery of the verse with an unadorned melody in D major. The main interest of the song lies in the harmony where, to simulate the bells, there are long passages of changing chords over syncopated tonic fifths in the bass, a device which foreshadows *Klokkeklang* (Bell sounds), no.6 of Book V of the *Lyric Pieces*, op.54, written two years later:

Ex.86

Osterlied

(in) al - len End - en und Lan - den, und from - me Her - zen ju - beln da - rein: Der (Lenz)

(Throughout all lands, and devout hearts rejoice in them: the [spring])

The chord clusters, as in *Foraarsregn*, are built up by the use — carefully indicated, bar by bar — of the sustaining pedal and finally, in the postlude, the bells fade away into the distance.

Two further settings of poems by Holger Drachmann also date from the summer of 1889. The first, *Simpel Sang* (Simple song) was written on 15 June, but was only published posthumously. It opens with a similar accompaniment figure and vocal line to *Lauf der Welt*, op.48 no.3, but unfortunately does not maintain the standard of the earlier song. The poem has five long stanzas and, with Grieg's constant use of repeated quaver figures, augmented triads and frequent changes of key, the song becomes tedious and anything but 'simple', except perhaps in its lack of inspiration. The 'simple song' of the title is that which is sung by the poet to give thanks for his escape from the wrecking of his small craft. The vocal line has a wide range and makes some use of ascending and decending octaves, a characteristic of Grieg's weaker vocal melodies throughout his life. The incessant rhythm is broken in the third stanza, where Grieg attempts to give some musical illustration of the waves that caused the shipwreck. The ending is an example of a device occasionally used by the composer, where the upper tonic is held in the vocal line over accompaniment chords in the subdominant, before the final resolution to the tonic.

*Du retter tidt dit Øjepar* (You often direct your eyes) was written on 4 July and fortunately the song has remained in manuscript, for neither the poem nor its setting is of any distinction. In four long stanzas Drachmann condemns the malicious rumours and jealousy of 'the mob' towards 'him who sits high above' – that is, the poet – and, as so often overstating his case, likens the experience to being burned at the stake. Although Grieg also sometimes felt himself misunderstood as an artist, it is difficult to see what attracted him to the ponderous poem. Perhaps to portray the eventual triumph of good over adversity, Grieg sets it to a hymn-like melody marked 'maestoso', but the music suffers from clumsy sequential phrases, all too frequently associated with his Drachmann settings. A pencil sketch of the song was also discovered by the author in Bergen, written on the back of the manuscripts of *Den hvide, røde rose* and *Der Jäger*, which shows some differences from the complete version: no piano interlude before the last line of each stanza; the vocal line, while similar, is not so drawn out; and the accompaniment chords, although still retaining a number of chromatically altered notes, are played with anticipatory lower octaves, not tremolando. In spite of the revisions, neither version was worthy of publication. Grieg apparently thought so too, for written in pencil at the bottom of the complete manuscript is the word 'slet (bad)', an opinion which is respected by the Grieg Committee, and the song is not printed in the *GGA*, although it is referred to in the Editorial Commentary.

The last years of the decade found Grieg still involved in a good deal of travelling, to Germany, England, Belgium and France, as well as nearer home. He and Nina spent the Christmas of 1887 in Leipzig, together with two more Norwegian composers, Sinding and Halvorsen, and occasionally

Delius too, and on New Year's Day 1888 they met Tchaikovsky at the home of the Russian violinist (and Halvorsen's teacher) Adolf Brodsky, who later became Director of the Royal Manchester School of Music.

Grieg's influence on contemporary French composers has already been mentioned in regard to *Foraarsregn*. The extent of these 'subtle and far-reaching cross influences'[1] is now generally accepted by Grieg's biographers. In an article written in 1943,[2] Percy Grainger recounted a conversation between Delius and Ravel, in which Delius claimed that contemporary French music was 'quite simply Grieg plus the Prelude to the third act of *Tristan*'. Henry Finck, Grieg's American biographer, wrote in another article in 1903, 'In the *Figaro*, Gabriel Fauré, the eminent composer, writes: "Among the most famous living composers, I know none who enjoys so much popular favour in France as Grieg does; none whose works have so deeply entered into our most intimate musical life as his compositions, which we find so natural, so charming, so refined, exotic and individual . . ."'[3] and Ravel, visiting Norway in 1926, said that he had never 'to this day written a work that was not influenced by Grieg'. For his part, Grieg, also in an article for *Le Figaro*, expressed the thanks 'that Scandinavian composers owe to French music'. He explained: 'We are North-Germans and therefore have much of the German tendency to melancholy and brooding. But we do not have the same compulsion . . . to express ourselves at length or verbosely. Far from it: we have always preferred to be short and sharp, clear and concise in expression . . . These characteristics are also the aim of our artistic endeavours.' He saw French art as having a 'light, unforced form' and 'transparent clarity', traits he obviously admired.[4]

There was a good deal of impressionism in much of the music Grieg was writing at this time, especially in the fifth book of *Lyric Pieces*, op.54, published in 1891, and John Horton comments on the similarity between *Morgenstemning* (Morning mood) from *Peer Gynt* and Debussy's piano piece *Reverie*, composed in 1890. Debussy, after a concert in Paris in 1903, dismissed Grieg disparagingly as a nationalist and while, unlike Ravel, he did not acknowledge any personal influence from Grieg's music, he did use the latter's String Quartet as something of a model for his own. However, it was one of Grieg's last compositions for piano, the *Slåtter*, op.72, which was to leave a lasting image not just on the younger French composers, but on others too. The *Slåtter* were Grieg's piano transcriptions of folk dances which the violinist and composer Johan Halvorsen had taken down from the Hardanger fiddle-player Knut Dale. Grieg wrote to Heinrich Hinrichsen of Peters in the summer of 1906, 'And in Paris — according to Halvorsen — the Slåtter have been discovered by some young musicians and they are crazy about "le nouveau Grieg" . . .'[5]

Grieg's music was received with great enthusiasm by French audiences — a letter to Beyer of 14 December 1889 tells of the concert hall being completely sold out – but in spite of his growing fame and reputation as a composer, the many tours were mostly necessitated by his popularity as a pianist and conductor and the remuneration such public appearances brought was always welcome. Grieg was, however, beginning to be plagued by bouts of ill-health and by 1889 had had to give up playing the solo part of his Piano Concerto. He was still conducting and accompanying and the October of 1889 saw performances in Christiania of the songs, opp. 48 and 49, sung by the dedicatees, Gulbranson and Lammers, and also the first performances in both Christiania and Copenhagen of the revised concert music to *Olav Trygvason*, which was published as op. 50 in 1888 in a piano edition and in score in 1890.

In April 1890 Grieg returned to Troldhaugen and in the next few months produced the *Old Norwegian Songs with Variations* for two pianos, op. 51, the piano transcriptions of various songs, op. 52, and the arrangement for string orchestra of *Fyremål* and *Det første møte*, published as op. 53. The performances in Christiania the year before had also provided an opportunity for him to renew his lapsed friendship with Bjørnson and, still hankering after a large-scale work and following the success with the concert music to *Olav Trygvason*, he suggested to the writer in a letter of 12 December 1890 the idea of an oratorio, a Requiem with a central theme of Peace. The proposition came to nothing, because Bjørnson wanted to treat the theme in a socio-political way, which would have been impossible to match in musical terms – at least, for Grieg – and although Bjørnson eventually published his whole text, *Fred* (Peace), the music comprised only one song, *Jeg elsket . . .* (I loved . . .), published much later in the second album of *Posthumous Songs*.

The poem concerns a young woman who has lost the man she loved, and it tells how she will share that loss with his mother, staying with her and thereby giving back a little of the love she has known. Grieg's setting, made in 1891, opens with a long piano introduction and is very mournful. The use of the sharpened fourth in the minor scale and the wealth of chromatic movement creates an angularity not unlike that in some of the Vinje settings, or in piano pieces like *Hjemve* (Longing for home), no. 6 of Book VI of the *Lyric Pieces*, and *Gjendines Bådnlåt* (Gjendine's lullaby) from the *Norske folkeviser* (Norwegian folksongs), op. 66. As Monrad Johansen commented, the use of so much chromaticism and the 'Grieg motif' here is so uninspired as to appear merely mannerism and the overall gloom is such that the final tonic *major* chords seem quite out of place. The vocal line is frequently doubled in the accompaniment right hand, particularly in the outer sections, and the whole song has a contrived feeling about it, so that it is scarcely surprising that it was not published during Grieg's lifetime.

Two important anniversaries occurred for Grieg in the early 1890s. First, on 23 November 1891, the twenty-fifth anniversary of his début in Christiania, which was marked by a concert and a banquet, attended by a number of eminent people, including Ibsen. Then, in June 1892, he and Nina celebrated their silver wedding at Troldhaugen with a large party of friends. Nina sang and Grieg played a piece he had written especially for the occasion, called *Gratulanterne kommer* (The wellwishers are coming), later called by its now well-known title, *Bryllupsdag ved Troldhaugen* (Wedding-day at Troldhaugen) and published as no.6 of the *Lyric Pieces* Book VIII, op.65.

Also during this time Grieg worked on the second suite of music from *Peer Gynt*, which was published in 1893 and, during the winter of 1892, he had revised the instrumental movements of the incidental music to *Sigurd Jorsalfar*, originally published as op.22. He made a further revision in 1898 for a new production of the play at the National Theatre in the Norwegian capital, but the first revisions, which appeared as op.56, involved a new Trio section for the *Hyldningsmarsj* (Homage march) and a fanfare-like section before the 'maestoso' ending of the same movement.

The two preceding winters had not been good ones for Grieg's delicate health. In December 1889 he wrote to Beyer that he could 'scarcely hold a pen, so weak and exhausted am I now with the sickness – influenza – which is now going around Europe'. He had influenza again at the beginning of 1892 and was also troubled by arthritis in his feet, which prevented him going to work in his composing hut just down the cliff path from Troldhaugen. He was ill for most of the summer after his silver wedding, although well enough to travel to Christiania in November for the first performance of the revised score to *Sigurd Jorsalfar*. Grieg and Nina then went on to Copenhagen, Leipzig and Berlin, where they celebrated Christmas with Sinding and Alnæs. Then it was back to Leipzig in February 1893, where Grieg conducted performances of the second *Peer Gynt* suite and his Piano Concerto.

In the spring he and Sinding were invited on a tour of the south of France by Peters' editor, Max Abraham, which did Grieg a great deal of good in terms of his health, if not his music. (The new set of *Lyric Pieces* Book VI, op.57, which was produced at this time, is regarded as being amongst the weakest of his piano works). Plans to go to England for concerts and to receive an honorary doctorate from Cambridge University had to be cancelled, once again because of ill-health, and by June he had, on doctors' advice, gone to take a cure at Grefsen Bad near Christiania. Grieg eventually received his degree in May 1894 and wrote to Delius, 'the first thing I had to do as a newly-fledged doctor was – to go to the doctor myself', and another spell followed at Grefsen Bad.

In spite of all the travelling and his own opinion that he was becoming more cosmopolitan, Grieg was if anything at this time becoming more patriotic. On the political front there was increasing unease amongst many people about the union between Norway and Sweden, but more personally Grieg missed Norway whenever he was away. The best of the *Lyric Pieces*

Book VI is the last, called *Hjemve* (Homesickness), which uses a Norwegian goat-horn melody and a dance theme. While taking a cure at Carlsbad in October 1887 Grieg wrote to Beyer that, in spite of Ibsen's opinion that it was best to belong to a great nation, 'I feel, the older I get, that I love Norway just because it is so humble, just because we are such cursed idiots in practical matters'.[6] Later he wrote, 'But to embrace Norway is, for me, the greatest thing and I do so every day in my thoughts.'[7]

He was able to enjoy some of Norway's natural splendour, which he loved, during the summer of 1891 when Röntgen and his family stayed at Lofthus, where they were visited by Grieg and Beyer. Trips were made into the Jotunheim mountains and it was on one of these occasions that Grieg heard a young woman, Gjendine Slaalien, sing a lullaby, which he promptly noted down. It became *Gjendines Bådnlåt* (Gjendine's lullaby), the last of the *Norske folkeviser* (Norwegian Folk-songs), op.66, arranged for piano and published in 1897. Folk music was still very much a living tradition at this time in the rural areas and particularly strong in the Hardanger region. Grieg enjoyed this summer enormously and wrote to Abraham on 10 August that he came back 'a new and better man – yes, ten years younger.'

Of all his music, the public liked best the Piano Concerto, the two *Peer Gynt* suites and the earlier songs, especially the Ibsen settings, but Grieg felt that he had more to offer and could develop further. With his love of Norway so much to the fore, it is not surprising that a good deal of his music at this time should be inspired by things Norwegian – folk music, nature and literature – and once again it was in the smaller forms that all these feelings found expression.

*Ave maris stella*, a setting of a Danish version (by Thor Lange) of the Latin hymn, which is nevertheless always referred to by its Latin title, is now also known to date from 1893. Grieg was by no means orthodox in his religious convictions and because he always had to have an empathy with the words he set, it is understandable that there is a dearth of religious music in his output. He often referred to feeling God's presence in nature and art and his upbringing in a Christian household led to his early aspirations to the priesthood. Many years later, however, he was to write to Delius, 'You know me well enough to realize that preachers viewed as a tribe are anathema to me'.[8] He certainly always felt a need to believe in a spirituality beyond everyday life, but required a faith that would also satisfy him intellectually, and eventually found something of a solution in the Unitarian Church, which he first encountered on a visit to Birmingham in 1888. Grieg, then, is not among the many Norwegian composers up to the present day who have added considerably to the church-music repertoire. Besides two of the songs for male-voice choir, op.30, *Deiligste bland kvinde* (Most beautiful among women) and *Den store hvide flok* (The great, white host) – later to be sung at the composer's funeral – there is an early fugue (1862) for unaccompanied choir, *Dona nobis pacem*, and the superb *Four Psalms*, op.74, for mixed choir with baritone solo. Among the songs, only *Morgenbønn på skolen* (Morning prayer at school), *Den syngende Menighed* (The singing congregation), *Sang til juletræet* (Song to the Christmas tree), op.61 no.2, *Julens Vuggesang* (Christmass cradle-song) and *Ave maris stella* have any religious theme.

With its simple, strophic, hymn-like setting and with the vocal line largely doubled in octaves in the accompaniment, *Ave maris stella* is nevertheless something outside the ordinary and contains a number of effects associated with Grieg's mature style. The most obvious of these is the abrupt change of key at bar 5 from the tonic F major to A major, which illuminates the words 'Redningsblus på Livets mørke Vover vilde (A rescuing light on life's dark waves so wild)'. Less overt but equally effective is the use of chords of the seventh, ninth and eleventh, and other unresolved dissonances, for example in bar 12:

Ex.87                                                          Ave maris stella

(a clear light in the night, an eye for all the blind)

In bar 8 Grieg makes use of one of his favourite cadential chords, the dominant eleventh, which is used again at the end of the strophe, this time preceded by the supertonic ninth. Other typical Griegian traits are the pedal tonic fifth of the first two bars of each strophe and the echoing of the last two bars of each section one octave higher in the accompaniment. While not a great composition, the song has a poignancy about it, but whether this reflects Grieg's longing for higher things or for final peace is speculative.

*Ave maris stella* was first published in 1893 by C.J. Kihl and Langkjær in Copenhagen with just the Danish text. A further edition, in both the original key and in a version for high voice in A flat, was published by Hansen's in 1900 with Latin, German, English and Danish words, although there are no indications of the identity of the translators. Grieg himself arranged the song for unaccompanied mixed choir in December 1898 and this version, again with the four languages as above, was published by Hansen's in 1899. This was the second of the *To religiøse kor* (Two sacred choruses) dedicated to the St Cecilia's Madrigal Choir of Copenhagen, and first performed by them on 30 January 1899. Other arrangements followed: for piano solo by Ludwig Schytte in 1905; for violin and piano by Carl Flesch in 1914; and for harmonium solo, harmonium with violin and harmonium with cello all by August Reinhard.

Grieg came home from a cure at Grefsen Bad at the end of June 1893, but in the autumn had to travel again, first to Christiania to play the latest of the *Lyric Pieces* (Book VI) and then, in November, to Copenhagen. There Nina had to go into a nursing home with kidney trouble, and although by then she rarely sang in public, Grieg still in his heart wrote his songs for her. Two of those he was currently engaged on he took with him when he went to visit her on her birthday, 24 November, at the clinic, describing them to Beyer as 'one to a new poem by John Paulsen, "Hjemkomst", and "Gretchen ligger i Kiste" [*Moderen synger*] by Krag. I am beginning to be in high spirits these days.' How much he felt in new heart for composition is also expressed in another letter to Beyer, written on 29 December, where he mentions the almost daily visits of a 'lovely girl', whom the letter goes on to identify as 'Fru Musa' – Madame Muse. He told Röntgen in a letter of January 1894 that, while Nina was away, he had written 'a heap of songs for her', enough to divide between three albums.

Before composing more than two songs for these albums, however, Grieg set another poem by Bjørnson. This was *Valgsang* (Election song), which was printed in the periodical *Verdens Gang* on 8 December 1893, Bjørnson's sixty-first birthday. In response to a query about the song from the present author, Nils Grinde has commented that 'the political situation between Norway and Sweden was tense at that time and Bjørnson's poem is the result of this',[9] and the political implications in the text were to prove an obstacle to the song's publication. In the version which appeared in *Verdens Gang* on 21 December 1893 Grieg set the poem for male-voice choir. Another version for solo voice and piano appeared in the same publication in the New Year of 1894,[10] although from a letter to Sigurd Hals it appears that this was, in fact, the original version: 'I am sending this morning to *Verdens Gang* a tune to Bjørnson's new "Valgsang". It is set out for male-voice quartet, but was written for one voice with piano.'[11] In the same letter Grieg offers the song to Hals for his publishing house, 'assuming that Dr Abraham of Peters . . . gives his consent'. Hals – and Peters – apparently turned the song down 'on political grounds', as Grieg was to complain in another letter to Hals,[12] and it never appeared independently. It will be reprinted in the *GGA*, where it will do nothing to enhance the composer's reputation.

In spite of its patriotic fervour, Grieg stressed to Hals that *Valgsang* was 'no song to be bawled on the streets'.[13] It hardly qualifies as a solo song at all, written as it is to a hymn-like melody with a chordal accompaniment that mostly doubles the vocal line. The male-voice setting is in G minor, while the solo version is in E minor and has a piano introduction and

postlude, both omitted in the former. The melody line is, as befits the poem,
very declamatory, but, like the weaker Drachmann settings, it abounds in
rising and falling octaves:

Ex.88                                                                    Valgsang

din Æ - re og din Fri - hed er i de sven - ske Sværd.

(your honour and your freedom are in the Swedish sword)

Unfortunately, 'Fru Musa' did not provide great inspiration for the first of
the three albums of songs Grieg produced at this time either. This was *Norge*
(Norway), published as op.58 and comprising settings of five poems by
Paulsen, the friend whose verses Grieg had not used since the op.26 songs of
1876. The poems he now selected were not as good as the earlier ones and
although, as in all the most recent songs, we must be grateful that he felt
such enthusiasm for his task, the results do leave much to be desired in
musical quality. John Horton suggests that Grieg 'must have been respond-
ing to the obligations of friendship'[14] and after his earlier triumphs with the
poetry of Ibsen, Bjørnson and Vinje, one cannot help but wonder what had
happened to his usually excellent literary judgement, for Paulsen's poems
here are little better than Drachmann's *Reiseminder*.

The first of the five songs is *Hjemkomst* (Homecoming) and it must have
been the sentiment behind it – of a traveller returning home from sunnier
climes, yet loving Norway for its bare rocks and misty shores – that appealed
to the composer, for there is no originality of thought or imagery in the three
stanzas. The opening series of spread supertonic seventh chords gives a rather
ambiguous feeling to the tonality and at the same time suggests water
lapping at the sides of the ship carrying the returning traveller. The vocal
line is very angular and is more recitative than melody. It is interrupted by
rests, so that many of the phrases begin with a syncopation, and there are
many wide intervals. It is, however, a dramatic line, anticipating later songs
like *Eros*, op.70 no.1, and sings well, the rising augmented fourths and
falling fifths well matched to the words: Ex.89.

Ex.89                                                                      Hjemkomst

med nø-gne skjær  og  hol-mer grå,  hvor   må-gen flag - rer  tyst.

(with bare rocks and grey islets, where the sea-gull flutters silently)

The second song, *Til Norge* (To Norway), is in many ways the best of the group. It is a short, sincere but unsentimental hymn of praise and Grieg uses the first two lines of Paulsen's single four-lined stanza once more at the end to almost the same music. The four-bar introduction is an embellished version of the first vocal phrase and, as might be expected of such a song, there are many elements of Norwegian music, from the opening 'Grieg motif' with its ornamentation to the piano echoes, also ornamented. Neither does the simple structure exclude chromatic writing, of which there is a good deal. The final decorated echo of the vocal line, which forms the postlude, is reminiscent of the similar figure in *Ein Traum*, op.48 no.6, and there is a wealth of feeling in the quiet ending, with the vocal line specifically marked 'senza cresc.': Ex.90.

With *Henrik Wergeland*[15] we are back in the rather pretentious realms of the Drachmann settings. Wergeland and his rival, Welhaven, were the two great figures of early nineteenth-century Norwegian literature. Their opposing standpoints have already been discussed in connection with Grieg's setting of Bjørnson's *Serenade til Welhaven*, op.18 no.9. With this new song the composer redresses the balance, although Paulsen's eulogy to Wergeland is not in the same class as Bjørnson's poem. Wergeland stood for the truly Norwegian development of his country's culture, without external influences, and so deserves Paulsen's epithet 'Norges skytsånd', Norway's guardian spirit. However, it is debatable whether he would entirely have approved Paulsen's rather grandiose description of the forest 'grieving for its lost singer', or of his own 'dauntless struggling' and his carrying of Norway's burdens 'until death'.

Grieg's setting is also rather pompous, 'like a Norse *dråpa*',* as he described a performance of the orchestrated version of the song to Beyer in a

---

*A Skaldic heroic song, usually in praise of a king or chieftain.

Ex.90                                                                Til Norge

(You are my mother, I love you; with that, everything is said!)

letter dated 29 March 1895. The spread chords in the piano accompaniment are marked 'Quasi arpa', and indeed are orchestrated for harps, again suggesting the skald's lay, and the whole song is set as a funeral march, 'andante solenne'. The stepwise movement of the 'walking' bass is unusual for Grieg and gives a certain heaviness to the song. The rather angular vocal line has a narrow range and gives an impression of improvization, again in keeping with the idea of a *dråpa*. The march rhythm is interrupted at bar 15, at the words 'da et suk i stilheden jeg fanger (then I caught a sigh in the stillness)' and, as so often in Grieg's songs, it is the second half of the strophe that holds the most harmonic interest, here a number of unusual key changes. However, after the more lyrical *Til Norge*, it is disappointing to find Grieg reverting in this song to a more *parlando* style.

It is difficult to understand how Monrad Johansen could have called *Henrik Wergeland* 'the most significant' song[16] in the op.58 album, although the composer himself was obviously pleased with it. He wrote to Lammers from Copenhagen in January 1894, 'three albums of songs are finished and there is almost none of them that will not lie beautifully for your voice. And one of the albums deals only with the Fatherland. There is a song in it, "Henrik

Wergeland", a poem by J. Paulsen, which I would be happy to travel up to the Holbergsgade, fourth floor, to hear. But you will not hear it until I myself can sit at the piano. That pleasure I will allow no-one to take from me.' [17] In the light of the next song, however, *Henrik Wergeland*, whatever its weaknesses, takes on a new stature.

*Turisten* (The tourist) has aptly been described as being almost a parody of the composer's style, so that, as David Monrad Johansen has commented, 'one must wonder that Grieg would have wanted his name on it'. [18] The poem is a trite little tale of a tourist who asks his way from a pretty girl, decides to stay the night where he is instead and then leaves her again the next morning, but it has none of the charm or impudence of, for example, *Die verschwiegene Nachtigall*. The musical style appears at first glance to be in the same mould as *Lauf der Welt* and *Nu er Aftnen lys og lang*, although the accompaniment is less elegantly written than these songs and does not lie so comfortably under the hands. Also, *Turisten* overdoes those Norwegian features which the earlier two songs use to good effect and so becomes 'folksy' rather than folk-like. The familiar sound of dominant chord over tonic pedal and the 'Grieg motif' are certainly present, but the changes of key are very contrived and there is no subtlety in the chromatic writing, so that after the first nine or ten bars the song seems to lose its sense of direction and intention.

The composer's reputation is redeemed to some extent by the last song of the set, *Udvandreren* (The emigrant). As with *Hjemkomst*, Grieg must have felt some sympathy for the poem, in which Paulsen bewails being far away from Norway now spring is there and, although the sentiments could have been expressed more succinctly than in these five stanzas, Grieg's music for the strophic setting contains some true elements from Norwegian music that he made so much his own. The strophes are very short and built on one melodic idea which is used sequentially, and the whole is surrounded by an allegro theme for piano, which could easily be one of Grieg's *Norwegian Dances*.

The vocal melody, constructed from a seventh chord in arpeggio, is quite haunting and anticipates the lovely melody Grieg was to compose for *Elsk* (Love), the fifth song of the *Haugtussa* cycle. Paulsen's poem here also uses the *nystev* form used by Garborg in *Elsk* and often found in verses whose intention is to suggest folk poetry, and in spite of the notation the accents fall on the words 'våres' and 'dale', so that the effect is of the three-note anacrusis associated with the *nystev* form: Ex.91. Grieg also makes use of one of his lovely modal cadences and there is a freshness to *Udvandreren*, not least in the chromatic alterations in the piano echoes, that transcends the undistinguished poem.

The op.58 songs are dedicated to Ingolf Schiøtt (1851–1922), a well-known singer and the cathedral organist in Bergen, and a choirmaster whom Grieg held in high esteem.

Ex.91                                                    Udvandreren

(Now surely spring is coming in Norway's valleys,)

The next album of songs, the *Elegiske Digte* (Elegiac Songs), op.59, do not show a much higher standard than *Norge*, but harmonically they are more ambitious. The first song of the six, *Når jeg vil dø* (When I shall die), is a setting of a lovely, melancholy poem, in which Paulsen says that it would be 'too difficult to say farewell in springtime' and he will only die in autumn, 'when Nature dies'. The accompaniment is conceived very much in piano terms and the semiquaver figure, which is used for much of the song, may well have been inspired by the opening line, 'Når løvet falder træt fra skogens kroner (When the leaves fall tired from the forest's crowns)'. The song makes extensive and occasionally unexpected use of pedal notes, especially in the middle section, although the basic harmonic structure is quite straightforward. The tonic G is used as a pedal for the first ten bars and the vocal melody, in its first two phrases, is anticipated in the accompaniment by one semiquaver's length, a construction that leads to a number of striking dissonances: Ex.92.

At bar 11 the music changes, the vocal line becomes more declamatory in style, and the falling diminished fifths help to illustrate the sinking sun and the colours and sounds dying away. The vocal line, although not quite so angular as in some of Grieg's recent songs, nevertheless still has a number of rising and falling intervals, occasionally diminished fourths and fifths, but the range is only just over one octave. The overall atmosphere of the music is more despondent than that of the words, but the song works well in performance.

*På Norges nøgne fjelde* (On Norway's bare mountains) is Paulsen's very accurate Norwegian version of Heine's *Ein Fichtenbaum steht einsam*, a short, pithy poem, which contrasts the fir-tree in the wintry north with the palm-tree, both discontented with their surroundings. Heine may have intended an allegory for two lovers far apart or just have been pointing out that,

Ex.92

Når jeg vil dø

(out over the earth, silent and cold and grey,)

wherever one is, another place always seems more attractive; in the words of another German poet, 'Dort wo du nicht bist, dort ist das Glück.'[19] Grieg's music, like the poem is succinct, but his setting offers no further illumination of the words. He sets the two stanzas in two through-composed sections and captures the bareness of the mountains with music that makes much use of fifths and octaves, and owes a good deal to folk music, not least in the hovering between the major and minor modes and in the decoration in the second bar of the introduction:

Ex.93        På Norges nøgne fjelde

The postlude is identical to the introduction, perhaps to illustrate that, in spite of what the trees may wish, their situations cannot change. Nevertheless, the song remains rather commonplace.

The words of the third song, *Til Én* (To One), also have a contrast of ideas and a brevity which makes the sadness of the poem all the more poignant. Grieg's setting underlines the contrast of 'spring' with 'autumn', here a metaphor for youth and age, by setting the first three lines in the major key and the second three in the minor. Although both the vocal line and the

accompaniment chords are fairly sparse, there is a warmth in the transition to
E major at bar 7, which underlines the new life found in spring.

The melody and accompaniment chords for the second three lines of the
poem begin in exactly the same way, but in the minor mode, until the words
'de brustne illusjoner . . . (those broken illusions)', where the music becomes
much more sustained, with a dissonant, accented G flat in the vocal line
sounded against the F natural of the accompaniment, quite different from the
rising phrase in the corresponding place in the first section. The 'illusions'
are further underlined by the descending diminished seventh chords that lead
into the last two lines. These contain the whole essence of the poem: that
spring and autumn do not belong together:

Ex.94                                                                    Til Én (I)

(But spring and autumn do not go together)

The resignation of the last line, 'og derfor nu vi skilles må (and therefore we
now must part)', is expressed in the sustained chords in the accompaniment
and the use of the lower register of both voice and keyboard. This song,
where conciseness is again so expressive, is more worthy of the composer of
the Ibsen settings.

The second song with the title *Til Én* is not quite so successful, mainly
because the agitation of the syncopated chords in the right hand of the
accompaniment overwhelms the rather more delicate sentiments of the
poem. Paulsen questions his beloved about the tears in her eyes: are they
there to enslave him or are they 'a message of pain'? He will kiss them away.
The poet's anxiety is in the music, and the vocal line – once more angular
and with syncopated entries – illustrates his questioning, which is also to be
found in the rising phrases of the accompaniment left hand. However, there
seems little justification in the poem for such harsh dissonances as are created
by the pedal E, held through much of the first section of the song and
sounded against, for example, D sharp and F natural in the right hand and
the vocal line. The tonality throughout is somewhat ambiguous and hovers
between E major and F major/D minor, although the song ends firmly in E

major. While the vocal line has the now familiar short range but wide intervals, the accompaniment has more pianistic interest than the two previous songs.

The fifth of the *Elegiske Digte, Farvel* (Farewell), entitled 'The Swan Song' in the Peters edition, has a flavour of its own. Paulsen's poem employs the Scandinavian image of the swan as a symbol of the soul, and the sight of a swan flying south brings the poet thoughts of bidding farewell to his beloved. Grieg's hymn-like setting with a largely chordal accompaniment follows the vocal line almost entirely. The melody again incorporates some wide intervals – sixths and sevenths – but is more lyrical than the previous songs in this album. The falling sixths at the words 'Elskte farvel (Beloved, farewell)' aptly express the poet's anguish at his loss. The postlude is a series of ascending diminished seventh chords, which leads from the end of the vocal line to the final tonic chords. As in a number of other songs, it seems a pity here that Grieg should use the passage after each stanza rather than after the second only, but such repetition is one of the major weaknesses of the *romanse* style. For all that, the song is pleasing enough, if conventional.

The final song of the six, *Nu hviler du i jorden* (Now you are resting in the earth), has, like *Til Én (II)*, some very unexpected harmonies created by the use of a pedal. Here it is an inverted pedal, comprising the last three quavers of each bar – D, F, D' – which remain constant throughout the song, except for four bars at the end of the strophe, where each note is sharpened. A number of striking dissonances are thus created, both with the vocal line and with the rest of the accompaniment: Ex.95.

The song is in strophic form, with two of Paulsen's four stanzas forming each strophe. The vocal line is much more legato than in the other songs in the album, moving stepwise for a good deal of its length. Unfortunately, the very lack of angularity in the vocal line here makes the melody rather static, an impression augmented by the ostinato quavers in the accompaniment. In the second strophe Grieg alters the rhythm of the vocal line, beginning some of the phrases on the second beat of the bar, as if to imply the poet's breaking voice as he recalls that he could not even send flowers for the grave of the girl he had loved in secret.

Although they are harmonically of more interest than *Norge*, the *Elegiske Digte* still belong to the least significant of Grieg's songs. They were dedicated to Hanchen Alme (née Wågård), a childhood friend of the Griegs.

One more song to a text by Paulsen, which exists in manuscript in Bergen, is to be published for the first time in the *GGA*. This is *Fædrelandssang* (Song to the Fatherland), which is undated, but which Nils Grinde has suggested as being 'composed at the latest in 1894, probably c.1893', as the text was printed 'with information that Grieg had written a melody to it'.[20] Although designated for voice and piano, like *Valgsang* it scarcely qualifies as a solo song, being a simple, hymn-like, strophic setting,

Ex.95                                                    Nu hviler du i jorden

(Now you rest in the earth, [you] who were my secret love.)

marked 'Maestoso', with the vocal line doubled throughout in the largely
homophonic accompaniment. The only point of minor interest is the
modulation from the tonic B flat major to D major in the sixteenth bar.

The last of the three albums written at this time contains settings of five
poems by Vilhelm Krag. Krag (1871–1933) was born in Kristiansand and
studied literature at the university there. He was the younger brother of the
famous novelist Thomas Krag, although his own writing was very much
influenced by Danish writers, especially Drachmann, and shows a variety of
colour, symbolism, religious fervour and fantasy, in poems, novels and
plays. Later in life, Krag became very involved with the people and the
countryside of his native Sørland, and this gave a new simplicity to his
writing.

Krag's first volume of verse, *Digte*, was published in 1891 and contained
one of his most well-known poems, the vivid *Fandango*, and one of his best,
the melancholy and symbolic *Der skreg en fugl*. His later collections, though
containing some good poems, do not reveal any true development. Although
many of his lyrical verses have been set to music, Grieg used only the five
that form the op.60 album. These, however, are a testimony to the

composer's dependence on good texts to write good songs, and it is difficult to believe that these Krag settings were written at the same time as the Paulsen songs, for the *Digte af Vilhelm Krag* are on quite a different plane, in terms both of vocal writing and of piano accompaniment. Most of the ambitious harmonic sequences of the other two albums have been discarded and in their place is a more conventional structure, but with the significant additions that are so typical of Grieg at his best.

The first song of the five, *Liden Kirsten* (Little Kirsten), is very like a folk-song, both in poetical content and in the simple melody to which Grieg sets it. The song is in ternary form, with the middle two stanzas of Krag's four forming the longer middle section, while the outer sections are filled out by interpolations of piano phrases into the melodic line. The semiquaver figure in the right hand in the introduction suggests the gentle movement of the loom, as Kirsten weaves her bridal linen, and the little hesitation in the third bar is reminiscent of Schubert's *Gretchen am Spinnrade*. The left hand has cuckoo-calls throughout the outer sections, suggested by the second line of the poem:

Ex.96                                                      Liden Kirsten

Gjø - gen gol ud - i grøn - ne Skov.                          Li-den

(Little Kirsten she sat so late, while the cuckoo called in the green wood.)

There is something bitter-sweet about the setting of 'mens Kirsten drømte om Kjæresten sin (while Kirsten dreamt of her beloved)', with its alternation of major and minor chords and the lingering on the word 'Kjæresten'. The setting of the final section is almost the same as the first and the introduction now becomes the postlude. The whole vocal melody is built from one phrase (bars 4 and 5 above), yet the song is as sophisticated and artistic as any of Grieg's, and it is the very artlessness that is so effective.

*Moderen synger* (The mother sings) is another poignant song about the death of a child, a theme always close to Grieg's heart. The treatment of sorrow is much simpler here than, for example, in *Når jeg vil dø*, and although the composer does revert to a *parlando* vocal melody, it does not have the numerous wide intervals of recent songs. The harmonic feeling is modal rather than minor, especially at the cadence points, but it is the middle section that once more holds the most interest. There are some striking dissonances, for example A natural sounded against A flat, but they are softened by the use of the higher register of the keyboard, the spread chords and the 'pianissimo' marking. There is a tragic resignation about the setting of the last stanza to the same music as the first, for Grieg makes no attempt to depict the storm that 'blows over the sea, taking all the flowers from little Gretchen's grave', as if the mother realizes that there was nothing she could do to prevent it.

The third song in the album, *Mens jeg venter* (While I am waiting), is by contrast bright and happy, full of light and the sounds of summer. The merriment is increased by the references to the children's song, *Ro, ro til fiskeskjær* (Row, row to the fishing-rock) and to *Bro, bro brille* (an untranslatable nonsense phrase), a popular singing game something akin to the familiar British *Oranges and Lemons*. Musically, the song has more variation of melody and phrase-length than is usually found in Grieg's songs.

The introductory figure in the accompaniment must have been suggested by the opening line of the third stanza, 'Vug mig, du blanke Vove, langt og let (Rock me, you smooth waves, far and lightly)', for here is water lapping gently against a boat – a lazy lapping, not the sensuous caressing of the water in *Vug, o Vove*, op.49 no.2. The accented appoggiaturas contained in the semiquaver figure have an impudent quality that immediately sets the scene for the rest of the song (bars 25 and 26 below; the introduction consists of the accompaniment to these bars, then repeated with the right hand one octave lower). Equally attractive is the jaunty picture of the duckling in his 'yellow socks', set to a descending chromatic melody and accompanied by syncopated chords. Grieg uses this passage to accomplish one of his magical modulations, where the G flat and B flat of the final syncopated chord are altered enharmonically to F sharp and A sharp, and from the tonic G major the tonality now moves to the distant key of F sharp major, until at bar 23 there is another lovely, unexpected modulation by way of an arpeggio of the dominant seventh to the tonic G major for the refrain 'Bro, bro brille' which ends each strophe:

Ex.97

Mens jeg venter

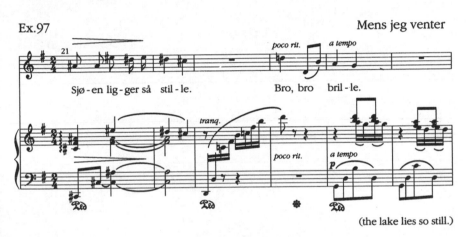

(the lake lies so still.)

The song is strophic, yet so multi-faceted is this setting that it amply matches all the images contained in the three stanzas, whether Krag is speaking of the wild geese, the dancing and violin music on St John's Eve (Midsummer Eve, 23 June) or the dreamy anticipation of marriage. The introductory figure serves as interlude and postlude, and the masterly working of this song, with its lovely vocal line and well-conceived accompaniment, makes it one of Grieg's most captivating and popular.

Craftsmanship of a different but no less masterly kind is seen in the fourth song, *Der skreg en fugl* (A bird cried). Here are no lightning changes of mood and variety of phrase-length, but a short, slow song that is entirely devoid of any unnecessary element. Krag's poem describes a bird crying in the 'autumn-grey day', as it flies 'on tired wings away over the sea'. Grieg matches the greyness and the bird's mournful cry with an unadorned though lyrical vocal line and a mostly chordal accompaniment, both of which are desolate in their simplicity. In fact the whole song, with the exception of the introduction and postlude, is tightly constructed over a bass which moves stepwise, up or down only a minor or diminished third from D or D sharp, G or G sharp.

In the first full bar after the introduction, Grieg uses the sharpened fourth – G sharp in the tonic D minor scale – so often found in Norwegian folk music, and this, together with the tonic pedal, augmented seconds and the suspensions in the vocal line, creates dissonances that underline the tension in the poem. Nevertheless, the melody glides slowly upwards like the bird. Further tensions are created by the chromatic movement of the bass in the following six bars, and the legato of the vocal line is broken at the words 'flaksed i brudte, afmægtige Slag (flapping is broken, powerless strokes)', echoed by the accompaniment, just as the sea-gull's normally smooth flight is broken:

Ex.98                                                        Der skreg en Fugl

flak - sed i brud - te,    af - mæg - ti - ge Slag,

The parallel seventh chords accompanying the last four bars of the vocal melody are pure impressionism, and the bird's exhaustion is mirrored in the use of the lower register of both voice and piano for the final phrase.

The most interesting thing about the song, however, is the music that forms the introduction and the identical postlude. This is based on a theme found after his death in one of Grieg's notebooks, an annotation of a 'sea-gull's cry heard in the Hardanger fjord', and harmonized by a single sustained tonic chord:

Ex.99                                                        Der skreg en Fugl

molto                                                        *ppp*

Nowhere else in his songs does he attempt so exact a portrayal of nature.

The poem has all the conciseness of thought associated with Ibsen's verse, which also inspired great music from Grieg, and although it has been set by other Norwegian composers, none of them achieves his veracity. Backer Lunde's setting has a similar legato vocal line, but it is much wider ranging, although interestingly he also uses the lower register of the voice for the last phrase. Sinding's setting also brings this phrase into the lower vocal range and he is more adventurous in his harmony than Backer Lunde, right from the opening ninth chord. However, his rising phrase for 'flaksed i brudte, afmægtige Slag' belies the waning strength of the bird.

Agathe Backer Grøndahl set ten of Krag's poems as her op.31, of which *Der skreg en fugl* is the third. This is a much bigger song than any of the other settings, drawn out by repeating each of the last three lines of the poem. The best feature is the rising and falling melody to 'seiled på sorte vinger (sailed on tired wings)':

Ex.100                                            Backer Grøndahl, Der skreg en Fugl

The accompaniment of repeated quaver chords in the upper register of the keyboard, however, does become monotonous.

For the last song of the op.60 album, *Og jeg vil ha mig en hjertenskjær* (And I will have me a sweetheart), Grieg goes back to the jaunty, carefree atmosphere of *Mens jeg venter*. Once again Krag's poem (also from the *Digte* of 1891) imitates a folk-song, although in the third stanza the 'heron's feather' referred to was also his symbol for the new things in contemporary poetry, the *nyromantikk*. Grieg's melody maintains the illusion of folk-song, this time for the most part with a strong, chordal accompaniment, so that the effect is not nearly as subtle as *Mens jeg venter*, but still full of humour.

The song is constructed entirely from the first theme, which is used in slightly different guises and in many different keys, without quite anticipating Balfour Gardiner's remark that the only thing one can do with a folk-song when it has been played once is to play it again – louder! The dance rhythm is accentuated by the accompaniment chords and the folk music image is further strengthened by the tonic pedal and the piano echoes of the vocal line.

The modulation to the dominant at bar 16 is not unexpected, nor is the next to the subdominant, but from then on Grieg's modulations are wide-ranging and audacious, managed with such brazen charm that they succeed. The delayed resolution at the end of each of these phrases, marked sforzando, also adds to the humour:

Ex.101                                           Og jeg vil ha mig en Hjertenskjær

(A heron's feather I will have in my hat, yes, yes, in my red hat.)

Arriving finally in the key of D flat major, one could be forgiven for expecting that to be an end to the modulations, but Grieg had not yet finished. Four bars later, the music slides upwards once again to the original tonic key, D major. However, one final surprise remains, for the rhythm of the vocal melody is suddenly augmented and, in a sequence not unlike the end of *Gruss*, op.48 no.1, Grieg conjures up the 'dugvåde Marker (dew-wet meadows)', over which the 'deilige Jonsoksnat (beautiful Midsummer night)' is carried. The song ends triumphantly in D major, with the last note of the vocal line providing an inverted tonic pedal. Monrad Johansen described this last passage as showing 'one of the means of surprise which only genius is master of'.[21]

Astra Desmond wondered whether the piano accompaniment might not be considered 'too brilliant', but it is never allowed to overwhelm the voice, only to underline the lively rhythm. Although shades of the more bravura Drachmann settings can be discerned here, *Og jeg vil ha mig en Hjertenskjær* is musically far superior.

The *Digte af Vilhelm Krag* are dedicated to the Dutch baritone, Johannes Messchaert, and were first performed at a concert in Copenhagen on 20 January 1894. The three sets of songs were published in three albums with Norwegian text by Hansen in September 1894 and shortly afterwards by Peters, again in three albums, with German words, the author of which is not named. Also in 1894, Augener of London published the three sets under the title *16 Songs with pianoforte accompaniment by Edvard Grieg*, with English words by Natalia Macfarren.

Lady Macfarren, who was born in Lübeck, presumably made her translations from the German, although she was in touch with the composer about them. There is a letter from her to Grieg — in English — concerning *Til Én I* in the Grieg Collection in Bergen:

> I am busy with the alterations and I think it needless to trouble you with them all, but as No.3 of op.59 had to be entirely altered (owing to the first three lines having to rhyme with the second three) I would like to have your assent before writing it under the music. Will you like it thus:
>
> > Thou art the vernal prime,
> > Life's thousand voices calling
> > Give thee a welcome cherish'd.
> > I am the autumn time,
> > When wither'd leaves are falling,
> > All my illusions perish'd.[22]

The rhyme-scheme referred to is that of the German translation, not of Paulsen's original, where only the second and fifth, third and sixth lines rhyme. Lady Macfarren also followed the German translator closely in altering names throughout these songs: *Liden Kirsten* is rendered in German as 'Margaretlein' and in English as the rather mannered 'Pretty Marg'ret'; in *Moderen synger* 'Gretchen' unexpectedly becomes 'Irmlein' in the German edition and thus 'Irma' for Lady Macfarren. Both translations also alter the titles of *Turisten, Når jeg vil dø* and *Og jeg vil ha mig en hjertenskjær*, the German becoming, respectively, 'Die Sennerin', 'Herbststimmung'[23] and

'Zur Johannisnacht', followed once more in English with 'The Shepherdess', 'Autumn Feeling' and 'Midsummer Eve'.

The most difficult song to translate from all three albums is *Mens jeg venter*, because of the nursery-rhyme element. 'Bro, bro brille' has no equivalent; the German version uses an equally nonsensical phrase, 'wo-wo-wille', echoed by Natalia Macfarren's 'vola-villa'. These at least fit the rhyme-scheme, but the idea was not quite captured by the 'heigh-ho nonny' of Lily David's English translation for a later, separate Peters edition. This song is also a case of a title misleadingly altered in translation, becoming 'Im Kahne' in German, 'On the water' to Lady Macfarren and 'Drifting' to Lily David. William Halverson in the *GGA* also calls his version 'On the water'; otherwise he has kept quite closely to Krag's original and has effected a neat solution to the problem of the last line with 'Hey, ho heying'.

After the deficiences of the opp.58 and 59 albums, the Krag settings come like a breath of fresh air and they began a period of great song-writing for Grieg, which would culminate in the *Haugtussa* cycle. Not least amongst the songs of this period was an unusual departure for the composer, the *Barnlige Sange* (Children's songs), op.61. These were written at the request of the educationist O.A. Grøndahl[24] in the summer of 1894, 'conceived', as Griege wrote to Sigurd Hals, 'to be able to be sung by youngsters, and therefore in schools!'[25] The texts were taken from a reading book compiled by Nordahl Rolfsen. Some were original, others selected by Rolfsen, who was a Bergen man and the author and publisher of educational books that were very popular throughout Norway. John Horton has said that these songs are the best children's songs written by any nineteenth-century composer and other Grieg scholars have concurred wholeheartedly with that opinion. They are unsentimental, have a good range of subject-matter and, with one exception, are well written for children's voices.

The first of them, *Havet* (The sea), was the one that Grieg considered the best of the seven. It is very Norwegian, with a strong rhythm, emphasized rather than detracted from by the syncopated chords in the accompaniment left hand, and basic tonic and dominant harmony. The most interesting feature, however, is the use of the sharpened fourth of the scale. Grieg wrote to O. Koppang, an organist and headmaster from Trondhjem, 'Of my "Barnlige Sange" I myself set "Havet" highest, because I believe it is the freshest and most full of character. It is the *C sharp*, which must sound like sea-salt'[26]: Ex. 102.

But not every writer has agreed with his assessment. Benestad and Schjelderup-Ebbe quote a remark from Grieg's German biographer, Richard Stein, who wrote, with regard to the *Barnlige Sange*, 'In Number 1, we Germans must be allowed to change the disturbing C sharp (leading-note to the dominant) to a C; even Norwegians here must feel that the C sharp is misplaced'![27] Benestad and Schjelderup-Ebbe themselves consider *Havet*

Ex.102                                                                     Havet

lo - sen lig - ger med flag paa top     u - den-for dø - ren og

luk - ker op     for al - le     ski - be som kom - mer.

(The pilot lies with his flag hoisted outside the bar
and opens it for all the ships that come.)

'melodically difficult',[28] an opinion with which the present author cannot
agree. The short vocal range of only a fifth places the song very comfortably
for young voices, and the notes are easy to project with the required vigour.

The second song of the *Barnlige Sanger*, *Sang til juletræet* (Song to the
Christmas tree), is to a poem by Johan Krohn, which in a setting by the Danish
composer C.E.F. Weyse has become one of the most popular Christmas
songs in Norway. The words are appealing without being sentimental and
Grieg sets the three stanzas strophically. The melody is quite straightforward, although the range is wider than in *Havet* and the final rising phrase
of each strophe would need careful breath control for young voices. A
typically Norwegian element is introduced in the first bar, where the high G
of the melody is sounded against the subdominant (A flat) chord. Otherwise
the harmonic structure, in spite of some chromatic movement, is simple.

*Lok*, a song for calling animals, is a setting of a poem by Bjørnson from his
novel *En glad Gut* (A happy boy) and the melody is built on four short
musical phrases, the fourth being a variation of the first. Some of the children
who sang these songs may well have been familiar with various *lokk* used in
the rural areas of Norway. The vocal range again is a comfortable one for
young voices, and Grieg added musical interest in the accompaniment, with
pedal notes – the whole of the second half of the song is written over the
tonic pedal – and with more chromatic movement in the inner parts than in
the first two songs: Ex.103.

Ex.103                                                                    Lok

(with your fine feathers! See, the grass is wet;)

The fourth song, *Fiskervise* (Fisherman's song), is the only one of the seven which is more art song than children's song. The vocal range is from the A sharp below middle C to high F sharp, an enormous range to expect from children, and the harmonic structure is far more complicated than elsewhere in the group. The words are taken from the great seventeenth-century poet Petter Dass, who loved the coasts of northern Norway, and who often wrote of the sea and the dangers of the fisherman's life. This poem is a vivid account of sea-fishing and the fisherman's task, matched by a vigorous melody from Grieg, while the rocking of the boat is felt in the 'presto con brio' tempo and the triple time. Grieg wrote to Thorvald Lammers, who was to perform the song, 'Remember: the "Fiskervise" fast and vigorous and rhythmically marked!'[29] It is not surprising that this difficult song does not seem to have been as popular with children as others in the group, although as an art song it is well worthy of performance.

With *Kveldsang for Blakken* (Evening song for Blakken – the name given to a duncoloured horse) we are once more completely in the realm of children's songs. The poem here is by Rolfsen himself, a gentle song of a child to his horse at the end of a long day. The horse's tired plodding is portrayed in the pedal tonic and dominant fifths and the syncopated rhythm of the accompaniment left hand, over which runs a tender, flowing melody that rises and falls with the horse's patient pulling. The seven stanzas are set strophically, but Grieg introduces some subtle alterations into the harmonization of the final strophe, with flattened sevenths and thirds which beautifully express the words: 'Dream of it, Blakken: just to eat, just to stand'. He also reverses the order of the second and third phrases, so that instead of increasing the tension, he now conjures up all the tiredness of the animal and the happy prospect of a day of rest.

*De norske fjelde* (The Norwegian mountains) is also a setting of a poem by Rolfsen and describes a number of mountains and peaks in the Gudbrands-dal, Dovre and Jotunheim ranges. Perhaps it was the mention of Rondane at the end of the third stanza that led Grieg, consciously or subconsciously, to begin the song with a phrase very similar to that which opens his famous Vinje setting, *Ved Rundarne*, op.33 no.9:

Ex.104 De norske fjelde

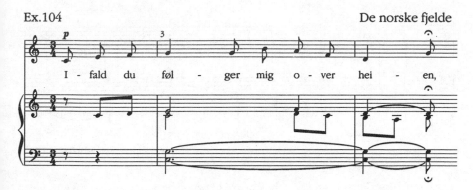

(In case you follow me over the moor,)

There are a number of folk music features here too: the *nystev* form of both verse and music, the pauses at the end of each phrase, the pedal tonic fifth of the first seven bars, the triple time and the unadorned melody. The spaciousness of the mountain ranges is felt in the spread chords of the postludes, with their flattened sevenths and thirds, all over a syncopated tonic pedal.

The last of the *Barnlige Sange* is a patriotic hymn, *Fædrelandssalme* (Hymn to the Fatherland). The poem is again by Rolfsen, after the Finnish 'national poet' Johan Ludvig Runeberg (who wrote in Swedish), and the strong sentiments, which fortunately never degenerate into mere pride or affectation, are matched by Grieg's vigorous melody. The six stanzas are set strophically and the harmonic structure is straightforward, although there is an interesting dissonance at the cadence point, created by the use of a supertonic ninth chord with a sharpened third: Ex.105.

Grieg got himself into some difficulty over the copyright for the *Barnlige Sange*. From 1889 Peters in Leipzig had the sole rights to all his music, but had given him the authority to do what he wanted with this particular album in Norway. He therefore offered the songs to Sigurd Hals, but unfortunately appears to have forgotten that Wilhelm Hansen had the sole Scandinavian rights as the agent of Peters, and in order that the latter company could eventually publish a collected edition of all Grieg's songs. Reminded of this, the composer was then annoyed that Hals wanted compensation from Hansen's to relinquish the songs, having expected co-operation from him in the matter, especially as Grieg has asked for only half the fee he would have

Ex.105                                                    Fædrelandssalme

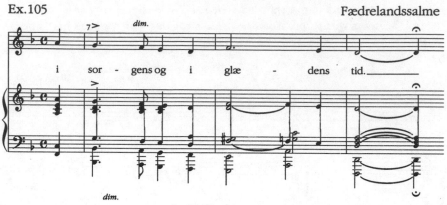

i    sor - gens og    i    glæ - dens tid._____

(in times of sorrow and happiness).

expected from Peters, and a rather heated correspondence ensued in December 1894.

The *Barnlige Sange* are dedicated to Nordahl Rolfsen and were eventually published by Brødrene Hals in February 1895, first in an album and then separately, and also subsequently by both Hansen and Peters, but the songs never did appear in a collected edition. There was also a contemporary English edition published by Augener in London in 1895, with the Norwegian texts and English translations by Natalia Macfarren, which, as with opp. 58, 59 and 60, appear to have been made from the German.

In a letter to Sigurd Hals Grieg reserved the right to let Rolfsen's *Læsebog* (reading book) 'have two of the melodies [*Havet* and *Fædrelandssalme*] for children's voices without accompaniment'.[30] He eventually arranged all the *Barnlige Sange* for three-part unaccompanied children's choir and these versions were published by Brødrene Hals in 1901. The composer further arranged *Fædrelandssalme* for four-part unaccompanied female voices, an arrangement also published by Hals in 1901. This edition, however, is in E minor, whereas the solo version and the children's choral version are in D minor. All these arrangements are now reprinted in Volume 17 of the *GGA*. There is some rearrangement of the chording in the choral versions, with a notable dissonance in *Fiskervise*, where in bars 13 and 14 the two upper voices have B and G sharp, and the third voice the A between them. (In the solo version, the G sharp is omitted altogether, while the A is held throughout the bar in the lower register of the keyboard rather than sounded separately). Similarly, a rearrangement in bars 19 and 20 results in the note-cluster D sharp, E and F sharp.

A number of other arrangements of the *Barnlige Sange*, both choral and instrumental, and including more than ten of *Fædrelandssalme*, were published before and after Grieg's own arrangements. In spite of this, his own four-part version of the last song and the letter to Lammers quoted above, Grieg was adamant that the songs were intended for children, writing again to Sigurd Hals: 'I hold very much to the words "For the school and the home" which I have written on the title page. It means what I have aimed for. It is all children's voices.'[31] Apparently Ellen Gulbranson sang one of the songs at a recital, which caused Grieg to write sternly to Hals: 'That Fru Gulbranson sang "Fædrelandssalme" in public was a great mistake. You should have asked my advice first . . . This song is absolutely for school and home and not for the concert hall, above all in this form for solo voice with piano. For choir – perhaps!'[32] It is strange, then, that the first performance of all the *Barnlige Sange* was given by Nina Grieg at a concert in Copenhagen on 26 April 1895.

The main feature of all the songs written during this period was the startling range of competence displayed in them. It is difficult to believe that the same composer, in a matter of weeks, could be responsible for both *Turisten* and *Der skreg en Fugl*. By 1894 Grieg was feeling much more optimistic about his abilities and in a letter to Max Abraham that January described all his songs of the time as being part of the 'Liederfrühling' that he and Nina were enjoying. He went on, 'It is incredible how much younger I have felt in the last few months. I have become so lyrical that songs pour out of my heart, better I think than ever before.'[33] In the last assumption he may have been right, but more was to come, for the following year he was to compose his greatest songs, the *Haugtussa* cycle.

## Notes

1   John Horton: *Grieg*, 1974, p.78.
2   P. Grainger: 'Personal Recollections of Edvard Grieg', *The Etude*, June 1943, quoted in Benestad and Schjelderup-Ebbe: *Edvard Grieg, mennesket og kunstneren*, 1980, p.340.
3   Finck: 'Musical News and Gossip'. The copy in the Grieg Collection is undated, but as it concerns Grieg's first concert in Paris after his involvement in the Dreyfus controversy, the article must date from 1903. A similar article with the same heading, dated 22 July 1905, was written for the *New York Evening Post*.
4   Grieg, article dating from October 1900, reproduced in *Edvard Grieg: Artikler og Taler*, ed. O. Gaukstad, 1957, pp.184–85.
5   Grieg to Hinrichsen, 29 June 1906.
6   Grieg to Beyer, 8 October 1887 from Carlsbad.
7   Grieg to Beyer, 10 March 1890 from Leipzig.
8   Grieg to Delius, 23 October 1903 from Christiania, included in *Delius. A Life in Letters*, ed. Lionel Carley, Vol.I, 1983, p.227.
9   Nils Grinde in a letter to the author.
10  Erroneously dated 1868 by Sverre Jordan: *En oversikt . . .*, 1954, pp.22–23 and

by Benestad and Schjelderup-Ebbe: *Edvard Grieg, mennesket og kunstneren*, 1980, p.353.

11   Grieg to Sigurd Hals (of Brødrene Hals publishing house in Christiania), 13 December 1893 from Copenhagen.
12   Grieg to Hals, 5 October 1894 from Bergen.
13   Grieg to Hals, 17 December 1893 from Copenhagen.
14   Horton: *Grieg*, p.186.
15   Spelt 'Vergeland' in Augener's English edition, 1894, presumably to ensure correct pronunciation.
16   Monrad Johansen: *Edvard Grieg*, 1934, p.361.
17   Grieg to Lammers, 12 January 1894 from Copenhagen.
18   David Monrad Johansen: *Edvard Grieg*, p.361.
19   Schmidt von Lübeck: *Der Wanderer* ('Ich komme vom Gebirge her').
20   Nils Grinde in a letter to the author.
21   Johansen: *Edvard Grieg*, p.362.
22   Natalia Macfarren to Grieg, 22 May; no year is given, but it must have been 1894. The translation is in fact what appeared in the Augener edition of that year, so Grieg must have approved.
23   Also the German title for *På Skogstien*, op.26 no.5.
24   The husband of Grieg's contemporary, the pianist and composer Agathe Backer Grøndahl.
25   Grieg to Hals, 21 September 1894 from Troldhaugen.
26   Grieg to O. Koppang, 7 September 1895.
27   Quoted in Benestad and Schjelderup-Ebbe: *Edvard Grieg, mennesket og kunstneren*, p.279.
28   Ibid.
29   Grieg to Lammers, 10 March 1898 from Leipzig.
30   Grieg to Hals, 5 October 1894 from Bergen.
31   Grieg to Hals, 6 October 1894 from Bergen.
32   Grieg to Hals, 17 November 1894 from Copenhagen.
33   Grieg to Max Abraham, 7 January 1894 from Copenhagen.

# 12 *Haugtussa*

For the fourth, final and undoubtedly most propitious time in his career, Grieg's song-writing genius was matched with great Norwegian verse. The lyricism of Garborg's *Haugtussa*, with its descriptions of nature and country life, was of the genre which Grieg understood best and to which he responded most successfully. The innate musicality of the *landsmål* language especially appealed to him and it is no small miracle that Garborg's finest work should also have found the composer at the summit of his powers as a song-writer, a combination which culminated in one of the greatest song-cycles of the nineteenth century.

Grieg first appears to have come across the work of Arne Garborg (1851–1924) when Beyer sent him a copy of the novel *Fred* (Peace), for which Grieg thanked him in a letter of February 1893: 'Dear Frants! Thank you for Garborg's Fred! It is a brilliant piece of work, a reflected image held out in front of the countryman. But I wonder if he saw himself in the mirror?'[1] – In so wondering, Grieg was very perceptive, for most of Garborg's work reflected himself and his own feelings, not least in *Fred*.

Arne Garborg was born near Stavanger and, although he never graduated, he studied at the university in Christiania and was at various times a teacher, journalist, writer and linguist. He was a great enthusiast for *landsmål* and the leader of the movement in his time, continuing and extending the work begun by Aasen and Vinje. He translated into *landsmål* many great works by, amongst others, Homer, Shakespeare, Molière and Goethe, and he saw the language become accepted when its use was permitted in schools in 1879 and when, by 1892, it had become a compulsory subject for teacher training. Apart from the *landsmål* movement, Garborg was concerned with many aspects of contemporary life – the plight of the country students in the city, religious and political matters – and his ever-changing subject matter reflects the ever-changing attitudes in Norwegian culture at the end of the 1880s. In 1887 he married a fellow writer, Hulda Bergersen, and moved back to the rural area near Stavanger, to Jæren, the region which provides the natural background to *Haugtussa*.

*Haugtussa* (the title denotes a girl or woman of the 'spirits who live in the hill') is justly considered to be Garborg's greatest work and was published in May 1895, during the period when Norwegian literature was changing from its preoccupation with social and political issues towards more concern with nature and lyricism – the *nyromantikk* or Neoromantic period. Garborg also shows great faith in the mystery of life itself and in the power of individuals to overcome temptations. *Haugtussa* is a poem-cycle which tells the story of Veslemøy (literally, 'little maid'), the 'haugtussa' of the title, a story of strength versus temptation, of Christianity versus trolldom and superstition, of light versus darkness; in other words, of good versus evil. Veslemøy has second sight and is seen by others in her community as strange. Second sight has both advantages and disadvantages: she can see the spirits of the other world – trolls, the hill-folk and even on one occasion the devil himself – but, because she *is* able to see them, she understands what is involved in the temptation she feels and is therefore better able to withstand it. She also finds it easier to cope with her gift while she has her love, Jon, but once he has deserted her, she listens to the hill-folk and hopes to escape her pain with them, and eventually she does go into the Blue Hill.

The poems abound in descriptions of nature and the imagery relies heavily on pathetic fallacy, so that love comes in summer, but when Veslemøy hears of Jon's desertion it is 'an evening towards autumn', and the trolls and spirits appear at night, in mist and cold and shadows. These last phenomena are also, in the poem *Gumlemål* (Gumle's speech), associated with the beginnings of the world, before the creation of sun and light. Garborg uses an extremely wide range of rhyme-scheme and meter within his cycle. Meter, like his imagery, is altered to fit the mood of the poem; thus serene scenes have smooth metric rhythms, bright and happy scenes have rapid, sometimes dance rhythms, and when Gumle is speaking of ancient times, the poet uses a meter and alliteration and even a title akin to those used in the Eddas.

It is small wonder that Grieg, with his well-developed sense of literary values, should have been so taken with the book when he read it soon after its publication. He wrote to Röntgen in June 1895, 'Recently I have been deep in a highly remarkable poem . . . "Haugtussa". It is a quite brilliant book, where the music is really already composed. One just needs to write it down.'[2] In another letter a few days later Grieg told August Winding, 'I have found "Haugtussa" so full of nature-mysticism that I couldn't resist it.'[3] Sigmund Torsteinson, the long-established former curator of Troldhaugen, remembers Camilla Grieg[4] recalling how the composer 'had sat and read long passages from Haugtussa' when the book first came out. Her description – 'He read so quietly . . . almost never raised his voice, but a little nuance here and there set it all beautifully in place'[5] – might equally be used of Grieg's musical settings. The composer also loved *landsmål*, describing it in a letter to Hulda Garborg in August 1898 as 'a world of unborn music', and he was obviously as captivated by Garborg's work as he had been by Vinje's. Garborg, in a letter of January 1898, professed himself pleased that Grieg had found his verses 'musically usable' and he went on to thank the composer, especially for his songs to Vinje's poetry, which he considered to be some of Norway's 'best national melodies'.[6]

Of the seventy poems which make up *Haugtussa*, Grieg originally chose twelve to set and eight more also reached various stages of completion. As he had done with *Den Bergtekne*, he at first conceived a large-scale work for voice, and perhaps choir, with orchestra, but eventually the cycle comprised just eight songs for mezzo-soprano and piano. The first page of the manuscript lists the original twelve poems chosen, although numbers 3 to 6 have been partially erased and the titles given here for those numbers are only a probable reconstruction: 1. *Det syng*, 2. *Veslemøy*, 3. *Sporven*, 4. *I slåtten*, 5. *Veslemøy undrast*, 6. *Den snille guten*, 7. *Blåbær-li*, 8. *Møte*, 9. *Killingdans*, 10. *Elsk*, 11. *Vond dag*, and 12. *Ved Gjætle-bekken*. The songs are listed in the manuscript in the same order as they appear in Garborg's book and all these poems are from the first part of *Haugtussa*, the majority of them from the section called *Sumar I fjellet* (Summer on the mountain). Grieg, significantly perhaps, chose to concentrate on one aspect of the book, that is the unrequited love of Veslemøy for Jon, and the cycle offers the performer a love story comparable to Schubert's *Die schöne Müllerin* or Schumann's *Dichterliebe* (although here seen from a female viewpoint), which ranges from ecstasy to desolation, from dreaminess to drama, and with two light-hearted episodes, all reflecting the complex nature of the central character, Veslemøy. Like Hugo Wolf, Grieg also occasionally implies in his music more than is actually stated in the poem, but aspects which the poet may well have had in mind.

The first song of the eight that comprise the final cycle is *Det syng* (The singing). The poem is in three sections and comes from the first part of the book, *Heime* (At home). (Veslemøy is a *seter*-girl and therefore only at home during the autumn and winter months; in spring and summer she lives up on the mountain pastures with her herds). The first part of Garborg's poem describes the mild weather, with mists and only fleeting glimpses of the moon, a time of trolldom, and the second how the lethargy affects Veslemøy, too. The 'singing' of the title floats from the misty, silent sea, enticing the girl into the Blue Hill where, in turning her silver spinning-wheel, she could forget earthly things. Grieg sets only the third and last section, the song itself, and uses three of Garborg's five stanzas here. The choice of the first and fifth of these, with the reiterated call to come into the Blue Hill, is obvious; the three middle stanzas describe the night, which is not to be feared for it hides sorrow, and of the three Grieg uses the second, which is the most gentle in terms of allurement and also the most alliterative.

The song opens with two spread supertonic seventh chords, their ambiguous tonality underlining the feeling of other-worldliness (Ex. 106). These chords later accompany the last two bars of each stanza and the first trill in the accompaniment was also given to the voice in the first manuscript, although it was omitted in the German manuscript and the printed editions of the song. The vocal melody of the first section is built largely on wide-ranging arpeggios, the first ascending in the tonic F minor, the second descending in D flat major, using one of Grieg's favourite transitions into the key of the flattened submediant:

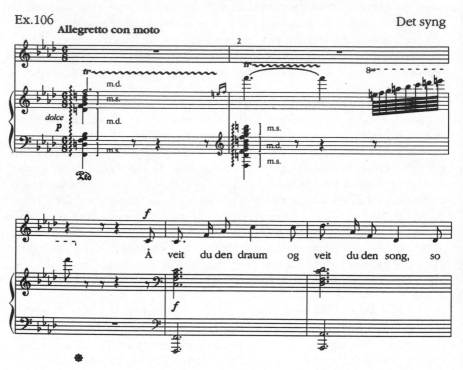

Ex.106                                                                                Det syng

(Oh, do you know that dream and do you know that song)

The second half of the strophe is set to a lilting melody in the tonic major, a melody that entices as much as the words it sets by returning three times to the leading-note (or to the dominant in the ensuing sequence) without rising again to the tonic until the very end of the passage. All this is accompanied by harp-like chords that hover between F major and D minor, followed by a series of seventh chords that similarly never resolve. The accompaniment of the first section, except for the echoes of the vocal line, all lies in the lower range of the keyboard and so the texture is considerably lightened by the use of the higher register for the second half, and this also adds to the feeling of allurement. The postlude figure, like the vocal melody in the second part of the strophe, falls away from the leading-note. It is very similar to the descending figure in *Ein Traum* (op.48 no.6) and is also found in other guises in the third and fourth songs of the *Haugtussa* cycle.

The second song, *Veslemøy*, describes the book's central character and comes from the second section, *Veslemøy synsk* (Veslemøy clairvoyant). The poem is in three stanzas and Grieg uses all but the first half of the last stanza, which describes Veslemøy sitting on her bed, lost in thought. All the essential information about her is in the song: her appearance, 'thin, dark and slender', and her character, with hints of her being able to see 'deep into another world'. How different this portrait is by both poet and composer from those in Drachmann's *Reiseminder*! This song is very subtle in that Grieg sets the poem to an unsophisticated vocal melody and uses the accompaniment to imply all the underlying currents in Veslemøy's character. The opening chords in E minor and the beginning of the vocal line are deceptively simple, although in the third bar he uses a subdominant seventh, as if to suggest that the adjective 'myrk' (dark) refers not only to Veslemøy's physical appearance, and similarly with 'augo *djupe* og grå' (eyes *deep* and grey) in the seventh bar.

The phrase at the end of the first section, which descends to the low register of the voice, gives the music a dreamy quality, while the increased chromatic movement in the second half of the strophe again implies that Veslemøy's lethargy is induced by other than natural causes:

Ex.107                                                              Veslemøy

(It is almost as if a drowsiness lay over the whole of her;)

The modal rather than minor tonality is reinforced at the cadence in the tenth bar, even though the modulation to the dominant key is straightforward enough. Some dissonance is also created by the use of suspensions in the inner parts of the accompaniment and the anticipated cadence in the tonic key at the end of the strophe is given new significance by the flattened fifth in the dominant seventh, which is used as the bass of the chord, and the seventh itself, which resolves through the *major* third of the tonic chord to the minor.

In the second stanza – the song is again set strophically – the three parallel dominant thirteenth chords beautifully underline Veslemøy's strangeness seen in her eyes, which 'shine as if behind a mist', and the dissonant second section portrays her beating heart and trembling mouth. The whole essence of Veslemøy is captured in the last two lines: 'She is quiveringly tender and weak, and at the same time she is fair and young', and the resolution from chromaticism and dissonance to the simplicity of the final tonic chords captures that exactly.

With *Blåbær-li* (Blueberry slopes) the scene moves up to the summer pastures, where Veslemøy tends her cows and goats. Happily tucking into the wild blueberries, she tells how she will deal with the wild creatures, should they happen along. She will give the wolf 'one on the nose' and the same treatment to the 'nice boy from Skare-Brote' if he comes, 'but preferably in another way!' The initial piano flourish establishes the happy mood and the six stanzas[7] of Garborg's seven (Grieg omits the second, where Veslemøy extols the virtues of the berries) are set to a wide-ranging F major melody in a brisk *springar* rhythm. The manuscript shows how much Grieg worked to improve the declamation and to keep the strength of the dance rhythm, by making a number of alterations to the beginnings of lines, so that the stress should fall better. For example, in the third strophe he changed his original:

Ex.108                                                    Blåbær-li

to

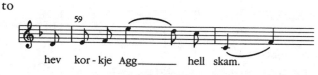

(and has neither resentment nor shame.)

and similarly in the last strophe with 'Han fekk vel ein på sin trut (He would certainly get one on the nose)', to place the stress on 'Han' rather than 'fekk'.

Even within the tonic-dominant structure, Grieg manages to introduce some singular effects, with a subdominant ninth chord in the fifth bar, a sharpened fourth in the eighth and repeated flattened sevenths in the second section, against which a D is sounded in the vocal line. The reiteration of the opening of the melody for the last line is harmonized not in the original tonic key (F) but in the subdominant, and the interval of a major seventh in the penultimate bar of the vocal line creates a supertonic thirteenth to precede the perfect cadence. The skipping of the animals is portrayed in the semiquaver figure of the interludes, which end with the same flourish as at the opening of the song, and thence into the next strophe: Ex.109.

Ex.109

Blåbær-li

The same music forms the postlude, but there it is followed by a simple 'tranquillo' figure, as if to bring us calmly down to earth. The happiness of the song is the more striking for being placed after the reflective *Veslemøy*. In Garborg's book it comes after the poem *Veslemøy lengtar* (Veslemøy yearns), which Grieg also set, but which was not incorporated into the cycle, where the girl is longing for home and her mother.

The printed version of the fourth song of the cycle, *Møte* (Meeting), has only the first two and the last of Garborg's eleven stanzas, although the manuscript of the original version has them all written in. The first version has the essence of the finished setting, especially in the accompaniment:

Ex.110

Møte (first version)

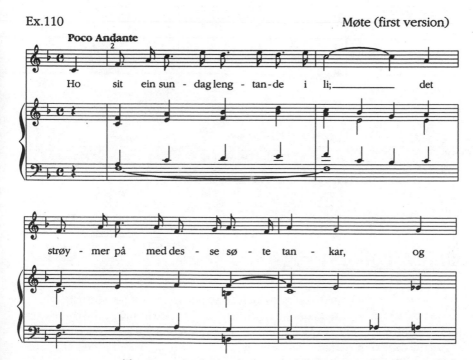

(She sits one Sunday longingly on the hill; these sweet thoughts crowd in)

but it lacks the smoothness and the combined anxiety and joy of the final version. Neither does this first setting allow for the long build-up to the climax of the song. The poem tells how 'the boy from Skare-Brote' does indeed come one Sunday, shares his lunch with Veslemøy and spends the afternoon with her. She is shy and prefers to listen to him talk about himself than tell him stories, and when the thunder comes, not wanting to part, they crawl into a little shelter under the overhanging rocks and spend the night in each other's arms.

Grieg's final setting opens with a folksong-like motif played by the piano, which is developed in the interludes between the strophes. The vocal melody begins simply enough in F major, but there is much more chromatic movement in this song than so far in the cycle and, as the music builds up in rising melodic sequences, we are made aware of the anxiety and confusion of Veslemøy's emotions:

Ex.111                                                                     Møte

The second part of the strophe, which sets the last two lines of each stanza, becomes much warmer and the texture fuller, with low octaves in the accompaniment. The harmony is also less chromatic here and Grieg uses one of his favourite modulations, up a major third to A major. Here, too, the piano and voice become much more interdependent, with the accompaniment playing the opening vocal phrase under a sustained C sharp in the vocal line. Thus Grieg's music matches Garborg's verse-form, in which the last two lines of each stanza are a resolution of the emotions contained in the preceding four lines.

Grieg reverses the order of the next two poems as they appear in Garborg's book, placing *Elsk* (Love) as the fifth song, in front of *Killingdans* (Kids' dance). The words of *Elsk* fall into two sections, the first comprising three stanzas, the second four, and Grieg sets all but the last two stanzas, which are Veslemøy's thoughts of Jon and her happy anticipation of the next Sunday. Each stanza uses the *nystev* form, that is, four lines rhyming in couplets, the first pair having a feminine rhyme, the second a masculine. The song is marked 'I stevtone' (like a *stev*) and Grieg retains the traditional structure by using a basically simple melody, which then undergoes variations. He also retains the three-note anacrusis and a sense of improvisation, with pauses at the end of some phrases. All the melodic material comes from the opening arpeggio figure, which appears in various guises and keys throughout the song, and which was first hinted at in *Udvandreren*, op.58 no.5. This opening phrase also resembles that of *Møte*, though now in the minor key, as if to intimate that Veslemøy already knows that this love-affair is not going to be a happy one:

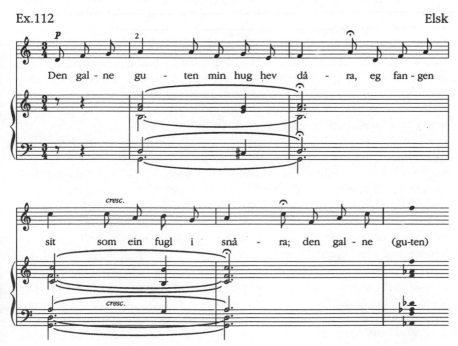

Ex.112          Elsk

Den gal - ne gu - ten min hug hev då - ra, eg fan - gen

sit som ein fugl i snå - ra; den gal - ne (gu-ten)

(The wild boy has ensnared my mind, I am caught like a bird in a snare;)

The first four notes of the melody are played first by the piano in bare octaves and the pensiveness of the first stanza is reflected in the dominant ninth and dominant eleventh chords, which accompany the first two vocal phrases. Veslemøy reflects that she will never be free of 'the wild boy' and the fuller texture and the disturbing chromatic movement at the end of the stanza again imply her unspoken presentiment that all will not end happily. In both this and the last stanza, where the music is identical, Grieg repeats the last line, and these two lines sum up the content of the rest of the song: Jon's knowledge of his power over Veslemøy — 'he knows that the bird will never be free' — and her doubts about him — 'will he really think of me this evening?'

For the second stanza the key changes from the tonic C major to E major and the rhythm to a vigorous *springar*, harmonized for most of its length over a tonic pedal alternating with a seventh chord on the flattened leading-note for the last four bars, and with the ninth added in the vocal line in bar 20. All this is then repeated a semitone higher to set the third stanza, ending on a dominant seventh in G, but not resolving as that might suggest.

In the fourth stanza, where Veslemøy again becomes pensive, thinking of Jon, the tonality is blurred by the use of diminished sevenths in the accompaniment, while the melodic structure remains similar, although the music is now written in $\frac{3}{2}$ instead of $\frac{3}{4}$. The piano interlude after this strophe is the longest there has been for some time and Grieg, with what Benestad and Schjelderup-Ebbe call his 'unerring sense of harmonic logic',[8] brings the music, via a series of elevenths and thirteenths, back to the original key for the last strophe. As so often with Grieg's best strophic or varied strophic songs, the melody suits the last stanza as much as the first, especially the two yearning phrases which use descending melodic minor scales and modal cadences. The final rising phrase and its cadence in C major, repeated by the piano as a brief postlude, contain a wistful note of hope.

*Killingdans* (Kids' dance) is to the second half of the cycle what *Blåbær-li* is to the first. Not unexpectedly, there are many elements of folk-song, but here so skilfully moulded into a deceptively simple-sounding song that one feels that this is where songs like *Lauf der Welt* (op.48 no.3 ) and *Nu er Afnen lys og lang* (op.49 no.4) were leading. The first section of each strophe is in a *halling* rhythm over a tonic pedal, but with a masterly use of the sharpened fourth of the scale in the accompaniment triplet figures, which opens up wider vistas than could be expressed by the diatonic scale alone: Ex.113.

In the second half of each stanza, Garborg has Veslemøy playing with the sounds of the goats' names and, as John Horton has suggested, the song is in some ways an extension of *Lokk* in the *Barnlige Sange*.[9] Certainly the rising vocal phrases at the end of each strophe suggest calls. The flattened sevenths in the chords that accompany the word-play bring another unexpected change of musical colour and, in the final cadence of each strophe, Grieg uses

Ex.113                                                          Killingdans

(Oh, hip and hop and tip and top on this day)

his favourite dominant thirteenth chord. The interludes and postlude are
built on the accompaniment figure of the first vocal phrases, but now the left
hand has syncopated tonic and dominant fifths instead of broken chords, and
the postlude is marked 'vivacissimo' as the goats skip away into the distance.
The happy atmosphere of the poem is perfectly captured in Grieg's setting,
and it seems strange that his original bright G major should have been
altered to G flat in the Hansen edition of the song. [10]

The cheerful mood is soon shattered, for when Sunday comes again, Jon
does not. *Vond dag* (Evil day) uses a theme that is very similar to that in *Møte*
and *Elsk*, but now in the minor key, with wider intervals and with a feeling
of resignation about it, as if this is what Veslemøy had expected all along.
Also where the ends of the opening phrases rose in *Elsk*, in *Vond dag* they fall
and the chromatic movement in the inner parts of the accompaniment here is
full of sorrow rather than hopeful anticipation: Ex.114.

The outburst over Jon's broken promise is underlined by a number of
dissonances, both within the accompaniment and between the accompaniment and the voice (especially in the eighth bar) and it is also felt in the
emphatic vocal melody. The chromatic movement becomes more insistent in
the last two lines, and the triple repetition of three notes in the final phrase —
the Grieg-motif in modal form — contains all Veslemøy's humiliation and

Ex.114

Vond dag

(She counts days and hours and late evenings until Sunday comes:
he has promised so faithfully)

disillusionment. The published song has only the first and last of Garborg's seven stanzas, although the manuscript shows that Grieg originally considered using some of the others too. The second stanza is written underneath the first, but is crossed out, and there is an amalgamation of lines from the fourth, fifth and seventh stanzas, also discarded. The stanzas that do not appear in the final version tell how Veslemøy at first cannot believe that Jon could be disloyal. Then, when she comes home from the mountain one Sunday in autumn, tired and anxious, she learns from her grandfather on his return from church that Jon has been on the 'courting path' and is to marry a rich woman from Ås. In the last stanza, like a wounded bird, Veslemøy creeps into her bed, 'sick and shaking' and weeps through the night. Grieg's strophic setting matches both the stanzas he uses, and the repeated phrase at the end especially suits the last anguished line, 'Now she must die; she has lost her boy.' This song is one of Grieg's most beautiful compositions and one can only agree with Shelley that 'our sweetest songs are those that tell of saddest thought.'

Finally, like the young man in *Die schöne Müllerin*, it is to the stream that Veslemøy goes for comfort in her pain. *Ved Gjætle-bekken* (By the Gjætle brook) is the consummation, not just of the *Haugtussa* cycle, but of the whole of Grieg's song-writing art. Here are all the now familiar elements — pedal notes, echoes, melodic sequences, changes of tempo, chords of the seventh, ninth, eleventh and thirteenth, sliding modulations, interruptions of the music, the portrayal of water — but all woven together in such artless simplicity as to make the song a masterpiece.

Garborg's poem is in three sections; Grieg sets the first, comprising five stanzas, in which Veslemøy talks to the brook, saying that beside it she will rest, dream, remember, forget and finally sleep. The second short section of the poem describes the sound of the harp which 'lures gently and softly, like the summer wind', and the third section is the song of the *hulder* who appears, promising Veslemøy that she will forget her sorrow and find happiness again in the Blue Hill.

Grieg's setting opens with an accompaniment figure, which is obviously a development of *Bekken* (The brook) from Book VII of the *Lyric Pieces*. From the beginning, the A major tonic triad has an added F sharp, both in accompaniment and the vocal melody, which effectively blurs the tonality, an effect increased by the use of the sustaining pedal. The song is built on two melodic themes, Exx. 115 and 116 but they are varied so much that the

Ex.115                                                    Ved Gjætle-bekken

(You swirling brook, you curling brook, here you lie cosily warm and clear.)

Ex.116

Ved Gjætle-bekken

(and glistens in the sun with gentle waves)

song appears almost through-composed. By a semitone slide from G sharp to G natural (bar 13) the key becomes C major, to be followed immediately by another similarly watery glide into B minor, all so skilfully managed that the effect is beautiful and never contrived, as had occasionally been the case elsewhere in his songs, and although the underlying atmosphere of conciliation does not preclude some dissonances, the long-drawn-out melody flows as smoothly as any stream. The subsequent cry of longing, 'Å her vil eg kvile (Oh, here I will rest)', returns melodically to the tonic A major, but over a chord of D minor in the accompaniment, to which the C sharp of the vocal line adds a major seventh. Grieg then uses the same musical idea for four of the five stanzas.

In the third strophe the music begins to develop. The accompaniment figure is interrupted, moves first to the tonic minor key and then to F major, the key of the flattened submediant once again. There is a lovely change to F minor (bar 27) at the words 'her fekk du seng under mosen mjuk (here you have a bed under the soft moss)', but the 'soft' is again not without dissonance, here D flat against C natural. The final phrase of the strophe is set higher here than in the rest of the song, as if Veslemøy's hopes rise for one last time as she says she 'will remember'.

The keys are constantly shifting like water through this and the next strophe and there is a hint of bitonality in the fourth, with the melody in A major and the accompaniment in F sharp minor, harmony which creates seventh and eleventh chords and where the blurring underlines Veslemøy's questioning of the brook. Suddenly, the dominant of A major becomes the leading-note of F, but once more the keys dissolve into one another like the brook's ripples and the chromatically descending bass emphasizes Veslemøy's anguish – 'Tru nokon du såg så eismal som eg (Surely you have seen no-one as lonely as I)' – and the oblivion she craves. For the only time in the song the final phrase is set to a *minor* seventh for the words 'her vil eg gløyma (here I will forget)', and here too the last word is repeated longingly, with a suspension of the B flat over the dominant seventh chord in D.

For the final strophe, while the setting is essentially the same as for the first two, Grieg draws out the music by echoing the vocal line in the accompaniment after each phrase and by overlapping melody and echo. The second part of the melody is also altered slightly with an accented appoggiatura at the words 'å syng kje om *det* som eg tenkjer no (oh, do not sing of *that*, which I am thinking of now)', and the word 'blunda (slumber)' is repeated as was 'gløyma (forget)', while the bass, low in the piano's compass, descends chromatically to the subdominant seventh:

Ex.117 Ved Gjætle-bekken

(Oh, let me slumber, slumber...)

The inner part alters the chord from major to minor and the whole resolves to the tonic A major, as the stream ripples lightly away into the distance. *Ved Gjætle-bekken* ends the *Haugtussa* cycle with the composer's most beautiful lyric song.

As with the Vinje songs, Grieg worked on a number of other *Haugtussa* poems not included in the cycle, which have remained either complete or in sketches in manuscript. The six complete songs, *Sporven*, *Veslemøy undrast*, *I slåtten*, *Dømd*, *Veslemøy lengtar* and *Ku-lokk*, are now to be published in the *GGA* and they and the sketches may be discussed in the order of their appearance in Garborg's book.

*Til deg, du hei* (To you, heath) is the prologue to the whole poetry cycle, and in Grieg's sketches the song also has the title *Prolog* in brackets. It is not included in the original list of twelve on the title-page of the manuscript and is not dated. The melody is slightly akin to those of *Det syng* and *Vond dag*, and has the familiar mixture of major and minor modes, and a number of piano echoes, while the accompaniment moves largely in minim-crotchet rhythm and is very chromatic:

Ex.118                                                                 Til deg, du hei

(To you, you heath and pale marsh with buck-leaves)

The extant sketches show a setting of the first two stanzas of the first part of Garborg's poem, but the music breaks off after the seventeenth bar. The words in the penultimate bar, 'Eg kjenner deg (I know you)', begin both the third and fourth stanzas, and the first of the next section of the poem, but as the manuscript has no more words written in, we are unable to judge which further stanzas Grieg intended to set. The poem dedicates 'my song of twilight and ghosts and hidden life' to the heath and marsh and, in its portrayal of natural phenomena and the pathetic fallacy of the third stanza, which links the 'grey troll-kingdom' with the 'shadowy night', it sets the scene for the whole book.

The sketches of *Veslemøy ved rokken* (Veslemøy at the spinning-wheel) are undated, but marked 'nr.5', although that number in the partially erased list would appear to be *Veslemøy undrast*. Also, the list is in the same order as the poems in Garborg's book and *Veslemøy ved rokken* would not fit as 'nr.5' here. The song has a tempo marking of 'allegro agitato' and there is a nineteen-bar piano introduction in which, with groups of semiquavers in the left hand and the insistent rhythm of the right, Grieg portrays the movement of the spinning-wheel:

Ex.119                                              Veslemøy ved rokken

He may also have intended it as a musical portrayal of the opening words of the poem: 'D'r haust. Det ruskar ute med regn og kalde vind (It's autumn. Outside it is drizzling with rain and cold wind)', for *D'r haust* is also the title of another sketch of the song. This sketch in Grieg's notebooks from the 1890s has the vocal line in two parts, mostly in thirds, and although no piano accompaniment is given, interludes between the vocal phrases, using material from the introduction, are:

Ex.120                                                       D'r haust

D'r haust.____ Det rus - kar u - te med regn og kal - de vird

In the next line the music is marked 'Sop. Ten' and the following line, after two bars interlude, 'Alt.Bass', so it seems that in his ideas for a large-scale work from *Haugtussa*, Grieg had considered this as a choral movement.

Another brief sketch in two and three parts, apparently for female voices, comes from the poem *Kvelding* (Evening), which immediately follows *Veslemøy ved rokken*. Autumn is giving way to winter and the snow has begun to fall. The few words in the manuscript come from the third of Garborg's seven stanzas and Grieg's *halling* rhythm matches the dancing meter of the poem.

*Sporven* (The sparrow) is complete, both in its original solo version, dated 25 May 1895, and in an arrangement for three-part ladies' choir, dated 2 September. Both are now printed in the *GGA*, volumes 15 and 17 respectively. The song is set in a folk-song style and makes some use of piano echoes of the vocal line. Although opening in G major, there are hints of B minor, E minor and C major within the first six bars, and a striking transition to A minor in the eighth bar, before a return to the tonic key: Ex.121.

Ex.121

Sporven

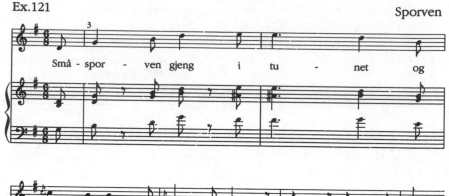

(The little sparrow walks in the yard and drops corn and picks straw)

The opening bars of the second half of the strophe are written over the dominant pedal and a chromatically descending bass also adds interest. Whether Grieg intended the choral version of *Sporven* as part of his projected large-scale work, or just as a separate arrangement, it is not now possible to tell.

Grieg's notebooks from the 1890s also contain some sketches of another song entitled *Veslemøy*, although the text, where it is written in, comes from the poem *Fyrevœrsel* (Premonition):

Ex.122

Veslemøy (Fyrevœrsel)

(Veslemøy lay dreaming in the grey morning hour)

Veslemøy has a vision of her dead sister, who tells her that she has 'the saddest destiny' and a 'dark path' to follow, 'but dear is the brightening morning after the hard night'. The opening melody occurs again for the words 'Du arme unge syster (You poor young sister)', but now in E major, and further sketches have words from the third stanza of the poem.

*Veslemøy undrast* (Veslemøy wonders) has been reconstructed by Nils

Grinde from Grieg's manuscript for inclusion in the *GGA*. The song is in E flat major, although the sketches have an apparent key-signature of four flats, and it is in a *halling* rhythm marked 'allegro con brio'. The folk-song element is to be found in the tonic fifth of the accompaniment and in the piano echoes of the vocal line. It does seem a rather lively setting for such a reflective poem, where Veslemøy is wondering about her future:

Ex.123                                                          Veslemøy undrast

Jen - ton' brei - er der  gu - tan' slær;_____  så  ro - par dei til kvar - an- (dre)

(The girls spread [the hay] where the boys mow, then they call to each other)

Each stanza, except the last which has a variation of the line, ends with the words 'Me veit, når det er så laga A — (I shall know, if it is meant to be)', once again illustrating Veslemøy's visionary gifts.

The folder in the Grieg Collection which contains one of the sketches of *Veslemøy undrast* is labelled *I slåtten* (In the hay-field), which is the overall title of that section of *Haugtussa* of which the former is the second poem. Sketches for the song actually entitled *I slåtten* are also in this folder, while the complete manuscript is in the Musikhistoriske Museum in Copenhagen, and another handwritten, though not autographed, copy is to be found in the British Library in London.

'Slåtten' here means 'the hay-field', but a *slått* is also a Norwegian dance, and Grieg uses the rhythm of the *gangar* form, marked 'allegro vivace'. The bouncing vocal line is underlined by the insistent rhythm of the accompaniment and only after the first phrase is there any echoing of the vocal line. Instead, the accompaniment echoes itself, right hand to left hand, and the brilliant piano writing, a little reminiscent of *Killingdans*, strengthens the impetuosity of the setting: Ex. 124.

In its very vigour and the full piano writing, however, the song is quite different from the other *Haugtussa* settings and would seem more suitable for a male voice than for the mezzo or soprano required for the cycle itself and for all the other songs except *Dømd*.

The sketches of *Dømd* (Doomed) are virtually complete except for some of the text and parts of the accompaniment, which is indicated if not written

Ex.124                                                                    I slåtten

(Things go so easily in the dew-soft meadow)

fully, and like *I slåtten*, complete manuscripts are to be found in Copenhagen and London. In the book *Dømd* is a section by itself, but comprises only one poem in three parts. Grieg uses the third, which begins 'Eg hev som vigde mammons træl (I have, like devoted mammon's slave)'. The song is written for a bass voice and this part of the poem is the song of an old man Veslemøy meets and nothing to do with the girl herself. Grieg cannot have intended it to be part of the cycle, but may have toyed with the idea of it forming part of the large-scale work he had at first envisaged *Haugtussa* becoming.

The vocal line is sombre, with a number of chromatically moving phrases and augmented intervals. The old man has been condemned for moving the stones used as boundary markers between farms, referred to in the mediaeval religious ballad *Draumkvedet* as a serious breach of the law and a punishable offence. His anguished cry 'Gud hjelpe meg i Jesu namn!' (God help me in Jesu's name!)' is vividly depicted at the end of the first and third stanzas, but given a much more resigned setting in the middle section of the song. The ends of the first four phrases of the vocal line are echoed in the accompaniment, but here in the lower register of the keyboard, which adds to the atmosphere of gloom:

Ex.125                                                                    Dømd

*Dømd* is a very strange song and seems quite out of place amongst Grieg's other *Haugtussa* settings, both in content and quality.

A further sketch in Bergen's collection has a text beginning 'Myrene søv under tåkefell (The marshes sleep under a cover of mist)' and comprises the third and fourth stanzas of the first section of the poem. The manuscript shows indications of two- and three-part writing, so again Grieg may have considered this section for his planned extended choral work.

For *Den snille guten* (The nice boy) Grieg apparently intended using only a small part of Garborg's long poem, which describes Jon, the boy rapidly growing into manhood who awakens Veslemøy's love. Only a few words of the text are written into the manuscript sketches and these indicate the second stanza, the last two lines of the final (fourteenth) stanza, and the whole of the third. The melody has a good deal in common with the first version of *Møte*, particularly the passage that ostensibly sets the second half of the second stanza:

Ex.126                                                  Den snille guten

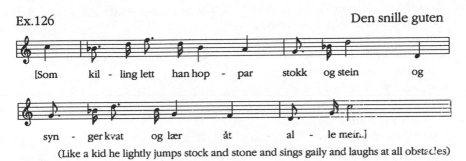

(Like a kid he lightly jumps stock and stone and sings gaily and laughs at all obstacles)

The sketch of *Veslemøy lengtar* (Veslemøy yearns) is dated 4 September 1895 and again exists in a complete version in Copenhagen and London. The first sketches are in E major and marked 'lento', while the complete song is in F and marked 'allegretto'. Veslemøy, as a *seter*-girl, lives up on the mountain pastures with her animals during the summer, often lonely and frightened and, as here, longing for her mother and home. The words 'ho mor (her mother)' occur like a refrain after the first, second and fourth lines of each stanza, something in the manner of the *omkved* in traditional ballad form, and this is also the subtitle of the completed song, although in the sketchbooks it bears the title 'No stend ho steller i kjøkenkrå, ho mor! (Now she stands working in the kitchen corner, her mother!)', the first line of the poem. The sketches also have some instrumental indications for cor anglais, strings and horn.

Once more the setting is strophic and the wide-ranging melody is very like a *lokk*. The left hand of the accompaniment consists largely of broken chords, while, except for the end of each strophe, the right hand echoes the vocal line at one bar's distance: Ex. 127.

Ex.127                                                        Veslemøy lengtar

No stend ho stel-ler i kjø-ken-krå, ho mor;_____

The key change at bar 8 from the tonic to A minor and the subtle chromatic movement in the second half of the strophe convey the wistful quality of the poem, especially the B natural to C in the inner parts (bar 18) and the G flat to F in the bass (bar 20), and one might also note the use made of the 'Grieg motif' in these last two phrases. This is a lovely song, which would not have been out of place in the cycle itself, adding as it does to the picture of the youthful and vulnerable Veslemøy.

Very brief sketches also exist with the title *Skog-glad* (Woodland joy). The poem, again from the section *sumar i fjellet* from which most of Grieg's choices were made, is Veslemøy's song to a 'poor little hare' she meets. The sketches are in E major with a time signature of $\frac{6}{8}$ altered to $\frac{2}{4}$. The dotted rhythm of the two-bar introduction and of the snatch of melody would appear to underline the skipping of the hare.

The last of the previously unpublished songs from *Haugtussa* is the beautiful and haunting *Ku-lokk* (Cow call),[11] which is more nearly a folk-song than any other of Grieg's songs. The postlude is in fact built on a phrase which the composer wrote down during the same tour of Jotunheim in 1886 when he noted *Gjendines Bådnlåt*. The vocal melody is unaccompanied for almost the whole of each strophe, each line echoed by the right hand, sometimes in its entirety, sometimes just the end of the phrase, and there is a sense of improvisation about the whole song, befitting the traditional style:

Ex.128                                                              Ku-lokk

Å  ky-ri mi ve-ne, å  ky - ri mi!_____

(Oh cows, my friends, oh my cows!)

There are many folk-song elements to be found in the decorations of the vocal line, the alternation of major and minor modes and in the sharpened fourth of the scale, as well as the familiar 'Grieg-motif'. The true *lokk* element is also felt at the end of the vocal line in each strophe, where the first line of the stanza is repeated to an angular melody built from the notes of the tonic chord. The chromatic cadence at the end of each strophe is formed by the use of the second inversion of the dominant seventh with the flattened fifth before the tonic major chord.

In the sketches of the song in Bergen there is a vocal cadenza at the end of the postlude, doubled a third higher by the piano right hand:

Ex.129                                                                    Ku-lokk

It appears, however, that Grieg changed his mind about this, for the complete manuscript omits the vocal line here. Once again in *Ku-lokk* Grieg was thinking in terms of orchestration; the sketches in his notebooks have the echoes of the vocal line designated for cor anglais, and some pencilled jottings in the manuscript of *Møte* read 'Ku-lok. Engelsk horn og sang selv (Cor anglais and voice only)'.

All the poems Grieg used come from the first and certainly better half of *Haugtussa*. The second part of the book deals with Veslemøy's life after she has gone into the Blue Hill, and it is difficult to see why Garborg then felt the need for a sequel, *I Helheimen* (In Helheim — the kingdom of the dead in Norse mythology, ruled over by Hel, daughter of Loki), for it never achieved the success of *Haugtussa*. Grieg's choice among the poems gives an overall picture of Veslemøy and particularly of her love for Jon and the devastation of his desertion. But, with the exception of *Det syng* and the hints of clairvoyance in *Veslemøy*, there are in the final song-cycle no references to the other-worldliness which is central to Veslemøy's character, and, to give a complete portrait of her, parts of *Synet* (The vision) and the poem entitled *Haugtussa* might have been appropriate. Grieg seems to have chosen to avoid the larger issues raised by Veslemøy's second sight; for example the illness it causes her, the inability or unwillingness of her mother to take the clairvoyance seriously (which brings to mind Goethe's *Der Erlkönig*), and Veslemøy's acceptance of her own gift, which shapes her philosophy of life:

'Oh, I would rather see with my eyes than go through the world deaf and blind and not make it out properly.'[12]

There is no doubt, however, that from all the poems he considered, his final choice of the eight that comprise the song-cycle was not at all arbitrary, for the order in which Grieg presents them has a calculated symmetry. The first song, the enticement of Veslemøy, is balanced by the last, where she finds peace beside the stream and ultimately in the Blue Hill; the narrative *Veslemøy* and the innocent joy of *Møte* have their counterparts in the fluctuating moods of *Elsk* and the anguished *Vond dag*; and each half of the cycle has its happy idyll in *Blåbær-li* and *Killingdans*. The reversal of the order of *Elsk* and *Killingdans* from Garborg's original allows the emotional climax of the cycle to be reached in the two middle songs, creating, as Torstein Volden has observed,[13] a strictly constructed curve. The cycle is also united musically by the tonic centre F. Four of the songs are in F major or minor, another begins in D minor and, by setting the final one in A major, Grieg utilizes one of his favourite modulations: up a major third from the F minor of the penultimate song.

As not all the manuscripts and sketches are dated, the order in which the songs were composed is not completely known. Garborg's book was published on 1 May 1895 and Grieg obviously obtained a copy very quickly, for the manuscript of the solo version of *Sporven* is dated 25 May. From the songs that are dated, it may be seen that *Killingdans* was written on 27 May, *Veslemøy* on 29 May, *Elsk* on 30 May, *Ved Gjætle-bekken* on 7 June, *Det syng* on 14 June and *Vond dag* on 25 June. The title-page of the manuscript carries the inscription 'Til [in hand] llte juni 1895', so it may be assumed that the twelve songs listed there were all in varying stages of composition by this date. The last dated of all is *Veslemøy lengtar* on 4 September.

A number of the songs have indications of instrumentation written on the manuscripts, Grieg, as we have seen, having originally envisaged using the book as a basis for his long dreamt-of large-scale work for soloist(s), chorus and orchestra. In a letter to Iver Holter of 10 September 1895 Grieg writes that he is 'writing music to "Haugtussa" by Garborg. It will be something for voice and orchestra'. Sketches of *Det syng* show the trill in the accompaniment marked 'violen tr.' and the subsequent flourish 'piccolo 8ve', while others also have indications for soprano and alto parts for the section beginning 'Å hildrande du'. In pencil under the final bar of the manuscript of *Ved Gjætle-bekken* is the figure:

Ex.130    Ved Gjætle-
                    bekken

This idea is continued on the next page of manuscript paper, as part of a score for strings, woodwind and horns, but there is no indication of whether or not this was a possible scoring for the song or something quite separate. Of the unpublished songs and sketches, *Veslemøy lengtar* has indications for 'Cor Ang.', 'Str.' and 'Cor'. It is clear that Grieg had some orchestration in mind, but when we consider the perfect combination of voice and piano he achieved in *Haugtussa*, we must be grateful that the notions of something larger did not come to fruition.

Nina apparently performed some of the *Haugtussa* songs for Julius Röntgen, when the families were together in Leipzig for Christmas 1895,[14] and the music and the performance, with Nina – significantly in the light of circumstances – singing and accompanying herself, greatly impressed him. Yet Grieg wrote to him from Troldhaugen the following June, 'Haugtussa for the time being still sleeps. I have, since Christmas when it was sung for you, never had the album[15] in my hands again.'[16] Others have speculated briefly on why Grieg, after his initial eagerness to set Garborg's work, seems to have lost incentive. Benestad and Schjelderup-Ebbe say that it was 'strange' that Grieg 'let the whole thing drop without going further and without trying to get it published.'[17] Torstein Volden asks why, if, as Grieg had written to Röntgen on 12 June 1895, 'the music to Haugtussa is really already composed. One just needs to write it down', he then waited over three years to publish the songs.[18] He suggests that ill-health may have been one reason, but it cannot have been the only one, for in spite of bouts of influenza, Grieg also had some good periods, and wrote to Beyer in November 1896 that he was feeling 'more healthy than . . . for many years.'[19] Grieg did mention in a letter to Matthison-Hansen that 'the texts unfortunately put obstacles in the way'[20] of his seeing how best to arrange his music, but this may have been because he was still contemplating a large-scale work. Later he was to blame the delay on the lack of understanding that he feared for the songs.

The true reason for the delay in preparing the songs for publication, however, is much more likely to have been similar to that which caused the long break in his song-writing in the early 1880s, that Grieg was once again infatuated with another woman; as has already been seen, when his marriage was in difficulties for whatever reason, he could write no songs. He had not been happy for some time and had told Beyer at the end of 1894 that he felt he ought to resign himself to accepting that his work was at an end, but that he could not do so, 'for energy and ambition are by no means extinct in me'.[21] Another letter to Beyer, written from Leipzig during the traumatic January of 1896, reveals that he was so unsettled during the summer he was writing the *Haugtussa* songs that he had even considered selling his beloved home: 'Now, as I sit here, I really cannot understand how so many times in the summer I could have been thinking of selling Troldhaugen. For at this moment it would give me the happiness and peace of mind I so sorely need.'[22]

The subject of the new infatuation was Isabella ('Bella') Edwards, an English pianist and teacher who studied at the Danish Music Conservatory in Copenhagen from January 1884 to December 1886. Six letters to her from Grieg, dated between November 1895 and January 1896, were acquired by Bergen Public Library in September 1963, but were only made public in May 1985. It is not known where or when the two met, but as Grieg was frequently in Copenhagen and they were both musicians, it is fair to assume that they met there. Grieg had been in the Danish capital at the end of 1894 and during the early months of 1895, and then again only briefly in October 1895 *en route* to Leipzig, so the situation between them must have developed before his encounter with *Haugtussa*. If so, he could perhaps already have seen a reflection of himself in Veslemøy: lonely and not always understood by those closest to him. By the end of the year the aspect of unrequited love had also entered the picture. Certainly after his initial eagerness to set Garborg's poems, Grieg appears to have lost incentive and on arrival in Leipzig he wrote to Beyer that, although he had intended to set to work again on *Haugtussa*, 'all that lies a hundred miles away. I haven't the slightest idea any more about their mood'.[23]

As he had to Beyer in the early 1880s, so Grieg in his correspondence with Bella Edwards wrote of his fruitless searching for happiness. On 1 December 1895 he declared, 'I live, live in order to search for something I will never find; that is my misfortune, and my misfortune as an artist and human being!' On Christmas Eve he wrote, 'I am a lonely man. Because of my eternal longing for deep sympathy. In art I found it, in life never!' There can be little doubt from the correspondence of the seriousness of Grieg's intentions. He had already, in October, told Beyer that he was hoping to go to Copenhagen over Christmas and, in the same letter to Bella of Christmas Eve, he was offering to forgo all his plans and travel there if she would just say the word. If not, she must be honest and tell him so, and 'then I *will* try to do the impossible. To forget you!'

He had told her 'you have taken all my heart', but she evidently would not commit herself, for on 30 December he wrote, 'It is like this then: you do not have the courage!' This must have hurt him deeply; so much so that at the end of January he told her, 'I cannot answer your letter without opening up all the wounds! Therefore, just this: Do not write any more!' After that decision was taken, it is most unlikely that Grieg would have been in any frame of mind to return to a song-cycle the subject of which all too closely mirrored his own situation, and it was another two years before *Haugtussa* was finally prepared for publication.

This was early in 1898, although the songs were not published until the September of that year. Grieg wrote to Lammers, 'The best songs I have

written will come out in the autumn. They are from Garborg's "Haugtussa"... If only some of the songs lay right for your splendid voice.'[24] The
first edition was published by Wilhelm Hansen, with Garborg's text and a
Danish translation prepared by John Paulsen and the composer. The Peters
edition followed in the same year, with translations into German and
English. The German version was by Eugen von Enzberg, who had been
recommended to Grieg by Garborg in a letter of 19 January 1898, although
Grieg wrote to Lammers that he had had 'a difficult task in obtaining a
German translation'.[25]

That the *Haugtussa* songs are scarcely known outside Scandinavia must
once again be blamed on the lack of good translations, although it should be
said that Garborg's vivid and descriptive poetry is very difficult to translate,
especially into singable verse. Also, the musical idiom was not understood
abroad, at least not in Germany. Grieg wrote to Finck of a critic in *Signale*
who 'a few years ago used six columns to show that he was as comprehending
of these songs as a bull of a red rag!' He complains, too, about the German
translations, which 'give absolutely no idea of the beauty and originality of
[Garborg's] story', so much so that one would indeed need to possess the
'fortunate gift of second sight' to understand them.[26]

In fairness it ought to be said that von Enzberg's translations are largely
accurate. Where they, and the unattributed English versions in the same
edition, fall short is in their failure to capture the softness and lyricism of
Garborg's language – that 'world of unborn music',[27] as Grieg described it –
and the other-worldly atmosphere that pervades so much of the book, but
which becomes much more prosaic in translation. For example, the spirit
which sings to Veslemøy in the first song of the cycle addresses her as
'hildrande', that is, wrapped up in her own imagination or creating an
illusion around herself, an idea not conveyed in the Danish 'tryllende'
(bewitching), nor in the German 'Strahlende' (radiant), and certainly not in
the English 'Enchanteress' (sic).

Astra Desmond commented of *Blåbær-li* that 'the words are amusing and
quaint in a way that cannot be reproduced in another language'.[28] She went
on to quote a German biographer (unnamed) of Grieg, who, recognizing this
difficulty, recommended singers to sing the song either in the original or in
English; he considered that the German version sounded 'zu vulgär', while in
Norwegian it would be 'urwüchsig' (natural, unspoilt) and in English
'beinahe so amüsant wie ein Niggersang'!

The most difficult song of the cycle to translate is *Killingdans*, with all the
playing on words for the goats' names in each stanza and, not least, the title.
Translations have also become rather anthropomorphic in describing the
kids' games. Rolf Stang, in his English translations in the *GGA*, manages
the name-play skilfully and his version of *Ved Gjætle-bekken* is both accurate
and truly lyrical. Elsewhere, in *Killingdans* and in other songs of the cycle, he

has unfortunately not always avoided the pitfalls of colloquialism.

It seems strange, except that Grieg's settings are definitive, that so few other Norwegian composers have used any of the *Haugtussa* poems. One who did was Catharinus Elling (1858–1942), who set six of Garborg's verses as his op.52 and six more as op.60 and his setting of *Sporven*, the fourth of his op.52 group, is the only one of his some two hundred songs that is generally known in Norway today. Because of the delay in preparing his own songs for publication, Elling's albums appeared before Grieg's, op.52 being published in Copenhagen in 1895 and op.60 in Christiania in 1896. Whether Grieg knew Elling's settings and, if so, his opinion of them, is not known.

Other music to *Haugtussa* includes a number of traditional melodies sung to the verses, collected, amongst the more than three thousand he wrote down in his lifetime, by Olav Sande (1850–1927). Settings of *'Dokka'* and *Elsk* were also made by Emil Jensen (1853–1934), a member of the board of management of the Bergen music society Harmonien. More recently Lillian Gulowna Taubo (b.1915) has set eighteen of the *Haugtussa* poems. The first twelve songs were written around 1950, the other six during 1985–86 and, although the music remains in manuscript, the cycle with its short prelude has been recorded. [29]

Grieg's cycle was dedicated to Dagmar Møller, a Norwegian-born singer living in Sweden, and Grieg sent her a copy of the first edition on 16 September 1898. The note that accompanied it may provide a further reason for the delay in publication: 'The songs have lain in my desk for over three years, because I doubted that they would be understood. However, interpreted by you, I still have hope.' Grieg also seems to have felt that the *landsmål* language would not be accepted, although after the reception given to his Vinje settings, this is unlikely; he was always inclined to blame outside forces rather than personal weakness for artistic lapses.

*Haugtussa* was published in two separate albums, each containing four songs, and four of them (*Det syng, Veslemøy, Møte* and *Elsk*) were sung at a concert in Christiania in October 1898 to very favourable reactions from audience and press alike, the critic in *Morgenbladet* describing them as 'a series of Norwegian songs which will find a path to everyone who has ears for the deep, moving atmosphere of our national music.' The first performance of the complete cycle, however, was not given until over a year later, in Christiania in November 1899, sung by Eva Nansen and with Agathe Backer Grøndahl accompanying, and a few days afterwards four songs were at last performed by the dedicatee, accompanied by the composer, in Stockholm. Garborg had received a copy of the songs in August 1898, according to a letter to the composer from Hulda Garborg, and he heard Eva Nansen's performance in the Norwegian capital. He wrote to Grieg, 'I was so pleased with them, more than I can say. It was exactly this deep, soft, muted, this underworld music, which I, in my way, tried to sing into words and rhyme, but which you have captured. And then suddenly once more sparkling, shining sun and summer rapture, as in the glorious Killingdans. But about the most truly moving is Bekken. Yes, I am now happy and proud, quite disgracefully proud, that you were able to use these verses. Thank you! Fru Nansen sang beautifully. I thought she *was* Veslemøy . . .'[30]

Nina's understanding of Grieg's songs was passed on mostly to Danish singers, principally Sylvia Larsen Schierbeck, whom she accompanied in the first performances in Denmark of the complete *Haugtussa* cycle (sung in *landsmål*) towards the end of 1924. The performance in Copenhagen on 1 November 1898 drew enthusiastic if descriptively limited praise from the critic Ejnar Fordhammer: 'And how beautiful this cycle is! How Garborg's beautiful words and Grieg's beautiful music blend together into an incomparable whole!'[31] Sylvia Schierbeck, accompanied by Otto Mortensen, also performed three of the unpublished *Haugtussa* settings, *Ku-lokk*, *I slåtten* and *Veslemøy lengtar*, at the Musikhistoriske Museum (which owns the autographed manuscripts) in October 1937 and, as related by Oddvin Mathisen,[32] recalled having sung them on occasion with Nina Grieg too.

Whatever his uncertainties about the acceptability of the *Haugtussa* songs, Grieg was in no doubt of their musical worth. He described them to Thorvald Lammers in March 1898 as 'the best songs I have written', with which one must heartily concur. The dearth of performances outside Scandinavia is a great loss to the rest of the musical world, for here as nowhere else is all Grieg had taken from Norway's national music, regenerated and returned in the form of great art song.

## Notes

1　Grieg to Beyer, 4 February 1893 from Leipzig.
2　Grieg to Röntgen, 12 June 1895 from Troldhaugen.
3　Grieg to Winding, 16 June 1895 from Troldhaugen.
4　Voice teacher and drama coach in Bergen.
5　Sigmund Torsteinson: *Med troll i tankene*, 1985, p.37.
6　Garborg to Grieg, 19 January 1898 from Christiania. It is interesting to note that Garborg's letters to Grieg are *not* in *landsmål*.
7　In the manuscript the third and fourth stanzas are crossed out, but are reinstated in the printed version.
8　Benestad and Schjelderup-Ebbe: *Edvard Grieg, mennesket og kunstneren*, 1980, p.292.
9　John Horton: *Grieg*, 1974, p.191.
10　A high-key version for soprano in B flat was also published separately by Peters in the series *Beliebte Lieder . . . von Edvard Grieg*, ?1905.
11　Like *Siehst du das Meer?*, *Ku-lokk* is also included on the record that accompanies the book *Edvard Grieg, mennesket og kunstneren*.
12　From 'Haugtussa', the fourth poem in the section *Veslemøy synsk*.

13    Torstein Volden: *Studier i Edvard Griegs Haugtussa-sanger*, 1967, p.50.
14    Benestad and Schjelderup-Ebbe: *Edvard Grieg, mennesket og kunstneren*, p.263, say the summer at Troldhaugen, which does not accord with Grieg's letter to Röntgen, 20 June 1896.
15    The songs are not named. We may assume it was the eight that comprise the cycle.
16    Grieg to Röntgen, 20 June 1896 from Troldhaugen.
17    Benestad and Schjelderup-Ebbe: *Edvard Grieg, mennesket og kunstneren*, pp.289–90.
18    Volden: *Studier i . . . Haugtussa-sanger*, pp.5, 6 and 7.
19    Grieg to Beyer, 5 November 1896 from Christiania.
20    Grieg to Matthison-Hansen, 16 September 1895 from Troldhaugen.
21    Grieg to Beyer, 29 December 1894 from Copenhagen.
22    Grieg to Beyer, 24 January 1896 from Leipzig.
23    Grieg to Beyer, 27 October 1895 from Leipzig.
24    Grieg to Lammers, 10 March 1898.
25    Ibid.
26    Grieg to Finck, 17 July 1900.
27    Grieg to Hulda Garborg, 18 August, 1898.
28    Astra Desmond in *Grieg: A Symposium*, ed. Gerald Abraham, 1948, p.90.
29    By Olav Eriksen (Bar) and Kaare Ørnung on Callisto 85015.
30    Garborg to Grieg, 7 November 1899 from Christiania.
31    Review by Ejnar Fordhammer, quoted by Oddvin Mathisen: 'Fire etterlate men fullstendige Haugtussa-sanger av Edvard Grieg (Four remaining but complete Haugtussa songs . . .)', *Norsk Musikktidsskrift*, March 1973.
32    Mathisen: ibid.

# 13 'Music's torch, which ever burns...'[1]

Whether it was because he realized the true worth of the cycle, or because after Garborg it was difficult to find any comparable verse in Norway, Grieg set only one more Norwegian poetry after *Haugtussa*, and his last two sets of songs are to Danish texts. Between 1895, when the *Haugtussa* songs were begun, and 1900, when the next albums appeared, almost all his original music was for piano. There is a setting of Jonas Lie's *Nu Pinsens klokker ringer* (Now Whitsun's bells are ringing), written in March 1896 under the title *Kristianiensernes Sangerhilsen* (The Christiania people's choral greeting), for male-voice choir with a baritone solo, conceived for 'a not unknown Norwegian Norseman who calls himself Thorvald Lammers'.[2]

The one Norwegian song Grieg did write is *Blåbæret* (The blueberry) to a short poem by Didrik Grønvold, intended by the poet as a children's song. He wrote to Grieg, enclosing the verses, from Sætersdal near Christianssand: 'On seeing the millions of blueberries . . . along the paths, I came to put [the poem] together. If there should be any musical-lyrical moments in it . . . then it might perhaps serve to bring a little love of the blueberry to our children across the country, especially if *you* will put one of your wonderful melodies to it.'[3] Grieg, however, was not inspired to any great melodic heights. The poem is about a small boy who, his heart full of resentment, is walking in the farmyard, until his mood is lightened by the blueberry, which promises him solace and refreshment. It is a little reminiscent of *Tytebæret* (op. 33 no. 4), although lacking Vinje's style, and of *Vesle gut*, while the folksong-like strophic setting also reminds one of *Langelandsk Folkemelodi* (op. 15 no. 3), not least in the monotonous rhythm of the accompaniment. There are occasional glimpses of interest, however, in the sequential phrases towards the end of each strophe: Ex. 131.

The manuscript is headed 'Troldhaugen 23/8/96' and the song is published for the first time in the *GGA*.

All through the final decade of the century, Grieg was still undertaking numerous journeys to perform and conduct, although his travels were increasingly dogged by ill-health. He had spent the winter of 1895–96 in Leipzig, where he once again met Brahms, there for a performance of his

Ex.131                                                                      Blåbæret

(right up to the dark moor with the light blue heather)

Fourth Symphony. After a summer spent on his beloved west coast of Norway, Grieg and Nina left for Stockholm in October for a series of four concerts of orchestral and choral music. The following month they went on to Vienna, via Christiania, for a further series of performances, but a proposed trip to Budapest had to be cancelled because of the composer's ill-health. The illness, described in a letter to Beyer as 'damned influenza and this time followed by bad bronchitis', also caused the temporary postponement of three of the Vienna concerts. On a lighter note, it was while he was in Semmering, near Vienna, that Grieg experienced one of the less pleasing aspects of his success: he wrote to Beyer: 'But popularity can sometimes be unpleasant. I found that out yesterday when, during dinner, a zither-player suddenly struck up with Solveig's song.'[4]

After the Christmas break, Grieg returned to Vienna for a Lieder concert on 6 January, where he was to accompany the Dutch bass-baritone, Anton Sistermans. Shortly afterwards he was back in Leipzig and wrote to Beyer that he had been ill again after the last concert in Vienna, 'miserably, like many years ago'. The illness, however, did not prevent him from going to the Netherlands for a concert tour organized by Röntgen, which was a great success with the public and with the Dutch royal family; 'universal congratulations, champagne with pasties, a grand reception with heaps of humbug', as Grieg described it.[5] By the middle of March he was back in Copenhagen, working amongst other things on the orchestration of the *Symphonic Dances*. Once more he and Nina spent the summer on the Norwegian west coast, first at Troldhaugen and then on a trip to Fossli, where they met with Röntgen and his wife.

In October 1897 Grieg began a tour of the United Kingdom, which in some eight weeks was to encompass ten concerts, in Manchester, Birmingham and Edinburgh, as well as London. He and Nina also performed to and were received by Queen Victoria at Windsor in December and Grieg described the queen, who liked his music very much and knew a great deal of it, as 'sweet'.[6] A vivid and shrewd contemporary description of the composer was noted by Arnold Bennett in his *Journals*, after a concert at St James's Hall, London. Bennett wrote: 'Grieg came on in a short jacket of black velvet which served to decrease still further his short stature. He has a large head with white hair and a bald patch, and the shrewd wrinkled face of a thinker. A restless man, weary and yet the victim of an incurable vivacity . . . He looked like one who has exhaused the joys of fame and of being adored.'[7] Christmas 1897 and the New Year were spent with the Röntgens in Amsterdam and then the Griegs were off on their travels once again, this time to Leipzig, where they stayed for three months. Once more Grieg suffered some ill-health in the early part of 1898 and had to decline an invitation to conduct a series of concerts in Italy.

In the summer of 1898 an exhibition of trade and industry was planned to be held in Bergen. Johan Bøgh, author of the poem Grieg set as a sixtieth-birthday tribute to Chr. Tønsberg, was secretary of the exhibition committee and it was he who suggested a music festival be held at the same time and accordingly consulted Grieg. After not a little rancour over the organization, the first Bergen Festival took place between 26 June and 3 July. Grieg had been overwhelmed by the splendid playing of the Amsterdam Concert-gebouw at their performance in Leipzig of Brahms' Fourth Symphony in January 1896, and insisted that the orchestra be invited to play at the festival in Bergen. The idea was not met with great enthusiasm, but Grieg even-tually had his way and the performances by the Concertgebouw orchestra were a tremendous success. They also had the effect of persuading the public that a really good orchestra was required in Norway, something Grieg had been advocating for a long time.

After the festival Grieg went on a mountain tour and then spent the autumn composing, turning down concerts in Europe and America in order to do so. In November he returned to Denmark and during the winter once more suffered a bout of bronchitis, this time so bad that he told Beyer he had been convinced he was going to die.

During the spring of 1899 he went to Italy, to Rome and Naples, where in between rehearsals and concerts, he revelled in the warmth and sunshine, 'full of gratitude to my lucky stars, which once more have led me here'.[8] The Griegs returned to Bergen late in May, travelling via Leipzig, Copenhagen and Christiania, and spent the summer at Troldhaugen and on a trip to Sunnmøre and Nordfjord. In September the new National Theatre opened in the Norwegian capital and Grieg conducted his incidental music to *Sigurd Jorsalfar*, one of the three plays produced for the opening season. He described 'the big day' to Beyer, and commented, 'So now I am a theatre capellmeister',[9] a thought which must have raised an ironic smile, after he had been refused exactly that post early in his career.

In the autumn Grieg became caught up in the notorious Dreyfus affair which rocked Europe, when, albeit with his permission, a letter was made public in which he refused a concert in Paris, not wanting to appear in a country that had allowed such a miscarriage of justice. Although most people admired the stand he took, the French were very angry, and it was several years before Grieg was able to appear in France again. He did appear most successfully, in spite of a recurrence of bronchitis, in four concerts in Stockholm, the first of which included performances of the choral arrangements of *Ved en ung hustrus båre* and *Ave maris stella*. Most of the latter part of 1899 and the turn into the new century, however, was spent in Denmark.

From 1900 onwards, Grieg's health became much more of a problem. In March he wrote to Beyer from Copenhagen, 'I have been really poorly recently. The vile influenza and bronchitis have assumed new forms',[10] and he began to draft his will. It is, then, little wonder that so few compositions appeared during these years or that inspiration for the next two albums of songs should have languished. Living in Copenhagen, it was perhaps also natural that he should turn to Danish poetry, although why, with one or two exceptions, he should have chosen the poems of such an indifferent poet as Otto Benzon is difficult to understand.

Musically, too, after *Haugtussa*, Grieg seems to have taken a backward step, and all the brilliant Norwegian distinctiveness he brought to that cycle is, with a few exceptions, dissipated here into musical tautology similar to that found in the Drachmann songs. Benzon's poetry is reminiscent of Drachmann, too, in its diffuseness, the opposite of those qualities of brevity and conciseness of thought which brought out the best in Grieg.

*Der gynger en Båd på Bølge* (A boat is rocking on the waves), the first of the album *Fem Digte af Otto Benzon*, op.69 has a lovely opening piano figure, which lures one into a sense of security that this is going to be one of Grieg's charming 'water' songs:

Ex.132     Der gynger en Båd på Bølge

This illusion, unfortunately, is soon shattered, for the song goes on to employ a number of mechanical effects, with cross-rhythms and repeated syncopated chords. The $\frac{6}{8}$ melody over an accompaniment in $\frac{3}{4}$ is interesting, but somewhat contrived and awkward in performance. The poem has something in common with the legend of the Lorelei, describing as it does a lovely girl, but with the warning at the end of each stanza: 'Men Slangen, den slår sine Bugter (But the serpent, it winds its coils)', although Grieg omits this line in his setting except in the first and last stanzas. The evil is hinted at in the music of the outer sections by a seventh (bars 19 and 20) which negates the anticipated return to the tonic key, and by the clash of C natural against C sharp (bar 24) on the word 'Bugter (coils)'.

The opening of the middle section provides quite a contrast in mood, largely because with the omission of the warning line, the song becomes a recital of the girl's virtues alone. The awkward cross-rhythms of the opening section are replaced by sustained notes in the left hand and syncopated chords in the right. The triplets in the vocal line add to the gentle mood and the modulations, while startling, are smoothly accomplished. The use of the reiterated syncopated chords becomes wearisome after fourteen bars, as does the repeated return to the upper D sharp in the vocal line, although the dissonances in the accompaniment at this point under the words 'og hendes Smil som den glade Sol (and her smile like the happy sun)' hint at the omitted warning. The modulation from the middle section into the modified recapitulation of the opening is worth noting: the D sharp which had been the third of the B major triad becomes the augmented fifth in a dominant seventh chord in C; but while individually passages of *Der gynger en Båd* work well, the constant changes of mood and tempo never become a cohesive whole, but remain a series of disjointed ideas.

*Til min Dreng* (To my son) is a light-hearted birthday greeting, written by Benzon from Maidstone, Kent in 1898. The poem is pleasant enough if conventional, but very mannered, with the poet constantly referring to himself as 'the old man'. It is a strange choice for setting by a composer like Grieg, who revelled in nature descriptions and poetic conceits. The humour is captured in the introductory figure with its ascending fourths and the abrupt pause before the voice enters. The key changes here are not the most subtle Grieg devised, but perhaps these and the syncopated accompaniment, together with the wide-ranging vocal line with its many intervals of fourths, fifths and octaves and even (bar 11) a ninth, were also intended to underline the humour. The song, however, remains contrived.

The third song of the op.69 album, *Ved Moders Grav* (Beside mother's grave), was one of Grieg's own favourites. In a letter to Thorvald Lammers, he wrote that 'it should sound like an Amati violin – or, more correctly, cello. Sombre. Gripping', and these comments provide a good guide to the singer about its style of performance. Perhaps to modern singers and audiences the song would be thought rather sentimental; as Astra Desmond has remarked: 'English ears . . . are loath to hear too much about dead mothers'.[11] Grieg, however, held his own mother in high regard and, unlike the first two songs of the album, this at least comes across with sincerity and a depth of personal expression, due almost entirely to the music and not to the largely uninspired poem. The vocal melody is legato with stepwise movement, except for the occasional telling use of syncopated entries and augmented intervals, this not being the moment for vocal display, while the rich chromatic writing and deliberate dissonances create an almost unbearably mournful atmosphere.

There could be no greater contrast than that between *Ved Moders Grav* and the next song of the album, *Snegl, Snegl* (Snail, snail). It is not clear from the poem if Benzon intended the snail of the title to be an allegory for people who will not look at what is around them, but there is much humour in the verse, even if it is rather pretentious. This setting at 116 bars is Grieg's longest through-composed song for some time and is unified by phrases that recur in a number of keys. The opening vocal melody recalls the style of the *lokk*, calling the snail out of its 'house', and the range is wide, from middle B to high F sharp. There is more direct imitation of the words by the music here than is usual in Grieg's songs, with, for example, ornaments and trills in the accompaniment at the words 'lysende Smil (bright smiles)' in bar 25, and a broadening of the rhythm and a low vocal register for 'de store sorte . . . Snegle (the large black snails)' in bars 72 and 73. The birds' songs and the sighing of the wind are matched by a chromatic melody, and a final upward seventh:

Ex.133                                                              Snegl, Snegl

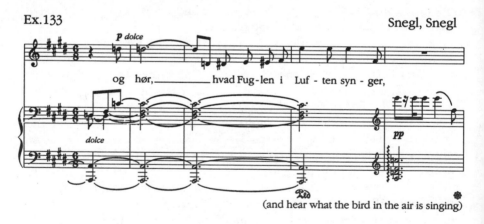

(and hear what the bird in the air is singing)

The piano writing is also more imaginative here and has more variety of figuration than in the earlier op.69 songs and, like so many of Grieg's songs, requires sensitive performers to bring it to life.

The poem set as the final song of the group, *Drømme* (Dreams), is, as so often with Benzon, unoriginal and longer than necessary for its content. The musical setting is a little disappointing, although it has some pleasing touches. The second part of the middle section unfortunately again makes use of repeated chords, albeit more judiciously than in *Der gynger en Båd*, and the modulations in this passage are almost Wagnerian in their sliding changes. The outer sections, with the unchanging rhythm of the accompaniment figure in the right hand used to good effect, are more subtle. They show, as John Horton has remarked, a 'strong French influence'[12] in their shifting, dreamy movement, bringing to mind such songs as Fauré's *Au bord de l'eau*:

Ex.134                                                                 Drømme

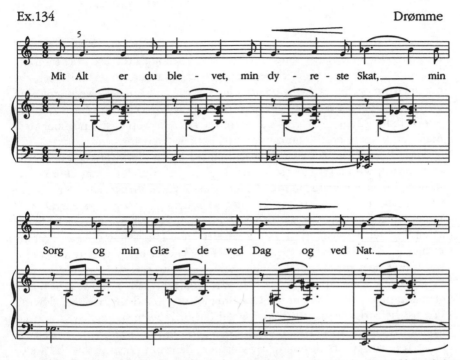

Mit Alt er du ble - vet, min dy - re - ste Skat,____ min Sorg og min Glæ - de ved Dag og ved Nat.____

(You have become my all, my dearest love, my sorrow and my joy by day and by night.)

The vocal line is wide-ranging, with long phrases that climb ever higher, accompanied by chromatically ascending chords used in sequence over a pedal note and creating some interesting dissonances. Unusually the echoes of the vocal line, where they occur, are in the lower register of the keyboard or in the inner parts. These last two songs do go some way to redeeming the otherwise poor standard of the op.69 album.

The sliding chromaticism heard to some extent in *Drømme* comes to fruition in the first song of the second album of Benzon settings (with the same title as the first), op.70. Each of the first three bars of the introduction of *Eros* immediately brings to mind *Tristan und Isolde*, although the chromatic movement later is not so subtle: Ex.135.

Ex.135                                                        Eros

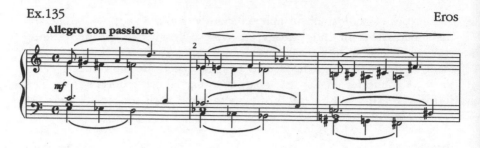

The same theme, in octaves, is used for the postlude, but with a gradual diminuendo, so that the song ends quietly. Although the use of chromaticism shows a Wagnerian influence, as also to a certain extent does the declamation of the song, the piano echoes of the vocal line are very typical of Grieg and there is a lovely effect in the minor-key echoing of a major-key phrase (bars 22 and 23) with the harmony altered from C sharp minor to C major after the words 'You cannot win back what is lost'.

The song falls into two sections, dictated by the form of the poem, the first ending with a series of sevenths, resolving to the dominant chord. The second stanza comprises fourteen short lines, which Grieg uses to build up the musical climax, similarly but not so subtly as in *Jeg giver mit Digt til Våren* (op.21 no.3), first with two chords to a bar, then four, each slowly ascending with constant chromatic alterations. The sequence does become rather tedious, however, especially as all the chords are played tremolando, but Grieg does make use of a wide range of piano and vocal colour.

The vocal line in *Eros* is largely declamatory, but a more lyrical declamation than that used in the Drachmann songs, and the strongly flowing line has helped to make the song a great favourite with singers. It is written in just the right part of the voice, middle C to high F, to allow the performer to achieve the effects the composer asks for. Benzon's poem extols the joy of love, 'den eneste virkelig store Lykke på Jord (the only truly great happiness on earth)', as opposed to the fruitless searching for what does not exist, and has received a better musical treatment than it deserved. An arrangement for the song for string orchestra, in E flat, was later made by Max Reger and published by Peters in 1914.

The second song of the op.70 album, *Jeg lever et Liv i Længsel* (I live a life of longing), is a very bitter poem of unrequited love, which drew from Grieg a gloomy setting that abounds in strange modulations and enharmonic changes. Understandably perhaps, after the Bella Edwards episode, the poet's assertions that all his happiness has been met with sorrow and pain are matched in the music by a feeling of resignation, coupled with a fairly narrow melodic range – although with some wide intervals – within each phrase. The first vocal phrases are echoed in the left hand of the accompaniment, causing some startling dissonances and adding to the atmosphere of pain and bitterness:

Ex.136                                                  Jeg lever et Liv i Længsel

(I have paid what I owed, met [happiness with sorrow])

Each of the three strophes ends with a remarkable chromatic sequence in which both hands of the accompaniment double the vocal line. This passage resolves to a chord of F flat major in second inversion – effectively the Neapolitan sixth – and finally to the tonic E flat minor. Unfortunately, any dramatic tension thus created is much reduced by the two repeats necessitated by the strophic structure and, although Grieg appears to have set great store by it, writing to Lammers of its 'wild, hidden passion and pathos', the song has not found any firm place in the repertoire.

All the disappointments of the op.69 and op.70 albums are, however, redeemed by the third song of the second set, *Lys Nat* (Light night). Here at last Benzon's poem has some of the lyricism of Garborg combined with the conciseness of thought that Grieg found so stimulating. The opening bars of the accompaniment have refined the more overt Wagnerian chromaticism to a new subtlety and the gentle movement here underlines the yearning expressed in the poem for the night, that time of love and dreams that is all too short during northern summers: Ex.137.

Even the reiterated chords of the middle section have a lightness to match the words: 'Er det alt Dagens Guld, som gryr? (Is that already the gold of day which is dawning?)'. The modulations, too, in this section, slide into one another as the sun's rays appear.

The vocal line is flowing and lyrical in the opening part of the song and gently declamatory in the middle, and much use is made of octave intervals and descending arpeggios, although the vocal range is only a tenth from middle C sharp. The return to the clarity of the opening for the last nine bars of the song lends a nostalgic quality to the words. The harmony is slightly simplified and the vocal line becomes almost recitative. The descending bass

Ex.137                                                                        Lys Nat

*(Was it not just now the sun sank behind the forests in the distance,)*

has a feeling of inevitability about it and Grieg is very careful to annotate exactly the declamation of these last two lines, to create a wistful lingering on the words 'drager du bort (you draw away)':

Ex.138                                                                        Lys Nat

*(Scarcely having come, you draw away!)*

The rise at the end of the vocal line, harmonized by a chord of the thirteenth resolving to a seventh, underlines the question 'hvi er du så kort? (why are you so short?)' and the echoing of that phrase a third higher as the piano postlude is a lovely detail, leaving one with a blend of happiness and sorrow. Unfortunately, the wordy and consonant-filled German translation detracts from the lightness engendered by the original Danish. Were it not for *Lys Nat*, one might well consider that Grieg would have been better to end his song-writing career with the *Haugtussa* cycle, but this gem of a song, in thirty-five short bars, makes one grateful he did not.

*Se dig for* (Beware) reverts to a straightforward folk-song style in strophic form, with the right hand of the accompaniment doubling the vocal line almost throughout. The chromatic writing is more subdued here than elsewhere in these Benzon settings and, where it does occur, has the effect of underlining the warning in the words. The vocal line of the song is also in the folk-song mould, essentially simple except for the descending chromatic phrase towards the end. The poem comprises a series of warnings about where one should choose one's path and, like *Til min Dreng*, is not an immediately obvious choice for musical setting. However, while the song is not particularly inspiring, it does not suffer from the banality of some of the other Benzon settings.

Both the two preceding poems were taken from Benzon's play *Anna Bryde*, published in 1894, Grieg's copy of which, inscribed 'To Edvard Grieg, in friendship from Otto Benzon', is part of the Grieg Collection in Bergen. The play concerns Anna Bryde, her husband (a naval officer) and her former lover. *Lys Nat* comes right at the beginning of the Prologue. The stage directions set the scene as 'a light summer night on the Sound [the Øresund]', with ships in the distance, while 'inland, singing and soft music is heard. There is a woman's voice' which sings 'Var det ej nylig...', although the words of the song 'are quavering only indistinctly'.

*Se dig for* comes from the end of the Prologue and is the song heard from five men on board a ship in the sound. Kaj Warming, Anna's former lover, says of the song, 'Nice melody – but ponderous words', which rather sums up Grieg's setting too. It is strange that the composer should have chosen to set this verse, rather than the song Kaj then sings to Anna, 'Snart er de lyse Nættens Tid forbi':

> Soon the time of the light nights will be over,
> and the darkness will rise behind the deep waters,
> and the wave will strike up its melody,
> which now is only hummed on the shore of the Sound...

This poem would also have provided a more fitting counterpart to *Lys Nat*.

The final song of the op.70 album, *Digtervise* (Poet's song), is quite different and reverts to the brash, quasi-operatic style of some of the Drachmann settings. Grieg, however, was very fond of it and wrote it with Thorvald Lammers in mind. The poem compares the differences between the poet, who sees and feels, and ordinary people, 'who are just heads and stomachs and arms and legs'. However, the contrasts drawn are so outrageous that one must assume Benzon was being ironic. Grieg's setting has a certain grim jollity, although the feeling appears to be external rather than part of any personal conviction.

The song opens with a march theme and fanfare-like figures, ideas which are continued in the vocal line. This passage is succeeded by a recitative-like section and a more declamatory vocal style over a mostly chordal accompaniment, which, while owing something to *Eros*, is more closely allied to the Drachmann songs. The changes of declamation to accommodate the different stanzas are typical of Grieg's attention to detail, but the song is not at all among his best. John Horton has suggested that the accompaniment needs orchestrating 'to bring it to life',[13] but even then the song would be unlikely to have great appeal.

Grieg several times insisted to Thorvald Lammers that he would like *Digtervise* and other songs in the op.70 album. From Copenhagen in March

1901 he wrote to the baritone: 'There are some [songs] which absolutely *must* suit you. I am certain that in spite of your grey hair you will both be crazy about the god *Eros* and can sing *Jeg lever et Liv i Længsel*, with all its wild, hidden passion and pathos. But above all it is the *Digtervise* that must suit you. This which sits up on Olympus and mocks the philistines below is really something for you.'[14] Lammers, however, was apparently not very enamoured of the song, for in a later letter from Troldhaugen Grieg again suggests it for inclusion in a concert programme, but adds, 'NB. only if it has become flesh and blood to you. For that we can quickly agree on: it must go "con amore" or else to hell with it.' David Monrad Johansen, quoting the last remark, commented that it was not difficult 'to predict that later times have come to choose the latter alternative'![15]

In spite of being intended for Lammers to sing – and the copy of the album in Oslo University's Music Library bears the inscription 'Thorvald Lammers med hjertelig Hilsen [with kindest regards] fra din Edvard Grieg. Kjbhvn. 2/2/1901' – the op.70 songs were dedicated to the Danish opera-singer Niels Juel Simonsen, and the op.69 album 'To the poet'. Both albums were published by Wilhelm Hansen in November 1900 with, as Benzon had requested, the texts of the poems printed separately at the front of each volume.

It seems incredible that Grieg, whose sense of self-judgement was usually so acute should have considered these songs as showing 'a sort of development', as he wrote to his friend the Danish composer Robert Henriques. He also wrote to Beyer, 'I think the album that begins with "Eros" is the best. It will hurt me if you don't come to the same conclusion.'[16] Yet the press did not receive their première in Copenhagen that month very enthusiastically and Grieg's expressed hope that time would mellow that opinion was totally ill-founded. A performance of some of the songs, given by Ellen Gulbranson and accompanied by the composer, in the Norwegian capital three years later was not particularly well received either. Grieg wrote bitterly to Beyer that, although he had 'deliberately chosen those of my *best* later songs, which they seldom or never hear',[17] the public would not allow him to develop, but only wanted to hear their favourite songs, which almost exclusively dated from his youth.

Grieg set one more text by Benzon, a song which has remained in manuscript in Bergen and which is published for the first time in the *GGA*. It is unusual in that the poem was written in English and it is, therefore, Grieg's only English setting. In a letter to the composer dated '12.5.00' Benzon mentions 'the English Devil-song' and says that it must 'be written first in English'. From another letter, from Paris later the same month, it is clear that he had intended Grieg to set the poem together with *Sneglen* and *Den lyse Nat* (sic), for possible inclusion in a second book of songs. Grieg was apparently not very happy about the poem, for in a further letter from Paris

Benzon asks if he can improve it, or, if not, offers instead another poem, *Forkynderen* (The advocate). This was written about the writer Emile Zola, after he had been convicted of libel following the publication of his open letter 'J'accuse' denouncing the actions of the French general staff in the Dreyfus case.

The poem, *To a devil*, is in much the same mould as *Til min Dreng*, and, if anything, even more mannered. The song, dated 19 February 1900, is marked 'allegro scherzando e amoroso', the 'amoroso' used for the only time in Grieg's songs. It opens with a two-bar introduction, marked 'vivace', and then a bar's rest before the voice enters, similar to the quasi-comic opening of *Til min Dreng* and *Den blonde Pige (I)*. The setting is described by Benestad and Schjelderup-Ebbe as having 'something of the British folk music style in a rousing, lively melody with original, fresh chord sequences in the accompaniment'. [18] The opening phrase, however, with the dominant rising to the leading-note and then descending, is more like Scandinavian folk music than English, where the dominant is more likely to lead directly to the tonic. The harmonization, with the frequent use of diminished triads and triads with added notes, and the key transitions, for example from B major to A flat major, are rather contrived, while the vocal line is often very angular and chromatic:

Ex.139                                                           To a Devil

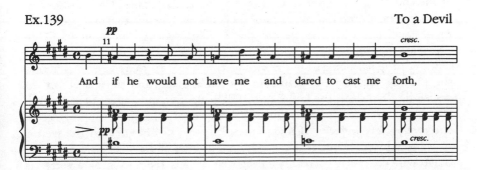

And if he would not have me    and    dared to cast me forth,

The English does cause some problems: Grieg's manuscript transcribes Benzon's word 'Allmightiness' as 'Allmightness' with only three syllables, and one wonders if either poet or composer was aware of the implications of the lines

> For [if] I can manage nothing else,*
> Then I can go to hell.

There are a few elements in the setting that lead one to think it might have been a better song if only the poem had been good, but with these words the music was really a waste of Grieg's time and energy.

---

*That is, after failing to bring his beloved back from heaven.

Another English poem which Grieg found was Kipling's *Gentlemen-Rankers*. The most commendable Norwegian translation, *Gentlemen-Menige*, which he set was by Rosenkrantz Johnsen and originally published in the journal *Verdens Gang*. Johnsen translated ten poems from Kipling's *Barrack Room Ballads* (1892) and other verses under the title *Soldat Sange*, which were published by Alb. Cammermeyer in Christiania in 1902, and a copy of this book, which is dedicated to Grieg and signed 'with respect and gratitude' by the translator, is in the Grieg Collection in Bergen.

The manuscript is dated 17 December 1900 and the song was written while Grieg was in the Voksenkollen sanitorium. The words are portrayed in the military style of Grieg's setting and the march rhythm is kept in the accompaniment, with crotchets in the left hand and crotchets on the weak beats only in the right. The song is marked 'allegro marcato' and there is a drumroll-like figure in the accompaniment in the introduction and at the end of the first two vocal lines (Ex. 140). The song uses all four stanzas, set strophically, but omits the famous refrain, 'We're poor little lambs who've lost our way'. Johnsen did translate the refrain, although he made no distinction between Kipling's 'Baa! Baa! Baa!', 'Baa-aa-aa!' and 'Baa! Yah! Bah!', giving all three as 'Bæ-Bæ-Bæ!'

The vocal line has a range of almost two octaves if the optional bottom G at the end of each strophe is sung. Some use is also made of wide intervals, even octaves, in the last five bars of each strophe, a trait that has previously been associated with the weaker songs. This setting, fortunately, is the exception to the rule. Although the first four bars of the vocal line are repeated, the harmonization the second time is much more aggressive, with the melody doubled in octaves in the right hand and with a chromatic descending phrase in the left: Ex. 140. The despair and anger of the poem is felt in the rhythm and the chromatic movement, although the song ends, effectively, very quietly. Benestad and Schjelderup-Ebbe regard the setting as 'a rushed job',[19] but it is a good, strong song and its publication in the *GGA* will do much to rectify Grieg's erroneous reputation as a setter of sentimental verse.

*Julens Vuggesang* (Christmas cradle song), a setting of a poem by the Danish author Adolf Langsted, was the penultimate song in the second album of those published posthumously. It was written in 1900 and apparently also first published that year: in a postcard to Grieg dated 30 December 1900 Langsted says that he was expecting the song to be printed in the Christmas number of *Musik og Sang* and although the song in question is not named, it is certainly *Julens Vuggesang*; Langsted had written to Grieg in March 1900 asking him to write 'a little Christmas song to the enclosed simple text', and this is the only setting of Langsted that Grieg made. Dismissed by the musicologists Benestad and Schjelderup-Ebbe as 'insignificant',[20] but not by the singer Astra Desmond who described it as 'simple' and 'moving',[21] the

Ex.140                                          Gentlemen-Menige

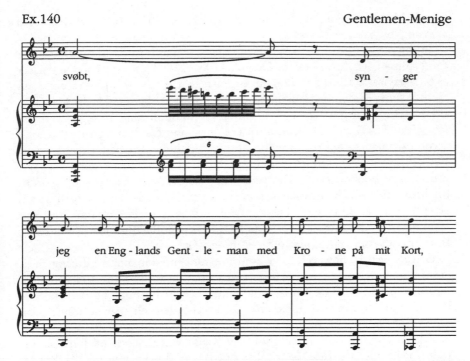

(wrapped [in sorrow], sing I, one of England's gentlemen with a crown on my tunic) *

song is attractive and very suitable for inclusion in a Christmas programme. The poem is subtitled 'The young mother beside the cradle' and it is a lullaby that contrasts the lowliness of the Christ-child's crib with the comparative richness of the one the mother is rocking here.

The melody is unusual for Grieg: the first phrase consists largely of a descending chromatic scale, while the second begins with two descending sevenths in arpeggio. Considering the delight Grieg had taken in *Gjendines Bådnlåt*, there is surprisingly little here that is associated with Norwegian folk music. The movement of the cradle is portrayed in the regular rhythm of the accompaniment, which also doubles the vocal line in part, and the first five bars are written over a tonic and dominant pedal. The harmony is unremarkable except for the use of the subdominant seventh chord with a minor third and the chromatically descending bass in the two penultimate bars of each strophe.

As well as the usual German and English versions published by Peters, the song was popular enough to merit a Swedish version, too. This was published as a separate song by Hansen in 1916, with the original words and

---

*A literal translation of the Norwegian, *not* Kipling's original words.

a Swedish translation, under the poem's subtitle 'Den unga moderen vid vaggan', by Sven Scholander.

In the early years of the new century Grieg was as busy as ever with concert tours abroad, visiting, besides Denmark, Sweden, Paris and London, places as far away as Warsaw and Prague. In Paris in 1903 he was well received, in spite of some demonstrations against him following the stand he had taken in the Dreyfus affair. At the concert Ellen Gulbranson sang *Solveigs Vuggevise, Fra Monte Pincio* and *En svane*, with the composer conducting the orchestral accompaniments, and the same programme included the performance of the two *Elegiac Melodies* which prompted Debussy's comments about Grieg's music as a 'bonbon rose'. The year 1903 also saw the composer's sixtieth birthday, for which occasion a special concert was held in Bergen and a reception at Troldhaugen. He received hundreds of letters and greetings from all over the musical world and two beautifully illuminated addresses from friends and colleagues in Sweden and Denmark.

Grieg's health, however, gave even greater cause for concern during these years and necessitated his twice staying in the newly-built Voksenkollen sanitorium just outside Christiania, and once in hospital in Bergen. His brother John committed suicide in 1901 and Grieg felt that he would soon follow, although not by his own hand. By 1905 he was in 'rather poor health', according to a letter from 'the Kansas City composer' Carl Busch, published under the title 'News about Grieg' in Finck's journal *The Musical Courier*. Busch wrote, 'When I bade him goodby I left with the impression that with the good care he takes of himself, Grieg may yet live a good many years. But will we get much new music from him? I believe not!'[22]

In the latter prediction he was to prove correct, although the very high quality of Grieg's last works more than compensates for the lack of quantity. These works are the *Slåtter*, op.72, written in 1902 and 1903, the *Stemninger* (Moods), op.73, composed between 1901 and 1905, both for piano solo, and the *Four Psalms*, op.74, for baritone solo and mixed choir, written in 1906.

There is also *Der Jäger* (The hunter), Grieg's last song, dated 15 July 1905, which was published as the final item in the second album of *Posthumous Songs* in 1908. It is strange that he should have chosen a German poem to set after so long, when his first known song was also to a German text some forty-six years earlier. Not that *Der Jäger* is anything like *Siehst du das Meer?* or the songs opp.2 and 4, nor even the op.48 album. The poem by Wilhelm Schulz is, in its happy unsophistication, reminiscent of some of those that Schubert set.

The song is a cheerful piece, the jauntiness underlined by the 'presto' marking and by the composer's instruction that the first and third crotchet of each bar should be 'short and accented'. The melody, as might be expected, is based on the typical calls of the hunting horn; however, with the use of the pedal tonic fifth for the first eight bars and the Griegian sounding of the dominant chord against it, this is apparently a Norwegian hunter rather than a German one:

Ex.141                                                                   Der Jäger

(The morning sun wakens the birds. [The hunter] has put a twig in his hat)

The harmony of the second half of each of the three strophes lifts the song out of the ordinary, with the employment of diminished chords and a number of unresolved sevenths and ninths. Finally the E flat, which has appeared in virtually every chord of this section, is altered enharmonically to D sharp and resolves, by way of a diminished seventh, to the tonic A major. The flattened seventh heard in the postlude evokes echoes both from Norwegian folk music and the harmonic series of the hunting horn, and the song makes a fresh and cheerful impact after some of the vagaries of the Benzon settings.

In September 1905 Norway at last gained her independence from Sweden. Feelings between the two countries earlier in the year had run very high, so much so that Grieg was unable to fulfil concert engagements in Finland because he could not, as a Norwegian, travel across Sweden. Many Norwegians had hoped that independence would bring with it a republic, but the majority was, like Grieg, royalist, and Prince Carl of Denmark was elected king and became the long-reigning Haakon VII.

In April 1906 Grieg undertook a concert tour of the Netherlands, where he was always popular, and then went on to England – in spite of his dislike of the sea-crossing – to accept an honorary doctorate from Oxford University. He also addressed the Norwegian Society in London on the first 17 May after independence.

The *Four Psalms*, written in September 1906, like the earlier *Slåtter*, show new departures in harmonic experiment for 'le nouveau Grieg'. They were arrangements of four old Norwegian hymn-tunes, with the melodies taken from Lindeman's famous collection, and were published by Peters in 1907. A new edition was published by Peters in 1925, arranged and with English translations by Percy Grainger. During the summer of 1907, Grainger, together with Röntgen, was a guest at Troldhaugen and Grieg seemed in better health, probably because he had so much looked forward to their visit.

After they left, however, he weakened, suffering from insomnia and experiencing difficulty in breathing, and he was not helped by the dreadful weather that year. He knew he would never see Röntgen again and told him so, as the Dutchman was to recall in a letter to Nina of 13 September. On 2 September Grieg was still planning, against advice, to travel once more to England, but his condition deteriorated and his friend and doctor Klaus Hanssen sent him to Bergen hospital. Here he sank into a coma and died of heart failure in the early hours of Wednesday 4 September, 'ruhig wie ein Kind eingeschlafen' as Nina wrote to Hinrichsen. [23]

Tributes and messages of condolence, including one from Queen Maud, flooded in, many of them published in Bergen's *Morgenavisen* on 5 September, and many thousands of people lined the route of the funeral cortège on 9 September.


That his last song, as his first, was to a German text, brings Grieg's song-writing a satisfying full circle, a circle which encloses a large but uneven output. One may truly summarize Grieg as 'a genius who, like all geniuses, could misfire, though never without interest.' [24]

Much reassessment of Grieg's music has taken place in the years since his death and we have come a long way from regarding him, as did Hugo Riemann in 1902, as 'beyond doubt the most important of the Scandinavian composers *after Gade*' (this author's italics)[25] – an opinion treated with some scorn by Henry Finck in the same year. [26] Yet the songs have largely been left out of any detailed studies of his music. Even Benestad and Schjelderup-Ebbe, whose splendid book contains the fullest account before this, dismiss many of them as weak or rushed, and completely ignore others. On purely musicological grounds they may be entitled to do so, but music is a performing art and the principal criterion for a 'good' song should be whether or not it succeeds in performance.

The unevenness in the quality of his songs stems partly from the external conditions Grieg was so fond of blaming, but also from the dichotomy in the character of the man himself: a romantic on the one hand, a realist on the other. 'The songs', as the poet Herman Wildenvey expressed it, 'live on with sweetness and salt harmoniously united.' [27] Even Grieg's attitude to Norwegian folk music is ambivalent. He loved the music he heard and recognized its worth, but seemed to regard it as unfinished and valuable mainly as raw material for development. In this he was very much a child of his time. Yet in his treatment of folk music, particularly in the *Slåtter*, op.72, he looks forward to the more purist usage of twentieth-century composers such as Bartók.

The success of Grieg's songs is largely due to his own great appreciation of literary qualities and although he always hankered after the larger musical forms, his talents were undoubtedly better suited to the smaller, where he could exercize his subtlety in detail and nuance. This is especially seen in the strophic form employed in so many of the songs. Grieg at last seems to have realized his strengths, comparing his own case with Liszt's remark about Thalberg: 'His province is the small genre, but in this he is great.'[28] Literature often provided inspiration when his own was flagging for purely abstract music, even though his critical acumen was not always as sharp as it could be, especially when it came to the work of friends, and words occasionally restricted the freedom of imagination to be found, for example, in some of the *Lyric Pieces*.

It was not just the texts, but also the sounds of the language, that were important to Grieg's word-setting and it is not accidental that his most lyrical melodies are to the most euphonious poems of Bjørnson, Vinje and Garborg. His natural ability for word-setting was augmented by the importance he placed on communication and it is small wonder that he had little patience with poor translations which circumvent that communication. His wish for the listener to understand the texts may also account for his very syllabic settings, even where the words might have suggested a more melismatic treatment. Grieg never used sound for its own sake, but only as a medium to underline the meaning of, and emotions behind, the text. Without a text, as in the *Elegiac Melodies*, a more descriptive title is felt necessary.

Like Wolf, Grieg sometimes used the music to express an idea which is not obvious from the text, but may have been in the poet's mind, and he made good use of preludes and postludes, as did his idol, Schumann. However, it is the words that are of supreme importance to him and so, as he wrote to Ravnkilde in 1884 in implied criticism of Brahms, 'if one takes words, then one should certainly keep to the word.'[29] Thus, if the poem calls for dramatic treatment, as in *Soldaten*, Grieg provides it in the musical setting; if it is a declamatory poem, as in *Eros*, then melody is subjugated to the declamation; if a soaring ecstasy, as in *Det første møte*, then that too is provided. Yet with all these varied characteristics, it is the vocal line that remains paramount, and although much use is made of piano echoes of the vocal phrases, the accompaniments are never truly independent of the melody. For this reason, the melodic line is almost always diatonic, the chromaticism and dissonances kept for the accompaniment, in particular, the inner parts.

There is no longer any reason to ignore Grieg's songs on the sole ground of the languages involved. If we accept that Musorgsky should be sung in Russian, and Bartók and Kodály in Hungarian, and with a number of good linguists among the younger generation of singers, then it is more than time for authentic performances of Grieg. For here is to be found a repertoire of songs for all types of voice and for all moods, which if performed, would provide the basis for a general reappraisal that must afford Grieg his rightful place in the hierarchy of the great song-composers.


## Notes

1    The opening line of a poem by Finn Simonsen, written for Grieg's sixtieth birthday and published in the 'Grieg Number' of *Bergens Tidende*, 17 June 1903.
2    Grieg to Lammers, 6 March 1896 from Leipzig.
3    Didrik Grønvold to Grieg, 13 August 1896 from Sætersdal near Christianssand.
4    Grieg to Beyer, 27 December 1896 from Semmering near Vienna.
5    Grieg to Beyer, 4 March 1897 from Amsterdam.
6    In her journal the Queen remembered the composer as 'small' and 'nice and simple'.
7    Arnold Bennett: *Journals*, entry for 22 November 1897.
8    Grieg to Beyer, 1 April 1899 from Rome.
9    Grieg to Beyer, 1 September 1899 from Christiania.
10    Grieg to Beyer, 10 March 1900 from Copenhagen.
11    Astra Desmond in *Grieg: A Symposium*, ed. Gerald Abraham, 1948, p.79.
12    John Horton: *Grieg*, 1974, p.192.
13    Ibid. p.193.
14    Grieg to Lammers, 2 March 1901 from Copenhagen.
15    David Monrad Johansen: *Edvard Grieg*, 1934, p.390.
16    Grieg to Beyer, 12 March 1901 from Copenhagen.
17    Grieg to Beyer, 17 November 1904 from Christiania.
18    Benestad and Schjelderup-Ebbe: *Edvard Grieg, mennesket og kunstneren*, 1980, p.308.
19    Ibid.
20    Ibid.
21    Astra Desmond in *Grieg: A Symposium*, p.80.
22    An article in an undated issue of *The Musical Courier* preserved in the Grieg Collection in Bergen. Busch's letter is dated 14 August 1905.
23    Nina Grieg to Hinrichsen, 11 September 1907 from Troldhaugen, reproduced in *Briefe an die Verleger der Edition Peters*, ed. Zschinsky-Troxler, 1932.
24    Sir Alec Guinness: *Blessings in Disguise*, Hamish Hamilton 1985, p.173, actually referring to the actor Charles Laughton.
25    Hugo Riemann: *Geschichte der Musik seit Beethoven (1800–1900)*, 1902, p.543.
26    Finck's review of Riemann's book, *New York Evening Post*, 24 September 1902.
27    From a poem in the style of Vinje's *Våren* often used as an introduction to events at Troldhaugen, quoted by Sigmund Torsteinson: *Med troll i tankene*, 1985, p.69.
28    Quoted by Benestad and Schjelderup-Ebbe: *Edvard Grieg, mennesket og kunstneren*, p.334.
29    Grieg to Ravnkilde, 21 July 1884 from Lofthus.

# Appendix A: Songs by Opus Number

| Opus No. | Opus and song titles | First edition |
|---|---|---|
| Op. 2 | *Vier Lieder für Altstimme und Klavier* (Four Songs for Contralto and Piano) 1. Die Müllerin (Chamisso); 2. Eingehüllt in grauen Wolken (Heine); 3. Ich stand in dunkeln Träumen (Heine); 4. Was soll ich sagen? (Chamisso) | C.F. Peters, Leipzig 1863 |
| Op. 4 | *Sex Digte af H. Heine, L. Uhland og A. von Chamisso for Altstemme og Pft.* (Six Songs by . . . for Contralto and Piano) 1. Die Waise (Chamisso); 2. Morgenthau (Chamisso); 3. Abschied (Heine); 4. Jägerlied (Uhland); 5. Das alte Lied (Heine); 6. Wo sind sie hin? (Heine) | Horneman & Erslev, Copenhagen 1864 |
| Op. 5 | *Hjertets Melodier af H.C. Andersen* (Melodies of the Heart by . . .) 1. To brune Øine; 2. En Digters Bryst; 3. Jeg elsker dig; 4. Min Tanke er et mægtigt Fjeld | Chr. E. Horneman, Copenhagen 1865 |
| Op. 9 | *Romancer og Ballader til Digte af A. Munch* (Songs and Ballads to Poems by . . .) 1. Harpen; 2. Vuggesang; 3. Solnedgang; 4. Udfarten | Horneman & Erslev, Copenhagen 1866 |
| Op. 10 | *Lette Sange med Piano* (Easy Songs with Piano) (Poems by Chr. Winther) 1. Taksigelse; | Chr. E. Horneman, Copenhagen 1866 |

267

| Opus No. | Opus and song titles | First edition |
|---|---|---|
| | 2. Skovsang; | |
| | 3. Blomsterne tale; | |
| | 4. Sang på Fjeldet | |
| Op. 15 | *Romancer af H. Ibsen, H.C. Andersen og* | Horneman & Erslev, |
| | *Chr. Richardt* (Songs by . . .) | Copenhagen 1868 |
| | 1. Margretes Vuggesang (Ibsen); | |
| | 2. Kjærlighed (Andersen); | |
| | 3. Langelandsk Folkemelodi (Andersen); | |
| | 4. Modersorg (Richardt) | |
| Op. 18 | *Romancer og Sange af danske og norske* | Horneman & Erslev, |
| | *Digtere* (Romances and Songs by Danish | Copenhagen 1869 |
| | and Norwegian poets) | (in two albums |
| | 1. Vandring i Skoven (Andersen); | containing, |
| | 2. Hun er saa hvid (Andersen); | respectively, nos 1–4 |
| | 3. En Digters sidste Sang (Andersen); | and 5–9) |
| | 4. Efteraarsstormen (Richardt); | |
| | 5. Poesien (Andersen); | |
| | 6. Ungbirken (Moe); | |
| | 7. Hytten (Andersen); | |
| | 8. Rosenknoppen (Andersen); | |
| | 9. Serenade til Welhaven (Bjørnson) | |
| Op. 21 | *Fire Digte af Bjørnsons 'Fiskerjenten'* (Four | Chr. E. Horneman, |
| | Poems from Bjørnson's 'The Fisher-girl') | Copenhagen 1873 |
| | 1. Det første Møte; | |
| | 2. God Morgen; | |
| | 3. Jeg giver mit Digt til Våren; | |
| | 4. Tak for dit Råd | |
| Op. 23 | *Incidental Music to Ibsen's 'Peer Gynt'* | C.C. Lose, |
| | 17. Peer Gynts Serenade; | Copenhagen 1876 |
| | 18. Solveigs Sang; | (excerpts, including |
| | 23. Solveigs Vuggevise | nos 17 and 18) |
| | | Edition Peters, |
| | | Leipzig 1908 (full |
| | | score, edited by |
| | | Johan Halvorsen) |
| Op. 25 | *Sex Digte af Henrik Ibsen* (Six Poems by . . .) | C.C. Lose, |
| | 1. Spillemænd; | Copenhagen 1876 |
| | 2. En Svane; | |
| | 3. Stambogsrim; | |
| | 4. Med en Vandlilje; | |
| | 5. Borte; | |
| | 6. En Fuglevise | |

| Opus No. | Opus and song titles | First edition |
|---|---|---|
| Op.26 | *Fem Digte af John Paulsen* (Five Poems by . . .) 1. Et Håb; 2. Jeg reiste en deilig Sommerkveld; 3. Den Ærgjerrige; 4. Med en Primula veris; 5. På Skogstien | C.C. Lose, Copenhagen 1876 |
| Op.32 | *Den Bergtekne* (The Mountain Thrall) | Wilhelm Hansen, Copenhagen 1882 |
| Op.33 | *Tolv Melodier til Digte af A.O. Vinje* (Twelve Melodies to Poems by . . .) 1. Guten; 2. Våren; 3. Den særde; 4. Tytebæret; 5. Langs ei å; 6. Eit syn; 7. Gamle mor; 8. Det fyrste; 9. Ved Rundarne; 10. Eit vennestykke; 11. Trudom; 12. Fyremål | Wilhelm Hansen, Copenhagen 1881 (in two albums, nos 1–6 and 7–12) |
| Op.39 | *Romancer Ældre og Nyere* (Songs Old and New) 1. Fra Monte Pincio (Bjørnson); 2. Dulgt Kjærlighed (Bjørnson); 3. I Liden høit deroppe (Lie); 4. Millom rosor (Janson); 5. Ved en ung Hustrus Båre (Monrad); 6. Hører jeg Sangen klinger (Heine/Rolfsen) | Wilhelm Hansen, Copenhagen 1884 |
| Op.44 | *Reiseminder. Fra Fjeld og Fjord* (Travel-Memories. From Mountain and Fjord – Poems by H. Drachmann) 1. Prolog; 2. Johanne; 3. Ragnhild; 4. Ingebjørg; 5. Ragna; 6. Epilog | Wilhelm Hansen, Copenhagen 1886 |

| *Opus No.* | *Opus and song titles* | *First edition* |
|---|---|---|
| Op.48 | *Sechs Lieder* (Six Songs) | C.F. Peters, Leipzig |
| | 1. Gruss (Heine); | 1889 |
| | 2. Dereinst, Gedanke mein (Geibel); | |
| | 3. Lauf der Welt (Uhland); | |
| | 4. Die verschwiegene Nachtigall (von der Vogelweide); | |
| | 5. Zur Rosenzeit (Goethe); | |
| | 6. Ein Traum (Bodenstedt) | |
| Op.49 | *Sechs Gedichte von Holger Drachmann* (Six Poems by . . .) | C.F. Peters, Leipzig 1889 |
| | 1. Saa du Knøsen; | |
| | 2. Vug, o Vove; | |
| | 3. Vær hilset, I Damer; | |
| | 4. Nu er Aftnen lys og lang; | |
| | 5. Julesne; | |
| | 6. Foraarsregn | |
| Op.58 | *Norge. Fem Digte af John Paulsen* (Norway. Five Poems by . . .) | Wilhelm Hansen, Copenhagen 1894 |
| | 1. Hjemkomst; | |
| | 2. Til Norge; | |
| | 3. Henrik Wergeland; | |
| | 4. Turisten; | |
| | 5. Udvandreren | |
| Op.59 | *Elegiske Digte af John Paulsen* (Elegiac Songs by . . .) | Wilhelm Hansen, Copenhagen 1894 |
| | 1. Når jeg vil dø; | |
| | 2. På Norges nøgne Fjelde; | |
| | 3. Til Én (I); | |
| | 4. Til Én (II); | |
| | 5. Farvel; | |
| | 6. Nu hviler du i Jorden | |
| Op.60 | *Digte af Vilhelm Krag* (Poems by . . .) | Wilhelm Hansen, Copenhagen 1894 |
| | 1. Liden Kirsten; | |
| | 2. Moderen synger; | |
| | 3. Mens jeg venter; | |
| | 4. Der skreg en Fugl; | |
| | 5. Og jeg vil ha mig en Hjertenskjær | |
| Op.61 | *Barnlige Sange* (Children's Songs) | Brødrene Hals, Christiania 1895 |
| | 1 Havet (Rolfsen); | |
| | 2. Sang til Juletræet (Krohn); | |
| | 3. Lok (Bjørnson); | |
| | 4. Fiskervise (Dass); | |

| Opus No. | Opus and song titles | First edition |
|---|---|---|
| | 5. Kveldsang for Blakken (Rolfsen); | |
| | 6. De norske Fjelde (Rolfsen); | |
| | 7. Fædrelandssalme (Runeberg/Rolfsen) | |
| Op.67 | *'Haugtussa' Sang-cyklus af Arne Garborgs Fortælling* ('Haugtussa' Song-cycle from Arne Garborg's story) | Wilhelm Hansen, Copenhagen 1898 (in two albums, nos 1–4 and 5–8) |
| | 1. Det syng; | |
| | 2. Veslemøy; | |
| | 3. Blåbær-li; | |
| | 4. Møte; | |
| | 5. Elsk; | |
| | 6. Killingdans; | |
| | 7. Vond dag; | |
| | 8. Ved Gjætle-bekken | |
| Op.69 | *Fem Digte af Otto Benzon* (Five Poems by . . .) | Wilhelm Hansen, Copenhagen 1900 |
| | 1. Der gynger en Båd på Bølge; | |
| | 2. Til min Dreng; | |
| | 3. Ved Moders Grav; | |
| | 4. Snegl, Snegl; | |
| | 5. Drømme | |
| Op.70 | *Fem Digte af Otto Benzon* (Five Poems by . . .) | Wilhelm Hansen, Copenhagen 1900 |
| | 1. Eros; | |
| | 2. Jeg lever et Liv i Længsel; | |
| | 3. Lys Nat; | |
| | 4. Se dig for; | |
| | 5. Digtervise | |
| | *Efterladte Sange I* (Posthumous Songs I) | Wilhelm Hansen, Copenhagen 1908 |
| | 1. Den blonde Pige (Bjørnson); | |
| | 2. Dig elsker jeg (Caralis); | |
| | 3. Taaren (Andersen); | |
| | 4. Soldaten (Andersen) | |
| | *Efterladte Sange II* (Posthumous Songs II) | Wilhelm Hansen, Copenhagen 1908 |
| | 1. På Hamars Ruiner (Vinje); | |
| | 2. Jeg elsket . . . (Bjørnson); | |
| | 3. Simpel Sang (Drachmann); | |
| | 4. Suk (Bjørnson); | |
| | 5. Julens Vuggesang (Langsted); | |
| | 6. Der Jäger (Schulz) | |

# Appendix B: Songs in Chronological Order of Composition

Where individual songs comprising or relating to one opus number were written at approximately the same time, they are listed in numerical order. Where their true order of composition differs from this, exact dates (where known) are to be found in the main text.

ES – *Efterladte Sange* (Posthumous Songs), published in two volumes in 1908. For the unpublished songs: Sky – exists in sketches only; MS – complete in manuscript; Bergen – Bergen Public Library, Grieg Collection; Oslo – Oslo University Music Library; Copenhagen – Musikhistoriske Museum, Copenhagen; GGA – published for the first time in Peters' *Grieg Gesamt-Ausgabe*.

| Opus no | Title | Poet | Date written | Date first published |
|---------|-------|------|--------------|----------------------|
| – | *Siebst du das meer?* (Do you see the sea?) | Emanuel Geibel | 31.12.1859 | Sk in Bergen (GGA) |
| – | *Den syngende Menigbed* (The singing congregation) | N.F.S. Grundtvig | July 1860 | MS in Bergen (NB not autograph) (GGA) |
| 2,1 | *Die Müllerin* (The miller-girl) | A. von Chamisso | 1861 | 1863 |
| 2,2 | *Eingebüllt in graue Wolken* (Shrouded in grey clouds) | Heinrich Heine | 1861 | 1863 |
| 2,3 | *Icb stand in dunkeln Träumen* (I stood in deep dreams) | Heine | 1861 | 1863 |

| No. | Title | Poet | Date | Note |
|---|---|---|---|---|
| 2,4 | *Was soll ich sagen?* (What shall I say?) | Chamisso | 1861 | 1863 |
| — | *Ich denke dein* (I think of you) | J.W. von Goethe | ?1862 | Not extant |
| 9,3 | *Solnedgang* (Sunset) | Andreas Munch | 1863 | December 1866 |
| 4,1 | *Die Waise* (The orphan) | Chamisso | 1863–64 | December 1864 |
| 4,2 | *Morgenthau* (Morning dew) | Chamisso | 1863–64 | December 1864 |
| 4,3 | *Abschied* (Parting) | Heine | 1863–64 | December 1864 |
| 4,4 | *Jägerlied* (Huntsman's song) | Ludwig Uhland | 1863–64 | December 1864 |
| 4,5 | *Das alte Lied* (The old song) | Heine | 1863–64 | December 1864 |
| 4,6 | *Wo sind sie hin?* (Where have they gone?) | Heine | 1863–64 | December 1864 |
| — | *Til kirken hun vandrer* (To church she walks) | Klaus Groth, trans. B. Feddersen | February 1864 | MS in Bergen (*GGA*) |
| — | *Clara Sang* from *Frieriet på Helgoland* (Clara's song from "The Courtship on Heligoland") | Ludwig Schneider/ B. Feddersen | Autumn 1864 | MS in Oslo (*GGA*) |
| 10,1 | *Taksigelse* (Thanksgiving) | Christian Winther | 1864 | 1866 |
| 10,2 | *Skovsang* (Woodland song) | Winther | 1864 | 1866 |
| 10,3 | *Blomsterne tale* (The flowers speak) | Winther | 1864 | 1866 |
| 10,4 | *Sang på Fjeldet* (Song on the mountain) | Winther | 1864 | 1866 |
| 5,1 | *To brune Øine* (Two brown eyes) | H.C. Andersen | 1864–65 | April 1865 |
| 5,2 | *En Digters Bryst* (A poet's heart) | Andersen | 1864–65 | April 1865 |
| 5,3 | *Jeg elsker dig* (I love you) | Andersen | 1864–65 | April 1865 |
| 5,4 | *Min Tanke er et mægtigt Fjeld* (My thoughts are like a mighty mountain) | Andersen | 1864–65 | April 1865 |
| 15,2 | *Kjærlighed* (Love) | Andersen | 1864 | December 1867 |
| 15,3 | *Langelandsk Folkemelodi* (A Langeland folk-song) | Andersen | ?1864 | January 1867 |
| — | *Min lille Fugl* (My little bird) | Andersen | 12.8.1865 | 1895 |

| Opus no | Title | Poet | Date written | Date first published |
|---|---|---|---|---|
| ES | Dig elsker jeg! (You I love!) | 'Caralis' | 1865 | 1908 |
| ES | Taaren (The tear) | Andersen | 1865 | 1908 |
| ES | Soldaten (The soldier) | Andersen | 1865 | 1908 |
| 18,4 | Efteraarsstormen (The autumn storm) | Christian Richardt | 1865 | 1869 |
| 9,1 | Harpen (The harp) | Munch | 1866 | December 1866 |
| 9,2 | Vuggesang (Cradle song) | Munch | 1866 | December 1866 |
| 9,4 | Udfarten (The outward journey) | Munch | 1866 | December 1866 |
| – | Vesle gut (Little boy) | Kristofer Janson | 1866 | MS in Bergen (GGA) |
| ES | Den blonde Pige (I) (The blonde girl) | Bj. Bjørnson | 1867 | 1908 |
| 15,1 | Margretes Vuggesang from Kongsemnerne (Margaret's cradle song from 'The Pretenders') | Henrik Ibsen | 1868 | December 1868 |
| 15,4 | Modersorg (A mother's sorrow) | Richardt | 1868 | December 1868 |
| 18,9 | Serenade til Welhaven (Serenade to Welhaven) | Bjørnson | 1868 | ?1869 |
| 18,1 | Vandring i Skoven (Wandering in the woods) | Andersen | 1869 | December 1869 |
| 18,2 | Hun er saa hvid (She is so pale) | Andersen | 1869 | December 1869 |
| 18,3 | En Digters sidste Sang (A poet's last song) | Andersen 1869 | December 1869 | |
| 18,5 | Poesien (Poesy) | Andersen | 1869 | December 1869 |
| 18,6 | Ungbirken (The young birch) | Jørgen Moe | 1869 | December 1869 |
| 18,7 | Hytten (The cottage) | Andersen | 1869 | December 1869 |
| 18,8 | Rosenknoppen (The rosebud) | Andersen | 1869 | December 1869 |
| 39,4 | Millom rosor (Among roses) | Janson | 1869 | December 1884 |

| | | | | |
|---|---|---|---|---|
| – | *Odalisken synger* (The odalisque sings) | Carl Bruun | 1870 | July 1872 |
| – | *Bergmanden* (The miner) | Ibsen | ?1870 | Sk. in Bergen |
| 21,1 | *Det første Møte* (The first meeting) | Bjørnson | 1870 | 1873 |
| 21,2 | *God Morgen* (Good morning) | Bjørnson | 1870 | 1873 |
| 39,1 | *Fra Monte Pincio* (From Monte Pincio) | Bjørnson | 1870 | December 1884 |
| – | *Prinsessen* (The princess) | Bjørnson | 1871 | 1871 |
| 21,3 | *Jeg giver mit Digt til Våren* (I will give my song to the spring) | Bjørnson | 1872 | 1873 |
| 21,4 | *Tak for dit Råd* (Thanks for your advice) | Bjørnson | 1872 | 1873 |
| – | *Den hvide, røde Rose* (The white, red rose) | Bjørnson | 1873 | MS in Bergen (*GGA*) |
| ES | *Suk* (Sighs) | Bjørnson | 1873 | 1908 |
| 39,2 | *Dulgt Kjærlighed* (Hidden love) | Bjørnson | 1873 | December 1884 |
| 39,5 | *Ved en ung Hustrus Båre* (Beside a young wife's bier) | O.P. Monrad | 1873 | December 1884 |
| 33,7 | *Gamle mor* (Old mother) | A.O. Vinje | 1873 | December 1881 |
| – | *Til L.M. Lindemans Sølvbryllup* (For L.M. Lindeman's silver wedding) | V. Nikolajsen | September 1873 | MS in Bergen (*GGA*) |
| – | *Til generalkonsul Chr. Tønsbergs 60te Fødelsdag* (For Consul-general Chr. Tønsberg's 60th birthday) | Johan Bøgh | December 1873 | MS in Bergen (*GGA*) |
| – | *Den blonde Pige* (II) (The blonde girl) | Bjørnson | 1874 | MS found in Leipzig (*GGA*) |
| 23,17 | *Peer Gynts Serenade* (Peer Gynt's serenade) | Ibsen | 1874–75 | 1876 |
| 23,18 | *Solveigs Sang* (Solveig's song) | Ibsen | 1874–75 | 1876 |
| 23,23 | *Solveigs Vuggevise* (Solveig's cradle song) | Ibsen | 1874–75 | 1876 |

| Opus no | Title | Poet | Date written | Date first published |
|---|---|---|---|---|
| — | Morgenbøn på Skolen (Morning prayer at school) | Fredrik Gjertsen | 1875 | December 1875 |
| 25,1 | Spillemænd (Minstrels) | Ibsen | 1876 | December 1876 |
| 25,2 | En svane (A swan) | Ibsen | 1876 | December 1876 |
| 25,3 | Stambogsrim (Album verse) | Ibsen | 1876 | December 1876 |
| 25,4 | Med en Vandlilje (With a waterlily) | Ibsen | 1876 | December 1876 |
| 25,5 | Borte! (Gone!) | Ibsen | 1876 | December 1876 |
| 25,6 | En Fuglevise (A bird-song) | Ibsen | 1876 | December 1876 |
| 26,1 | Et Håb (A hope) | John Paulsen | 1876 | December 1876 |
| 26,2 | Jeg reiste en deilig Sommerkveld (I went one lovely summer evening) | Paulsen | 1876 | December 1876 |
| 26,3 | Den Ærgjerrige (The ambitious one) | Paulsen | 1876 | December 1876 |
| 26,4 | Med en Primula veris (With a primrose) | Paulsen | 1876 | December 1876 |
| 26,5 | På Skogstien (On the woodland path) | Paulsen | 1876 | December 1876 |
| 33,5 | Langs ei å (Beside a stream) | Vinje | 1877 | December 1881 |
| 32 | Den Bergtekne (The mountain thrall) | (Old Norse) | 1877–78 | 1882 |
| — | Dyre Vaa (Dyre Vaa) | Welhaven | ?1880 | Sk. in Bergen |
| 33,1 | Guten (The youth) | Vinje | 1880 | December 1881 |
| 33,2 | Våren (The spring) | Vinje | 1880 | December 1881 |
| 33,3 | Den særde (The wounded one) | Vinje | 1880 | December 1881 |
| 33,4 | Tytebæret (The wild cranberry) | Vinje | 1880 | December 1881 |
| 33,6 | Eit syn (A vision) | Vinje | 1880 | December 1881 |
| 33,8 | Der fyrste (The first thing) | Vinje | 1880 | December 1881 |
| 33,9 | Ved Rundarne (At Rundarne) | Vinje | 1880 | December 1881 |
| 33,10 | Eit vennestykke (A broken friendship) | Vinje | 1880 | December 1881 |

| | | | | |
|---|---|---|---|---|
| 33,11 | Trudom (Faith) | Vinje | 1880 | December 1881 |
| 33,12 | Fyremål (The goal) | Vinje | 1880 | December 1881 |
| – | Jenta (The girl) | Vinje | 1880 | MS in Bergen (GGA) |
| – | Attegløyma (The old maid) | Vinje | 1880 | MS in Bergen (GGA) |
| ES | På Hamars ruiner (On Hamar's ruins) | Vinje | 1880 | 1908 |
| 39,3 | I Liden høit deroppe (In the meadow high above) | Jonas Lie | 1884 | December 1884 |
| 39,6 | Hører jeg Sangen klinge (When I hear the song resound) | Heine, trans. N. Rolfsen | 1884 | December 1884 |
| 48,1 | Gruss (Greeting) | Heine | 16.9.1884 | 1889 |
| 48,2 | Dereinst, Gedanke mein (One day, my thoughts) | E. Geibel | 17.9.1884 | 1889 |
| – | Under Juletræet (Under the Christmas-tree) | Nordahl Rolfsen | 1885 | 1885 |
| 44,1 | Prolog (Prologue) | Holger Drachmann | 1886 | December 1886 |
| 44,2 | Johanne (Johanne) | Drachmann | 1886 | December 1886 |
| 44,3 | Ragnhild (Ragnhild) | Drachmann | 1886 | December 1886 |
| 44,4 | Ingebjørg (Ingebjørg) | Drachmann | 1886 | December 1886 |
| 44,5 | Ragna (Ragna) | Drachmann | 1886 | December 1886 |
| 44,6 | Epilog (Epilogue) | Drachmann | 1886 | December 1886 |
| 49,5 | Julesne (Christmas snow) | Drachmann | 1886 | 1889 |
| 49,6 | Foraarsregn (Spring rain) | Drachmann | September 1887 | 1889 |
| – | Østerlied (Easter song) | Adolf Böttger | 7.6.1889 | 1904 |
| – | Du retter tidt dit Øiepar (You often direct your eyes) | Drachmann | 4.7.1889 | MS in Bergen |
| 48,3 | Lauf der Welt (The way of the world) | Uhland | August 1889 | 1889 |

| Opus no | Title | Poet | Date written | Date first published |
|---|---|---|---|---|
| 48,4 | Die verschwiegene nachtigall (The discreet nightingale) | Walther von der Vogelweide | August 1889 | 1889 |
| 48,5 | Zur Rosenzeit (At rose-time) | Goethe | August 1889 | 1889 |
| 48,6 | Ein Traum (A dream) | F. Bodenstedt | August 1889 | 1889 |
| 49,1 | Saa du Knøsen? (Did you see the lad?) | Drachmann | 1889 | 1889 |
| 49,2 | Vug, o Vove (Rock, oh waves) | Drachmann | 1889 | 1889 |
| 49,3 | Vær hilset, I Damer (Greetings, ladies) | Drachmann | 1889 | 1889 |
| 49,4 | Nu er Aftnen lys og lang (Now the evening is light and long) | Drachmann | 1889 | 1889 |
| ES | Simpel Sang (A simple song) | Drachmann | 1889 | 1908 |
| ES | Jeg elsket . . . from Fred (I loved . . . from 'Peace') | Bjørnson | 1891 | 1908 |
| — | Valgsang (Election song) | Bjørnson | 1893 | 1894 |
| — | Fædrelandssang (Song to the Fatherland) | Paulsen | ?1893 | MS in Bergen (GGA) |
| — | Ave maris stella (Hail, star of the sea) | trans. Gustav lange | ?1893 | 1893 |
| 58,1 | Hjemkomst (Homecoming) | Paulsen | November 1893 | September 1894 |
| 60,2 | Moderen synger (The mother sings) | Vilhelm Krag | November 1893 | 1894 |
| 58,2 | Til Norge (To Norway) | Paulsen | 1893–94 | September 1894 |
| 58,3 | Henrik Wergeland (Henrik Wergeland) | Paulsen | 1893–94 | September 1894 |
| 58,4 | Turisten (The tourist) | Paulsen | 1893–94 | September 1894 |
| 58,5 | Udvandreren (The emigrant) | Paulsen | 1893–94 | September 1894 |
| 59,1 | Når jeg vil dø (When I shall die) | Paulsen | 1893–94 | September 1894 |
| 59,2 | På Norges nøgne Fjelde (On Norway's bare mountains) | Paulsen after Heine | 1893–94 | September 1894 |
| 59,3 | Til Én (I) (To one) | Paulsen | 1893–94 | September 1894 |
| 59,4 | Til Én (II) (To one) | Paulsen | 1893–94 | September 1894 |

| No. | Title | Text | | |
|---|---|---|---|---|
| 59,5 | *Farvel* (Farewell) | Paulsen | 1893–94 | September 1894 |
| 59,6 | *Nu hviler du i Jorden* (Now you are resting in the earth) | Paulsen | 1893–94 | September 1894 |
| 60,1 | *Liden Kirsten* (Little Kirsten) | Krag | 1893–94 | September 1894 |
| 60,3 | *Mens jeg venter* (While I am waiting) | Krag | 1893–94 | September 1894 |
| 60,4 | *Der skreg en Fugl* (A bird cried) | Krag | 1893–94 | September 1894 |
| 60,5 | *Og jeg vil ha mig en Hjertenskjær* (And I will have me a sweetheart) | Krag | 1893–94 | September 1894 |
| 61,1 | *Havet* (The sea) | N. Rolfsen | 1894–95 | February 1895 |
| 61,2 | *Sang til Juletræet* (Song to the Christmas-tree) | Johan Krohn | 1894–95 | February 1895 |
| 61,3 | *Lok* (Call) | Bjørnson | 1894–95 | February 1895 |
| 61,4 | *Fiskervise* (Fisherman's song) | Petter Dass | 1894–95 | February 1895 |
| 61,5 | *Kveldsang for Blakken* (Evening song for Blakken) | Rolfsen | 1894–95 | February 1895 |
| 61,6 | *De norske Fjelde* (The Norwegian mountains) | Rolfsen | 1894–95 | February 1895 |
| 61,7 | *Fædrelandssalme* (Hymn to the Fatherland) | Rolfsen after Runeberg | 1894–95 | February 1895 |
| 67,1 | *Det syng* (The singing) | Arne Garborg | 1895 | 1898 |
| 67,2 | *Veslemøy* (Veslemøy) | Garborg | 1895 | 1898 |
| 67,3 | *Blåbær-li* (Blueberry slopes) | Garborg | 1895 | 1898 |
| 67,4 | *Møte* (Meeting) | Garborg | 1895 | 1898 |
| 67,5 | *Elsk* (Love) | Garborg | 1895 | 1898 |
| 67,6 | *Killingdans* (Kids' dance) | Garborg | 1895 | 1898 |
| 67,7 | *Vond dag* (Evil day) | Garborg | 1895 | 1898 |
| 67,8 | *Ved Gjætle-bekken* (By the Gjætle Brook) | Garborg | 1895 | 1898 |

| Opus no | Title | Poet | Date written | Date first published |
|---|---|---|---|---|
| — | Prolog: Til deg, du bei (Prologue: To you, heath) | Garborg | 1895 | Sk. in Bergen |
| — | Veslemøy ved rokken (Veslemøy at the spinning wheel) | Garborg | 1895 | Sk. in Bergen |
| — | Kvelding (Evening) | Garborg | 1895 | Sk. in Bergen |
| — | Sporven (The sparrow) | Garborg | 1895 | MS in Copenhagen (GGA) |
| — | Fyreversel (Premonition) | Garborg | 1895 | Sk. in Bergen |
| — | I slåtten (In the hayfield) | Garborg | 1895 | MS in Copenhagen (GGA) |
| — | Veslemøy undrast (Veslemøy wonders) | Garborg | 1895 | Sk. in Bergen (GGA) |
| — | Dømd (Doomed) | Garborg | 1895 | MS in Copenhagen (GGA) |
| — | Den snille guten (The nice boy) | Garborg | 1895 | Sk. in Bergen |
| — | Veslemøy lengtar (Veslemøy yearns) | Garborg | 1895 | MS in Copenhagen (GGA) |
| — | Skog-glad (Woodland joy) | Garborg | 1895 | Sk. in Bergen |
| — | Ku-lokk (Cow-call) | Garborg | 1895 | MS in Copenhagen (GGA) |
| — | Blåbæret (The blueberry) | Garborg | 1895 | MS in Bergen (GGA) |
| 69,1 | Der gynger en Bad på Bølge (A boat is rocking on the waves) | Didrik Grønvold | 23.8.1896 | MS in Bergen (GGA) |
| 69,2 | Til min Dreng (To my son) | Otto Benzon | 1900 | November 1900 |
| 69,3 | Ved Moders Grav (Beside Mother's grave) | Benzon | 1900 | November 1900 |
| 69,4 | Snegl, Snegl (Snail, snail) | Benzon | 1900 | November 1900 |
| 69,5 | Drømme (Dreams) | Benzon | 1900 | November 1900 |
| 70,1 | Eros (Eros) | Benzon | 1900 | November 1900 |
| 70,2 | Jeg lever et Liv i Længsel (I live a life of longing) | Benzon | 1900 | November 1900 |

| | | | |
|---|---|---|---|---|
| 70,3 | *Lys Nat* (Light night) | Benzon | 1900 | November 1900 |
| 70,4 | *Se dig for* (Beware) | Benzon | 1900 | November 1900 |
| 70,5 | *Digtervise* (A poet's song) | Benzon | 1900 | November 1900 |
| — | *To a Devil* | Benzon | 19.2.1900 | MS in Bergen (*GGA*) |
| — | *Gentlemen-Menige* (Gentlemen-rankers) | Rudyard Kipling, trans. Johnsen | 17.12.1900 | MS in Bergen (*GGA*) |
| ES | *Julens Vuggesang* (A Christmas cradle-song) | Adolf Langsted | 1900 | 1908 |
| ES | *Der Jäger* (The hunter) | Wilhelm Schultz | 15.7.1905 | 1908 |

# Appendix C: Personalia

ABRAHAM, MAX (1831–1900)   Born in Danzig (Gdansk), he was editor for and then a partner in the publishing house of C. F. Peters, Leipzig, eventually becoming its sole proprietor in 1880. He inaugurated the famous Edition Peters and was succeeded by his nephew, Henri Hinrichsen (see below). Because of his position he became a regular correspondent and a good friend of Grieg.

ALNÆS, EYVIND (1872–1932)   Norwegian organist, accompanist and composer who studied in Christiania, Leipzig and Berlin. His works include two symphonies, a piano concerto, chamber and piano music. Amongst his songs, which number around eighty-five, are settings of poems by Vinje, Krag and Ibsen, some of which were also set by Grieg.

AUGUNDSON, TORGEIR (1801–72)   Known as 'Myllarguten', the Miller's Boy. One of Norway's most celebrated Hardanger fiddle players, with an especially great talent for improvization. He was taken up by Ole Bull, who arranged a number of concerts with him from 1849. Augundson also played in southern Norway and in Copenhagen.

BEYER, FRANTS (1851–1918)   An amateur musician and composer, born in Bergen. A one-time pupil of Grieg's in Christiania, Beyer became his closest friend for more than thirty years. A driving force in Bergen's musical life, he was chairman of Harmonien for many years and the society's only honorary member. He published six albums of songs and was a great admirer of Norwegian folk music. He loved the countryside, especially the Jotunheim area. He was the recipient of innumerable letters from Grieg, some of which were published by his wife Marie in 1923, and many more edited by Bjarne Kortsen, published in 1978, which are invaluable as source material.

BENZON, CARL OTTO VALDEMAR (1856–1927)   Born in Copenhagen, Benzon wished first to be a doctor. However, he bowed to his father's wishes, qualified as a pharmacist and went into the family firm. Also a noted sportsman, he was a pioneer in contemporary sports movements. His career as a dramatist began with a one-act play *Surrogater* (Substitutes) in 1882, which received its first performance at the Royal Theatre in Copenhagen. He went on to write many plays between then and 1922, including the one regarded as a masterpiece, *Forældre* (Parents, 1907). His play *Anna Bryde*, produced in 1894 and from which Grieg set two songs, was not a success. Benzon was director of the Royal Theatre in 1913–14.

BULL, OLE BORNEMANN (1810–80) Norwegian virtuoso violinist, entrepreneur and composer, described by Nils Grinde as 'the great fairy-tale in Norwegian musical history'. Born in Bergen and intended by his father to be a clergyman, he began to play the violin at about five years of age. He made rapid progress and was frequently a soloist with the local music society. His playing was thought to be so 'magical' as to be inspired by a *fossegrim*, a water-sprite, and it is this idea that is depicted in his statue in Bergen. A nationalist all his life, he came into contact with folk music as a child and it was to have a great influence on him. Bull used folk-tunes as themes for improvisation and for larger-scale composed works, as well as playing the music for its own sake, and his interest extended to the folk music of other countries too. His fantastic villa on Lysøen, an island off the coast a little south of Bergen, which he used as a summer residence, now provides a lovely venue for concerts of folk music. Related to the family by marriage, it was Bull who first recognized Grieg's talent and suggested he be sent to study in Leipzig.

BØGH, JOHANN (1848–1933) A Norwegian art historian who took an active interest in conserving the arts and crafts of his native Bergen. Among other things he helped to re-establish Den national Scene, Bergen's theatre, and had the initial idea for, and asked Grieg's help with the musical aspect of the now internationally famous Bergen Festival. Also a journalist and author, Bøgh published a collection of stories under the title *Fra Bergenskanten* (From the Bergen district) in 1888.

DALE, KNUT (1834–1921) Norwegian Hardanger fiddle player from Telemark, from whom Halvorsen took down a number of *slåtter* in 1901, which provided the material for Grieg's *Slåtter*, op.72, and Halvorsen's own *Norwegische Bauerntänze* of 1905. Further melodies played by Dale have been taken down and transcribed by other composers. Most show considerable rhythmic complexity and much double-stopping. Halvorsen's *Fossegrimen* (The water-sprite), the first work for Hardanger fiddle and symphony orchestra, was undoubtedly also inspired by Dale.

DASS, PETTER (1647–1707) Norwegian writer and the only figure of seventeenth-century Norwegian literature who is of more than historical interest. Born on the coast of northern Norway, he always loved the sea and the dangerous life of the fisherman. His most famous work is *Nordlands Trompet*, describing Norway and its people and their lives in folk-like verse. Dass shows an accurate observation with a sense of humour and an eye for amusing detail and a sense of reality, and he often makes use of Norwegian dialect words. Grieg set one of his poems amonst the *Barnlige Sange* (Children's Songs), op.61.

DESMOND, ASTRA (1893–1973)    English contralto who studied at the Royal Academy of Music in London and later in Berlin. After a recital début in London in 1915, she made some appearances with the Carl Rosa Opera Company and also at Covent Garden. She was, however, chiefly known as a concert and oratorio singer, particularly noted for her performances as the Angel in Elgar's *Dream of Gerontius*. She specialised in Grieg's songs, giving numerous recitals in the original languages and making English translations. In recognition of this work, she was awarded the Norwegian medal of St Olav. In England she was awarded a CBE in 1949.

ELLING, CATHERINUS (1858–1942)    Norwegian teacher and publisher, and the composer of some two hundred songs, including two sets (twelve songs in all) to poems from Garborg's *Haugtussa*. Elling studied music in Leipzig and philology in Christiania. He was recommended by Grieg for a government stipend and went to Berlin. Besides songs, his compositions include a symphony, a violin concerto and chamber music.

FEDDERSEN, BENJAMIN JOHAN (1823–1902)    Danish author and music teacher. He met Grieg in Denmark in the early 1860s and became something of a mentor to him. Grieg dedicated the *Poetiske tonebilder* (Poetic Tone-Pictures), op.3, to him and also the Andersen setting *Min lille Fugl*. Feddersen became one of Grieg's closest friends and wrote an article about him, *Fra Griegs Ungdom* (From Grieg's Youth), in 1899.

FINCK, HENRY THEOPHILUS (1854–1926)    American music historian, journalist, editor and author. He graduated from Harvard in 1976 with honours in philosophy and later furthered his studies in music. He became one of the most influential critics of his day, writing for *The Nation* and the *New York Evening Post* and editing the *Musical Courier*. He wrote a total of twenty-four books; his biography of Grieg was published in London in 1906, and another book, *Grieg and his Music*, was published in New York in 1909. His *Chopin and Other Musical Essays* was, to judge from its reviews, written in a typically journalistic style: it was described by the *Boston Post* as being 'enlivened by anecdotes and touches of enthusiasm' and by the *Boston Advertiser* as 'a charming description of the inner life of the musical giants'. The letters Finck received from Grieg in answer to his queries for his books and articles, written in German, are preserved in Bergen Public Library, together with a number of magazine articles, all of which are valuable source material. Other books by Finck include *Songs and Song Writers*, published in New York in 1900, and *Success in Music and How it is Won*, published in 1909. Finck also edited *50 Master Songs* (1902), *50 Schubert Songs* (1903) and *50 Grieg Songs* (1909).

GADE, NIELS WILHELM (1817–90)   Danish composer, the son of a Copenhagen instrument-maker, who studied in Denmark and in Leipzig. His First Symphony was performed by the Leipzig Gewandhaus orchestra under Mendelssohn. Gade held several musical posts in Copenhagen. His compositions include eight symphonies and many choral, orchestral and chamber works, and it was on his advice that Grieg wrote his own Symphony.

GJERTSEN, FREDRIK (1831–1904)   A schoolmaster, principally teaching Norwegian and French, with a deep literary understanding. He was well regarded as a public speaker and gave the address at the unveiling of Kjerulf's statue. He wrote some verse and also edited school books and the illustrated children's paper *Nordisk illustreret Børneblad*. His hymn *Morgenbønn på skolen* (Morning prayer at school) was set by Grieg in 1875.

GRINDE, NILS (b. 1927)   Norwegian university lecturer, musicologist and author, who studied at the University and the Music Conservatory in Oslo. His *Norsk Musikkhistorie* (Norwegian Musical History) was published in 1971 and in 1978 his edition of Kjerulf's songs was published in two volumes in Oslo. He is also the co-editor (with Dan Fog) of Grieg's songs for Peters' *Grieg Gesamt-Ausgabe*.

GROVEN, EIVIND (1901–77)   Norwegian musicologist and composer. A collector of Norwegian folk music, he was the folk music consultant for NRK, the Norwegian broadcasting company. Groven was also an excellent Hardanger fiddle player and wrote articles on the instrument and its music.

GRUNDTVIG, NIKOLAI FREDERIK SEVERIN (1783–1872)   Danish minister, author and hymn-writer. His *Sangværk til den danske Kirken* (Songs for the Danish Church) eventually comprised more than fourteen hundred hymns. He preached tolerance, both nationally and in a religious context, and 'glade Kristendom' (happy Christianity), which had a lasting influence on other writers. He became a romantic writer after he 'discovered' Norse mythology, but was a manic-depressive who went through a series of crises, both personal and literary as well as spiritual. Grieg set only one of his hymns, the early *Den syngende Menighed* (The singing congregation).

GRØNDAHL, AGATHE (NÉE BACKER) (1847–1907)   Norwegian pianist and composer who studied with Winter-Hjelm and Kjerulf. She married O.A. Grøndahl in 1875. Her concert tours throughout Scandinavia, Germany and England were greeted with great acclaim. She wrote about 190 songs and over 120 piano pieces. She was a friend of Grieg and a frequent performer of his music.

GRØNVOLD, DIDRIK HEGERMANN (1855–1928)   Norwegian teacher, author, composer and writer on music. He was born in Bergen and took a degree in humanities as well as studying piano and harmony in Munich.

Later he studied piano with Agathe Backer Grøndahl and harmony with Johan Selmer in Christiania. He became the music critic for *Bergens Tidende* and *Bergensposten* and was the author of a concise history of Norwegian literature. He also wrote plays and novels, an epic poem and other poetry, as well as sketches and music reviews. He was chairman of the management committee of Harmonien for four years. His own compositions comprise a number of solo songs and pieces for male-voice choir, including a setting of Garborg's *Gud signe Norigs land* (God Bless Norway). Grieg set his poem *Blåbæret* (The blueberry).

GULBRANSON, ELLEN (NÉE NORDGREN) (1863–1947)    Swedish-born singer who was especially renowned for her Wagnerian roles. She sang Brünnhilde in *Die Walküre* at the opera's first performance in Scandinavia, in Copenhagen in 1891, conducted by Johan Svendsen. Later she sang many Wagnerian roles in Bayreuth and made concert appearances all over Europe. She retired from the stage in 1916, but continued to give recitals until 1923. Grieg thought very highly of her and she performed many of his songs. Her voice has been described as 'a dark, rich mezzo-soprano of great volume and size . . . even and supple in all registers' (*Musikken og vi*).

HALVORSEN, JOHAN (1864–1935)    Norwegian violinist, composer and conductor. He studied in Stockholm as well as in Norway, and then studied violin under Adolf Brodsky in Leipzig. He conducted Harmonien in Bergen and also the National Theatre orchestra in Christiania. He wrote incidental music to a number of plays by, amongst others, Drachmann, Hamsun, Holberg and Brandt. He also wrote three symphonies, a violin concerto and the two famous *Norwegian Rhapsodies*, as well as other orchestral works. It was Halvorsen who took down the *slåtter* from Knut Dale's playing, which became the basis of Grieg's *Slåtter*, op.72. His *Fossegrimen* was the first work written for Hardanger fiddle and orchestra.

HARTMANN, JOHAN ERNST (1726–93)    German-born musician who settled in Copenhagen in 1762. In that year, too, he took down some melodies to Skaldic verses, sung by a group of visiting Icelanders, which give some idea of traditional melodies. His compositions include the singspiel *Balders Død* (The death of Balder) with the poet Ewald, based on Norse mythology, and the opera *Fiskerne* (The Fishermen).

HARTMANN, JOHANN PETER EMELIUS (1805–1900)    Danish composer, the son of J.E. Hartmann (see above). He wrote operas, ballet music, one symphony and much chamber music. His daughter married Niels Gade.

HARTMANN, WILHELM EMILIUS (1836–98)    Danish composer, the son of J.P.E. Hartmann (see above). He was a fellow student with Grieg in Leipzig. His compositions include seven symphonies, three concertos and the symphonic poem *Haakon Jarl* (Earl Haakon).

HENRIQUES, ROBERT (1858–1914)   Danish cellist, conductor and composer, and a good friend of Grieg. He made orchestral arrangements of some of Grieg's *Norwegian Dances*, op.35, the first three of which were used in the ballet for the scene in the Dovregubb's Hall in *Peer Gynt*, for the Copenhagen production in 1886. His own compositions include an overture *Olaf Trygvason*, a symphonic sketch *Aquarellen*, and a number of pieces for cello.

HINRICHSEN, HENRI (or Heinrich) (1868–1942)   The director of the publishing house of Peters in succession to Max Abraham (see above) and a correspondent of Grieg's. He was forced into exile by the Nazis and died in Auschwitz. His son Max (1901–65) worked with him until 1937, when he came to London to direct that division of Peters and founded Hinrichsen Edition Ltd.

HOLTER, IVER (1850–1941)   Norwegian composer with no particularly individual style and of rather limited production. He played the violin in Grieg's orchestra for the subscription concerts and also in the Music Society orchestra in Christiania. He studied with Svendsen, while also studying medicine, and later in Leipzig and Berlin. He succeeded Grieg as conductor of Harmonien and later of the Music Society orchestra, giving performances of many contemporary works.

HORNBECK, LOUIS (1840–1906)   Danish teacher and composer. A friend of both Grieg and Nordraak, he was probably responsible for introducing them to each other. He married a cousin of Nordraak's. His compositions included six albums of songs and he was described by Grieg as having a 'clear, critical nature' and 'a lovely lyrical talent for composition'. He was involved with Grieg and Emil Hornemann in the society Euterpe.

HORNEMAN, CHRISTIAN FREDERIK EMIL (1841–1906)   Danish composer and a fellow student and friend of Grieg. His style resembled that of Brahms, whom he greatly admired, and he was considered to have had some stylistic influence on Nielsen.

JOHNSEN, PETER MARCUS GJØE ROSENKRANTZ (1857–1929)   Norwegian writer, born in Bergen. He wrote stories and novellas, novels and poetry, beginning with *Nygifte og andre fortællinger* (The Newly Weds and other stories) in 1885. Amongst a number of good translations are ten of Kipling's *Barrack Room Ballads* and other verses, which were published in 1902 under the title *Soldat Sange* and from which Grieg set *Gentlemen-Menige* (Gentlemen-rankers).

KJERULF, HALFDAN (1815–68)   Norwegian composer of Danish descent, highly regarded by Grieg. He lived for most of his life in Christiania, but went to Paris in 1840 where, besides music by the Viennese classicists and the early romantics, he also heard works by Berlioz. In the summer of 1849 he toured the Hallingdal, Hardanger and Sogn regions of Norway and heard much folk music first hand; otherwise, most of what he knew was through Lindeman's collections. He studied music first in Christiania and only later with Niels Gade in Copenhagen and E.F. Richter in Leipzig. His background and training account for the wide choice he made among poets for his songs. Most of his songs are strophic and very much in the *romanse* tradition, and, perhaps because he was the first song-composer to gain a wide currency in Norway, he is often called 'the Norwegian Schubert'.

KRIEBEL (also KRIBEL), ANNA (1863–1926)   Norwegian soprano, much admired by Grieg. She married the Italian capellmeister Vittorio Vanzo. She performed in opera and concert, both in Norway and abroad.

KROHN, JOHAN (1841–1925)   Danish schoolmaster and author, who graduated in theology in 1867. He wrote a number of books for children and is best known for *Peters Jul* (Peter's Christmas), published anonymously in 1866, which contains the *Sang til Juletræet* set by Grieg in the *Barnlige Sange*, op.61, and by C.E.F. Weyse.

LAMMERS, THORVALD (1841–1922)   Norwegian singer, conductor and composer. He first practised as a lawyer, coming to music later, studying singing only after 1870, first in Stockholm and then in Milan, where he made his début in 1873. He was the resident bass at the Christiania Theatre until the fire of 1877, and he settled in the Norwegian capital as a singer and teacher in 1879. His greatest contribution as a singer came after 1880, when he gave the first performances of several of Grieg's songs, and became particularly well-known as an interpreter of the Vinje settings, op.33. His own compositions were mostly songs and choral works, the large majority written after 1900, including a large-scale oratorio on Bjørnson's *Fred* (Peace) – a project abandoned by Grieg – but died shortly after its first performance.

LANGSTED, ADOLF CHRISTOFFER (1864–1919)   Danish author and schoolmaster. He first studied French and was much influenced by Rousseau, and later worked as a journalist in Paris. He published some small collections of poetry, including several poems set as hymns and *Julens Vuggesang*, set by Grieg.

LINDEMAN, LUDVIG MATHIAS (1812–87)   Norwegian organist, composer and teacher, born in Trondhjem. All his musical studies were with his father, who was steeped in the Bach tradition, which in turn influenced his own music. With other organists, he inaugurated the new organ at the Royal Albert Hall in London in 1871, where his talent for improvisation was greatly acclaimed. He also began an organists' school in Christiania, which eventually became Oslo's Music Conservatory. However, his real importance to later generations was as a collector of Norwegian folk music, which culminated in the *Ældre og nyere norske Folkemelodier* (Old and New Norwegian Folk Tunes), published between 1867 and 1907 and comprising over 600 tunes. Other collections include *Halvhundre norske Fjeldmelodier* (Half a Hundred Norwegian Mountain Tunes), arranged for male voice choir, published in 1862; *30 norske Kjæmpevise-melodier* (Thirty Norwegian Giant-songs), arranged for three equal voices (1863); and *Norske Kjæmpevise-melodier*, arranged for mixed choir (1885). He also produced hymn-books, books of songs for school use, and works for organ, piano and string quartet.

LUNDE, JOHAN BACKER (1874–1958)   Norwegian pianist and composer. He wrote four symphonies, around two hundred songs, orchestral works and piano and chamber music. He was an excellent pianist and much in demand as an accompanist. His music is pleasant but with insufficient individuality to hold a firm place in the repertoire.

MACFARREN, NATALIA (1828–1916)   Born Clarina Thalia Andrae in Lübeck. A contralto and linguist who translated a number of Grieg's songs, including opp.58, 59, 60 and 61. She married Sir George Macfarren, who became Director of the Royal Academy of Music in London. Lady Macfarren also composed a number of songs and piano pieces herself, and published an 'Elementary course for vocalising and pronouncing the English language'. She was also the editor of many German and Italian operas.

MATTHISON-HANSEN, JOHAN GOTTFRED (1832–1909)   Danish organist and composer. He was a friend of Grieg's from his days in Copenhagen and a co-founder of the music society Euterpe.

MESSCHAERT, JOHANNES MARTINUS (1857–1922)   Dutch baritone, a friend of Röntgen and one of Grieg's favourite singers. He first studied violin, then changed to singing, and was a pupil of J. Stockhausen in Frankfurt. He began his career as a choral conductor in Amsterdam before appearing as a singer. He specialised in Lieder and the works of Bach, becoming a noted interpreter of the role of Christus in the St Matthew Passion. He taught at a number of European conservatories, finally moving to Zurich in 1920. Two volumes of Schubert's songs with Messchaert's dynamic markings were published in Mainz in 1928.

MOE, JØRGEN (1813–82)   Norwegian clergyman and writer best known for his work, with his friend Asbjørnsen, in collecting the traditional stories of his country, the Norwegian equivalent of the work of the brothers Grimm in Germany. He also wrote words to Bull's melody for the song *Sæterjentens Søndag*, 'På solen jeg ser', so popular in Norway, and was the author of *Ungbirken*, set by Grieg amongst the op.18 songs.

MONRAD, OLAF PEDER (1849–1920)   Norwegian clergyman and writer. He studied aesthetics and art history in Copenhagen and eventually settled there, after several posts as chaplain and parish priest in various parts of Norway. He preached a true congregational ideal and worked a good deal for young people, in youth clubs, choral groups and so on. He wrote books about Kierkegaard and Grundtvig and was the father of the singer Cally Monrad. Grieg set his poem *Ved en ung Hustrus Båre* (Beside a young wife's bier) both as a solo and choral song.

MØLLER, DAGMAR HENRIETTE (NÉE BOSSE) (1866–1956)    Norwegian opera and concert singer, born in Christiania and settled in Sweden. Her memoirs, *Griegminne*, were written in 1940 and contain some interesting comments on the standards the composer set for his performers. Grieg dedicated the *Haugtussa* songs to her and she was known as a performer of his songs and those of other Scandinavian composers, including Agathe Backer Grøndahl, Sjøgren and Stenhammar. Her sister, the actress Harriet Bosse, married August Strindberg.

NANSEN, EVA SARS (1858–1907)    Norwegian mezzo-soprano who married Fridtjof Nansen, the polar explorer. She studied with Thorvald Lammers, amongst others, and made her début in Christiania in 1881. Highly regarded as a concert singer, she toured all over Scandinavia. She gave the first performance of the complete *Haugtussa* cycle, accompanied by Agathe Backer Grøndahl, in Christiania in November 1899.

NISSEN, ERIKA (NÉE LIE) (1845–1903)    Norwegian pianist, who studied first with her older sister, then with Kjerulf in Christiania and later with Theodor Kullack in Berlin. She became an internationally known artist and undertook many concert tours abroad, as well as teaching and performing in Christiania. She was the soloist in the first performance in Christiania of Grieg's Piano Concerto.

NORDRAAK, RIKARD (1842–66)    Norwegian composer. He was a cousin of Bjørnson and his setting of Bjørnson's poem 'Ja, vi elsker dette Landet' has become the Norwegian national anthem. He was originally intended by his family to be a businessman, but he studied music instead, first in Copenhagen and later in Berlin. His studies in Germany, however, lasted only six months, before he returned to study piano and composition in Christiania. He was greatly influenced by Ole Bull's attitude to folk music and was very enthusiastic about all things Norwegian. He met Grieg in Copenhagen in 1864 and was involved with him in setting up Euterpe, their society dedicated to performing contemporary Scandinavian music. Nordraak composed mainly songs and piano music, the style mostly simple, but with a certain refinement. His sixteen songs are all strophic, with supportive piano accompaniments which frequently double the vocal line, although – like Grieg – he used the postlude to some effect. He is considered by Nils Grinde to be 'the only one of Grieg's contemporaries to remain quite independent of

Grieg's style'. Nordraak also wrote some music for male voice choir, and incidental music to Bjørnson's plays *Sigurd Slembe* and *Maria Stuart i Skotland*. He died in Berlin from tuberculosis.

PREETZMAN, CASPARA (1792–1876)  Danish painter, who was a nun at the convent of Gisselfeld. Her paintings include religious works and copies of the Italian masters, none of them particularly noteworthy. She translated English and American verse into Danish and also wrote her own poetry under the pseudonym 'Caralis'. Grieg set her poem *Dig elsker jeg!* (You I love!) in 1865.

RAVNKILDE, NIELS C.T. (1823–90)  Danish piano teacher and composer. He later lived in Rome and was president of the Scandinavian Society there. He was also one of Grieg's closest friends while he was in Rome.

RICHARDT, CHRISTIAN (1831–92)  Danish poet, who eventually became a priest. His first book of poems was published in 1860 and shows a great range of styles. His travels to Rome, Greece and Palestine resulted in the travel book *Det hellige Land* (The Holy Land) in 1870. He was a life-long friend of Georg Brandes, who encouraged Richardt in his writing. Several of his poems were set to music and he also wrote the libretto for Heise's *Drot og Marsk* (King and Marshal) of 1878. He was chairman of the student choral society in Copenhagen.

ROLFSEN, NORDAHL (1848–1928)  Norwegian educationist, writer and publisher, born in Bergen. His educational books were known for many years throughout Norway and his selection of poetry (some original) for a school reading-book provided the texts for Grieg's *Barnlige Sange*, op.61. He also translated a number of poems by German writers into Norwegian.

RÖNTGEN, JULIUS (1855–1932)  Dutch pianist, violinist and composer, born in Leipzig. He became a professor of violin at Leipzig Conservatory and leader of the Gewandhaus orchestra before eventually settling in Amsterdam, where he became director of the Conservatory. He was one of Grieg's greatest friends and published a biography of the composer in 1930 and a collection of his own letters to Grieg in 1934.

SCHIØTT, INGOLF (1851–1922)  Norwegian singer, choirmaster and the cathedral organist in Bergen. Grieg regarded him very highly as a choral conductor, and he directed the choir and sang the solo in the performance of *Den store hvide Flok* op.30 no.10, at Grieg's funeral. He was also the dedicatee of the Paulsen songs, op.58.

SCHJELDERUP, GERHARD (1859–1933)  Norwegian musicologist and composer, born in Kristiansand and brought up in Bergen. He originally studied humanities, then cello and composition in Paris. Between 1889 and 1916 he settled in Germany. His compositions include symphonies and other orchestral works, incidental music and songs, but he is especially remembered for his ten operas and the symphonic poem *Brand*, after Ibsen's play. He wrote a biography of Wagner and, with O.M. Sandvik, a history of Norwegian music, published in 1921. He was Grieg's first Norwegian biographer.

SIMONSEN, NIELS JUEL (1846–1906)   Danish operatic baritone who gave many performances of Grieg's songs, in particular of *Den Bergtekne*. He was also the dedicatee of the Benzon settings, op.70.

SINDING, CHRISTIAN (1856–1941)   Norwegian composer, violinist and pianist, who came from a very artistic family, one brother being an artist, another a sculptor. He was a pupil of L.M. Lindeman and later studied in Leipzig and Munich. He is often regarded as Grieg's 'heir' in Norwegian musical history, but Sinding was more successful in the larger forms. He lived for long periods in Germany, which caused him to be much maligned during the German occupation of Norway in the Second World War. He wrote four symphonies, concertos for violin and for piano, and other orchestral works, besides piano pieces (including the famous *Rustle of Spring*), chamber music and some 250 songs to Norwegian, Danish and German texts.

STEENBERG, JULIUS (1830–1911)   Danish concert and opera singer, who made his début at the Royal Opera in Copenhagen in 1856, and remained with the company, singing lyrical tenor and high baritone roles until 1888. Grieg met him in Copenhagen in the 1860s. He had a very high regard for Steenberg's artistry and wrote him a testimonial in which he described him as 'a song-poet and a poetical singer by the grace of God'. In 1891, at the composer's request, Steenberg prepared an account of Nina's singing for inclusion in a German biography of Grieg.

SVENDSEN, JOHAN SEVERIN (1840–1911)   Norwegian violinist and composer. He had his first lessons from his father, a military musician, and studied violin, although even as a child he had begun to compose. He later studied in Leipzig, where he was accepted as a student on the strength of his *Caprice* for violin and orchestra. Although he married an American in New York, he returned to Scandinavia and also travelled to Italy, France and England. He finally settled, as a conductor, in Copenhagen where he died. His compositions are mostly for orchestra, including two symphonies, concertos for violin and for cello, and the well-known *Rhapsodies*, based on tunes from Lindeman's collections, and he also wrote some songs and chamber music. Certain nationalist characteristics are apparent in his music, for example in the *Norwegian Artists' Carnival* and the *Four Norwegian Rhapsodies*.

SÆVERUD, HARALD (b. 1897)   Norwegian composer, acknowledged as one of the greatest of the twentieth century. He studied at the conservatory in Bergen and later in Berlin, but is also influenced by folk music, especially that for the Hardanger fiddle. He was prolific from an early age – his first symphony was performed in Oslo in 1920 – and his works now include nine symphonies, concertos, chamber music, songs and piano pieces. The new incidental music to *Peer Gynt*, which Sæverud wrote in 1948, has become popular in its concert form of twelve orchestral pieces. He is an admirer of Grieg's music, but considers Nordraak to be the greater influence on his own.

SÖDERMAN, JOHAN AUGUST (1832–76)   Swedish composer, who studied at the Stockholm Conservatory. He was coeditor, with Grieg and Hornemann, of the *Nordiske Musikblade* (Scandinavian Music Paper). He wrote mostly stage music, including incidental music to *Peer Gynt* BEFORE Grieg, although this has been lost and has apparently never been performed with the play. Writing and arranging theatre music became his main occupation and his use of elements of Swedish folk music, for example in *Ett Bondbröllop* (A country wedding), has been a considerable influence on later composers.

TØNSBERG, NILS CHRISTIAN (1813–97)   Norwegian publisher born in Bergen. His childhood was impoverished and he had to fit in an education in the early mornings and evenings while he earned a living during the day. After his marriage he moved to Christiania, where he worked and furthered his education, finally graduating in law in 1845. He set up as a publisher and his list included some of the greatest books of the day; for example, Wergeland's *Samlede skrifter* (Collected Writings), P.A. Munch's *Det norske folks historie* (A History of the Norwegian People) and Landstad's *Norske folkevise* (Norwegian Folk-songs). He also published the famous pictorial book *Norske nationaldragter* (Norwegian National Costumes). In spite of all this and state loans, he went bankrupt, and in 1861 became a customs officer. He was also consul and consul-general for a number of small states, including Bavaria, Rumania and Liberia. After his retirement he took up publishing again on a small scale and produced several works, including the first travel book on Norway, in two editions in 1874 and 1879. Grieg set Johan Bøgh's eulogy on Tønsberg on the occasion of his sixtieth birthday.

WELHAVEN, JOHAN SEBASTIAN (1807–73)   Norwegian poet born in Bergen. He went to Paris in 1836 and lectured there in philosophy from 1840. His poetry is somewhat melancholy, but always elegantly written, with a serious religious element coming into his later verse. His cosmopolitan style angered Wergeland, who wanted a more authentic Norwegian aspect, while the latter's more slapdash style irritated the scholarly Welhaven, who denounced his contemporary in a long dissertation in 1832.

WERGELAND, HENRIK (1808–45)   Norwegian playwright and poet. He was born in Kristiansand and educated in Christiania, where he graduated in theology. He considered his writing to be a call from God and that the writer should be both prophet and guide, living among the people and, through his work, entering into their daily toil. He tried to improve popular education, and founded public libraries and wrote textbooks. He wanted to sever all links, cultural and business, with Denmark, and had an almost life-long conflict of ideals with his contemporary Welhaven.

WINDING, AUGUST HENRIK (1835–99)   Danish composer and pianist. He was a friend of Grieg's from his time in Copenhagen in the 1860s, and accompanied Grieg to Italy in 1869. He studied with Gade and became a professor at Copenhagen Conservatory in 1867 and its director from 1891 until his death. His compositions include a symphony, a piano concerto, two violin sonatas and many piano pieces.

WINTER-HJELM, OTTO (1837–1931)   Norwegian composer and teacher, born in Christiania. He first studied theology before music, then became a pupil of Kjerulf and later a student at Leipzig Conservatory. He had great success as a private teacher and wrote many teaching manuals. In his later years he taught singing at Christiania cathedral school. However, his first attempt to start his own music school in 1864 lasted barely two years, and his later attempt with Grieg was not successful either. He was conductor of the Philharmonic Society in Christiania, and in 1861 became the first Norwegian composer to write a symphony.

WINTHER, CHRISTIAN (1796–1876)   Danish writer. The two principal motifs in his work are nature and love and these are often, directly or indirectly, interwoven. The inspiration of love can be seen in three separate ways, which correspond to particular periods in his life: the many loves of his youth; the cynicism of the early 1830s caused by a personal crisis, together with his meeting with Byron in Italy; and finally his great passion for Julie Werlin, whom he first met in 1836 and eventually married, after her divorce, in 1848. He spent a good many of his later years abroad and died in Paris. Unfortunately, Grieg set none of his better verse, only four trifles as op. 10.

# Appendix D: Norwegian Folk-song: Musical Forms and Instruments

## 1. Musical Forms

*Folkeviser*

The term *folkevise* (folk-song) is a very general one. Nils Grinde is of the opinion that *folkeviser* – in the widely accepted sense of ballads rooted in the Middle Ages – came to Norway from England during the twelfth and thirteenth centuries, together with the *kjededans* (chain dance), and that the form became popular in a very short time.[1] The *folkevise* was first taken up as a fashionable trend among the nobility, but soon spread to all classes of society. In spite of the apparent borrowing from England, with the translation and rewriting which that borrowing implies, the melodies known today seem typically Norwegian in style, and the same song may be sung to different melodies in various regions of the country.

The songs are divided according to their subject-matter: *kjempeviser* concern giants; *trollviser* – also called *tryllviser* – concern trolls and witchcraft; *heilagviser* are sacred songs and *historiske viser* are historical tales; *ridderviser*, tales of knights and courtly love, and *skjempeviser*, jesting or mocking songs. There is, however, no similar division in the types of melody, although there are two different verse constructions which affect the melodies: a four-lined stanza, with the same rhyme-scheme as the *gammelstev* (see below), and a two-lined stanza.

The four-lined stanza also has an *omkved* (refrain), often divided into two parts, with the *innstev* (inner verse) or *mellomsleng* (middle refrain) coming between the first and second lines, and the *endestev* (end verse) or *ettersleng* (after refrain) after the second line. The two-lined stanza form has the whole *omkved* at the end of the second line. These single and double refrains are often found in Scottish ballads and Negro spirituals, while in English folk-song it is more usual to find the whole refrain at the end of the stanza or, where it is split, after the second and fourth lines, rather that after the first and second.

The *heilagviser* were always to Catholic texts, while the *religiøse folketoner* (religious folk-tunes) were to Protestant texts. (The *folketoner* are not folk music at all in the pure sense, for the texts are usually by named poets and the melodies a remodelling of others, and so best described as 'traditional'). These religious songs concern the lives of saints and Biblical stories, or are moral tales, in which innocence triumphs and evil is punished.

W.J. Entwistle, in *European Balladry*, says that 'the rise of the *viser* corresponds with the fundamental change in prosody from alliteration [so frequently encountered in Old Norse poetry] to assonance, and this change must have taken place during the twelfth century. But much of the older alliterative poetry continued to be heard, and with such frequency and acceptance that it has been transformed into *viser*.'[2] Some of the same subject-matter of heroes and supernatural figures continues from historical to modern times and Entwistle goes on: 'In Norway particularly, where the conditions of life are peculiarly forbidding, ballads of malicious trolls and kobolds are so numerous as to constitute a distinguishing mark of the region.'[3] The older tales of gods were superseded by the spine-chilling accounts of natural dangers and horrors, for example the sea swallowing up ships and sailors. Even the Christian faith was not enough to dispel the fear of trolls and dragons, elves and mermaids, and an atmosphere of mystery is frequently conveyed with great skill. The wooden stave-churches, which date from the eleventh century, also show a fascinating blend of the Christian and the pagan, decorated as they are with both crosses and dragons' heads, as if the worshippers wanted to make absolutely sure of their protection from ill, whatever its source.

There is everywhere in the *viser* a singular earnestness; even the *skjempeviser* are not totally lighthearted. As Entwistle sums it up, 'the graver emotions are exploited with ingenious mastery: love as strong as death, jealousy, death, treachery and the formless, viewless horror of an evil world ever beside man's elbow.'[4] It is easy to see the continuation of the tradition into more modern literary works, such as Ibsen's *Peer Gynt* and Garborg's *Haugtussa*.

*Stev*

The *stev* (verse) is a traditional, four-lined verse-form found in folk poetry in Norway and is found in two related types: the old form, *gammelstev*, and the new, *nystev*. In the *gammelstev*, the fourth line of the stanza rhymes with the second, and each of these lines has three stresses, while the first and third lines have four stresses each. In the *nystev*, each line has four stresses and the stanza is rhymed in couplets; the second couplet, both textually and melodically, forms a parallel with the first, and the music is frequently characterised by a three-note anacrusis. In both forms, the number of unstressed syllables in each line may be varied. Grieg often referred to *Den*

*Bergtekne* (The mountain thrall), op.32, as a 'stev' and the poem is written in the *gammelstev* form. There are many examples of the *nystev* form in his settings, that form being frequently used by writers trying to evoke an 'old world' atmosphere.

Contests in improvising *stev*, called *stevjast*, were popular in former times, but the practice has now died out. The traditional *stev* were employed, suitably 'modified' to suit the current circumstances, but unfortunately these modifications often became vulgar, maligning local personalities.

### Lokk

*Lokk* is the general term for the calls used to gather animals, whether on the homestead or up on the *seter*. Nils Grinde is of the opinion that the 'tonal and melodic features of many of the old *lokker* confirm that they belong to the oldest [Norwegian] folk music tradition'.[5] The *lokk* has no clearly defined form, but is built up from short motifs which are improvised upon by the herdsman, the complexity of the improvisation being totally dependent on the proficiency of the individual. The short motifs used to build up the melody of *Lok*, the third of Grieg's *Barnlige Sange* (Children's Songs), op.61, may be cited as an example of the simplest form. More complex is the use of motifs in *Ku-lokk*, one of the extra songs from Garborg's *Haugtussa*, where the vocal range, wide intervals, melodic development and resultant haunting quality are most memorable. O.M. Sandvik, in his book on the Østerdal region quoted by Nils Grinde, described a form of *ku-lokk* he heard, where a *seter*-girl called her different animals by name.[6] A similar idea was reflected by Garborg and Grieg in *Killingdans* (Kids' dance) from *Haugtussa*. Sandvik also wondered whether some motifs could be considered to be attempts to imitate the animals' own 'language'.[7]

The *huving* (otherwise *hujing* or *hauking*) and the *laling* (or *liljing*) were forms of *lokker* used for calling people, herdsman to herdsman for example. The *huving* was often a particular snatch of melody that would identify a specific person, while in some areas the *laling* was also used antiphonally in a kind of musical conversation.

### 2.  Instruments

### Lur

The *lur* is almost certainly the oldest Scandinavian instrument. It has been depicted in carvings dating back to 1000 BC and the bronze examples found in excavations in Norway and Denmark date back to the second century BC. Apparently always made in pairs, *lurer* are assumed originally to have been fashioned from the tusks of mammoths, although other forms existed using other animals, for example goats' horns. There was also a long version, something akin to the Alpine horn, wound around with birch-bark, which is referred to in the sagas. Interestingly, the cup-shaped mouthpieces of the *lur*, which are a composite part of the instrument, are very like those used with modern brass instruments. The three-quarter intervals given by the *lur* had a good deal of influence on other folk instruments and the music they produced.

### Hardingfele

The *hardingfele* or Hardanger fiddle is still today the chief instrument used in Norwegian folk music and is thought to have developed into its present form some time between the mid-sixteenth and mid-seventeenth centuries. Smaller than the orchestral violin, the instruments are, like the *langeleik*, frequently highly decorated, with painting on the wood and inlaid mother-of-pearl on the fingerboard. The drone element is present in the four sympathetic strings, which run under the bridge beneath the four upper strings which are played normally. The upper strings may be tuned to a variety of *stille* or note-series, the most usual being A,-D-A-E'; that is, similar to normal violin tuning, except for the bottom string, which is a tone higher. The sympathetic strings are usually tuned to the tonic, supertonic, mediant and dominant of the major chord being used, a series which, as has often been pointed out, comprises the notes – backwards and forwards – of the opening phrase of *Morgenstemning* (Morning mood) from Grieg's *Peer Gynt* music.

The bridge on a Hardanger fiddle is higher than that on a violin, in order to accommodate the sympathetic strings, but is at the same time less curved, making double- and triple-stopping easier to accomplish. It may be this feature that led Ole Bull to adapt his violin bridge to accommodate his own predilection for multiple-stopping.

### Notes

1   Nils Grinde: *Norsk Musikkhistorie*, 1971, p.75.
2   W.J. Entwistle: *European Balladry*, 1939, p.210.
3   Ibid., p.211.
4   Ibid., p.226.
5   Grinde: *Norsk Musikkhistorie*, p.72.
6   Ibid.
7   Ibid.

# Select Bibliography

## A. Books and Articles

ABRAHAM, GERALD (ed.): *Grieg. A Symposium*, Lindsay Drummond, London 1948; reissued Oxford University Press 1952

ALANDER, BO (trans. P. Britten Austin): *Swedish Music*, Swedish Institute, London 1956

ALEXANDER, MICHAEL (trans.): *Beowulf*, Penguin Books, Harmondsworth, 1973

BENESTAD, FINN and SCHJELDERUP-EBBE, DAG: *Edvard Grieg, mennesket og kunstneren*, Aschehoug, Oslo 1980

BERGEN PUBLIC LIBRARY: *Catalogue of Grieg Exhibition, 19th–30th September 1962*, Bergen 1962

—— *Catalog over manuskripter*, Bergen 1986; revised 1987

BEYER, EDVARD: *Utsyn over norsk litteratur*, J.W. Cappelen, Oslo 1971

—— (Trans. Marie Wells): *Ibsen: The man and his work*, Souvenir Press, London 1978

BEYER, MARIE (ed.): *Breve fra Edvard Grieg til Frants Beyer 1872–1907*, Steenske forlag Christiania 1923

BREDSDORFF, ELIAS: *Hans Christian Andersen*, Readers' Union, Newton Abbot 1975

BÆKKELUND, KJELL (ed.): *Norske komponister*, Tiden Norsk forlag, Oslo 1977

CARLEY, LIONEL (ed.): *Delius, A Life in Letters* (Volume I), Scolar Press, 1983

DAHL, WILLY: *Bjørnson* (series: *Norske forfatter i nærlys*), Aschehoug, Oslo 1977

—— *Ibsen* (series: *Norske forfatter i nærlys*), Aschehoug, Oslo 1974

DJUPEDAL, REIDAR: Notes to *Vinje: Dikt*, Noregs boklag, Oslo 1974

DOWNS, B.W.: *Modern Norwegian Literature, 1860–1918*, Cambridge University Press 1966

ENTWISTLE, W.J.: *European Balladry*, Oxford University Press 1939; revised 1951

FIEDLER, H.G.: *Das Oxforder Buch deutscher Dichtung*, Oxford University Press 1915

FOG, DAN: *Edvard Grieg – Værk fortegnelse*, typescript 1966, Oslo University Music Library and Bergen Public Library

GARRETT, F.E.: *Lyrics and Poems from Ibsen*, J.M. Dent and Sons, London 1912

GAUKSTAD, ØYSTEIN (ed.): *Edvard Grieg: Artikler og taler*, Gyldendal Norsk forlag, Oslo 1957

GORDON, E.V. (Revised by A.R. Taylor): *Introduction to Old Norse*, Oxford University Press 1981

GRINDE, NILS: *Norsk musikkhistorie*, Universitetsforlag, Oslo 1971; revised 1975

HOLLAND, A.K.: *The Songs of Delius* (series: *The Musical Pilgrim*), Oxford University Press 1951

HORTON, JOHN: *Scandinavian Music, A Short History*, Faber & Faber 1963

—— *Grieg* (series: *The Master Musicians*), J.M. Dent and Sons, London 1974

—— *Grieg* (as above; Norwegian edition, expanded), Dreyer, Oslo 1978

JOHANSEN, DAVID MONRAD: *Edvard Grieg*, Gyldendal Norsk forlag, Oslo 1934

JORDAN, SVERRE: *Edvard Grieg: Et oversikt over hans liv og verker*, Grieg Fund, Bergen 1954

KLEM, LONE and NIELSEN, ERLING: *Navne i dansk litteratur*, Gyldendal, Oslo 1974

KORTSEN, BJARNE (ed.): *Griegs brev til Frants Beyer*, Kortsen, Bergen 1973

LANGE, KRISTIAN: *Norwegian Music, A Survey*, Tanum forlag, Oslo 1971

LERVIK, ÅSE HIORTH: *Elementær Verslære*, Universitetsforlag, Oslo 1972

MEYER, MICHAEL: *Ibsen*, Pelican Books, Harmondsworth, 1974

MYHRE, REIDAR: *Oversikt over norsk litteratur*, Lutherstiflesen, Oslo 1969

ROBERTSON, J.G. (ed. Dorothy Reich): *A History of German Literature* (6th edition), W. Blackwood, Edinburgh 1970

SCHJELDERUP-EBBE, DAG: *A Study of Grieg's Harmony*, University Press, Oslo 1953
────── *Edvard Grieg: 1858–1867*, Universitetsforlag, Oslo 1964; English translation, Allen & Unwin, London 1964

STØVERUD, TORBJØRN: *Milestones of Norwegian Literature*, Tanum forlag, Oslo 1971

SVENDSEN, ARNE RUNAR: *Edvard Griegs Vinjesanger*, unpublished thesis (no.3674), Oslo University Library, 1971

SVENSEN, ÅSFUD: Notes to *Garborg: Haugtussa*, Aschehoug, Oslo 1974

TIME, SVEINUNG: *Garborg* (series: *Norske forfatter i nærlys*), Aschehoug, Oslo 1979

TORSTEINSON, SIGMUND: *Med troll i tankene*, Gyldendal Norsk forlag, Oslo 1985

VOLDEN, TORSTEIN: *Studier i Edvard Griegs Haugtussa-sanger*, unpublished thesis (no.2831), Oslo University Library, 1967

ZSCHINSKY-TROXLER, ELSA VON (ed.): *Briefe an die Verleger der Edition Peters 1866–1907* Peters, Leipzig 1932

## B. Editions of Songs Cited

*Edvard Grieg. Romanser og Sanger*
Vol. 1:    Opp.4, 5, 9, 10 and 15
Vol. 2:    Opp.18 and 21
Vol. 3:    Opp.23, 25, 26, *Odalisken synger* and *Princessen*
Vol. 4:    Opp.33 and 39
Vol. 5:    Opp.44 and 48
Vol. 6:    Opp.49 and 58
Vol. 7:    Opp.59 and 60
Vol. 8:    Op.67
Vol. 9:    Opp.69 and 70
Vol. 10:   Efterladte Sange
Norsk Musikkforlag A/S, Oslo (Edition Wilhelm Hansen)

*Den Bergtekne*, op.32
Wilhelm Hansen, Copenhagen 1882

*Edvard Grieg. 20 Selected Songs* (with English versions by R.H. Elkin)
Op.5; op.9 nos 2 and 3; op.15 nos 1, 2 and 4; op.18 nos 1, 2, 7 and 8; op.21 no. 2; op.23 nos 18 and 23 (actually designated nos 1 and 2); op.33 nos 2, 6, 7 and 9
Enoch & Sons (Edwin Ashdown), London 1901

*Edvard Grieg. 18 Selected Songs* (With English versions by R.H. Elkin)
Op.9 nos 1 and 4: op.10 no.1; op.15 no.3; op.18 nos 3, 4 and 6; op.21 nos 1, 3 and 4; op.33 nos 1, 3, 4, 5, 8, 10, 11 and 12
Enoch & Sons (Edwin Ashdown), London

*Grieg Album of Twenty-Three Songs* (with English translations by Th. Marzials and Mrs. J.P. Morgan)
Opp.5, 9, 15, 18 nos 1–4 and 6–8; op.21
Pitt & Hatzfeld, London 1888

*Grieg Album, Volume 2* (with English translations by Marzials and Morgan)
Op.23 nos 18 and 23; op.33; op.44
Pitt & Hatzfeld, London 1888

*16 Songs . . . by Edvard Grieg* (with English words by Lady Macfarren)
Opp.58, 59 and 60
Augener, London 1894

*Seven Children's Songs . . . by Edvard Grieg*, op.61 (with English versions by Lady Macfarren)
Augener, London 1894

*Reminiscences of Mountain and Fiord*, op.44 (with English versions by R.H. Elkin)
Enoch & Sons (Edwin Ashdown), London 1906

*Grieg-Album*
Vol.1:   Op.9 nos 2,3 and 4; op.15 no.1; op.18 nos 2, 3 and 8; op.21 nos 2, 3 and 4; Die Prinzessin; Die Odalisken
Vol.2:   Op.4 nos 2–5; op.5 nos 2 and 3; op.15 nos 2 and 4; op.18 nos 1, 4 and 6; op.21 no.1
Vol.3   Op.5 nos 1 and 4; op.23 no.8[17]; op.25 nos 1–5; op.26 nos 1, 2, 4 and 5
Vol.4:   Op.33 nos 1–12
Vol.5:   Op.4 nos 1 and 6; op.9 no.1; op.15 no.3; op.18 nos 5 and 7; op.23 no.9[18]; op.39 nos 1, 2, 4, 5 and 6
C.F. Peters, Leipzig 1911–12

*Grieg Gesamt-Ausgabe: Edvard Grieg Samlede Verker* (Collected Works)
Vol.14:   Opp.2–49
Vol.15:   Opp.58–70 and songs without opus numbers
Edition Peters, Frankfurt ?1990

*I love you*, op.5 no.3
*Solveig's Song*, op.23 no.18
*A Swan*, op.25 no.2          (with English translations by Astra Desmond)
*The Spring*, op.33 no.2
*A Dream*, op.48 no.6
Augener, London 1961

# Discography

This discography represents the author's attempt to list all commercial recordings, though recent reissues and remasterings are not exhaustively covered. A number of the recordings listed have not been distributed outside Scandinavia.

Grieg's oeuvre is listed in order of opus number, works without opus numbers at the end; any complete recordings of an opus are listed first. Singers are listed alphabetically within each opus number. The list comprises recordings for solo voice with piano, instrumental or orchestral accompaniment, but does not include choral arrangements of solo songs. The language being sung, where it differs from the language of the song's title, is indicated where known, as is the year of issue of the recording. All records listed are 33⅓rpm Stereo LP, unless otherwise indicated.

*Abbreviations*: (m) – mono; (78) – 78 rpm; (45) – 45 rpm; (ss) – single side; (d) – digital recording; (CD) – compact disc; (R) – Reissue or remastering of older recording, broadcasts, compilations etc.

OP.2.   VIER LIEDER FÜR ALTSTIMME
(1. *Die Müllerin*; 2. *Eingehüllt in grauen Wolken*; 3. *Ich stand in dunkeln Träumen*; 4. *Was soll ich sagen?*)

| | |
|---|---|
| 2,3 | Dietrich Fischer-Dieskau (Bar), Hartmut Höll   EMI EL 067 27 0219 (d) (1985) |
| 2 | Tuula Nienstedt (A), Uwe Wegner   Acanta/Aristocrate EA 22 437 |

OP.4.   SEKS DIGTE
(1. *Die Waise*; 2. *Morgenthau*; 3. *Abschied*; 4. *Jägerlied*; 5. *Das alte Lied*; 6. *Wo sind sie hin?*)

| | |
|---|---|
| 2–6 | Dietrich Fischer-Dieskau (Bar), Hartmut Höll   EMI EL 067 27 0219 (d) (1985) |
| 2–4, 6 | Dietrich Fischer-Dieskau (Bar), Aribert Reimann   EMI 1C 065 02 673 |
| 2,5 | Tuula Nienstedt (A), Uwe Wegner   Acanta/Aristocrate EA 22 437 |

302

| | |
|---|---|
| 2 | Aulikki Rautawaara (S), Michael Raucheisen   Acanta 40 23 559 (1986R) |
| 4 | Willi Domgraf-Fassbaender (Bar), Michael Raucheisen Acanta DE22 695/Acanta 40 23 559 (1986R) |
| 5 | Feodor Chaliapin (B), Max Rubinowitsch   EMI 1C 147 486/ 7M (m) |

## OP.5. 'HJERTETS MELODIER'

(1. *To brune Øine*; 2. *En Digters Bryst*; 3. *Jeg elsker dig*; 4. *Min Tanke er et mægtigt Fjeld*)

| | |
|---|---|
| 1–4 | Olav Eriksen (Bar), Einar Steen-Nøkleberg   Lu-Mi LU 40 10 48 |
| 1,3 | Aksel Schiøtz (T), Folmer Jensen   HMV X 6924 (78); HMV X 7203 (78) |
| | Anita Soldh (S), Arnold Östman   Caprice 1114 |
| 2,4 | Dietrich Fischer-Dieskau (Bar), Hartmut Höll [in German] EMI EL 067 27 0219 (d) (1985) |
| 1 | Anne Bolstad (S), Audun Kayser   EMI TROLD 01 (1981) |
| | Edi Laider (Bar), Ole Willumsen   HMV OCS 1006 (78) |
| | Thor Mandahl (–), –   Gramophone GC 82 684 (78) |
| | Helge Rosvænge (T), Michael Raucheisen [in German] Acanta BB 22 505 (m)/Acanta 40 23 559 (1986R) |
| | Lillemari Østvig (S), Erik Werba   DGG 30 201 EPL (45) |
| 3 | Elly Ameling (S), Dalton Baldwin   HMV ASD 2902 (m) |
| | Victoria de los Angeles (S), LSO/de Burgos   HMV ASD 651 (m); Angel SCB 3728–83 |
| | Rolf Bjørling (T), Jan Eyron   HMV EBS 26 (45) |
| | W. Booth (T), Gerald Moore   HMV B 9497 (78) |
| | Kim Borg (B), Robert Levin   DGG EPL 30 571 (45) |
| | Karin Branzell (A), –   Lebend. Vergangenheit LV 182 |
| | Richard Crooks (T), [orch.] [in English]   HMV DA 1394 (78) (1935) |
| | Anton Dermota (T), Ivor Newton [in German]   Decca M 620 (78) (ca. 1946) |
| | Astra Desmond (A), Gerald Moore   Decca K 962 (78) |
| | Helena Döse (S), Thomas Schuback   Electra SLT 33 247 |
| | Ranveig Eckhoff (S), ensemble/Kruse   Aurora AR 1900 (1985) |
| | Olav Eriksen (Bar), Audun Kayser   EMI TROLD 02 (1982) |
| | Kirsten Flagstad (S), Edwin McArthur   HMV OCS 390-91 (78); HMV DA 1520 (78) (1936)/DACO 168 (R); Decca LXT 5264 (m) (1957); Victor 1804AB; Decca ECS 622 (1971R) |

Kirsten Flagstad (S), Edwin McArthur [in German]    HMV
    DA 1505 (78) (1936)
    Kirsten Flagstad (S), BBC SO/Sargent    Rococo 3 RR 5380
    (m)
Porla Frijsch (S), –    HMV 32 3556–57 (m)
Nicolai Gedda (T), –    HMV ASD 2574
Per Grønneberg (–), Robert Levin    HMV AL 3026 (78)
Ingrid Günther (A), Rhein SO/Günther    Garnet 40 101
Svanhild Helland Hansen (S), Arne Dørumsgaard    HMV AL
    2980 (78)
Caroline Kaart (–), Cor Lemaire    Parlophone PM DH 1201
    (78)
Adalbert Kraus (T), Roland Keller    Carus 63 103
Mario Lanza (T), –    RCA ERA 9770 (45); RCA 2648 069
    DP (m)
Marjorie Lawrence (S), Ivor Newton    Decca DR 10434–5
    (78)
D. Lloyd (T), Gerald Moore    Columbia DB 2131 (78)
Aase Nordmo Løvberg (S), Robert Levin    Odeon PASK 2002
Kari Løvaas (S), Justus Frantz    Ariola 200 155–366
Otakar Marak (T), [pf] [in Czech]    HMV AM 266 (78)
    (1926)
Kenneth McKellar (T), Denis Woolford [in German]    Decca
    SKL 4663
Lauritz Melchior (T), –    HMV B 9446 (78)
Lauritz Melchior (T), Ignaz Strasfogel    Victor 1882 (78)
Melitta Muszely (S), Günther Weissenborn    Europa E 325
Tuula Nienstedt (A), Uwe Wegner    Acanta/Aristocrate EA
    22 437
Birgit Nilsson (S), Leo Taubman    RCA LSC 2578 B; RCA SB
    6543
Birgit Nilson (S), Lars Roos    Bluebell BEL 109
Ruggiero Orofino (T), Dresden PO/Masur    Fontana 6747
    114; Fontana 6736 008; Fontana K 71 BC 801; Fontana
    6545 016
Hermann Prey (Bar), Herbert Heinemann    Columbia SMC
    80 941
Hermann Prey (Bar), Leonard Håkonson    Denon CD 1254
    (CD)
Eva Prytz (S), Ivar Johnsen RCA LPNA 4 (78)
Marie Rappold (S), [orch]    Edison 4890 4944 (78)
Aulikki Rautawaara (S), Michael Raucheisen [in German]
    Acanta 40 23 559 (1986R)

Anneliese Rothenberger (S), Günther Weissenborn    EMI 1C
065 28 979
Karl Schmitt-Walter (Bar), Franz Rupp    Telefunken A 2040
Rudolf Schock (T), Berlin SO/ —    Ariola 0 27 223 U; Ariola I
86 86411
Peter Schreier (T), Berlin SO/Hanell    DGG 2536 292;
Polydor 2562 039
Elisabeth Schwarzkopf (S), Gerald Moore    Columbia SAX
2265
Elisabeth Schwarzkopf (S), Geoffrey Parsons    HMV ASD
2634
Frank Sinatra, —    Columbia DB 2346 (78)
Anita Soldh (S), Columbia SO/Kostelanetz    CBS 30 004;
CBS 61 955
Grete Stückgold (S) [orch.]    Lebend. Vergaugenheit LV 188
Elisabeth Söderström (S), Martin Isepp    Bluebell BEL 111
Elisabeth Söderström (S), New Philh./Davis    CBS 76 527;
US Columbia M 34 531; CBS DC 40 143
Richard Tauber (T), [orch.]    Parlophone RO 20 191 (78);
Odeon 0 4532 (78); US Decca 20 251 (78)
Edith Thallaug (MS), Oslo PO/Jansons    Philips 411 315–1
(1983)

4.          Knut Skram (Bar), Eva Knardahl    Bis LP 49 (1976)


OP.9.    ROMANSER OG BALLADER
(1. *Harpen*; 2. *Vuggesang*; 3. *Solnedgang*; 4. *Udfarten*)
2          B. Martin (S), [ens.]    US Columbia 50 030 (78); US Columbia 35 612 (78)
4          Willi Domgraf-Fassbaender (Bar), Michael Raucheisen [in
German]    Acanta 40 23 559 (1986R)
Aksel Schiøtz (T), [pf.]    HMV Z 279 (78)


OP.10.    FIRE ROMANSER
(1. *Taksigelse*; 2. *Skovsang*; 3. *Blomsternes tale*; 4. *Sang på Fjeldet*) —


OP.15    ROMANSER
(1. *Margretes Vuggesang*; 2. *Kjærlighed*; 3. *Langelandsk folkemelodi*; 4. *Modersorg*)
2,4        Marianne Hirsti (S), Audun Kayser    VNP 0085186 (1985)
1          Kari Løvaas (S), Justus Frantz    Ariola 200 155–366
2          Astra Desmond (A), Gerald Moore    Decca K 962 (78)
4          Kirsten Flagstad (S), —    Harvest H1004 (78) (1929); Legendary Recordings LR120–3 (R from Scandinavian HMV of
1929)

Borghild Langaard (S), [orch.]    Pathé N 1003 (78)
Aulikki Rautawaara (S), Michael Raucheisen [in German]
Acanta 40 23 559 (1986R)

OP. 18.    ROMANSER OG SANGE
(1. *Vandring i Skoven*; 2. *Hun er saa hvid*; 3. *En Digters sidste Sang*; 4.
*Efteraarsstormen*; 5. *Poesien*; 6. *Ungbirken*; 7. *Hytten*; 8. *Rosenknoppen*; 9.
*Serenade til Welhaven*)

| | |
|---|---|
| 2,3 | Dietrich Fischer-Dieskau (Bar), Hartmut Höll [in German] EMI EL 067 27 0219 (d) |
| 4,7 | Tuula Nienstedt (A), Uwe Wegner    Acanta/Aristocrate EA 22 437 |
| 1 | Helge Rosvænge (T), Michael Raucheisen    Acanta BB 22 505 (m) Acanta 40 23 559 (1986R) |
| 2 | Aase Nordmo Løvberg (S), –    RCA Program 2869–70 (m) (1955) |
| 3 | Waldemar Johnsen (Bar), –    RCA Program 2869–70 (m) (1955) |
| 4 | Astra Desmond (A), Gerald Moore    Decca M 491 (78) |
| | Kirsten Flagstad (S), Gerald Moore    Seraphim M 60 046 |
| | Kirsten Flagstad (S), LSO/Fjeldstad    Decca SXL 2145; Decca SDD 209 |
| | Margarete Klose (A), Michael Raucheisen [in German] Acanta 40 23 559 (1986R) |
| 5 | Olav Eriksen (Bar), Auden Kayser    EMI TROLD 02 (1982) |
| | Marianne Hirsti (S), Audun Kayser    VNP 0085–86 (1985) |
| 7 | Kirsten Flagstad (S), Edwin McArthur    Decca LXT 5264 (m) (1957); Decca ECS 622 (1971R); Richmond R 23 220 (m) |
| | Randi Helseth (S), Kåre Siem    WOR Program 2671–72 |
| | Herman Iversen (Bar) Kenton Read RCA Program 2747–48 |
| | Aase Nordmo Løvberg (S), Robert Levin    Odeon PASK 2002 |
| | Eva Prytz (S), Ivar Johnsen    RCA LPNA 4 (78); RCA LPNE 54 (78) |
| | Sophie Schönning (S), Boyd Neel Str. O    Decca K 1208 (78) |
| 8 | Eva Prytz (S), –    RCA Program 2959–60 |

OP. 21.    FIRE DIGTE AF 'FISKERJENTEN'
(1. *Det første Møte*; 2. *God Morgen*; 3. *Jeg giver mit Digt til Våren*; 4. *Tak for dit Råd*

| | |
|---|---|
| 1–4 | Kari Løvaas (S), Justus Frantz    Ariola 200 155–366 |
| 1,3 | Kirsten Flagstad (S), Edwin McArthur    Decca LXT 5264 (m) (1957); Decca ECS 622 (1971R); Richmond R 23 220 (m) |
| | Anita Soldh (S), Arnold Östman    Caprice 1114 |

1,4 Helena Döse (S), Thomas Schuback  Electra SLT 33 247
2,4 Ranveig Eckhoff (S), ensemble/Kruse  Aurora AR 1900 (1985)
3,4 Signe Amundsen (S), −  HMV Z 280 (78)
1 Astra Desmond (A), Gerald Moore  Decca K 962 (78)

Kirsten Flagstad (S), BBC SO/Sargent  Rococo 3 RR 5380 (m)

Kari Frisell (S), Kaare Ørnung  RCA Program 3081 (1965)

Asta Jørgensen (−), Willy Johansens trio  Odeon NW 2275 (78)

Aase Nordmo Løvberg (S), Robert Levin  Columbia 33 cx 1409 (m) (1957)

Kaja Eide Norena (S), [orch.]/Coppola  HMV DA 4828 (78)/ HMV 7 EBN 8 (45m)/US Club '99' CL 99−32 (R)

Jon Otnes (T), Edwin McArthur  RCA Program 2787−88

Aulikki Rautawaara (S), Michael Raucheisen [in German] Acanta DE 22 637 (m)/Acanta 40 23 559 (1986R)

Elisabeth Schwarzkopf (S), Geoffrey Parsons [in German] HMV ASD 2844; EMI C 063 02 331

2 Anne Bolstad (S), Audun Kayser  EMI TROLD 01 (1981)
3 Erna Berger (S), Michael Raucheisen [in German]  Acanta 40 23 559 (1986R)

Kirsten Flagstad (S), LSO/Fjeldstad  Decca SXL 2145; Decca SDD 209

Waldemar Johnsen (Bar), Kåre Siem  WOR Program 2654−55

Tuula Nienstedt (A), Uwe Wegner  Acanta/Aristocrate EA 22 437

4 Ritva Auvinen (S), Pentti Koskimies  Finlandia FA 326

Astra Desmond (S), Gerald Moore  Decca M 492 (78)

Dietrich Fischer-Dieskau (Bar), Hartmut Höll [in German] EMI EL 067 27 0219(d) (1985)

Kirsten Flagstad (S), Philh./Braithwaite  HMV DB 21 020 (78); HMV HQM 1057 (m); EMI 1C 147 01 491/2M (m)

## OP.23.  SONGS FROM 'PEER GYNT'

(17. *Peer Gynts Serenade*; 18. *Solveigs Sang*; 23. *Solveigs Vuggevise*)

17 Asbjørn Hansli (Bar), LSO/Dreier  Unicorn RHS 361/2 (1978)

Urban Malmberg (Bar), Gothenburg SO/Järvi  DGG 423 079−2 (1988)

18,23 Elly Ameling (S), San Fran. SO/Waart [in German]  Philips 411 038−2 (CD)

Ingrid Bjoner (S), Berlin PO/Eichhorn  Ariola 41 170 CK (45)

Anne Bolstad (S), Norw.Op.O/Dreier    Polygram NRF 30
055 (1983)
Barbara Bonney (S), Gothenburg SO/Järvi    DGG 423 079–2
(1988)
Toril Carlsen (S), LSO/Dreier    Unicorn RHS 361/62 (1978)
Elisabeth Grümmer (S), Berlin SO/Dietz [in German]    EMI
EX 29 121 03
Kari Løvaas (S), Justus Frantz    Ariola 200 155–366
Lucia Popp (S), Acad. St. Martin's/Marriner [in German]
EMI 1C 067 43 440T (d)
Aulikki Rautawaara (S), Berlin PO/Schmidt-Isserstedt
Telefunken E 1795 (78)
Adele Stolte (S), Leipzig Gewandhaus/Neumann [in German]
Philips Sequenza 6257 086
T. Valjakka (S), Dresden Staatskap./Blomstedt    EMI EG 29
0266–61; HMV ASD 3640

18.    Iselin Alme (S), Norw.Str.Quartet    DB Records DBLP 001
Sheila Armstrong (S), Hallé/Barbirolli    HMV TWO 269
Maria Barrientos (S), – [in Spanish]    EMI 1C 061 91 860 (m);
XAR 492 318961
Erna Berger (S), Berlin Staatsop./ – [in German]    Polydor 47
061B (78) (1934)
Bergljot Bergh (S), [trio]    Odeon NW 897 (78)
Emmy Bettendorf (S), [orch.]    Lebend. Vergangenheit LV
156
Judith Blegen (S), Philadelphia/Ormandy    RCA VL 845 18
Eugenia Burzio (S), Martin Schøyer    Pathé 844 82–83 (78)
April Cantelo (S), RPO/Gibson    Classics for Pleasure HR 41
8125–4
Helen Donath (S), Bamberg SO/Eschenbach [in German]
Ariola Eurodisc 207 047–425
Kirsten Flagstad (S), –    HMV X 1940 (78) (1923)/Legendary
Recordings LR 120–3 (R); Harvest (US) H 1004 (78)
Kari Frisell (S), orch./Bergh    Musica N 810–11 (78)
Rina Gigli (S), ROH orch/Rignold [in Italian]    HMV DB
6931 (78)
Frieda Hempel (S), Conrad v. Bos    Edison 7362. 7738 (78)
Ilse Hollweg (S), RPO/Beecham    HMV SXLP 30 423 (m);
ASD 258 (m)
Borghild Langaard (S), [orch.]    Gramophone GC 83 648 (78)
(1908); EMI RLS 743 (m); HLM 7181–93 (m)
Aase Nordmo Løvberg (S), [orch.]/Levin    HMV AL 3336
(78)

Kaja Eide Norena (S), [orch.] LPML 940–41
Eva Prytz (S), Oslo PO/Grüner-Hegge SK 15 526 (78);
RCA LPNE 69 (78)
Elisabeth Rethberg (S), [orch.] [in German] Brunswick
15069B (78) (193?)
Anneliese Rothenberger (S), Günther Weissenborn EMI 1C
065 28 979
Elisabeth Schumann (S), [orch.] [in German] HMV DA
1544 (78) (1937)
Joan Sutherland (S), New Philh./Bonynge Decca SXL 6619
Elisabeth Söderström (S), New Philh./Davis CBS DC 40
143

23.          Anne Bolstad (S), Audun Kayser EMI TROLD 01 (1981)
Brita Hertzberg (S), [orch.] [in Swedish] HMV X 2506 (78)
(1927 or 1928)
Aulikki Rautawaara (S), Michael Raucheisen [in German]
Acanta 40 23 559 (1986R)

OP.25.  SEX DIGTE AF IBSEN
(1. *Spillemænd*; 2. *En Svane*; 3. *Stambogsrim*; 4. *Med en Vandlilje*; 5. *Borte!*; 6.
*En Fuglevise*)

1–6          Ellen Westberg Andersen (S), Jens Harald Bratlie Simax
PS 1011; PSC 1011 (CD) (1987)
Olav Eriksen (Bar), Einar Steen-Nøkleberg Lu-Mi LU 40
10 48
Marianne Hirsti (S), Audun Kayser VNP 0085–86 (1985)
1–3          Knut Skram (Bar), Robert Levin Philips 6507 001 (1970)
2,4,6        Anne Bolstad (S), Audun Kayser EMI TROLD 01 (1981)
Lillemari Østvig (S), Erik Werba DGG 30 201 EPL (45)
2,3          Feodor Chaliapin (B), Max Rubinowitsch EMI 1C 47 01
486/7 (m)
Ranveig Eckhoff(S), ensemble/Kruse Aurora AR 1900 (1985)
2,4          Helena Döse (S), Thomas Schuback Electra SLT 33 247
3,4          Astra Desmond (A), Gerald Moore Decca K 961 (78)
2            Jussi Bjørling (T), Frederick Schauwecker RCA Victor
EBRP 5225
Rolf Bjørling (T), Jan Eyron HMV EBS 26 (45m)
Anne Bolstad (S), Norw. Op.O/Dreier Polygram NRF 30
055 (1983)
Astra Desmond (A), Gerald Moore Decca M 491 (78)
Kirsten Flagstad (S), Edwin McArthur [in German] Victor
M342-3-4 (78); HMV DA 1513 (78)/Danacord DACO
168(R)

Kirsten Flagstad (S), Philh./Braithwaite    HMV DA 1879
(78); HMV HQM 1057 (m); EMI 1C 147 01 491/2 (m)

John Forsell (–), [orch.]    Gramophone GC 83 632 (78);
Pathé 100 857 (78)

Nicolai Gedda (T), Jan Eyron    EMI 1C 063 28 023 (m)

Joseph Hislop (T), Percy Kahn    HMV 7 82212/13 (78)

Annelies Kupper (S), –    Heliodor 89 857tr (m)

Lorri Lail (A), –    Lebend. Vergangenheit LV 141

Aase Nordmo Løvberg (S), Robert Levin    Odeon PASK 2002

Lauritz Melchior (T), Ignaz Strasfogel    HMV DA 1648 (78)

Gunvor Mjelva (S), Johan Øian    CBS GM 41 082 (1982R)

Melitta Muszely (S), Günther Weissenborn    Europa E 325

Tuula Nienstedt (A), Uwe Wegner    Acanta/Aristocrate EA
22 437

Birgit Nilsson (S), Leo Taubman    RCA LSC 2578B

Birgit Nilsson (S), Vienna Op.O/Bokstedt    Decca LXT 6185
(m)

Kaja Eide Norena (S), [orch.]    Odeon A 147 327 (78)

Helge Rosvænge (T), Michael Raucheisen [in German] Acanta
BB 22 505 (m)

Anneliese Rothenberger (S), Günther Weissenborn    EMI 1C
065 28 979

Erna Sack (S), Michael Raucheisen [in German] Acanta 40 23
559 (1986R)

Joseph Schwarz (Bar), [orch.]    Lebend, Vergangenheit LV 87

Elisabeth Schwarzkopf (S), Geoffrey Parsons    Decca SXL
6943 (1981)

Knut Skram (Bar), Eva Knardahl    Bis LP 49 (1976)

Elisabeth Söderström (S), New Philh./Davis    CBS 76 527;
US Columbia M 34 531; CBS DC 40 143

3    Kirsten Flagstad (S), Gerald Moore    HMV DA 1957 (78)

Bernhard Sönnerstedt (B), Folmer Jensen    HMV DB 10506
(78)

4    Ritva Auvinen (S), Pentti Koskimies    Finlandia FA 326

Isobel Baillie (S), Gerald Moore [in English]    Columbia DO
2763 (78) (ca. 1927)

Willi Domgraf-Fassbaender (Bar), Michael Raucheisen [in
German]    Acanta DE 22 695 (m)/Acanta 40 23 559
(1986R)

Fanny Elsta (A), Svend Tollefsen    WOR Program 2665–66

Kirsten Flagstad (S), –    HMV DA 1957 (78)

Kirsten Flagstad (S), Gerald Moore    HMV HQM 1057 (m)

Kirsten Flagstad (S), Edwin McArthur    Decca LXT 5264(m)/

Decca ECS 622 (1971R); Richmond R 23 220 (m); Decca 6
35 406 DT (m)
Povla Frijsh (S), C. Dougherty   HMV DA 1324 (78)
Randi Helseth (S), Sigvart Fotland   ProMusica PP 9014 (m)
(1986R)
Tuula Nienstedt (A), Uwe Wegner   Acanta/Aristocrate EA
22 437
Eva Prytz (S), Ivar Johnsen   RCA LPNA 4 (78); RCA LPNE
54 (78)
Elisabeth Schwarzkopf (S), Geoffrey Parsons   HMV ASD 2634
Anita Soldh (S), Arnold Östman   Caprice 1114
Elisabeth Söderström (S), Martin Isepp   Bluebell BEL 111
Esther Østby (MS), Svend Tollefsen   RCA Program 2801–02

OP.26.   FEM DIGTE AF JOHN PAULSEN
(1. *Et Håb*; 2. *Jeg reiste en deilig Sommerkvæld*; 3. *Den Ærgjerrige*; 4. *Med en
Primula veris*; 5. *På Skogstien*)

| | |
|---|---|
| 1,2 | Sophie Schönning (S), Boyd Neel Str.O   Decca K 1208 (78) |
| | Lillemari Østvig (S), Erik Werba   DGG 30 201 EPL (45) |
| 1,4 | Anne Bolsted (S), Audun Kayser   EMI TROLD 01 (1981) |
| | Anita Soldh (S), Arnold Östman   Caprice 1114 |
| | Bernhard Sönnerstedt (B), Folmer Jensen   HMV DB 10506 (78) |
| 3,4 | Kirsten Flagstad (S), Edwin McArthur   Decca LXT 5264 (m)/Decca ECS 622 (1971R) |
| 1 | Kirsten Flagstad (S), Edwin McArthur   HMV DA 1516 (78)/ Danacord DACO 168 (R) |
| | Kirsten Flagstad (S), BBC SO/Sargent   Rococo 3 RR 5380 (m) |
| | Birgit Nilsson (S), Lars Roos   Bluebell BEL 114 |
| 2 | Borghild Langaard Bryhn (S), [orch.]   Gramophone GC 83 693 (78) |
| | Randi Helseth (S), Johan Øian   ProMusica PP 9014 (m) (1986R) |
| | Klara Hultgren (S), −   Pathé 90347–8 (78) |
| | Helge Rosvænge (T), Michael Raucheisen [in German] Acanta 40 23 559 (1986R) |
| | Randi Heide Steen (S), Robert Levin   HMV AL 2930 (78) |
| 3 | Kirsten Flagstad (S), Edwin McArthur   Richmond R 23 220 (m) |
| 4 | Signe Amundsen (S), −   HMV X 6925 (78) |
| | Signe Amundsen (S), Amund Raknerud   HMV AL 2816 (78) |
| | Isobel Baillie (S), −   EMI RLS 714 |

Elisabeth Cooymans (A), Rudolf Jansen    EMI 1C 065 24 782 (m)

Astra Desmond (A), Gerald Moore    Decca M 492 (78)

Helena Döse (S), Thomas Schuback    Electra SLT 33 247

Kirsten Flagstad (S), Edwin McArthur    HMV DB 3392 (78)

Øystein Frantzen (–), Einar Groths orch.    Odeon D 6978 (78)

Ingrid Günther (A), Rhein SO/Günther    Garnet 40 101

Aase Nordmo Løvberg (S), Robert Levin    Odeon PASK 2002; Columbia 33CX 1409 (m) (1957)

Kari Løvaas (S), Justus Frantz    Ariola 200 155–366

Eva Prytz (S), Ivar Johnsen    RCA LPNE 4 (78); RCA LPNE 54 (78)

Helge Rosvænge (T), Michael Raucheisen [in German] Acanta BB 22 505/Acanta 40 23 559 (1986R)

Elisabeth Schwarzkopf (S), Geoffrey Parsons [in German] HMV ASD 2844 (m); EMI 1C 063 02 331 (m)

Conchita Supervia (S), orch.    Odeon P 0180 (78)

Elisabeth Söderström (S), James Shomate    RCA ERA S 198 (45)

5.          Dietrich Fischer-Dieskau (Bar), Hartmut Höll [in German] EMI EL 067 27 0219(d) (1985)

Tuula Nienstedt (A), Uwe Wegner    Acanta/Aristocrate EA 22 437

Aulikki Rautawaara (S), Michael Raucheisen [in German] Acanta 40 23 559 (1986R)

OP.32.    'DEN BERGTEKNE'
Kåre Bjørkøy (Bar), LSO/Dreier    Polydor NKF 30 040 (1981); Unicorn KP 8003

Waldemar Johnsen (Bar), Bergen SO/Garaguly    RCA Program 2871–72 (m) (1955)

Knut Skram (Bar), Göteborg Kammerorch./Schuback    Bis LP 49 (1976)

OP.33.    VINJE-SANGER
(1. *Guten*; 2. *Våren*; 3. *Den særde*; 4. *Tytebæret*; 5. *Langs ei å*; 6. *Eit syn*; 7. *Gamle mor*; 8. *Det fyrste*; 9. *Ved Rundarne*; 10. *Eit vennestykke*; 11. *Trudom*; 12. *Fyremål*)
1–12          Olav Eriksen (Bar), Einar Steen-Nøkleberg    Lu-Mi LU 40 10 48

John Magnusson (Bar), Knut Albrigt Andersen    VNP 0086–12 (1986)

1,3–6,12 Knut Skram (Bar), Robert Levin Philips 6507 001 (1970)
2,4–7,9,12 Olav Eriksen (Bar), Audun Kayser EMI TROLD 02 (1982)
2,3,5,9 Aase Nordmo Løvberg (S), Robert Levin Odeon PASK 2002
2,5 Helena Döse (S), Thomas Schuback Electra SLT 33 247
2,9 Iselin Alme (S), Norw. Str. Quartet DB Records DBLP 001
  Anne Bolstad (S), Audun Kayser EMI TROLD 01 (1981)
  Astra Desmond (A), Harold Craxton Decca M 536 (78)
3,9 Kirsten Flagstad (S), Philh./Braithwaite HMV 7 EBN 9 (45m)
1 Jostein Eriksen (–), Sigvart Fotland NorDisc 2413 001
  Kirsten Flagstad (S), Philh./Braithwaite HMV HQM 1057 (m)
  Kirsten Flagstad (S), – HMV DA 1992 (78)
2 Eva Berge (S), Kjell Olsson Felix FX 239–40 (78)
  Bergljot Bergh (–), trio Odeon D 4140 (78)
  Anne Bolstad (S), Norw.Op.O/Dreier–Polygram NRF 30 055 (1983)
  Borghild Langaard Bryhn (S), – Pathé 90326 (78)
  Margareta Einarson (S), Fritjof Kjellberg Barben BEP 72 (45m)
  Kirsten Flagstad (S), – Harvest H 1004 (78) (1924); HMV DA 1904 (78); Legendary Recordings LR 120–3 (R from Scandinavian Odeon of 1926)
  Ingrid Günther (A), Rhein SO/Günther Garnet 40 101
  Ellen Strygg Jensen (–), Hans Meyer Petersen TONO L 28103–1–2 (78)
  Erling Krogh (T), [orch.] Polydor AB 623 014 (78)
  Annelies Kupper (S), – Heliodor 89 857tr (m)
  Kari Løvaas (S), Justus Frantz Ariola 200 155–366
  Gunvor Mjelva (S), Leo Taubman CBS GM 41 082 (1982R)
  Tuula Nienstedt (A), Uwe Wegner Acanta/Aristocrate EA 22 437
  Birgit Nilsson (S), Vienna Op.O/Bokstedt Decca SXL 6185
  Rei Nishiuchi (MS), Volker Reinicke [in German] DGG ME 1090
  Kaja Eide Norena (S), [orch.] HMV DB 4849 (78)
  Siff Petersen (S), Finn Nielsen Troll TRLP 5 (m)
  Anneliese Rothenberger, (S) Günther Weissenborn [in German] EMI 1C 065 28 979
  Aksel Schiøtz (T), – HMV X 6924 (78)
  Peter Schreier (T), Berlin Radio O/ – DGG 2536 292
  Elisabeth Schwarzkopf (S), Geoffrey Parsons HMV ASD 2634

Harald Steen (–), [orch.]    Odeon A 147 102–3 (78)

Elisabeth Söderström (S), Martin Isepp    Bluebell BEL 111

Richard Tauber (T), –    Parlophone RO 20 191 (78); Odeon
    0 4532 (78); VP DaCapo 2109/10 (m); EMI 1C 147 28
    596/7 (m)

Olav Werner (–), Rolf Holger (org)    Odeon ND 7222 (78)

3    Kim Borg (B), Robert Levin    DGG EPL 30 571 (45m)

Kirsten Flagstad (S), Philh./Braithwaite    HMV DB 21020
    (78); EMI 1C 147 01 491/2 (m)

5    Rolf Bjørling (T), Jan Eyron    HMV EBS 26 (45m)

Ranveig Eckhoff (S), [ens.]/Kruse    Aurora AR 1900 (1985)

Aulikki Rautawaara (S), Michael Raucheisen [in German]
    Acanta 40 23 559 (1986R)

Knut Skram (Bar), Eva Knardahl    Bis LP 49 (1976)

Randi Heide Steen (S), Robert Levin    HMV AL 2929 (78)

6    Waldemar Johnsen (Bar), [pf.]    WOR Program 2648–49

Karl Schmitt-Walter (Bar), Michael Raucheisen [in German]
    Acanta 40 23 559 (1986R)

7    Jacob Endregaard (–), [orch.]    Odeon A 147 278 (78)

Sigurd Hoff (–), [pf.]    Gramophone 290 10 (78)

Erling Krogh (T), [orch.]    HMV X 3453 (78)

Gunvor Mjelva (S), Sigvart Fotland    CBS GM 41 082 (1982R)

G. Østby (T), A. Engesvik (org)    Tone Art 9 (78)

9    Willi Domgraf-Fassbaender (Bar), Michael Raucheisen [in
German]    Acanta 40 23 559 (1986R)

Kirsten Flagstad (S), –    HMV DA 1992 (78)

Øystein Frantzen (–), Einar Groths O [in *bokmål*]    Odeon D
    6978 (78)

Erling Krogh (T), –    HMV AL 2003 (78)

Erling Krogh (T), [orch.]    Victrola 4030B (78)

Øivind Lunde (–), [trio]    Parlophone B 41 105 (78)

Aase Nordmo Løvberg (S), Gerald Moore    Columbia 33 CX
    1409 (m) (1957)

Aksel Schiøtz (T), H. Koppel    HMV X 6924 (78)

Aksel Schiøtz (T), Folmer Jensen    Odeon MOAK 20 (m)

Peder Tønnesen (T), Thomas Berg    RCA Program 2883–84

Esther Østby (MS), Svend Tollefsen    RCA program 2801–02

11.    Erling Krogh (T), [orch.]    HMV X 3041 (78)

12.    Kirsten Flagstad (S), BBC SO/Sargent    Rococo 3 RR 5380 (m)

## OP.39.    ROMANSER ÆLDRE OG NYERE

(1. *Fra Monte Pincio*; 2. *Dulgt Kjærlighed*; 3. *I Liden høit deroppe*; 4. *Millom rosor*; 5. *Ved en ung Hustrus Båre*; 6. *Hører jeg Sangen klinger*)

| | |
|---|---|
| 1,3,4 | Kirsten Flagstad (S), Edwin McArthur   Decca LXT 5264 (m); Decca ECS 622 (1971R); Richmond R 23 220 (m) |
| 1,2 | Tuula Nienstedt (A), Uwe Wegner   Acanta/Aristocrate EA 22 437 |
| 1,3 | Eva Prytz (S), Ivar Johnsen   RCA LPNA 4 (78); RCA LPNE 54 (78) |
| 1,4 | Aase Nordmo Løvberg (S), Robert Levin   Columbia 33 CX 1409 (m) (1957) |
| | Anita Soldh (S), Arnold Östman   Caprice 1114 |
| 1 | Anne Bolstad (S), Norw. Op.O/Dreier   Polygram NRF 30 055 (1983) |
| | Kirsten Flagstad (S), Philh./Braithwaite   HMV DAN 1905 (78) |
| | Kari Frisell (S), Kaare Ørnung   RCA Program 3081 (1965) |
| | Borghild Langaard (S), [orch.]   Pathé N 1003 (78) |
| | Birgit Nilsson (S), Vienna Op.O/Bokstedt   Decca SXL 6185 |
| | Kaja Eide Norena (S), [orch.]/Coppola   HMV DB 4849 (78) |
| | Sophie Schönning (S), Boyd Neel Str. O   Decca K 1208 (78) |
| | Elisabeth Söderström (S), New Phil./Davis   CBS 76 527; US Columbia M 34 531; CBS DC 40 143 |
| 2 | Nicolai Gedda (T), Jan Eyron [in German]   EMI 1C 063 28 023 |
| | Ingrid Günther (A), Rhein SO/Günther   Garnet 40 101 |
| 4 | Kirsten Flagstad (S), –   Harvest H 1004 (78) (1929); Legendary Recordings LR 120–3 (R) |
| | Margarete Klose (A), Michael Raucheisen [in German] Acanta 40 23 559 (1986R) |
| 6 | Dietrich Fischer-Dieskau (Bar), Aribert Reimann [in German] EMI 1C 065 02 673 |
| | Dietrich Fischer-Dieskau, Hartmut Höll [in German]   EMI EL 067 27 0219 (d) (1985) |

OP.44.   'REISEMINDER FRA FJELD OG FJORD'
(1. *Prolog*; 2. *Johanne*; 3. *Ragnhild*; 4. *Ingebjørg*; 5. *Ragna*; 6. *Epilog*)

| | |
|---|---|
| 3,5 | Knut Skram (Bar), Eva Knardahl   Bis LP 49 (1976) |
| 3 | Borghild Langaard Bryhn (S), [orch.]   Gramophone GC 83 670 (78) |
| | Randi Helseth (S), Johan Øian   ProMusica PP 9014(m) (1986R) |
| | Aase Nordmo Løvberg (S), Robert Levin   Columbia 33 CX 1409 (1957) |
| | Elisabeth Munthe-Kaas, (–) –   Pathé 17982 (78) |
| 5 | Signe Amundsen (S), –   HMV Z 280 (78) |

OP.48.    SEKS SANGE
(1. *Gruss*; 2. *Dereinst, Gedanke mein*; 3. *Lauf der Welt*; 4. *Die verschwiegene Nachtigall*; 5. *Zur Rosenzeit*; 6. *Ein Traum*)

| | |
|---|---|
| 1–6 | Marianne Hirsti (S), Audun Kayser    VNP 0085–86 (1985) |
| 1–3,5,6 | Dietrich Fischer-Dieskau (Bar), Hartmut Höll    EMI EL 067 27 0219 (d) (1985) |
| 1,3–6 | Ingrid Bjoner (S), Robert Levin    Forum FOREP 1301 (45m) |
| 1,2,5 | Bernhard Sönnerstedt (B), Falmer Jensen    HMV DB 10 507 (78) |
| 1,3,4 | Randi Helseth (S), Johan Øian    ProMusica PP 9014 (m) (1986R) |
| 2,3 | Dietrich Fischer-Dieskau (Bar), Aribert Reimann    EMI 1C 065 02 673 |
| 2,4,5 | Kari Løvaas (S), Justus Frantz    Ariola 200 155–366 |
| 3,5 | Elisabeth Schwarzkopf (S), Geoffrey Parsons    HMV ASD 2844 |
| 5,6 | Kim Borg (B), Robert Levin    DGG EPL 30 571 (45m) |
| 2 | Tuula Nienstedt (A), Uwe Wegner    Acanta/Aristocrate EA 22 437 |
| 3 | Erna Berger (S), Michael Raucheisen    Acanta 40 23 559 (1986R) |
| | Elisabeth Söderström (S), New Philh./Davis    CBS 76 527; US Columbia M 34 531; CBS DC 40 143 |
| 4 | Gwen Catley (S), Wilfrid Parry [in English]    HMV B 10 340 (78) |
| 9 | Willi Domgraf-Fassbaender (Bar), Michael Raucheisen    Acanta DE 22 695 (m)/Acanta 40 23 559 (1986R) |
| 6 | Victoria de los Angeles (S), Geoffrey Parsons    DGG 2383 389 |
| | Isobel Baillie (S), – [in English]    EMI RLS 714 |
| | Jussi Bjørling (T), Frederick Schauwecker    RCA Victor EBRP 5225 |
| | Rolf Bjørling (T), Jan Eyron    HMV 7 EBS 26 (45m) |
| | Karin Branzell (A), –    Lebend. Vergangenheit LV 182 |
| | Richard Crooks (T), Frederick Schauwecker [in English] HMV EG 16 2177A (78) (ca. 1930) |
| | Ranveig Eckhoff (S), ensemble/Kruse    Aurora AR 1900 (1985) |
| | Olav Eriksen (Bar), Audun Kayser    EMI TROLD 02 (1982) |
| | Kirsten Flagstad (S), orch.    HMV DB 21 021 (78) |
| | Kirsten Flagstad (S), Edwin McArthur [in Norwegian] Decca ECS 622 (1971R) |
| | Kirsten Flagstad (S), Edwin McArthur    HMV DA 1505 (78)/ Danacord DACO 168 (R); HMV 7 EBN 9 (45m); Decca LXT 5264 (m); Richmond R 23 220 (m) |

Nicolai Gedda (T), Jan Eyron   EMI 1C 063 28 023
Beniamino Gigli (T), Berlin State Op.O/Seidler-Winkler [in
   French]   HMV DA 1504 (78) (1936)
Beniamino Gigli (T), D. Ferdi [in French]   HMV ALP 1329
   (m)
Gunnar Graarud (T), –   HMV 30 5917–18 (78)
Arne Hendriksen (T) Robert Levin   HMV AL 3019 (78)
Erling Krogh (T), –   HMV X 6928 (78)
Maria Markau (S), Haraldur Sigurdsson   HMV X 6041 (78)
Birgit Nilsson (S), Lars Roos   Bluebell BEL 109
Erik Schmedes (T), [pf.]   Lyrophon W 7118 (78) (1904)
Rudolf Schock (T), Berlin SO/ –   Ariola 0 27 223; Eruodisc
   77 173
Richard Tauber (T), –   Odeon 0 5007 (78); Parlophone RO
   20 553 (78)
Peder Tønnesen (T), Thomas Berg   RCA Program 2883–83
   (m) (1956)
Martin Öhman (–), –   Nordiska Polyphon 6803

OP.49.   SEKS DIGTE AF HOLGER DRACHMANN
(1. *Saa du Knøsen*; 2. *Vug, o Vove*; 3. *Vær hilset, I Damer*; 4. *Nu er Aftnen lys og
lang*; 5. *Julesne*; 6. *Foraarsregn*)

| | | |
|---|---|---|
| 3,6 | Aksel | Schiøtz | (T), |
| | Gerald | |
| | Moore   HMV 7 EBK 1005 (45m) | |
| 2 | Astra Desmond (A), Gerald Moore   Decca K 961 (78) | |
| 3 | Svanhild Helland Hansen (S), Svend Tollefsen   WOR Program 2659–60 | |
| | Aksel Schiøtz (T), Folmer Jensen   Odeon MOAK 3 (78) | |
| | Bernhard Sönnerstedt (B), Folmer Jensen   HMV DB 10506 (78) | |
| | T. Thygesen (T), –   HMV X 3371 (78) | |
| 5 | Willi Domgraf-Fassbaender (Bar), Michael Raucheisen [in German]   Acanta DE 22 695 (m)/Acanta 40 23 559 (1986R) | |
| 6 | Astra Desmond (A), Gerald Moore   Decca M 492 (78) | |
| | Randi Helseth (S), Sigvart Fotland   ProMusica PP 9014 (m) (1986R) | |
| | Marianne Hirsti (S), Audun Kayser   VNP 0085–86 (1985) | |
| | Kari Løvaas (S), Justus Frantza   Ariola 200 155–366 | |

OP.58.   'NORGE'
(1. *Hjemkomst*; 2. *Til Norge*; 3. *Henrik Wergeland*; 4. *Turisten*; 5. *Udvandreren*)
2         Signe Amundsen (S), –   HMV Z 280 (78)

Willi Domgraf-Fassbaender (Bar), Michael Raucheisen [in German]   Acanta DE 22 695 (m)/Acanta 40 23 559 (1986R)

Olav Eriksen (Bar), Audun Kayser   EMI TROLD 02 (1982)

Lauritz Melchior (T), [orch.]   HMV DA 1827 (78)

Siff Petersen (S), Finn Nielsen   Troll TRLP 5 (m)

Gerard Souzay (Bar), Dalton Baldwin   EMI HQS 1295 (m)

Randi Heide Steen (S), Robert Levin   HMV AL 2934 (78)

3 — Anne Bolstad (S), Norw. Op.O/Dreier   Polygram NRF 30 055 (1983)

4 — Tuula Nienstedt (A), Uwe Wegner   Acanta Aristocrate EA 22 437

5 — Dora Labbette (S), –   Columbia C 9423 (78)

## OP.59.  ELEGISKE DIGTE

(1. *Når jeg vil dø*; 2. *På Norges nøgne Fjelde*; 3. *Til En (I)*; 4. *Til En (II)*; 5. *Farvel*; 6. *Nu hviler du i Jorden*)

2–4 — Dietrich Fischer-Dieskau (Bar), Hartmut Höll [in German]   EMI EL 067 27 0219 (d) (1985)

3,4 — Kirsten Flagstad (S), LSO/Fjeldstad   Decca SXL 2145; Decca SDD 209

4 — Edith Thallaug (MS), Oslo PO/Jansons   Philips 411 315–1 (1983)

## OP.60.  DIGTE AF VILHELM KRAG

(1. *Liden Kirsten*; 2. *Moderen synger*; 3. *Mens jeg venter*; 4. *Der skreg en Fugl*; 5. *Og jeg vil ha mig en Hjertenskjær*)

1–5 — Ellen Westberg Andersen (S), Jens Harald Bratlie   Simax PS 1011; PSC 1011 (CD) (1987)

Edith Thallaug (MS), Robert Levin   NKF 30 059 (1984)

3,5 — Birgit Nilsson (S), Leo Taubman   RCA LSC 2578B

Karl Aagaard Østvig (–), –   Nordisk Polyphon S42 010–11 (78)

1 — Erna Berger (S), Michael Raucheisen [in German]   Acanta 40 23 559 (1986R)

Kirsten Flagstad (S), Edwin McArthur   Decca LXT 5264 (m); Decca ECS 622 (1971R); Richmond R 23 220 (m)

Randi Heide Steen (S), Robert Levin   HMV AL 2930 (78)

2 — Ernestine Schumann-Heink (–), [in English]   HMV 1625 (78)

3 — Signe Amundsen (S), –   HMV X 6925 (78)

Ritva Auvinen (S), Pentti Koskimies   Finlandia FA 326

Kirsten Flagstad (S), Edwin McArthur [in German]   HMV DA 1513 (78)/Danacord DACO 168 (R)

Elena Gerhardt (S), Ivor Newton [in German]   Vocalion B
  3107 (78) (1936)
Borghild Gundersen (–), –   Pathé 17562–63 (78)
Randi Helseth (S), Johan Øian   ProMusica PP 9014 (m)
  (1986R)
Arne Hendriksen (–), Robert Levin   HMV AL 3019 (78)
Joseph Hislop (T), Percy Kahn   HMV 7 82212–13 (78)
Kari Løvaas (S), Justus Frantz   Ariola 200 155–366
Elisabeth Munthe-Kaas (–), –   Pathé 17982–83 (78)
Rei Nishiuchi (MS), Volker Reinicke [in German]   DGG ME
  1090
Hermann Prey (Bar), Herbert Heinemann   Columbia EPC 40
  917 (45m)
Hermann Prey (Bar), Berlin SO/Eisbrenner   Eurodisc 77 941
  KK
Anneliese Rothenberger (S), Günther Weissenborn   EMI 1C
  065 28 979
Karl Schmitt-Walter (Bar), Michael Raucheisen [in German]
  Acanta 40 23 559 (1986R)
Ernestine Schumann-Heink (–), – [in German]   HMV 1625
  (78); Victor 87170 (78ss)
Joseph Schwarz (Bar), – [in German]   Lebend. Vergan-
  genheit LV 87
Anita Soldh (S), Arnold Östman   Caprice 1114

4      Astra Desmond (A), Gerald Moore   Decca K 962 (78)
  Tuula Nienstedt (A), Uwe Wegner   Acanta/Aristocrate EA
  22 437

5      Jostein Eriksen (–), Sigvart Fotland   NorDisc 2413 001
  Olav Eriksen (Bar), Audun Kayser   EMI TROLD 02 (1982)
  Kirsten Flagstad (S), Edwin McArthur   HMV DB 3392 (78)
  Kirsten Flagstad (S), LSO/Fjeldstad   Decca SXL 2145; Decca
  SDD 209
  Ellen Gulbranson (MS), –   Pathéfon 6317 (78)
  Waldemar Johnsen (Bar), Kåre Siem   WOR Program 2654–
  55
  Edith Thallaug (MS), Oslo PO/Jansons   Philips 411 315–1
  (1983)

OP.61.   BARNLIGE SANGE
(1. *Havet*; 2. *Sang til Juletræet*; 3. *Lok*; 4. *Fiskervise*; 5. *Kveldsang for
Blakken*; 6. *De norske Fjelde*; 7. *Fædrelandssalme*)
2,5     August Werner (–), –   HMV AL 1057 (78)
3      Hulda Frisk Gran (S), –   Columbia DN 217 (78)

Elisabeth Schwarzkopf (S), Gerald Moore [in German] Columbia SAX 2265

5        Gjertrud Sand (–), Hjalmar Lindbergs ens.    Columbia GN 1077 (78)

Randi Heide Steen (S), Robert Levin    HMV AL 2931 (78)

7        Alfred Helgeby (–), [orch.]    Gramophone 28 2918–19 (78) (1915)

Erling Krogh (T), –    HMV X 6927 (78)

OP.67.    'HAUGTUSSA'
(1. *Det syng*; 2. *Veslemøy*; 3. *Blåbær-li*; 4. *Møte*; 5. *Elsk*; 6. *Killingdans*; 7. *Vond dag*; 8. *Ved Gjætle-bekken*)

1–8      Ellen Westberg Andersen (S), Jens Harald Bratlie    Simax PS 1011; PSC 1011 (CD) (1987)

Torgun Birkeland (S), Audun Kayser    VNP 0086–10 (1986)

Kirsten Flagstad (S), Edwin McArthur    HMV DB 5833–36 (78) (1940); RCA LM 1094 (m) (1950); Decca LXT 5327 (1956); Decca ECS 622 (1971R); London 23 242 (m); RCA HR 228 (m)

Aase Nordmo Løvberg (S), Robert Levin    HMV 7 EBN 1/2 (78)

Kari Løvaas (S), Erik Werba    DGG 2555 004

Randi Heide Steen (S), Amund Raknerud    Nordisk Polyphon NORLP 329

Edith Thallaug (MS), Kjell Bækkelund    Philips 854 006 AY

Edith Thallaug (MS), Robert Levin    NKF 30 059 (1984)

Siv Wennberg (S), Geoffrey Parsons    HMV HQS 1345 (m) (1973)

3        Eva Prytz (S), Ivar Johnsen    RCA LPNA 4 (78); RCA LPNE 54 (78)

4        Margarete Klose (A), Michael Raucheisen [in German] Acanta 40 23 559 (1986R)

6        Erna Berger (S), Michael Raucheisen [in German]    Acanta 40 23 559 (1986R)

Tuula Nienstedt (A), Uwe Wegner    Acanta/Aristocrate EA 22 437

OP.69.    FEM DIGTE AF OTTO BENZON
(1. *Der gynger en Båd på Bølge*; 2. *Til min Dreng*; 3. *Ved Moders Grav*; 4. *Snegl, Snegl*; 5. *Drømme*)

1        Kirsten Flagstad (S), Edwin McArthur    HMV DA 1515 (78)/ Danacord DACO 168 (R); Decca LXT 5264 (m); Decca ECS 622 (1971R); Richmond R 23 220 (m)

OP.70.    FEM DIGTE AF OTTO BENZON
(1. *Eros*; 2. *Jeg lever et Liv i Længsel*; 3. *Lys Nat*; 4. *Se dig for*; 5. *Digtervise*)
1    Kirsten Flagstad (S), [orch.] HMV DA 1879 (78)

    Kirsten Flagstad (S), Edwin McArthur Decca LXT 5264
     (m); Decca ECS 622 (1971R); Richmond R 23 220 (m)

    Per Grønneberg (–), Robert Levin HMV AL 3026 (78)

    Margarete Klose (A), Michael Raucheisen [in German]
     Acanta 40 23 559 (1986R)

    Walter Ludwig (–), F. Leitner [in German] HMV EG 3243
     (78)

    Lauritz Melchior (T), Ignaz Strasfogel HMV DA 1827 (78)

    Norman Myrikk (T), Samuel Lewenssohn RCA Program
     2889–90 (m) (1956)

    Rei Nishiuchi (MS), Volker Reinicke [in German] DGG ME
     1090

    Karl Schmitt-Walter (B), Michael Raucheisen Telefunken A
     2178 (78)

    Joseph Schwarz (Bar), – [in German] Lebend. Vergan-
     genheit LV 87

    Richard Tauber (T), [orch.] Parlophone RO 20 553 (78)

3    Erna Berger (S), Michael Raucheisen [in German] Acanta 40
     23 559 (1986R)

    Kirsten Flagstad (S), Edwin McArthur HMV DA 1515 (78)/
     Danacord DACO 168 (R); HMV HQM 1057 (m)

    Marianne Hirsti (S), Audun Kayser VNP 0085–86 (1985)

    Aase Nordmo Løvberg (S), Robert Levin Columbia 33 CX
     1409 (1957)

    Tuula Nienstedt (A), Uwe Wegner Acanta/Aristocrate EA
     22 437

    Eva Prytz (S), Ivar Johnsen RCA LPNA 4 (78); RCA LPNE
     54 (78)


SONGS WITHOUT OPUS NUMBERS
*Ave maris stella*
Alice Babs (S), Åke Leven (org) Teledec SLT 33 197 (1969)
Erling Krogh (T), H. Lund-Christiansen HMV AL 2818 (78)
Erling Krogh (T), – HMV X 6927 (78)

*Dig elsker jeg!*
Gunvor Mjelva (S), Sigvart Fotland CBS GM 41 082 (1982R)

*Der Jäger*
Dietrich Fischer-Dieskau (Bar), Hartmut Höll    EMI EL 067 27 0219 (d) (1985)
   Margarete Klose (A), Michael Raucheisen    Acanta 40 23 559 (1986R)

*Julens Vuggesang*
   Margarete Klose (A), Michael Raucheisen [in German]    Acanta 40 23 559
(1986R)

*Prinsessen*
Kirsten Flagstad (S), −    HMV DA 1957 (78)
Kirsten Flagstad (S), Gerald Moore    HMV HQM 1057 (m)
Kari Frisell (S), Kaare Ørnung    RCA Program 3081 (1965)
Kari Løvaas (S), Justus Frantz    Ariola 200 155–366
Tuula Nienstedt (A), Uwe Wegner    Acanta/Aristocrate EA 22 437
Rei Nishiuchi (MS), Volker Reinicke [in German]    DGG ME 1090
Aulikki Rautawaara (S), Michael Raucheisen [in German]    Acanta 40 23 559 (1986R)
Elisabeth Söderström (S), New Philh./Davis    CBS 76 527; US Columbia M 34 531; CBS DC 40 143
Aalrud Tillisch (−), −    Victor 73759A (78)

# General Index

Note: the Scandinavian letters Æ and Å/AA occur at the end of the alphabet.

# Index of Songs